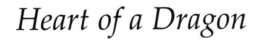

Heart of a Dragon

By the same author

The VCs of Wales and the Welsh Regiments
Old Wrexham Vols 1–5
Old Pwllheli Vols 1–2
Against the Odds, the life of Group Captain Lionel Rees, VC, OBE, MC, AFC
Commandant of the Transvaal, the life of General Sir Hugh Rowlands, VC, KCB
The Encyclopaedia of Wrexham

With Kevin Matthias

A Wrexham Collection

Heart of a Dragon

— the VCs of Wales and the Welsh Regiments

1854–1902

W. Alister Williams

bridge
books

Heart of a Dragon
First published in Wales in 2006
by
BRIDGE BOOKS
61 Park Avenue, Wrexham
LL12 7AW

www.bridgebooks.co.uk

Cover illustration:
Detail from 'The Formidable 24th'
The defence of Rorke's Drift, 22nd/23rd January 1879
David Cartwright

ISBN 1-84494-027-6

A CIP entry for this book is available from the British Library

Printed and bound by
Cromwell Press Ltd
Trowbridge, Wiltshire

To

Sue

'That valour lies in the eyes o' the lookers on, And is called valour with a witness.'

BEN JOHNSON

'In valour there is hope.'

TACITUS

'No thought of flight,
None of retreat, no unbecoming deed
That argued fear; each on himself relied,
As only in his arm the moment lay
Of victory.'

JOHN MILTON

CONTENTS

Outline of the Defence of Rorke's Drift, 22/23 January, 1879   125

INTRODUCTION

This book is not a history of the Victoria Cross. Rather, it is an attempt to enlarge upon the details of a number of individual VC actions and other significant events in the lives of the men concerned. Numerous researchers have tried to find a common link between the recipients of the coveted Cross but to no avail. Each individual is linked only to the others by the exceptionally high degree of courage exhibited by them all. Some writers have tried to cast doubts upon the validity of some VC actions, stating that some of the earlier ones bear no comparison with those made in later wars. This is a futile exercise. Each award was made because the individual concerned had shown great gallantry *in the eyes of his contemporaries*. It is not possible to judge one act of valour against another. We will never know whether it took more or less courage to face up to a Zulu impi than it took to fight against the German SS. The only assessment which we can make today is that, in the case of all VCs, the most likely outcome of the individual's action was death. As the reader makes his way through the awards recorded in this first of two volumes covering all the VCs of Wales and the Welsh regiments, it will become obvious that the citations become more detailed as the story progresses which has tended to devalue the earlier awards because of the lack of information available. This is hardly the responsibility of the man concerned and his fear, pain and courage were quite possibly the same. The VC is not the prerogative of the young and foolhardy, but has been awarded to every possible classification of society. Unfortunately, over the years, the biographical details of some VC recipients have been lost. Wherever possible, I have made use of primary sources and, as a consequence, the keen reader will discover some details which disagree with those published elsewhere. I have made every effort to ensure that the data which is reproduced here is accurate. Any errors which may have slipped through are my sole responsibility.

The men whose biographical details appear here are not all Welshmen. They are, however, all connected with Wales either by birth, residence, death or military service. Purists would argue that those VCs awarded to the 24th Regiment of Foot before 1881 should not be included in a work of this nature as the regiment was then the 2nd Warwickshire Regiment and had no more of a territorial connection with Wales than any other regiment in the army. To exclude them would be even more confusing as the modern standard bearer of that illustrious regiment (and its predecessors, the Royal Regiment of Wales, the South Wales Borderers, the Welch Regiment and the Monmouthshire Regiment) is The Royal Welsh and the regimental museums are located in Brecon, Powys and Cardiff. Similarly, the Queen's Dragoon Guards have, since 1959, served as the cavalry regiment for Wales.

Since 1984, an awareness of 'Welshness' has become much more pronounced in society and people have become genuinely interested in what our small country has produced.

The policy of the British government in 2006 meant that sad and dramatic changes to the face of those regiments traditionally associated with Wales took place. A new regiment, The Royal Welsh has been created from the Royal Welch Fusiliers and the Royal Regiment of Wales. Whilst retaining its Welsh identity, this new amalgamation has meant that more links with the military tradition and history of Wales have been modified, if not broken. With regard to the Queen's Dragoon Guards — who can doubt their Welshness having seen them in action in Iraq in 2003, Red Dragon flying and constantly referred to by the media as 'The Welsh Cavalry'.

Twenty-two years have passed since I first went into print on this subject, a period which has seen the award of only one Victoria Cross (Private Johnson Beharry, Iraq, 2005) and yet interest in the decoration continues unabated. During this period, numerous VC biographies have been published as well as books of a more general nature but, undoubtedly, the most significant publication was *Monuments to Courage* by the late David Harvey. The 150th anniversary of the actions which brought about the award of the first VCs has resulted in considerable media interest and the publication of a number of books dealing with this most prestigious of all decorations.

The VCs of Wales and the Welsh Regiments was well-received in 1984 and, as a consequence, numerous individuals and organisations contacted me with additional information and amendments. I feel that sufficient time has now elapsed to allow a new generation of individuals to become interested in the VC. The publishers feel that modern printing methods will enable a much more comprehensive and attractive edition to be published. The deep-rooted reason, however, was not commercially motivated. Having been passionately interested in the Victoria Cross since childhood, I felt that access to information on the 'Welsh' VCs should be readily available in a format that would appeal to the twenty-first century student. Whilst conducting research for this book, I discovered two individuals whose qualification as a 'Welsh VC' had been overlooked in 1984 and whose details appear here for the first time (Captain Mansel-Jones [1900] and Temporary Lieutenant-Colonel Burges [1918]).

No author can claim that a book of this nature is the result of his own unaided efforts. By its very nature, it must be the compilation of knowledge from numerous individuals and organisations who have willingly shared their knowledge and time. Below, I have tried to acknowledge all those who have assisted me with my searches but I feel certain that there will be some whom I have overlooked. May I express my most sincere thanks and apologies as the case may be to all who have kindly co-operated with me since I began this project thirty years ago. Certain names must, however, be given prominence as their contributions have been of great general value. My gratitude must go, above all, to the eminent naval historian and novelist, the late John Winton, who allowed me access to the voluminous files on all recipients of the Victoria Cross prepared and researched by his late mother, Mrs Margaret Pratt, who sadly died before being able to fulfil her ambition to write the definitive book on the subject. One of the first avenues for any VC researcher must be the files prepared during a lifetime of study by the late Rev. Canon William Lummis, MC. His kindness and generosity were well known to students of British military history.

Research of this nature brings one into contact with numerous 'fellow travellers', some of whom become more than names on an envelope or voices at the end of a telephone. My original research produced two such people — Chris Bacon and Clive Hughes. For their fellowship, advice, assistance and enthusiasm, I shall always be grateful. In this new work, I must give particular thanks to my friend of over thirty years, Gwynne Belton, for his assistance and companionship on the highways and byeways of Wales, England, France and Belgium. I must also thank 'Sapper' Graham Mason (Llangefni) who has an unrivalled knowledge of the men at Rorke's Drift.

The Imperial War Museum; The National Army Museum; The National Maritime Museum; The National Archives (Kew); The British Library (London); The National Library of Wales (Aberystwyth); The Commonwealth War Graves Commission (Maidenhead); The Australian War Memorial (Canberra); The Royal Naval Museum (Portsmouth); The Royal Welch Fusiliers Museum (Caernarfon), particularly Colonel Peter Crocker and Mrs Ann Pedley; The Royal Regiment of Wales Museum (Brecon), particularly Major Martin Everett and Mrs Celia Green; The Royal Regiment of Wales Museum (Cardiff), particularly the late Lieutenant Bryn Owen, RN (Retd) and Mr John Dart; The Queen's Dragoon Guards Regimental Museum (Cardiff), particularly Mr Clive Morris; The Durham Light Infantry Museum & Arts Centre (Durham); The Royal Artillery Historical Trust (Woolwich); 55th (The Residency) Field Battery, Royal Artillery; The Royal Military Academy, Sandhurst; The King's Own Yorkshire Light Infantry Museum (Doncaster); The Prince of Wales's Own Regiment of Yorkshire Museum (York); The Dorset Military Museum (Dorchester); The Queen's Own Royal West Kent Regimental Museum (Maidstone); The Royal Green Jackets Museum (Winchester); Derby Museum and Art Gallery; Newark Museum; The Victoria Cross and George Cross Association, particulalrly Mrs Didy Grahame, MVO; The Powysland Museum (Welshpool); the Diocese of Monmouth & Newport; the Diocese of Brecon & Swansea; Wrexham Library and Arts Centre, particularly Mr Hedd ap Emlyn; Llanelli Public Library; The University of Wales (Bangor) Library and Archives; Edinburgh University Library; Edinburgh Libraries & Information Services; Dorset County Library; Dyfed Library Service; Gwent County Library; Gwent Record Office (Cwmbran); Newport Leisure Services;

Alexander Turnbull Library (Wellington, New Zealand); Carmarthenshire Archive Service (Carmarthen); Carmarthen County Museum (Carmarthen); Gwynedd Archives Service (Caernarfon); Tyne and Wear Archivist's Department (Newcastle-upon-Tyne); Hampshire Record Office (Winchester); Herefordshire Record Office (Hereford); Staffordshire County Museum (Shugborough); City of Philadelphia Department of Records; New Zealand Electronic Text Centre; memorials.inportsmouth.co.uk; the South African Military History Society; *The London Gazette*; Edinburgh Academy; Sherbourne College; Marlborough College; Rugby School; Eton College; Harrow School; Westminster School; Brecon Cathedral; St Patrick's College (Dublin); HM Coroner (Hereford); Tony Jones (Essex) for details of the background of William Jones, VC and his complex family; Mr & Mrs Mal Stokes (Bridgend); Miss Mary Greer; Mrs Isabel Findlay; Mr O. Gethin Evans (Aberystwyth); Mr Kenneth Williams (Conwy); Mr Gethin Davies; Mrs Mary Sullivan; Mr A. J. D. Morgan; Lady Bettina Thomson; Mr O'Brian; Mrs Freda Orr; Mr Gus Jones; Mr Wilfred Leonard (Shaw); Mr Edward Lloyd; Mrs Joyce Hill-Ervey; Mrs Victoria Howard; Mr Robert Howard; Mr W. J. Davies; Mrs M. Booth; Major Herbert Lloyd-Johnes, OBE, TD; Mr Walter Ireland; Mr H. E. R. Bunting (Gloucester); Mr Bernard Baldwin, MBE; Mr & Mrs William Dodd (St Albans); Mrs E. Whitmill (Brecon); the late Lieutenant-Colonel G. C. S. Coode, MBE (Cornwall); Mr Bryan H. Coode (Cornwall); Major C. J. Wilson (Winchester); Mr Donald Morris (Texas); Mr Stephen Morris; Mrs Wanda Pugh; Mrs J. Ridley; Mr G. E. Moody; Mrs S. Toogood; Miss W. Hempenstall (Reading); Major B. H. Jones; Mrs V. Partridge; the late Mrs Frances M. Douglas (Ontario, Canada); Mrs G. E. Moody; Miss J. Lewis; Mr David Christie-Murray (Harrow); Mr Gordon Everson; Mrs Diane Edwards (Oswestry); the late Wing Commander Frederick Carrol; Mr Vivian Smith; Mr Lyn John (Llanelli); Commodore Dacre Smyth, AO, RAN (Victoria, Australia); Mrs Anne German (Lincolnshire); Mrs Diana Bailey (Pershore); Mrs Monica Foster (Newport); Mrs Ruth Webley (Slough); Mrs Jayne Roper (Newport); Stuart Cameron (Cwmbran); Mrs Gillian Evans (Efail Isaf); Ms Vanessa Leslie (Lostwithiel); Mr W. Stuart Cameron (Cwmbran); Mr Mike Wilson (Blackwood); Mrs Diana Bailey (Pershore); Brigadier M. E. Browne, CBE (Nottinghamshire); Mr Mick Crumplin, FRCS (Wrexham); Mr Brian Best (The Victoria Cross Society); Mr Simon Gaine; Mr Ralph Raby (London); Mr Philip E. Raby (Bath); Lieutenant-Colonel Peter Blaker (Oxfordshire); the Right Reverend Michael Mann, KCVO (Gloucestershire); Mr David P. Evans (Welshpool); Mrs Angela Scott (Cirencester); Mrs Ethel M. Lumb (Huddersfield); Mr Sean Farrell (London); Mrs J. C. Furness (Gloucester); Mr Barry Johnson (Birmingham); Ian Hunter (Gloucester); David Keyworth (Brigg); Mrs Elizabeth Griffiths (Goodwick); Bob Hinton; Philippa Morris (Australia); Reverend William Pearsall, SJ (London); Alkit & Christine Savage (Llandysilio); the numerous owners of houses once occupied by VC recipients and the diligent caretakers at the many corporation, parish and Commonwealth War Graves cemeteries.

I accept full responsibility for any interpretation that I have given to the information obtained.

W. Alister Williams
Wrexham
2006

AUTHOR'S NOTE

1. The main body of the text details those Victoria Cross recipients who were born in Wales, born elsewhere but of Welsh parentage, died in Wales or who gained the award whilst serving with a regiment which is today regarded as serving Wales. The entries are listed in the order of the action for which the VC was awarded.

2. Each entry is divided into two sections. The first section deals with the basic biographical details and the VC citation. Place names have been given their modern spelling e.g. Caernarfon not Caernarvon, except in citations and quotations where the original, often archaic, spelling is retained, particularly in India e.g. Bulandshahr not Bolundshahur. The names on medal clasps are shown as they appear e.g. Ashantee not Ashanti. The second section provides a more detailed account of certain aspects of the individual's life e.g. a more detailed account of the VC action or the account in the recipient's own words (in certain instances no attempt has been made to alter or correct spelling, punctuation and grammar).

3. Wherever possible, citations have been included for decorations other than the Victoria Cross. Unfortunately, not all awards carried a published citation in the *London Gazette* and therefore a great many such details are not available.

4. Some of the entries lack certain background details. In most cases this is as a result of the total absence of any such data in the official military or civil records. In very few cases, data has been withheld at the request of the individual's family.

5. Each entry in this book carries the sub-heading 'Location of Victoria Cross'. Where the VC is held by an organisation which has display facilities, e.g. regimental museums, the entry will indicate whether the VC is held by that organisation. This does not mean that the actual VC is on public display and often, the VC shown in the photograph of the museum display is a replica, the original being held in a secure location. When a VC is held by the family, or is in a private collection, the location is not given.

ABBREVIATIONS

ADC	Aide-de-Camp
AMS	Army medial Services
CB	Companion of the Order of the Bath
CinC	Commander-in-Chief
CMG	Companion of the Order of St Michael and St George
CMO	Chief Medical Officer
DAAG	Deputy Assistant Adjutant-General
DAQMG	Deputy Assistant Quartermaster-General
DCM	Distinguished Conduct Medal
DL	Deputy Lieutenant
DLI	Durham Light Infantry
DSO	Distinguished Service Cross
FRGS	Fellow of the Royal Geographical Society
FRHistS	Fellow of the Royal Historical Society
FRS	Fellow of the Royal Society
GCB	Knight Grand Cross of the Order of the Bath
GOC	General Officer Commanding
HM	His/Her Majesty
HS	High Sheriff
KCB	Knight Commander of the Order of the Bath
KinA	Killed in Action
LLB	Batchelor of Laws
LLD	Doctor of Laws
LRCS	Licentiate of the Royal College of Surgeons
LSA	Licentiate of the College of Apothocaries
MA	Master of Arts
MB	Batchelor of Medicine
MC	Military Cross
MD	Doctor of Medicine
MinD	Mention in Despatches
MM	Military Medal
MRCS	Member of the Royal College of Surgeons
OC	Officer Commanding
PoW	Prisoner of War
QDGs	Queen's Dragoon Guards
RC	Roman Catholic
RE	Royal Engineers
RHA	Royal Horse Artillery
RHQ	Regimental Headquarters
RMA	Royal Military Academy, Woolwich/Sandhurst
RMC	Royal Military College, Sandhurst
RN	Royal Navy
RNM	Royal Naval Museum, Portsmouth
RRW	Royal Regiment of Wales
RWF	Royal Welch Fusiliers/Royal Welsh Fusiliers
SMO	Senior Medical Officer
SWB	South Wales Borderers
VC	Victoria Cross

THE VICTORIA CROSS

The obverse and reverse of the Victoria Cross awarded to Major Lionel Rees for his action on 1 July 1916. Note the date engraved in the centre of the reverse and the name on the reverse of the suspender bar.
[Eastbourne College]

The Victoria Cross was instituted by royal warrant on 29 January 1856, as a reward for acts of valour carried out by British servicemen (or foreign nationals in the service of the British Crown) in the face of the enemy. This warrant states that the award was to be granted 'with a view to place all persons on a perfectly equal footing in relation to eligibility for the Decoration it is hereby declared that neither rank, nor long service, nor wounds, nor any circumstances or conditions whatsoever save the merit of conspicuous bravery shall be held as sufficient claim to the honour.' Consideration that such an award should be established stemmed from questions being asked in the House of Commons by Captain Scobell, MP, on 19 December 1854. The idea was taken up by Prince Albert and, through him, by Queen Victoria herself.

Since the original warrant was issued, there have been several amendments made. The most notable of these being: the award of VCs to members of the Honourable East India Company's forces (1857); the award of VCs to non military persons bearing arms as volunteers (1858); the award of VCs to local forces in New Zealand and the colonies and their dependencies (1867); the award of posthumous VCs (1902); the award of VCs to members of the Royal Air Force (1919).

Throughout the period when the Victoria Cross has existed, only 1,355 men have received the award (including one to the American Unknown Warrior of the Great War). In addition, three men have received a second Victoria Cross which is indicated by a bar on the ribbon of the original award.

The Victoria Cross was originally issued with two ribbons — blue for all naval awards and crimson for all army awards. The establishment of the Royal Air Force in 1918 led to the crimson ribbon being issued for all awards, irrespective of the service involved.

When the proposals for the establishment of the Victoria Cross were being made in the 1850s, the military authorities desired that it should be an 'Order' but were overruled by Queen Victoria who insisted that it should be a 'Decoration'. Despite this, Lord Panmure carried on treating it as an Order which meant that every recipient had not only to survive the action for which it was awarded, but also be alive at the time of recommendation and confirmation by the monarch.

It was a generally held principle that an order of chivalry could not be awarded posthumously and was not valid until the recipient had been invested with it by the Crown.* This procedure was short-circuited during the Indian Mutiny when the GOC was granted the right to make an immediate award of a VC without recourse to London and the Crown. Five servicemen were awarded the VC who later died before the matter could be confirmed by the Queen. The awards were allowed to stand, but a new ruling ensured that similar circumstances would not arise again and all awards would only be made to living recipients.

In 1858, Pte Edward Spence of the Black Watch died from wounds received in an action where his comrades were awarded the VC. A memorandum to those awards stated that Spence would also have been recommended for the decoration had he survived.

The issue of posthumous VCs arose frequently during the second half of the nineteenth century and various officials made attempts to 'fudge' the rules in order to allow some awards to be made as it was quite conceiveable for two men to be involved in an act of gallantry with one playing a leading role and the other supporting him. If the former were killed he would not be awarded the VC whilst the latter, having survived, might be awarded the decoration. The whole procedure was both indefensible and totally unacceptable to the British public who could see no difference between an act of gallantry in which a man died and that of his comrades who survived.

The awards made to the men detailed in this work are of particular interest as they cover a wide spectrum of actions and circumstances including:

- the first Army awards — Luke O'Connor and Edward Bell
- the first man to wear the Victoria Cross — Henry Raby
- five of the six 'non-combat' awards — 24th Regiment, Andaman Islands
- the best known multiple VC action — Rorke's Drift, 1879

In the second volume, further interesting awards include those to:

- the first official fighter pilot — Lionel Rees
- a Tank Regiment award — Richard Wain
- a balloted award — William Williams
- a bomber pilot — Hughie Edwards
- a submariner — Tubby Linton
- the only award to a transport pilot — David Lord

---

* This ruling was not always strictly applied e.g. during the First World War, Brigadier John Gough VC was created a posthumous KCB.

HISTORICAL BACKGROUND TO THE WELSH REGIMENTS

1st KING'S DRAGOON GUARDS
Raised in 1685 during the rebellion of the Duke of Monmouth and known as the 2nd, or Queen's, Regiment of Horse, it first saw action at the Battle of the Boyne in 1690. In 1714, the regiment became known as the King's Own Regiment of Horse and in 1746, the 1st King's Dragoon Guards. During the 18th century, it saw service throughout Europe and in 1815 was present at Waterloo. It served in the closing stages of the Crimean War and in the China, Zulu, First Boer and Second Anglo-Boer Wars. During the Great War it saw action on the Western Front and was mechanised in 1937. For most of the Second World War it served in the Mediterranean area. On 1st January 1959, the 1st King's Dragoon Guards amalgamated with the 2nd Dragoon Guards (Queen's Bays) to become the 1st Queen's Dragoon Guards. The regiment's RHQ is at Maindy Barracks, Cardiff and the museum is at Cardiff Castle.

2nd DRAGOON GUARDS (QUEEN'S BAYS)
Raised in 1685 during the rebellion of the Duke of Monmouth, and known as the 3rd Regiment of Horse, it first saw action at the Battle of the Boyne in 1690. In 1746, it became known as the 2nd, or Queen's, Regiment of Dragoon Guards (later, due to the fact that its mounts were bay horses, it became known as The Queen's Bays). During the 18th century it saw active service throughout Europe. In 1857, the regiment was sent to India where it served with distinction during the Indian Mutiny. Its next major involvement was in South Africa during the Second Anglo-Boer War. It served throughout the Great War on the Western Front and began to be converted to a mechanised regiment during the mid-1930s. For most of the Second World War it served in the Mediterranean area. On 1st January 1959, the 2nd Dragoon Guards amalgamated with the 1st King's Dragoon Guards to become the 1st Queen's Dragoon Guards. The regiment's RHQ is at Maindy Barracks, Cardiff and the museum is in Cardiff Castle.

THE WELSH GUARDS
The Welsh Guards are the youngest of the five regiments of Foot Guards having only been formed in 1915. During its short period of service the regiment has already earned the respect of the other regiments and has won considerable glory in both World Wars and on active service throughout the world. The RHQ and the Guards Museum are both at Wellington Barracks, London. A private museum to the Welsh Guards is located at Parkwall, Oswestry.

THE ROYAL WELCH FUSILIERS (23rd Regiment of Foot)
Raised in 1689, by Lord Herbert of Chirbury in Shropshire, it was originally known as Herbert's Regiment, which recruited in Wales and the border country and had its headquarters at Ludlow in Shropshire. The regiment first saw action at the Battle of the Boyne in 1690 since when it has had an unbroken record of service and has featured in almost every major campaign in which the British Army has been involved. In 1702 it became known as 'The Welsh Regiment of Fusiliers' and, in 1714, 'The Prince of Wales's Own Regiment of Welch Fusiliers'. In 1751 it became the 23rd Regiment of Foot and, in 1756, formed a second battalion at Leicester which, two years later, became the 68th Regiment of Foot (later the Durham Light Infantry). In 1804 another second battalion was raised which recruited in north Wales. During the First World War it raised forty-two battalions, twenty-two of which served overseas in almost every theatre of operations. The regimental depot has been at Hightown Barracks, Wrexham since 1877 and the museum is at Caernarfon Castle. The Government's defence review of 2005 decided that the Royal Welch Fusiliers would merge with the Royal Regiment of Wales and the Royal Welsh Regiment (T.A.) to form a new regiment, The Royal Welsh. This is the first amalgamation in the regiment's history. The first battalion of the new regiment would bear the name: 1st Bn The Royal Welsh (Royal Welch Fusiliers).

The word 'Welch' or 'Welsh' appeared in the regiment's title at various times in its history. From the late nineteenth century until 1920, it was 'Welsh' since when it has used the old English spelling of 'Welch'.

THE SOUTH WALES BORDERERS (24th Regiment of Foot)

Raised in 1689 as a regiment of foot soldiers, by Sir Edward Dering, Bt, of Surrenden in Kent, it was originally known as Dering's Regiment and first saw active service in Ireland. In 1751 it was designated the 24th Regiment of Foot, serving throughout the Duke of Marlborough's campaigns against the French and later in North America and the Peninsula. In 1756 the regiment raised a second battalion in Nottinghamshire and Derbyshire which, two years later became the 69th Regiment of Foot (see Welch Regiment below). In 1804 another second battalion was raised. At Chilianwala, India, in 1849, the 24th (2nd Warwickshire) Regiment, lost nearly half its strength in action against the Sikhs. Thirty years later history repeated itself at Isandlwana, Zululand where the 1/24th and 2/24th lost a total of 596 officers and men. In 1881 the regiment's territorial title was changed to The South Wales Borderers, taking the name from a local militia regiment, the Royal South Wales Borderers Militia. It served with distinction throughout the two World Wars. In 1969, the regiment amalgamated with The Welch Regiment to become The Royal Regiment of Wales. The museum (24th/41st Foot) is at Brecon Barracks, Brecon. The Government's defence review of 2005 decided that the Royal Regiment of Wales would merge with the Royal Welch Fusiliers and the Royal Welsh Regiment (T.A.) to form a new regiment to be called the Royal Welsh Regiment. The second battalion of the new regiment would bear the name: 2nd Bn The Royal Welsh (Royal Regiment of Wales).

THE WELCH REGIMENT (41st/69th Regiment of Foot)

Raised in 1719 as a regiment of infantry it was recruited from Out Pensioners at the Royal Hospital, Chelsea and known as 'The Invalids'. Its duties were to garrison Britain's coastal defences and guard prisoners of war in order that the regular line regiments could be released for foreign service. In 1751 the regiment was designated the 41st Regiment of Foot and in 1787 dropped the title Invalids when it became a regular regiment of the line. In 1756, the 24th Regiment of Foot (see South Wales Borderers above) raised a second battalion which, became the 69th Regiment of Foot in 1758 and the 69th (South Lincolnshire) Regiment of Foot in 1781. Shortly afterwards the 69th served for a short period as marines. These two regiments, 41st and 69th, served with distinction throughout the world during the 19th century and, in 1881, amalgamated to become the 1st and 2nd Battalions, The Welch Regiment. The regiment served in the Anglo-Boer War and throughout the two World Wars. In 1969, the Welch Regiment amalgamated with the South Wales Borderers to become The Royal Regiment of Wales. The museum (24th/41st Foot) is in Cardiff Castle. The government's defence review of 2005 decided that the Royal Regiment of Wales would merge with the Royal Welch Fusiliers and the Royal Welsh Regiment (T.A.) to form a new regiment, the Royal Welsh. The second battalion of the new regiment would bear the name: 2nd Bn The Royal Welsh (Royal Regiment of Wales).

MONMOUTHSHIRE REGIMENT

Formed in 1908 from the 2nd, 3rd and 4th Volunteer Battalions South Wales Borderers, as part of the newly created Territorial Force. The regiment served with distinction in both World Wars. Units of the Monmouthshire Regiment disappeared with the restructuring of the Territorial Army in 1967.

The VCs of Wales
and the Welsh Regiments

*Colour-Sgt Luke O'Connor
[RWF Museum]*

LUKE O'CONNOR
Sergeant
23rd (Royal Welch Fusiliers) Regiment of Foot

Full Name: Luke O'Connor.
Place of Birth: Elphine, County Roscommon, Ireland.
Date of Birth: 20 February 1831.
Father: —
Mother: —
Father's Occupation: —
Education: —
Pre-Service Employment: —
Service Record: Enlisted as a private soldier, 23rd Regiment of Foot, 21 July 1849; corporal, 15 May 1850; sergeant, 18 May 1851; colour sergeant, 22 September 1854; served Crimean Campaign, 1854–56 (present at the Alma and during the Siege of Sebastopol), severely wounded 20 September 1854; dangerously wounded 8 September 1855; commissioned as an ensign, 76th Regiment of Foot, 19 October 1854 (without purchase as a reward for his gallant conduct at the Battle of the Alma); exchanged to 23rd Regiment of Foot, 5 November 1854; lieutenant, 9 February 1855 (without purchase); served Indian Mutiny 1857–8 (present at the relief and capture of Lucknow and at Cawnpore); captain, 24 August 1858 (without purchase); served Gibraltar, 1863–6; served Canada, 1866–7; brevet major, 5 July 1872; served Ashanti War, 1873–4; served Gibraltar, 1874–80; major, 19 August 1874; brevet lieutenant-colonel, 1 April 1874; lieutenant-colonel, 21 June 1880; colonel, 17 August 1879; half-pay, 1886; retired 2 March 1887; honorary major-general, 9 March 1887; Honorary Colonel, Royal Welsh Fusiliers, 3 June 1914.
Decorations, Medals and Rewards: Victoria Cross (for action at the Battle of the Alma, 20 September 1854 and before Sebastopol, 8 September 1855); CB (*London Gazette,* 29 June 1906); KCB (*London Gazette,* 3 June 1913); Crimea Medal (clasps for Alma and Sebastopol); Indian Mutiny Medal (clasps for Relief of Lucknow and Lucknow); Ashanti War Medal, 1873–74 (no clasps); Turkish Order of the Medjidie, 5th Class (1856); Turkish Crimea Medal; Sardinian Crimea Medal; received the thanks of Sir George Brown and Sir William Codrington on the field of the Alma (1854); Reward for Distinguished Service; received one year's pay as lieutenant and a temporary pension as brevet lieutenant-colonel for his services during the Ashanti Campaign of 1873–4.
Post-Service Employment: Retired general officer; Colonel, Royal

L–R: CB, Victoria Cross, Crimea Medal, Indian Mutiny Medal, Ashantee War Medal, Order of the Medijie (Turkey), Sardinian Crimea Medal, Turkish Crimea medal, KCB. [RWF Museum, Caernarfon]

Welsh Fusiliers.

Married: Unmarried.

Children: None.

Died: Clarges Street, London, 1st February 1915.

Buried: Plot 1100, St Mary's RC Cemetery, Kensal Rise, London, 4 February 1915.

Memorials: St Mary's RC Cemetery, Kensal Rise, London; plaque opposite the altar to Our Lady of Lourdes, Church of the Immaculate Conception, Farm Street, London; portrait RWF Museum, Caernarfon; Connor Crescent, Wrexham; Luke O'Connor House, Wrexham.

Location of Victoria Cross: RWF Museum, Caernarfon Castle.

Citation for the Victoria Cross: *London Gazette,* 24 February 1857. 'Was one of the centre Sergeants at the Battle of the Alma and advanced between the Officers carrying the colours. When near the Redoubt, Lieutenant Anstruther, who was carrying a Colour, was mortally wounded and he was shot in the breast at the same time and fell, but recovering himself, snatched up the Colour from the ground, and continued to carry it till the end of the action although urged by Captain Granville to relinquish it and go to the rear on account of his wound: was recommended for and received his commission for his services at the Alma (September 20th, 1854). Also behaved with great gallantry at the assault on the Redan 8th September 1855, where he was shot through both thighs.'

VC Investiture: By HM Queen Victoria at the first investiture in Hyde Park, London, 26 June 1857. His departure for India with his regiment was delayed to allow him to attend the investiture.

Colonel Luke O'Connor, VC in the full dress uniform of the Royal Welch Fusliers. [RWF Museum]

Luke O'Connor, VC, centre right with the officers of the RWF.[RWF Museum]

The grave of Major-General Sir Luke O'Connor, VC at Kensal Rise, London

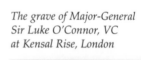

Luke O'Connor, seated centre wearing a hat, Plymouth, 1880. [RWF Museum]

Luke O'Connor is often cited as an example of how a common soldier could prosper in the nineteenth century British Army, rising from the rank of private to that of major-general. It is perhaps, therefore, of interest to trace his background and early career. Other than his date of birth (20 February 1831), few details of his background were known until the discovery in the archives of the Royal Welch Fusiliers of a magazine article, written by O'Connor himself in 1900.

Major-General Luke O'Connor, VC, c.1912.
[RWF Museum]

> I was born near Elphin, co. Roscommon, in 1832, and owing to the troubles in those days my parents, with a large portion of their numerous family, emigrated to Canada in order to go in for farming, and took me, being one of the youngest children, with them. Crossing the Atlantic was a tedious business then, and we did it in a slow sailing vessel. During the long voyage my father died at sea. My widowed mother reached Quebec in the midst of an epidemic of small-pox and fever, when she too, was taken ill and died, also one of my brothers, leaving me to the care of an elder sister, who brought me back to Ireland.
>
> My first recollection in life is my return to Boyle, a military town containing barracks …. Here I was handed over to an uncle, as my sister returned immediately to America, where many of my relations still are; some of them attained to high positions during the American War. It was not strange that my earliest ideas had a military tendency, for Roscommon is famous for giving soldiers to the service, and, indeed, many of my own relatives have served in the Army all over the world. My first and greatest delight was in playing at soldiers and drilling other children in the street; also occasionally making raids into the barracks, in defiance of the sentries, instead of attending school, for which I often received a severe thrashing. Little did I then think that later in life I should become a captain commanding a two-company detachment in the same quarters.

Although this account gives little away as regards O'Connor's social background there are one or two assumptions that can be made with a degree of certainty. Although he mentions 'the troubles of those days', the family emigrated from Ireland in the pre-famine period. Despite the tragic loss of both his parents, the surviving children had sufficient money to pay for Luke and his sister to return to Ireland and for his sister to then re-join her other siblings in North America. This would suggest that, although Irish, Roman Catholic and a large family, the O'Connors were not without some financial standing in their homeland. This is confirmed by Luke's description of how he came to enlist in the Army.

> It was intended at first to make me a priest, and this notion sometimes took hold of my fancy. My uncle, however, wished me to return to Canada to join my people; but all at once he died. There was a first cousin of mine, however, in London in medical practice, who had served as a surgeon under Sir de Lacy Evans in Spain. I resolved to visit this relative, and see what he could do for me.
>
> My cousin promised to do his best, but said it would take some time. Meanwhile, having met some young fellows of my own age, we went about town and were soon attracted at Westminster by sergeants flaunting gay ribbons in their caps anxious to secure recruits. Being like most of my countrymen very fond of horses, I took the Queen's shilling for the 17th Lancers.
>
> When I told my cousin of this the next day he said: 'I hope you'll do something better than that,' and I got off by paying the 'smart money' before being regularly attested.
>
> In spite of this my wish to soldier became too strong for me, and shortly afterwards when again in Westminster I was struck by the gallant appearance of a fine-looking recruiting sergeant of the Royal Welsh Fusiliers, a regiment I had never heard of before, and its title caught my fancy. I took the shilling once more, a few of my young friends followed my example, and we enlisted in the same regiment. I said nothing to my cousin this time, and in a few days found myself in the barracks at Winchester, where the Royal Welsh were quartered in July 1849.

Again, this rather sparse information is sufficient to confirm that Luke O'Connor's family were of some substance and that he only entered the ranks of the Army because of his own headstrong nature and not because of necessity or insufficient status to gain a commission. In these few sentences, he passes over a lengthy period of his life, ranging from arrival back in Ireland (his earliest recollection) probably aged not much beyond 5 years, to being recruited into the 17th Lancers (when he would have been in his late teens). Much of this time must have been spent with his uncle at Boyle and his consideration of the priesthood would suggest that, despite his truancy, he had attained an acceptable level of education. His later life in London with his medical cousin (probably the son of the uncle from Boyle), would also indicate that the family was reasonably comfortably off.

Luke O'Connor enlisted as a private soldier in the 23rd Regiment of Foot (Royal Welch Fusiliers) on 21 July 1849,

Captain Luke O'Connor, VC, c.1860.

in London and joined the regiment which was then stationed at Winchester. On joining I was told off to a Barrack-room and placed in charge of an old Welshman, Tom Jones by name, who was told to look after me. This veteran soldier took great interest in this duty and showed me how to clean my things and turn out smart for parade, and I felt much gratitude to him for his kind attention. In those days a soldier's rations were very bad, the bread served out to us was black and so badly baked it would stick to the wall. With spare money of my own I used to buy some of a better quality, which I shared with my elder comrade, besides standing him beer. The sergeant of my room, a fine tall man, who played the fiddle, was also very kind to me. Strange to say, years afterwards this sergeant, Kneightly by name, was my quartermaster when I commanded the regiment. Within a fortnight of joining I had so mastered my drill that I was noticed by my adjutant and sergeant-major and called out to drill a squad in their presence to see if I could do it just as I had been taught.

Proud of the opportunity, I repeated the necessary cautions and gave the words of command completely to their satisfaction.

Next day I was brought to the orderly-room before my colonel, Arthur Wellesley Torrens, a man well known in the service. Formerly adjutant to the Guards, very much to the disgust of the older officers of the Royal Welsh he had been promoted to the command of their regiment. Yet, no doubt, he was a thoroughly clever, competent officer, and, I can now say, was very far advanced in military subjects for that period … and, although very severe, seemed devoted to his profession, and loved to encourage young soldiers.

To my great delight, on that day he gave me my stripe as a lance-corporal, which I am always proud to remember. In June 1850, I was promoted full corporal and to lance-sergeant the same year, and twelve months later on, when the regiment was at Plymouth, I became a sergeant, just two years after joining it.

His natural intelligence and ability had made him stand out amongst his comrades and the rate of his promotion was quite exceptional and a clear indicator of things to come. In 1853, he was detached from the regiment to drill and train the Montgomeryshire Militia at Welshpool and then to repeat the exercise with the Anglesey Militia and the 3rd Lancashire Militia in Liverpool. He had obviously developed into a man who could give as well as receive orders and whose presence carried some weight.

In 1854, the 23rd Regiment embarked aboard the SS *Trent* for Turkey, forming part of the Allied army supporting the Turks in their conflict with Russia. They took part in the campaign in Bulgaria where the only event of note was the loss of one officer and 36 other ranks to cholera which seemed endemic to all the armies involved. In August, the British and French governments issued directives that their armies in Bulgaria were to embark at Varna and then endeavour to capture the Russian naval base at Sebastopol in the Crimea. On 14 September the British army began to land troops at Kalamita Bay, north of Sebastopol and the first regiment ashore (from the prophetically named *Victoria*) was the 23rd Foot. The unopposed landings lasted for four days and on 19 September the advance south towards Sebastopol began. That night they encamped near the village of Bulganak, close to the northern bank of the river Alma. The eastern bank, and the route south, was dominated by a ridge, some 400 feet high and six miles long, which commanded the approach which the Allies would have to take. At the top this ridge was the Russian army in prepared positions.

Early on the morning of 20 September the French (who were on the right of the line, between the British army and the sea) began their advance, expecting to be closely supported. The British Staff, however, due to generally poor organisation, failed to order the advance until 3pm when Field Marshal Lord Raglan ordered the 2nd and Light Divisions, supported by the 3rd and 1st Divisions, to advance up the slopes directly in front of them. The Royal Welch formed part of the Fusilier Brigade of the Light Division. As they advanced towards the river they passed through vineyards and began to scramble over stone walls, activities which began to break up their formation and they became the target of a heavy bombardment from the Russian guns on the heights ahead of them. Once across the river, they commenced up the slope which had no natural cover. Almost immediately, the advance slowed and in places, began to falter. General Codrington, commanding the Fusilier Brigade ordered his men to fix bayonets and attack the Russian positions. The Royal Fusiliers on the right of the line were forced to form to the right to repel a large Russian column that was attempting to outflank them. The Royal Welch, and the 33rd Foot, were joined by a regiment from the 2nd Division and the 19th Regiment and surged up the hill.

Early on the morning of the 20th … the Light Division was deployed into line, and halted for some time. Our adjutant came to my captain and asked him to let me go as one of the escort for the colours. He replied I was wanted where I was. The adjutant returned with the colonel's commands for me to be sent as directed. I went away delighted with the distinction of being with the colour party, and was appointed centre sergeant. On the line being told to advance, I took the usual six paces to the front as guide to the right brigade, of which the Royal Welsh was the battalion of direction.

The general, however, called me back, as we were now under a heavy fire of shot and shell, and told me to take the usual place between the colours. … We pushed through the river, which was very deep in some places … here the men began to drop very fast.

As they reached the Russian line which was protected by an earthwork, the Colours of the Royal Welch were being carried by eighteen-year old Lieutenant Anstruther and Ensign Butler. This duty, although deemed a great honour, was highly dangerous. Viscount Wolseley later wrote that a 'general who would condemn anyone to carry a large silk colour under close musketry fire ought to be tried for murder'. Within minutes Butler was shot dead and the pole broken by a musket ball. The fallen Regimental Colour was then picked up by Lieutenant-Colonel Chester and then passed to Sergeant Honey Smith who carried it for the remainder of the day. Lieutenant Anstruther, carrying the Queen's Colour, was urged by Sergeant O'Connor to move forward, believing that it was safer close to the earthwork than it was lower down the slope. Suddenly the Russians began to limber up their artillery and Anstruther charged forward leading a number of men intent on foiling the enemy's plan.

We then ran up the slope until about eighty yards from the redoubt when I remarked: 'If we go further the colours may be taken, for we are far ahead of the men.' We halted; at that moment the poor officer was killed and I was knocked over at the same time by a bullet striking me in the breast and breaking two ribs. Private Evans came up and helped me on my legs; I then snatched up the flag, rushed to the earthwork and planted it on the parapet. … The silk standard was riddled with shot, but the redoubt itself sheltered my body.

When O'Connor fell the Queen's Colour had actually been taken up by Welshman, Private William Evans and he held it up to indicate that the Royal Welch were the first to reach the enemy positions, before passing it to Corporal Luby who then relinquished it back to O'Connor. Captain Granville urged the wounded sergeant to relinquish the Colour and to go to the rear for medical treatment but he refused until loss of blood forced him to pass it to Captain Bevil Granville. There followed a period of fierce fighting before the Russians finally withdrew and left the field of battle to the Allies. The Royal Welch had 8 officers and 44 men killed and five officers and 154 men wounded, amongst whom was Sergeant Luke O'Connor whose battlefield promotion to colour-sergeant was confirmed two days later. The Queen's Colour borne by O'Connor had been pierced by twenty-six bullets.

O'Connor was one of the fortunate men who, having been severely wounded in action, managed to survive the ministering of the medical services in the field and at Scutari in Turkey. After recovering from his wound and being discharged by the hospial on 20 October, he was laid low by disease whilst en route back to the Crimea and was returned to Scutari. On 19 October he had been commissioned (without purchase) as an ensign (2nd lieutenant) in the 76th Regiment of Foot (2nd Bn Duke of Wellington's Regiment) as a reward for his action at the Alma. It was normal to commission an NCO into another regiment as it was felt that such a promotion within the same regiment would

place him in a difficult position with regard to his former comrades. Despite this, however, the losses sustained by the Royal Welch as a result of enemy action and, more importantly, disease, meant that on 5 November he was able to exchange back into his 'natural home' the 23rd Regiment of Foot. On 9 February 1855, he was promoted to lieutenant (without purchase). It would appear that much of this took place without O'Connor's knowledge, possibly as a result of poor communications in the theatre of war and with his absence from the regiment.

I reached Scutari Hospital on 26th [September], and was discharged on October 20th. I again embarked for the Crimea, but caught a fever on board, was landed at

Chevalier Louis Désanges's painting of Sergeant Luke O'Connor's VC action at the Battle of the Alma. [RWF Museum]

Major-General Sir Luke O'Connor, VC, KCB, c.1913. [RWF Museum]

the Balaclava Hospital and sent back to Scutari, where I received much kind attention from Miss Nightingale and the Sisters of Charity. I was most anxious to rejoin my regiment, but when somewhat better was appointed acting sergeant-major to take charge of invalid British soldiers on board a Turkish man-of-war until I picked up more strength. Meanwhile, in February, I received the good news I had been promoted to an ensign's commission in the Royal Welch Fusiliers, and this was subsequently antedated to November 5th, 1854.

On 8 September Lieutenant O'Connor took part in the British assault on the Redan, one of two major Russian defensive works outside Sebastopol. The storming party dashed across nearly 300 yards of open ground towards a twenty-foot wide and fourteen-foot deep ditch. Unfortunately, when they began their attack, the men of the 23rd Foot who were in support were still some distance from the front line. Lieutenant Boscawen Trevor Griffith wrote in a letter home:

'We rushed madly along the trenches … Several officers we met coming back wounded said that they had been in the Redan and that the supports were only wanted to complete the victory … We gained the 5th parallel (trench line), our most advanced trench, and 'On, Twenty Third! This way!' cried the staff officers. We scrambled out of the trench on to open ground. That was a fearful moment. I rushed across the space … shot striking the ground all the way and men falling down on all sides. When I got to the edge of the ditch … I found our men all mixed up in confusion but keeping a steady fire against the enemy … over the next glacis — here were lots of men of different regiments all huddled together — scaling ladders placed against the parapet crowded with our fellows. Radcliffe and I got hold of a ladder and went up it to the top of the parapet where we were stopped by the press — wounded and dead men kept tumbling down upon us ….

Well, do as we could, we could not get the men to come up the parapet in sufficient numbers … Suddenly a panic seized our men and I grieve to say they deserted their comrades inside and retreated in confusion towards our trenches.

O'Connor had volunteered to command one of the storming parties which had to run 180 yards in the open, straight into an intense enemy fire. Half his men fell before they reached the parapet of the Redan but he managed to reach the top before being shot through both thighs and falling back into the ditch and being knocked unconscious. He was carried back to the British trenches where, for a time, it was thought that he might have to have one leg amputated. On 25 September he was invalided to Britain aboard the *Robert Lowe*, arriving in Portsmouth on 10 November when he was admitted to Haslar Naval Hospital. He rejoined his regiment at Aldershot in December.

After the Crimean War, O'Connor continued to serve in the Royal Welch Fusiliers and again saw action during the Indian Mutiny and in the Ashanti War, eventually rising to command one of the regiment's battalions. On retiring, he was made an honorary major-general, Colonel of the Royal Welch Fusiliers and, in 1913, was knighted. He died at his home in Clarges Street, Mayfair in 1915. It is of interest that, being unmarried and with no immediate family, he left most of his estate to various Roman Catholic charities. The biggest single beneficiary was the Incorporated Society of the Crusade of Rescue to which he left £1,500, the bulk of which was to be used 'towards the expenses of emigration to Canada of two children, male and female'. This was an unusual, but understandable gesture, when one considers his own experiences as a child when trying to emigrate to Canada with his parents.

Major-General Luke O'Connor, VC, front row wearing spats, on one of his last visits to the RWF Depot at Hightown Barracks, Wrexham, Alma Day, 1913. The Queen's Colour which he carried at the Alma is being held left centre. [RWF Museum]

Major-General Luke O'Connor, VC, regularly attended the annual regimental dinners of the RWF. Seen here at the 1905 dinner, he is seated in the centre of the photograph, on the right of General Sir Edward Bulwer (Colonel of the Regiment), on whose left sits HRH The Prince of Wales (Colonel in Chief of the Regiment).
[RWF Museum]

Luke O'Connor's action at the Battle of the Alma was the first for which the Victoria Cross was awarded to a member of the British Army although, because of the reference to the award being made for two events, twelve months apart, this honour has been claimed by others.

The memorial plaque to Sir Luke O'Connor in the Church of the Immaculate Conception, Farm Street, Mayfair, London.
The inscription reads:

+ OF YOUR CHARITY PRAY FOR THE SOUL OF
MAJOR-GENERAL SIR LUKE O'CONNOR, VC, KCB,
A CONSTANT WORSHIPPER IN THIS CHURCH.
HE ENLISTED IN THE ROYAL WELSH FUSILIERS 1849
AND ROSE TO BE COLONEL OF HIS REGIMENT.
HE RECEIVED THE VICTORIA CROSS FOR GALLANTRY
AT THE BATTLE OF THE ALMA 1854 AND ALSO SERVED
IN THE INDIAN MUTINY AND ASHANTI.
DIED 1ST FEBY 1915, AGED 83.
A GOOD SOLDIER OF CHRIST JESUS, II TIM. 2.3.
R.I.P.

Captain Bell, VC. [Mrs Diana Bailey]

Kempsey Lodge, the childhood home of Edward Bell.
[Mrs Diana Bailey]

Bell's VC, decorations and medals in Caernarfon Castle.
L–R: CB; VC; Crimean Medal, Indian Mutiny Medal,
Order of the Medjidie; Turkish Crimea Medal.
The Legion of Honour appears to be missing.
[RWF Museum]

EDWARD BELL
Captain
23rd Regiment of Foot (Royal Welch Fusiliers)

Full Name: Edward William Derrington Bell.

Place of Birth: Landguard Fort, Essex. The family home was at Napleton Cottage, Kempsey, then Kempsey Lodge, Worcestershire. They also owned The Lodge, Kempsey where the cottage was named Alma Cottage.

Date of Birth: Not known. He was baptised on 19 January 1824. He had a younger brother, Lieutenant Montagu Wigley Bell, 28th Regiment, (died Sebastopol, 7 January 1855), and a younger sister, Caroline Isobella (who married Vice Admiral Alexander Philips).

Father: Lieutenant-General Edward Wells Bell, (died 1870, formerly 7th Regiment of Foot & 29th Regiment of Foot, of Ravenhurst, Staffordshire and Kempsey Lodge, Worcestershire).

Mother: Mary Anne Chapman (died 1870), the daughter of Sir Benjamin Chapman, Bart, of Killua Castle, Co. Westmeath, Ireland and great aunt of T. E. Lawrence (Lawrence of Arabia). Her family claimed descent from Sir Walter Raleigh. Her name is sometimes written 'Marianne'.

Father's Occupation: General officer, former lieutenant-governor of Jamaica (1856–7). He had served with the 7th Regiment of Foot (Royal Fusiliers) and had fought at Vittoria and Salamanca. Present at the Battle of New Orleans. Colonel 66th Regiment, 1859–70.

Education: Sandhurst School; RMA Sandhurst.

Service Record: Commissioned as an ensign, 23rd Regiment of Foot, 15 April 1842 (without purchase); served North America 4 November 1842–25 July 1845, 9 May 1846–19 March 1850, 15 May 1852–25 July 1853; lieutenant, 17 November 1843 (by purchase); captain, 18 December 1848 (without purchase); served Crimean Campaign, 1854–6 (present at the Alma, Inkerman and Sebastopol); brevet major, 12 December 1854 (for distinguished service in the field); major, 13 March 1855 (without purchase); brevet lieutenant-colonel, 30 December 1856; served Indian Mutiny (present at the capture of Lucknow) 18 November 1857–20 March 1858; lieutenant-colonel, 30 March 1858; CO 2nd Bn Royal Welch Fusiliers, 1858; served Malta, 1859–63; served Canada, 1866–7; colonel, 10 August 1862; CO Regimental Depot, Wrexham; major-general, 6 March 1868; GOC Belfast District, 28 February 1875–9.

Edward Wells Bell, the father of Edward Bell, VC. [Mrs Diana Bailey]

33 The Promenade, Cheltenham as it is today. [Ian Hunter]

Decorations, Medals and Rewards: Victoria Cross (for action at the Battle of the Alma, 20 September 1854); CB (1856); Crimean Medal (clasps for Alma, Inkerman and Sebastopol); Indian Mutiny Medal (clasp for Lucknow); Turkish Crimea Medal; Turkish Order of the Medjidie, 5th Class (1856); Legion of Honour, 5th Class (1856); MinD (Crimea and Indian Mutiny — twice); mentioned in general orders by Lord Raglan for his distinguished conduct while in command of a working party under heavy fire on 2 April 1855; Reward for Distinguished Service.

Married: (1) Alice, daughter of Captain Francis Capper Brooke, (Grenadier Guards), at Ufford Parish Church, Suffolk, 27 May 1857 (she was aged 17 years). Divorced. (2) Charlotte Wadsworth Davies (widow of Surgeon John Davies, ex-49th Regiment, served Crimea, resided 30 The Promenade, Cheltenham), at St Mary's Church, Cheltenham, 3 August 1869. She was the daughter of Robert Wadsworth Bartell, Esq. At the time of his marriage, Bell resided at 33, The Promenade, Cheltenham. She died 19 April 1892.

Children: One son, Colonel Edward Bell, CMG, from his first marriage. He served in the Worcestershire Regiment and was Adjutant of the City of London Volunteers in South Africa, 1900–02. His daughter Mary was the sister-in-law of Clement Robertson, VC and his daughter Dorothy was the sister-in-law of Maurice Dease, VC. From his second marriage, Bell had one son, Captain William Edward Derrington Bell, JP, born 1874 (Worcestershire Militia,

Captain Bell, VC. [RWF Museum]

The 16lb-gun captured by Bell, on display at the Royal W elch Fusiliers Museum, Caernarfon Castle.

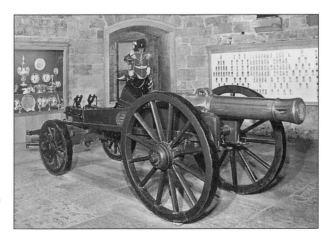

served South Africa and Worcestershire Regiment and Middlesex Regiment, 1914-18, temporary major, honorary captain) — and three daughters — Caroline Mary Anne (Edwards), Margaret Derrington (Longhurst), Katherine Arabella (Boucher). He also had two step-daughters by his second marriage.

Died: Lisbreen House, Fort William Park, Belfast, Ireland, 10 November 1879 of 'Gout in the head'.

Buried: Kempsey Churchyard, Kempsey, Worcestershire, 15 November 1875, his body being brought from Ireland for burial in the family vault.

Memorials: Kempsey Churchyard, Kempsey, Worcestershire.

Location of Victoria Cross: RWF Museum, Caernarfon Castle (on loan).

Citation for the Victoria Cross: *London Gazette*, 24 February 1857.
'Recommended for his gallantry, more particularly at the Battle of the Alma, where he was the first to seize upon and capture one of the enemy's guns which was limbered up and being carried off. He moreover, succeeded to the command of that gallant regiment which he brought out of action; all his senior officers having been killed or wounded.'

VC Investiture: By HM Queen Victoria on Southsea Common, Hampshire, 2 August 1858.

The Bell family vault at Kempsey.

The inscription on the Bell's family vault is now virtually indecipherable. It reads:

IN A VAULT UNDER THIS STONE
ARE DEPOSITED THE REMAINS OF
GENERAL EDWARD WELLS BELL
COLONEL 66TH REGIMENT
WHO DEPARTED THIS LIFE
AT KEMPSEY OCTOBER 9TH 1870
AGED 81 YEARS.
ALSO OF
MARY ANNE HIS WIFE
WHO DEPARTED THIS LIFE
MARCH 19 1870(?)
AGED 73 YEARS.
THEY WERE BEAUTIFUL IN THEIR LIVES
AND IN DEATH THEY WERE NOT DIVIDED.
ALSO OF
MAJOR-GENERAL EDWARD
WILLIAM DERRINGTON BELL VC, CB,
COLONEL 2 BA (?)
(?)
(?) NORTHERN DISTRICT,
(?) BELFAST
ON THE 10 OF NOV 1879 AGED 51 YEARS
? BATH
?
ALSO HIS WIFE
CHARLOTTE WADSWORTH BELL
BORN JUNE 18TH 1838(?), DIED APRIL 19TH 1892
THY WILL BE DONE.

Captain Bell winning the Victoria Cross, a painting by Chevalier Louis Désanges. [RWF Museum]

Edward Bell came from a military family. His father, Lieutenant-General Edward Wells Bell, had served with the Royal Fusiliers and fought at Vittoria and Salamanca in the Peninsular War and was later Governor of Jamaica. Edward was born at the family home, Kempsey Lodge in Worcestershire and educated at Sandhurst School and Sandhurst Military College before receiving his commission as a 2nd Lieutenant in the 23rd Regiment of Foot (Royal Welch Fusiliers) on 15 April 1842.

At the beginning of the battle of the Alma on 20 September 1854, he was a captain in the Royal Welch Fusiliers which formed part of the Fusilier Brigade of the Light Division. As the regiment advanced up the steep slopes of Kourgané Hill, towards a heavily defended position known as the Redoubt, the Russian artillery covering the slope were ordered to limber up and withdraw — the Tsar having given express orders that no artillery piece was to be allowed to fall into the hands of the invading British and French armies. Bell realised what was happening and led a charge against the remaining guns in the position. One, a brass 24-pounder, was reputedly seized by an officer of the 33rd Foot named Donovan who claimed to have scratched his name on it before it was taken away — the veracity of this claim is in serious doubt! Bell then noticed a Russian artillery driver trying to whip up his team at the rear of the Redoubt in order to pull away a 16-pounder. Alone, Bell rushed towards the gun, drew his revolver and pointed it at the Russian's head, making clear signs as to what he thought should happen. The artillery driver was under no illusions as to what would happen if he remained where he was and leapt from his saddle and ran towards the Russian lines. Bell seized the reins on the lead horse and, assisted by Private Pyle of the Royal Fusiliers, began to lead the team down the slope towards the British rear.

While this had been going on, a mounted figure had appeared who shouted at the men of the Light Division to cease firing as they were being approached not by the Russians but by their French allies. Lieutenant-Colonel Chester, commanding the Royal Welch, ignored the warning and ordered his men to keep firing before being shot dead by men who were very definitely Russians. It was too late, however, as the fire from the British line slackened and the

Colonel Edward Bell VC, wearing winter gear during his service in Canada as CO 2nd Bn Royal Welch Fusiliers, 1866–7. The rather haphazard method of wearing the VC and medals was the norm at this time.

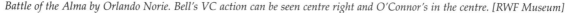

Battle of the Alma by Orlando Norie. Bell's VC action can be seen centre right and O'Connor's in the centre. [RWF Museum]

Russians were able to re-capture the Redoubt. As the now disorganised and unsupported men of the Fusilier Brigade fell back towards the river they sustained heavy casualties. Chester's second in command, Captain Campbell, was also badly wounded. As Bell made his way down the slope he came across Sir George Brown, his divisional commander, who, furious that the captain had left his company in order to claim the gun as a prize, ordered him to return to the front. Bell pointed the horses towards the rear and then returned to the remnants of his company where Brigadier-General Codrington gave him the command of the Royal Welch. Gradually, the retreating line was steadied and the British troops recaptured the ground they had lost and eventually drove the Russian army off the heights above the river Alma.

Bell's gun arrived safely at the foot of the slope and became the only Russian gun to be captured in the battle. It eventually made it back to Britain where, for some years, it was displayed at Woolwich before being moved to Hightown Barracks in Wrexham in 1885, where it remained until 1960. Today, the gun is located in the Royal Welch Fusiliers Museum in Caernarfon Castle.

When Bell's name was put forward for consideration as a recipient of the Victoria Cross, there appears to have been some controversy. Sir George Brown's disapproval of Bell leaving his company to secure the gun carried some considerable weight. Bell obviously thought this was unfair and argued, as the officer commanding the

Artist's impression of Captain Bell capturing the Russian gun for which he was awarded the Victoria Cross. [Mrs Diana Bailey]

Major-General E.W.D. Bell, VC, CB, with his ADC Captain Hutton, a photograph taken at Belfast shortly before his death in 1879. [RWF Museum]

2nd Battalion Royal Welch Fusiliers, that he could not support the nomination of Sergeant O'Connor unless his own nomination also went forward. As things transpired, both nominations were put forward and approved and Bell's award therefore merits consideration as possibly the first army VC (O'Connor's having been awarded for two actions).

During the General Election of 1868, rioting broke out in Newport, south Wales which caused the authorities to call out the Royal Welch Fusiliers in an effort to disperse the rioters. The troops, under the command of Colonel Bell, VC, were ordered to fix bayonets and clear the streets. As a result of this, Mrs Mary Grant, an innocent bystander, was

Major-General Edward Bell VC. [Mrs Diana Bailey]

killed whilst trying to get into her home. The inquest returned a verdict of 'accidental death' and declared that 'no blame whatsoever attached to the military'.

In 1857, Bell had married Alice Brooke, by whom he had one son, Edward who served with distinction in the South African War where he was adjutant of the City Imperial Volunteers. For his services, Edward was promoted to brevet lieutenant-colonel and given the CMG. It is believed that he was, at the time, the youngest lieutenant-colonel in the British Army. The marriage of Edward Bell senior and Alice, ended in divorce and he had little contact with his son for the remainder of his life. In 1869, he married Charlotte Davies, the widow of his friend, Surgeon John Davies, who lived close to him at The

Above: Lieutenant-Colonel Edward Bell, CMG, the eldest son of Major-General Edward Bell, VC, CB. [Mrs Diana Bailey]

Parade, Cheltenham. The family were told that this marriage stemmed from Surgeon Davies requesting Bell to take care of his widow and daughters. From this marriage, he had a second son, William, and three daughters. Sadly, there were no grandsons and the name Bell died out with the death of William in 1937.

Bell was the first Freemason to be awarded the Victoria Cross.

Left: Captain William Bell, the second son of Major-General Edward Bell, VC, CB. [Mrs Diana Bailey]

AMBROSE MADDEN
Colour Sergeant
41st Regiment of Foot (The Welch Regiment)

A photograph believed to be of Ambrose Madden, taken in the 2nd Division camp, 1856.

FULL NAME: Ambrose Madden.
PLACE OF BIRTH: Cork, Ireland.
Date of Birth: *Circa* 1820.
Father: —
Mother: —
Father's Occupation: —
Education: —
Pre-Service Employment: Labourer.
Service Record: Enlisted 2nd Dragoon Guards at Cahir, 24 May 1838 (Service No. 550); transferred to 41st Regiment of Foot at Dublin, 31 October 1845 (Service N°. 2195); corporal, 16 June 1848; sergeant, 7 September 1849; colour sergeant, 1 May 1853; served Crimean Campaign, 1854–6 (present at Alma, Little Inkerman, Inkerman and Sebastopol); acting sergeant-major, 7 August 1855; sergeant-major, 2 October 1856; resigned and reverted to colour sergeant, 12 October 1858; voluntary transfer to 2nd West India Regiment, 31 October 1858; company sergeant-major, 1 November 1858; commissioned ensign, 2nd West India Regiment, 13 December 1858; served in Baddiboo War, West Africa, 1861 (present at the bombardment of Sowarracunda Creek, 16 February 1861, the storming and capture of Carawan, Kinty Cunda and Saba) where he suffered a severe attack of fever but continued to carry out his duties; lieutenant, 20 August 1861; transferred to 3rd West India Regiment, April 1861, as garrison adjutant at Gambia, West Africa; transferred to 4th West India Regiment, 7 April 1862.
REWARDS, DECORATION AND MEDALS: Victoria Cross (for action at Little Inkerman, 26 October 1854); Crimean Medal (clasps for Alma, Inkerman and Sebastopol); French Medaille Militaire; Turkish Crimea Medal.
Married: Bridget Furlong at Tuam, Galway, Ireland, 10 September 1847.
Children: Son (George) and daughters (Kate, Mary, Julia and unknown).
Died: Jamaica, 1 January 1863, of fever.
Buried: Location of grave not known but likely to have been buried in Up Park Military Cemetery, Jamaica.
Memorials: None recorded.
Location of Victoria Cross: RRW Museum, Cardiff.
Citation for the Victoria Cross: *London Gazette*, 24 February 1857. 'For having headed a party of men of the 41st Regiment and having cut off and taken prisoner one Russian officer and fourteen privates, three of whom he personally and alone captured.'
VC Investiture: By Major-General E. W. Bell, Lieutenant Governor and GOC Jamaica, (the father of Captain Bell, VC, see above) on 7th August 1857.

The medals and decorations of Ambrose Madden as displayed in the RRW Museum, Cardiff .
L–R: Victoria Cross, Crimea Medal, Medaille Militaire, Turkish Crimea Medal.

Very little is known of the background of Ambrose Madden other than that he was born in Cork, Ireland. Like so many of his compatriots, he found enlistment in the British Army the only route out of an impoverished background. He initially enlisted in the 2nd Dragoon Guards (The Scots Greys), almost certainly because they were serving in the Munster area of Ireland at the time. Seven years later, at Dublin, he transferred to the 41st Foot (The Welch Regiment) which had only recently returned from a period of service in India. He was soon promoted and may well have been one of the NCOs who benefited from the introduction into the regiment in 1849 of an examination system for promotion to the higher grades of NCO. His first experience of overseas service was in 1851 when the regiment was posted to the Ionian Islands, followed by Malta in 1853 and Turkey the following year. That Madden was highly regarded by his superior officers is evidenced by his promotion to colour sergeant in May 1853, the rank he held at the time of his VC action in November 1854. He was certainly present at the battle of the Alma in September 1854 but it is for his actions at the little known battle of Little Inkerman that his name came to the fore.

Following the march south from the Alma to the hills above the village of Inkerman, the British Army began to prepare for what many believed was an imminent assault on the city of Sebastopol. On 17 October, the British artillery opened their bombardment of the Russian defences on the south side of the city, successfully opening a breach in the position known as the Redan and silencing the enemy's artillery. An explosion in the French magazine put all thoughts of an assault out of the minds of the generals and, as dawn broke each morning, the enemy's ability to repair the damage caused during the previous day's bombardment was only too clear. While all this was taking place, the men of the 41st Regiment (as part of the 2nd Division) were encamped on the Heights of Inkerman, a site that was 'as much open to attack as it was unsuitable for defence.'

On 25 October, the situation took a turn against the Allies when the British force in the valley above Balaclava was forced to fight for its survival and the small success achieved by the Russians made the position of the Allies far more precarious. The next day, the pickets of the 2nd Division, under the command of Major Eman of the 41st, were posted as usual (including one company, furnished by his own regiment, which was positioned on the West Jut above the Careenage ravine). The morning was described as 'particularly beautiful' and quiet until, at about noon, reports were received that large numbers of Russians were moving up the slope of Cossack Hill towards their position. Advancing in three columns, the Russians (estimated at some 6–7,000 men) were met with accurate artillery fire as soon as they came within range of the British guns and were forced to retire shortly after 2pm. Under the protective fire of the British artillery, the Light Company of the 41st Regiment, under the command of Lieutenant Harriott moved forward to support two companies of the 49th Regiment. Nos 5 and 6 companies of the 41st advanced in skirmishing order towards the main road and Quarry Ravine. Sir de Lacy Evans then ordered the whole of the 2nd Division to advance in pursuit of the enemy and, because of the nature of the terrain, all semblance of military precision quickly vanished. Small groups of officers and men became involved in numerous skirmishes before the Russians withdrew behind their defences at Sebastopol. Losses were estimated to have been well in excess of 200 killed and 80 men taken prisoner, whilst the 2nd Division had 9 men killed and 4 officers and 58 men wounded. During this pursuit, some men from the 30th and 41st regiments made their way down into the Careenage ravine where they supported the Coldstream Guards' sharpshooters. Amongst these men was Ambrose Madden who led a detachment of soldiers towards the enemy troops who were sheltering in caves along the far side of the ravine, in an abandoned quarry. Entering a cave, Madden's group captured one officer and fourteen privates whom they succeeding in bringing back to the British lines. For this action, Madden was later nominated for the award of the Victoria Cross and Corporal Crawford was nominated for the Sardinian Medal.

Madden went on to serve at Inkerman and in the abortive assaults on Sebastopol, and ended the war as an acting sergeant-major. He returned with the regiment to Britain but seems then to have entered an unsettled period of his life. Having been promoted to sergeant-major in October 1856, he quickly volunteered to revert to colour sergeant ten days later and then, on 31 October, voluntarily transferred to the 2nd West India Regiment where he was immediately promoted to company sergeant-major and then commissioned as an ensign (2nd lieutenant). This rapid change in his career would suggest that his position within the 41st had become untenable and that the traditional 'pecking order' of the British line regiments may have had some part to play. By transferring into the West India Regiment, he was leaving a socially desirable regiment for one that had very little status but where he, an Irishman of possibly peasant stock, could receive a commission.

The two remaining uncertainties about Madden are what he looked like and where he is buried. For many years there were no known images of him at any time during his life. Some twenty-five years ago, whilst conducting research for the first edition of this book, the author and Lt Bryn Owen, RN (then curator of the Welsh Regiment Museum in Cardiff) spent many hours searching through a variety of images of regimental members serving in the Crimea. As a result of this, one figure emerged as a strong candidate for Ambrose Madden. In one of the group photographs taken in the British Army camp at Sebastopol in 1856, there is an imposing figure of an NCO. Careful study of his uniform and badges led us to the conclusion that this was almost certainly a photograph of Madden. This picture was then published in the first edition of this work under the caption: 'Colour Sergeant Ambrose Madden, VC, taken in the camp at Sebastopol, 1856. This is believed to be a photograph of this man but no officially identified picture of him exists'. Since that time, the picture has been reproduced in other works and identified simply as 'Ambrose Madden, VC'. Without further evidence, there is still great uncertainty about the identity of the individual in this photograph.

Madden appears to have had two Victoria Crosses, one of a few instances where this is known to have occurred — both named to the same man, and possibly both genuine. In 1935, the Welch Regiment bought the VC, Medaille Militaire, Crimea Medal and Turkish Crimea Medal awarded to Ambrose Madden from Spink & Son. The Crimea medal had been re-named 'A. Maddon' (being an incorrect spelling of his name). The Turkish medal was unnamed (as was the norm). In 1952, a second VC named to Ambrose Madden came into the possession of Spink & Son. As the 1st Bn The Welch Regiment was serving overseas (and had the 1935 VC with them) it was not possible to make a comparison until they returned. On examination, Spinks were unable to confirm which was the genuine Victoria Cross, although one was named to 'SERJT MAJOR AMBROSE MADDEN 41ST REGT', and dated '25 OCT 1854' and the other to 'SERGT MAJOR AMBROSE MADDEN 41ST REGT', and dated '5 NOV 1854'. Both VCs, despite the discrepancies, were sent to Hancocks (the jewellery firm that has manufactured all Victoria Crosses) for checking and they were also unable to decide which was the genuine Cross. In 1954, Colonel Morrey Salmon bought the second VC and another pair of Crimea and Turkish Crimea medals from Spink, correctly named to Madden, and presented them to the regiment. This second VC was displayed at Maindy Barracks until 25 April 1964 when it was stolen during a burglary and has never been recovered. It seems likely that the VC marked SERJT and dated (correctly) 25 OCT 1854 is the original, issued in 1857. The second VC, and possibly the second medal pair, may have been made for Madden at another date, perhaps because he was serving overseas at the time of the presentation and was unable to gain access to the original or, perhaps, he was issued with an incorrectly engraved Cross and then issued with another which had been correctly engraved. This was not unprecedented. M. J. Crook in his definitive study of the Victoria Cross cites a number of occasions where duplicate medals were issued and where the particulars engraved on Crosses have had to be altered e.g. Lieutenant Symons' VC was wrongly dated as 18 Oct 1854 when it should have been 6 Jun 1855. In the case of Private Thomas Ashford, the medal was incorrectly named to Private John Ashford. These examples were changed by Hancocks at the request of the War Office but it is not beyond the realms of possibility for the original, incorrectly engraved VC, to be returned to the recipient. In the case of Private Farmer, a VC was sent out to Natal for presentation to him by the GOC but, by the time it arrived, Farmer had returned to the UK and a second Cross was produced for presentation by Queen Victoria. The original Cross was then returned to the War Office. Conversely, Lieutenant English was decorated with an unnamed Cross by the Prince of Wales in 1902 which was later replaced by an engraved Cross with the original being returned to the War Office.

In Madden's case, he was serving in the West Indies when the first investiture took place in London in June 1857. Perhaps a wrongly named or dated Cross was sent out to Jamaica which was later replaced by a corrected Cross at a later date but the original was not returned to London. Sadly, due to the 1964 theft and disappearance of one of the two Crosses, the use of modern forensic methods cannot be used to ascertain if only one of them was genuine.

In 1891, in St Johns, New Brunswick, Canada, a Michael Maddigan was exposed as an impostor. He claimed to have served in the Crimea campaign with the 41st Regiment of Foot for which he had been awarded a Victoria Cross for his gallantry at Inkerman. The similarity between his surname and that of Madden is striking and, indeed, Maddigan and Madden both derive from the same origin. His claim to have received the VC for his action at Inkerman (rather than Little Inkerman) fits in with the incorrect date on one of the two Madden VCs. There is a possibility that there is a link between this impostor and the inaccurately engraved VC.

The two VCs 'awarded' to Ambrose Madden. The variations in colour are quite acceptable due to variations in the composition of the bronze used in the manufacture and the amount of polishing which each medal has received.
[RRW Museum, Cardiff]

Major Hugh Rowlands shortly after his return from the Crimea — the VC, although awarded had not been presented and an inaccurate impression of the award has been drawn onto the photograph.

Private McDermond, 47th Regiment, assisting in saving the life of Lieutenant-Colonel Haly. A painting by Chevalier Louis Désanges. [Loyal Lancashire Regiment Museum, Preston]

HUGH ROWLANDS
Captain
41st Regiment of Foot (The Welch Regiment)

FULL NAME: Hugh Rowlands.
PLACE OF BIRTH: Plastirion, Llanrug, Caernarfonshire.
Date of Birth: 6 May 1828. He was the second of three children, having an elder brother John, and a sister Elizabeth.
Father: John Rowlands.
Mother: Elizabeth Anne Rowlands (née Hastwell).
Father's Occupation: Gentleman landowner, Deputy-Lieutenant of Caernarfonshire, Justice of the Peace, officer in the Caernarfonshire Militia.
Education: Beaumaris Grammar School, Anglesey, 1837–42; Mr John Taylor's Cramming Academy, Woolwich, July–August 1849.
Service Record: Commissioned ensign 41st Regiment of Foot, 25 September 1849 (by purchase); lieutenant, 21 April 1851; captain, Grenadier Company, 24 August 1854 (by purchase); served Crimean Campaign (present at the Alma, Little Inkerman, Inkerman and throughout the siege of Sebastopol); wounded severely in the arm at Inkerman and slightly during the second assault on the Redan, September 1855; brevet major, 2 November 1855; Town Major of Sebastopol, September 1855; Brigade Major, 2nd Brigade, 2nd Division, Sebastopol, 1 October 1855; major, 13 December 1857; half pay, 6 November 1857; staff major at Aldershot, July 1858; major 3/7th Regiment at Chatham, August 1858; half-pay, 26 August 1859; major, 100th Regiment, December 1860; major, 41st Regiment, 5 February 1861; brevet lieutenant-colonel, May 1865; lieutenant-colonel, 41st Regiment, 23 March 1866; colonel, 23 March 1871; CO 1st Border Regiment, 12 May 1875; Special Service Officer, Cape Colony, March 1878; Inspector of Colonial Forces, Transvaal, May 1878; Commandant of the Transvaal, 13 August 1878; OC campaign against the Pedi in Eastern Transvaal, 1878; CO Nᵒ· 5 Column, Transvaal, January 1879; OC defences of Pretoria from threat of Boer attack, March 1879; brigadier-general (temporary rank), 21 May 1879; GOC brigade Lower Tugela River, Zululand, June 1879; half-pay, August 1879; AAQMG, North British District, 1 July 1880; brigadier-general, Peshawar Brigade, Bengal, January 1881; major-general, 1 July

The awards and decorations of General Sir Hugh Rowlands as displayed in the RRW Museum, Cardiff. Top: KCB, CB. Bottom: VC, Crimea Medal, South Africa Medal, Legion of Honour, Medjidie, Turkish Crimea Medal.

1881; GOC, 3rd Infantry Brigade, Aldershot, 19 August 1882; GOC, Bangalore Division, Madras, 21st April 1884; GOC (temporary), Madras Army, August 1885–March 1886 and October–December 1886; unattached officer, April 1889; lieutenant-general, 1 January 1890; Lieutenant of the Tower of London, 21 June 1893; GOC, Scottish District, 5 January 1894; general, 16 October 1894; retired, 6 May 1896; Honorary Colonel, Duke of Wellington's (West Riding) Regiment, 8 October 1897.

Decorations, Medals and Rewards: Victoria Cross (for action at Inkerman, 5 November 1854); KCB (*London Gazette,* 24 May 1898), CB (*London Gazette,* 29 May 1875, for services in the Crimean War); Reward for Distinguished Service (31 January 1880, for services in South Africa, 1878–9); Crimean Medal (with clasps for Alma, Inkerman and Sebastopol); South Africa Medal (with clasp for 1878–9); MinD (Crimea and South Africa); Legion of Honour (21June 1856); Order of the Medjidie (1856); Turkish Crimea Medal; Deputy-Lieutenant of Caernarfonshire; Justice of the Peace (Caernarfon and the Transvaal).

Post-Service Employment: Retired general officer, landowner, Justice of the Peace. Founding committee member of the New United Services Club, Regent Street, London. Served on the committee of the 1901 Military Exhibition, Earls Court, London.

Married: Isabella Jane Barrow (daughter of Thomas James Raikes Barrow, RN, of Randwick, Stroud, Gloucester) at Serampore, India, 2 November 1867. She was the granddaughter of William Griffiths of Rhosfawr and Bodegroes, Pwllheli.

Children: One daughter and one son, Violet Margaret Isabel and Hugh Barrow. Hugh served with the Suffolk Regiment in South Africa and with the Central/King's African Rifles in Ashanti and Somaliland. He died of wounds received whilst serving as a Major in Somaliland in 1903. Violet married Captain Arthur Hume and their daughter, Marjorie, became a well-known British stage and film actress.

Died: 1 August 1909, at his home, Plastirion, Llanrug, Caernarfonshire.

Buried: St Michael's Churchyard, Llanrug, Caernarfonshire.

Memorials: St Michael's Churchyard, Llanrug, Caernarfonshire; Welch Regiment Chapel, Llandaff Cathedral, Cardiff; biography, *Commandant of the Transvaal* by W. Alister Williams, 2001.

Lady Isabella Rowlands, c.1905.

The grave of General Sir Hugh and Lady Rowlands, Llanrug.

Plastirion, Llanrug, where Hugh Rowlands was born and died.

The forage cap worn by Hugh Rowlands during the second assault on the Redan. [RRW Museum, Cardiff]

Location of Victoria Cross: On loan at the RRW Museum (Cardiff).
Citation for the Victoria Cross: *London Gazette*, 24 February 1857.
'For having rescued Colonel Haly, of the 47th Regiment, from Russian soldiers, Colonel Haly having been wounded and surrounded by them, and for gallant exertions in holding the ground occupied by his advanced picquet against the enemy, at the commencement of the Battle of Inkerman.'
VC Investiture: By Major-General Sir Abraham Josias Cloete, KCB, at Barbados, 5 August 1857.

Lieutenant-General Hugh Rowlands, VC, CB in the uniform of Lieutenant of the Tower of London, 1893.

Hugh Rowlands was the first Welshman to be awarded the Victoria Cross. His family were minor gentry in north-west Wales and claimed descent from Madog ap Cynfyn, Prince of Powys and Dafydd ap Gruffydd, Prince of Wales. There was no military tradition in the family other than a distant cousin who had served in the West Indies in the late eighteenth century. Rowlands is a classic example of a younger son forced to seek a career as the family inheritance was scheduled to pass to his older brother. After considerable difficulties, he was offered a commission in the 53rd Regiment (the Shropshire Light Infantry) which was immediately changed to the 41st Regiment (The Welch) before he had actually joined in 1849. He was posted overseas to the Ionian Islands and Malta before the regiment formed part of the 1854 expeditionary force sent to Turkey in support of that country in its conflict with Russia by which time Rowlands was the captain commanding the Grenadier Company, regarded by many as the élite company in any regiment.

He faced enemy fire for the first time at the battle of the Alma in September 1854 where he admitted his nerves began to affect him and there were butterflies in his stomach. Suddenly, a voice called out from the ranks behind him *'Rwan yr hen Blastirion! Rwan am biff!'* [Now old Plastirion! Now for a fight!] It was the voice of a man from his own village. The realisation that he was being watched focused his attention and he was able to calm himself knowing that the honour of his family was at stake:

> The nearer the Alma was approached, the more plunging was the fire. I believe all our loss was from artillery, and so plunging was the fire that I saw the head of a rear rank man shot off without touching the front rank man.

It is highly likely that Rowlands played some part in the fighting at Little Inkerman in October but it was the following month at Inkerman that his name became known throughout the army.

The night of 4/5 November was cold and wet. The hot, disease ridden days of the Crimean summer, which had provided such a good breeding ground for the spread of cholera, were giving way to the first touches of winter. On the heights above the ruins of Inkerman, the British Army slept protected as usual by a ring of pickets, the men of the Light Division guarding Victoria Ridge and Careening Ravine, the pickets of the Guards Division on a prominence looking north along Careening Ravine and the 2nd Division pickets on the Heights of Inkerman itself. As the night advanced, the dampness changed into a fog which clung to the ground in the numerous ravines and slowly made its way up the slopes onto the higher ground.

The most advanced picket on the Heights was that of the 95th Regiment, positioned on Shell Hill, under the command of Captain Vialls. The position was a miserable one and afforded its occupants no protection from the elements and they were delighted when, in the early hours of 5 November, Major Goodwyn of the 41st, who was Field Officer for that area, ordered them to withdraw down to the foot of the south-eastern slope of Shell Hill, where they found a more sheltered position. This move, coupled with the dark and the advancing fog, caused a great deal of confusion amongst the soldiers making up the picket and, in consequence, Captain Vialls ordered the withdrawal to continue as far as the Old Post Road so that they might regain some semblance of order.

Between 2 and 3am, several of the picket positions had reported the sound of wheels carrying up the slopes from the direction of Sebastopol. It would appear that, without exception, the officers who received these reports paid little heed to them, assuming the sound to be coming from some innocent source. Lieutenant Ward of the 47th Regiment crawled forward beyond Shell Hill and, on his return, reported that the noise was coming from British ammunition

Brevet Major Hugh Rowlands (standing third from the right) with fellow officers of the 41st Regiment, British Army Camp, Sebastopol, 1856.

wagons which were moving up to the artillery batteries. Major Bunbury of the 23rd Regiment, positioned further to the British left, came to the conclusion that the sound was that of Russian ammunition wagons moving up to the batteries protecting the city. Suspicions were not even aroused about an hour later when the bells in the distant city began to ring; those that heard them recalled that it was Sunday and placed no significance on the unusually early hour.

At a little before dawn, the men who were to make up the day pickets, paraded for inspection in the camp of the 2nd Division. The Officer of the Day for the 2nd Brigade of the 2nd Division was Lieutenant-Colonel William O'Grady Haly of the 47th Regiment who later recorded the events which followed:

> … the Picket of the Second Division paraded on that part of the Inkerman Road running through the camp of the Division. I proceeded in Command of the Picket forming the line of advanced posts from the road or Shell Hill to the Ravine running between the 2nd and Light Divisions, the most advanced Picket being under the brow of Cossack Hill near the Ravine.

As dawn began to break over the valley of the Chernaya, one of the pickets of the Light Division, comprising an officer and about 30 men, saw what they thought to be British troops approaching them out of the fog. Too late, they realised their mistake and they were captured without a shot being fired. On Shell Hill, the advanced picket

The battlefield of Inkerman. Shell Hill, the scene of Hugh Rowlands's VC action can be seen in the centre distance with Sebastopol top right.

commanded by Vialls, and accompanied by Major Goodwyn, was relieved by the Grenadier Company of the 41st, commanded by Captain Rowlands. The relieving picket was also accompanied by Lieutenant-Colonel Haly who was informed by Major Goodwyn that all was quiet and that nothing unusual had been observed during the night.

The tents of the Second Division are pitched on the verge of the plateau which we occupy, and from the right flank of the camp the ground rises gently for two or three hundred yards to a ridge covered with scrubby brushwood, so thick that it is sometimes difficult to force a horse through it. These bushes grow in tufts, and are about four feet in height. On gaining the ridge you see below you the valley of the Tchernaya, a green tranquil slip of meadow, with a few white houses dotting it at intervals, some farm enclosures, and tufts of green trees. From the ridge the hill-side descends rapidly in a slope of at least 600 feet high. The brushwood is very thick upon it, and at times it is almost impervious. At the base of this slope the road winds to Inkermann, and thence to Sebastopol.

In a letter home, Rowlands described the scene as his men assumed their duties:

When I passed through the night picket you cannot imagine a more cheerless aspect. I halted the company about half way up and went to plant sentries about one hundred and fifty yards over the hill.

Rowlands had therefore resumed the occupation of the position which had been evacuated by Vialls during the night and was situated on the highest point in the area. Evidently all was still quiet and the advancing Russian force still remained undetected by any of the pickets — any firing which would have occurred on the two forces making contact would have been heard by Rowlands and his men. Both Lieutenant-Colonel Haly and Lieutenant Allan confirmed Rowlands' later report that all was quiet. The Light Division pickets were certainly not engaged at this time as is borne out by the histories of the regiments involved and the report of *The Times'* correspondent, William Howard Russell:

It was a little after five o'clock when Brigadier-General Codrington, in accordance with his usual habit, visited the outlying pickets of his own brigade of the Light Division. It was reported to him that 'all was well' and the General entered into some conversation with Captain Pretyman, of the 33rd Regiment, who was on duty on the ground, in the course of which it was remarked that it would not be at all surprising if the Russians availed themselves of the gloom of the morning to make an attack on our position, calculating on the effects of the rain in disarming our vigilance and spoiling our weapons. The Brigadier … turned his pony round at last, and retraced his steps through the brushwood towards his lines. He had only proceeded a few paces when a sharp rattle of musketry was heard down the hill and on the left of the pickets of the Light Division. It was here that the pickets of the Second Division were stationed.

The credit for detecting the Russian advance lies fairly and squarely with the pickets of the 2nd Division and, indeed, with the Grenadier Company of the 41st Regiment. Lieutenant Allen wrote:

We had just taken up our day position, and posted our sentries when … our left sentries shouted that 'The Russians are in front'. We had no more than time to get under arms, and extend the main body of the picket, when shots were exchanged, and the enemy advanced up the slopes in dense masses, preceded by skirmishers…

The firing which then commenced was undoubtedly that heard by Codrington's men and it told the Russians that, at last, their attack had been detected. A few more minutes would have taken them within striking distance of the British camp but, even without them, a rush up the slope would carry them through the thin line of pickets and on towards the still sleeping or barely awake Allied camp.

Rowlands' own description matches that recorded by Allan, but adds more detail:

I returned to the company, which had just piled arms, and ordered the men to take off their packs, when the sentries commenced firing in a most determined way. I ran up to enquire the cause, when one shouted that there were columns of Russians close to them. I stood to my arms and advanced in extended order, thinking it was a sortie something like that on the 26th … On getting to the top of the hill, I found myself close upon, very truly, thousands of Russians. I immediately gave the order to retire, which was done for about 200 yards, when I halted on the next bit of high ground [a continuation of Shell Hill where the right of this picket linked up with the pickets of the 1st Brigade] and lay down, quietly waiting for them. Fitzroy [Lieutenant G], who was in support of me, then came up with the Light Company. His men I likewise extended to reinforce my own. When we retired the Russians came on with the most fiendish yells you can imagine. We commenced firing. To my dismay I found that half the flint-locks missed fire, which dispirited the men. At this period the Russian columns opened with their field pieces, pouring in grape and shell. We then got some reinforcements of the 55th and 30th, but we were gradually obliged to retire … I begged and entreated Colonel Haly to allow me to charge, which he did … and after a little hand-to-hand work we turned them and drove them back about 500 yards, when we were met by a fresh column, who compelled us to retire.

Lieutenant-Colonel Haly was himself in the thick of the fighting as he described in a letter:

The only known photograph of Private McDermond, VC.

… as soon as our bayonets told on the foremost of the enemy they turned back up the hill towards the heavy columns which now showed on the brow. In leading that charge, the first of the day, being somewhat ahead, I got surrounded by Russians, & was bayoneted off my horse … the Russians then bayoneted me on the ground and disabled me.

Haly's situation was critical. On losing his seat on the horse, the officer's foot had become caught in the stirrup and he sustained a very heavy fall. He had already sabred three Russian soldiers in the charge and expected the worst. As the grey clad soldiers surrounded him he could see only a grisly end.

… a bayonet thrust grazing my left shin bone, left leg, and coming through the thick of the calf. Another small prod in the back and the thigh. A probe in the ribs and a thrust in my face which grazed my temple … My life was providently saved.

Rowlands saw what had befallen Haly and, accompanied by Privates McDermond and Kelly of the 47th Regiment, he rushed to his assistance. Forcing their way through the advancing Russians they reached the disabled officer and were involved in a short but very deadly struggle during which Kelly was killed and Rowlands was severely wounded in the arm. Despite this, Haly was lifted up and carried back to the comparative safety of the British lines. The lieutenant-colonel later gave the full credit for saving his life to Rowlands, McDermond and Kelly and recommended that the former be awarded an immediate promotion to brevet major. Lieutenant-General Pennefather, commanding the 2nd Division, informed Haly that he had already urged such an award with Lord Raglan and had high hopes that it would be acted upon very shortly. As it happened, Rowlands was to endure a further twelve months of front-line service before such an honour was bestowed upon him. In the meantime, after a period at the military hospital in Scutari, he continued his service at the front and became known to the officers in the Crimea as 'the man who began the Battle of Inkerman'. Private McDermond of the 47th Regiment was awarded the Victoria Cross for this action.

Rowlands' story is however incomplete as a few months later he again distinguished himself and, when the nominations for the award of a Victoria Cross were made, he received two separate citations, thereby making him possibly the first man to ever be nominated for two VCs (as opposed to one VC for two actions). This second nomination, signed by Lieutenant-General Pennfather, reads:

> Distinguished on an hundred occasions in action and in the trenches. Particularly gallant and devoted in jumping out of the trenches under a terrific fire and rallying soldiers of the Light Division, beaten back by the Russians. Attack on the Redan, 18th June 1855.

The nomination for a second VC for Brevet-Major Hugh Rowlands.

The choice of words in this citation, which was initially accepted by the War Office committee, was unfortunate as they can only be described as vague in the extreme and, had Pennefather taken greater care, then this might have been the citation for which the eventual award was made. Two awards could not, however, be made to the same person as the regulations, if strictly interpreted, did not allow for such a circumstance. Clause 4 of the Royal Warrant stated:

… that any one who, *after having received the Cross,* shall again peform an act of bravery which, *if he had not received such Cross,* would have entitled him to it, such further act shall be recorded by a Bar attached to the ribband by which the Cross is suspended. [author's italics]

As no VC had been awarded before 1857 there was no Crimean recipient who had already received the decoration and therefore no claims to bars could be accepted in relation to acts of gallantry performed during that campaign. Another consideration when looking at the two nominations and trying to decide which should merit the award are the circumstances surrounding each. At Inkerman, Rowlands had played a significant role in a military action which, although confused, resulted in a resounding British victory whereas the first assault on the Redan, gallant though it may have been, was an abject failure. One further point on the case for a second award to Hugh Rowlands concerns his actions on 8 September during the second assault on the Redan. There can be no question that his actions on that day were regarded by all as having displayed the highest levels of gallantry. Amongst those who, like Rowlands, attacked the Redan on that fateful day, no fewer than nine received the Victoria Cross. Whether the omission of Rowlands from this list was because it was felt that he had already been adequately rewarded for his actions on that day by being promoted to brevet major or whether there was some other unknown reason we shall never know. In order to provide a full picture of Hugh Rowlands' gallantry it is probably worth a closer examination.

Andrew Moynahan, VC, whose life was saved by Hugh Rowlands, 18 June 1855.

The Allied plans were that the French would attack the Malakoff shortly after noon. Once the French had captured that position the British troops would leave their trenches and assault the Redan. The French had only 25–40 yards of open ground to cover and reached the Russian positions without a shot being fired and within minutes the Tricolor was flying above the Malakoff. The British spotted the flag and immediately stormed out of their trenches across the 300 yards of open ground. As soon as the Light Division left cover they were met by a hail of small arms and artillery fire and sustained heavy casualties. The next wave comprised the men of the 2nd Division and the first to go over the top were the Grenadier Company of the 41st led by Hugh Rowlands. Ahead of them their path was blocked by the Light Division which was desperately seeking cover from the withering Russian fire. Rowlands got his men to push their way through and to cross the defensive ditch in front of the Redan but, in doing so, they lost both momentum and cohesion. Rowlands led a small group of his men through a burning opening in the wall and found themselves almost alone inside the Redan.

The first British soldier to enter the Russian defensive work that day was almost certainly Sergeant Andrew Moynihan of the 9th Light Infantry who later recorded that 'To stay here was certain death; to retreat was not the soldier's way; so I jumped down into the Redan, a distance of about four yards, into the midst of the enemy.' He was joined by a private of the 90th and Lieutenant Graham of the 41st and together the three charged the Russian trench but to no avail and only Moynahan survived. He was then joined by another six or seven men commanded by Rowlands and they took up a position in the centre of the Redan which they managed to hold for five minutes before being forced to seek cover. They were joined by a further six men of the Buffs and Lieutenant-Colonel Maud and together held their ground for a further fifteen minutes. Another officer, Lieutenant Swift of the 90th Regiment was badly wounded and in danger of being killed by a Russian soldier when Moynihan rushed forward and killed the assailant, but was then himself bayoneted and taken prisoner by two Russians. Rowlands led a small group to his rescue and succeeded in recovering the gallant sergeant.

As the struggle became more desperate by the minute, fresh Russian troops could be seen moving into the positions ahead of the small band of British troops. Both sides were running low on ammunition and resorted to throwing any missiles which they could get their hands on. Rowlands was struck in the eye and knocked to the ground by some grapeshot thrown by a Russian. No

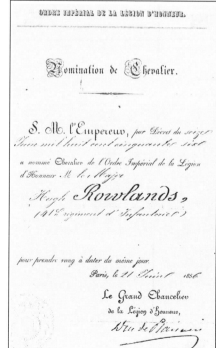

The nomination of Brevet Major Hugh Rowlands as a Knight of the Legion of Honour.

General Hugh Rowlands, VC, CB, c.1900. [RRW Museum, Cardiff]

sooner was he back on his feet than he was hit by a similar missile in the other eye and again fell to the ground. Outside the Redan the attacking force was beginning to fall back and Rowlands and his companions saw the last chance of success slipping away and they too began to withdraw. As well as the blows to his face, Rowlands later discovered that a bullet had entered his forage cap and passed through his hair and that his clothing was pierced in five places by bullets. Major Goodwyn, his commanding officer, wrote to Colonel Windham: 'I am glad to report that the conduct of all the officers of the Regt has been highly satisfactory & exemplary — but more especially that of Captains Rowlands and Every'.

Amongst the VCs awarded for that day's actions were those given to Lieutenant-Colonel Maud and Sergeant Andrew Moynihan.

Hugh Rowlands went on to have a distinguished military career, serving for many years in India. The one low point was the period which he spent as a Special Service officer in South Africa (1878–9) when he commanded the British force sent to quell the disturbances in the north-eastern Transvaal instigated by the Pedi chief Sekukuni. Here Rowlands displayed great caution when sending poorly prepared Imperial troops against an unassessed native force. As a result of this, the assault on Sekukuni's stronghold was aborted and it was left to a much stronger force under the command of Sir Garnet Wolseley to complete the job shortly after the final defeat of the Zulus. As a consequence, Rowlands had

to endure considerable unwarranted criticism from Lord Chelmsford, Evelyn Wood and Redvers Buller, the first and last of which were to eventually destroy their own reputations through lack of adequate forethought and respect for their enemy.

Hugh Rowlands was followed into the Army by his only son, Hugh Barrow Rowlands, who had an adventurous and promising career as a junior officer, serving in Ashanti, South Africa and Somaliland where he died following a wound received whilst speaking to Major Johnnie Gough during the action at Bohtle in 1903. Reports suggested that the bullet which struck

Colonel Rowlands (seated right) with Captain Fred Carrington, Sir Bartle Frere and Colonel Owen Lanyon at Pretoria, 1879.

Rowlands in the arm was actually aimed at Gough who moved away at the last moment. Gough was later awarded a Victoria Cross for his gallantry during this action.

Hugh Rowlands, VC, attained the highest rank of any Welsh Victoria Cross recipient.

Major Hugh Barrow Rowlands.

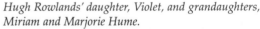

Hugh Rowlands' daughter, Violet, and grandaughters, Miriam and Marjorie Hume.

The New Zealand Medal awarded to Sergeant John Byrne [DLI Museum]

7 Crown Street, Maindee, Newport (centre) where John Byrne was living at the time of his death.

JOHN BYRNE
Private
1/68th Light Infantry (Durham Light Infantry)

FULL NAME: John Byrne.

PLACE OF BIRTH: Castlecomber, Kilkenny, Ireland.

Date of Birth: *Circa* September 1832.

Father: —

Mother: —

Father's Occupation: —

Education: No education certificate. His signature was very clumsy which would indicate that he was probably illiterate.

Pre-Service Employment: —

Service Record: Enlisted 68th Light Infantry at Coventry, 27 July 1850 (Service N° 2832); served Crimean Campaign, 1854–6 (present at Alma, Inkerman, Balaclava and Sebastopol), slightly wounded in the foot 13 January 1855; corporal, 21 January 1861; sergeant, 7 March 1866; served East Indies and in New Zealand during the Maori War, 1860–6; discharged at Cork, 14 May 1869; served as sergeant, Queen's County Militia, May–October 1869; re-enlisted 68 Light Infantry, October 1869 as a sergeant; discharged, 14 May 1872; served as colour sergeant, 2nd North Durham Militia, 1872, believed to have been discharged in the same year '… for insubordination and highly improper conduct.'

Decorations, Medals and Rewards: Victoria Cross (for action at Inkerman, 5 November 1854, and in the trenches before Sebastopol, 11 May 1855); Distinguished Conduct Medal (for action at Tauranga, New Zealand, 21 June 1864); Crimea Medal (clasps for Alma, Balaclava, Inkerman and Sebastopol); New Zealand Medal, 1861–66; Turkish Crimea Medal; three Good Conduct Badges (he would have received four had he not been promoted and five had he served a further five days and not been promoted).

Post-Service Employment: Little information is available on this period of his life. When he left the army his intended place of residence was given as Durham. In 1878 he obtained employment in Bristol as a labourer with the Ordnance Survey.

Married: No record of marriage.

Children: None.

Died: 10 July 1879, 7 Crown Street, Maindee (where Byrne was lodging). For many years it was mistakenly believed that John Byrne had died on 6 December 1872.

Buried: Grave RC E15, Block 14, St Woolo's Cemetery, Newport, 12 July 1879. This is part of the lawn cemetery.

Memorials: Originally buried in an unmarked, pauper's grave. A headstone, commissioned by the Durham Light Infantry Charitable Fund, was dedicated at St Woolo's Cemetery, Newport, on 4 November 1985 when a wreath was laid by Major-General de la Billière, GOC Wales; DLI VC Memorial, DLI Museum, Durham.

Location of Victoria Cross: Not known. His New Zealand Medal is held by the Durham Light Infantry Museum but his Crimean Medal is missing.

Citation for the Victoria Cross: *London Gazette*, 24 February 1857.

'At the Battle of Inkerman, when the regiment was ordered to retire, Private John Byrne went back towards the enemy, and, at the risk of his own life, brought in a wounded soldier, under fire.

'On the 11th May 1855, he bravely engaged in a hand to hand contest with one of the enemy on the parapet of the work he was defending, prevented the entrance of the enemy, killed his antagonist, and captured his arms.'

VC Investiture: By Major-General Sir George Buller, GOC Ionian Islands, at Corfu, 22 July 1857. Major Thomas de Courcy Hamilton of the 98th Regiment was decorated at the same investiture.

Citation for DCM: *London Gazette*, 16 September 1864. There is no actual citation for this award but the despatch from which it originates was published in the *London Gazette* on the above date:

'Corporal J. Byrne, VC (68th) who, when the order to charge was given, was the first man of his company into the rifle pits. A maori whom he transfixed with his bayonet seized his rifle with one hand and holding it firm with the bayonet through him, this time endeavoured to cut him down with his tomahawk and his life was saved by Sergeant Murray.'

The grave of Sergeant John Byrne in St Woolo's Cemetery, Newport.

Many people have a mistaken belief that the Irish love a good fight and that Ireland is the perfect recruiting ground for soldiers. Whilst a very large percentage of the pre-1914 British Army was made up of Irish volunteers, this was more a reflection on the economic state of that country rather than the fighting talents of the Irish nation. For so many Irishmen, taking the Queen's/King's shilling was the only escape from a life of abject poverty. In the mid-1840s this route was flooded by young men fleeing from the effects of the potato famine which was to claim the lives of over a million of their countrymen. There were however some men of all nationalities to whom a good fight was an important feature of their everyday life and there is no doubt that many of these, be they Irish, Welsh, Scots or English, found their way into the ranks, where most of them learned, through the discipline imposed upon them, to harness their aggressive tendencies and channel them into activities acceptable to the Crown.

John Byrne, from County Kilkenny in the south east of Ireland left his homeland in search of a better life in England and, whilst living in Coventry, enlisted in the 68th Regiment of Foot in 1850. Ironically, in light of the scope of this book, the 68th Regiment had been formed in May 1758 from one of the two battalions of the 23rd Regiment (Royal Welch Fusiliers). Byrne's attestation papers show him to have been 5 feet 7 inches tall, with grey eyes, brown hair and a fresh complexion. There is no evidence that he had received any education and his signature on this document is an almost illegible scrawl. He did not, however, fit easily into army life and, as a result, served his first period of custody in November 1853, when he was sent to a military prison for six months. Nineteenth century civil prisons were notoriously unpleasant institutions and military prisons, under the rule of martial law, were infinitely worse. He was released from custody in May only to reoffend in July and be returned to custody. Unfortunately, there is no record of what he was guilty of but his later life would suggest that he had a talent for fighting, possibly coupled with a propensity to consume large amounts of alcohol. In August he was released from custody in order to join his regiment for service in the Crimean War.

Byrne had his first taste of action at the Battle of the Alma on 20 September 1854 where the 68th Regiment, which formed part of the 4th Division, was under the command of Lieutenant-General Cathcart. Six weeks later came the Battle of Inkerman where Byrne was to distinguish himself for the first time. The initial Russian attack which began shortly before 6am caught the British

Some NCOs and men of the 68th in the Crimea, photograph taken by Robertson, 1855. Unfortunately, Byrne was not included in the group.

unawares and had it not been for the gallant resistance offered by the officers and men of the 2nd Division, the camp on the heights above Inkerman would have been overrun. By 7am reinforcements from the other British divisions were being pushed forward into the line to stop the Russian advance. Amongst these was the 4th Division which included some 200 men of the 68th Regiment, one of whom was Private John Byrne. Immediately caught up in the chaos caused by swirling fog and rough terrain, the men of the 68th were soon fighting in small groups against unknown numbers of Russians. It was close-quarter, hand-to-hand fighting, quite unlike the drilled formation volley firing and manoeuvring of the Napoleonic period which the men had been trained for. As their ammunition ran out and the Russians seemed about to overwhelm them, the 68th began to fall back, abandoning their wounded. This type of fighting suited Byrne. He was not a well-disciplined soldier, and seemed to prefer to rely on his own quick wits rather than the well-drilled precision of parade ground soldiering. Whilst aggressive by nature, he was also a man who was loyal to his comrades. As the Russians moved forward, he turned to face them and, seeing Private Anthony Harman, one of his regiment, lying injured on the ground, rushed forward directly into the face of the Russian fire, to assist him. Miraculously he reached Harman unscathed, picked him up and carried him back to the British lines. Byrne had certainly redeemed himself for his offences back in Britain.

By the spring of 1855, the Allied forces had endured a winter of appalling conditions without proper accommodation or equipment but, nevertheless, had managed to construct a system of trenches which were gradually creeping forward towards the defences of the city of Sebastopol. In April and May, Allied troops captured the Russian rifle pits in front of their trenches, thereby eliminating much of the sniper fire which had proved fatal to so many during the course of the winter. On 10 May the Russians launched an assault upon the British trenches which, after a struggle of about two hours, was repelled. During the very wet night of 11/12 May 1855, a large Russian force came out of Sebastopol to attack the British trenches near the Worenzoff road which were held by two companies of the 68th Regiment. The soldiers became involved in hand-to-hand combat and Byrne again distinguished himself by becoming engaged with one Russian on the trench parapet. The Irishman eventually managed to bayonet his opponent and capture his gun in a fight which in no small way inspired the British troops and led to them driving back the Russians. Once again Byrne had excelled where the action was based upon an individual act of valour. For his gallantry on 5 November 1854 and 11/12 May 1855, Byrne was awarded the Victoria Cross.

Although he served for the remainder of the campaign in the Crimea and in Burma, Byrne's name did not again come to prominence in the story of the 68th Regiment until 1864. He appears to have settled more to military life and, perhaps partly as a result of his VC award, was promoted to corporal in 1861. Two years later, the regiment was posted to New Zealand, arriving at Auckland in January 1864, mid-way through the Maori Wars. From the late eighteenth century, European settlers had arrived in New Zealand in relatively small numbers which, unlike Australia, were not supplemented by the forced transportation of convicts. In 1837, the New Zealand Company was set up to encourage the settlement and development of the colony but, despite this, relations between the Maori and the Europeans were amicable (the latter being outnumbered by sixty to one). Gradually, however, concern grew about the buying up of Maori land by Europeans and the British, fearing that some other world power might lay claim to the islands, drew up the Treaty of Waitangi in 1840 which gave the British Crown the right to buy land and, in return, the Maori were granted all the rights and privileges of British subjects. For a short time relations between the two races were relatively peaceful but, gradually, small skirmishes broke out over small land disputes. In 1860, the Te Ati Awa tribe, controlling the area around Taranaki in the west of North Island, refused to accept a land deal and the British government marched troops onto the land to seize it by force. As a result, the North Island tribes united against what they saw as an act of aggression which then erupted into full scale war. Although unsophisticated in terms of weaponry and tactics, the Maori had adopted some European military methods and were formidable and courageous warriors who sensibly avoided pitched

The Gate Pa battlefield, now disappearing in a suburb of Tauranga, is bisected by the main Tauranga–Rotorua road. The memorial plaque, which is located in front of the white church at the top of a hill, reads: 'On 29th April 1864 the battle of Gate Pa was fought on this site. This plaque commemorates the chivalry displayed by both Maori and Pakeha [Euorpeans], which has helped unite the two races. Kua iwi kotahi Tatou.' 'In memory of the unnamed Maoris who were killed at this battle and buried here.'

The site of the battle of Te Ranga. The main Maori rifle pits, extending from left to right, were used for the burial of more than 100 Maoris killed during the battle. The Teranga–Rotorua road (via Pye's Pa) runs behind the hedge on the right. The battle memorial (close-up on the left) can be seen centreground left.

battles wherever possible. Despite their talent for combat, the Maori had also devised a code of conduct, drawn up by Henare Taratoa which regulated their treatment of the enemy, particularly the wounded. In accordance with this code (which was strictly adhered to), all wounded soldiers were to be spared, any soldiers captured were to be dealt with by the rule of law and it was forbidden to harm any European women and children. In January 1864, the British moved troops into Tauranga Moana, the traditional home of the Ngaiterangi, the Ngati Ranginui and the Ngati Pukenga, the area around the modern town of Tauranga on the Bay of Plenty where, on a spit of land, the Maori had established a formidable redoubt called Gate Pa. This defensive work was highly sophisticated in its design and incorporated trenches, anti-artillery bunkers and rifle pits, similar to those previously encountered by the British at Sebastopol. Inside its defences was a garrison of some 230 Maoris armed with obsolete hunting guns, muskets and traditional Maori weapons such as axes and clubs. They had no artillery. The British forces (under the command of General Cameron) numbered some 1800 troops (armed with Enfield rifles) with 14 artillery pieces including one gun, 'Big Bertha', capable of firing a 120-pound explosive. In his report, General Cameron wrote:

> On the 27th I moved the 68th Regiment and a mixed detachment of 170 men … towards the rebel entrenchments of which I made close reconnaissance. It was constructed on a neck of land about 500 yards wide, the slopes of which fell off into a swamp on either side. On the highest point of this they had constructed an oblong redoubt, well palisaded and surrounded by a post and rail fence, a formidable obstacle to an assaulting column and difficult to destroy with artillery. The intervals between the side faces of the redoubt and the swamp were defended by an entrenched line of rifle trenches. I encamped the [force] about 1,200 yards from the enemy's positions.

At 7.15am on 29 April, the artillery batteries supporting the troops bombarded the strongpoint for nearly nine hours.

> Having received information that moving a force along the beach … at low water it was possible for a body of troops to pass outside the swamp on the enemy's right and gain the rear of his position, I ordered Colonel Greer to make the attempt with the 68th regiment after dark on the evening of the 28th, and in order to divert the attention of the enemy from that side, I ordered a feigned attack to be made on his front. Colonel Greer's movement succeeded perfectly and [he] took up a position in rear of the enemy which cut off his water supply, and made his retreat in daylight impossible

The following day the artillery knocked a breach in the parapet and, at 4pm, the order was given to storm the position from the front. Within minutes almost every officer in the assaulting party had become a casualty and the men fell back. The 68th Regiment were still to the rear of the position, blocking the enemy's escape route. An attempt by the Maori to break out at 5pm was defeated (killing two chiefs, Te Kani and Keni) and they then waited until darkness had fallen before making their escape into the mountains, leaving Gate Pa to the British. Hori Ngatai, a survivor wrote in 1903:

We adhered strictly to the terms of the battle-covenant, and harmed not the wounded nor interfered with the bodies of the dead. In the night ... recognising that our defences no longer existed we abandoned the ruined pa ... retiring in good order and spirits. We crept quietly through the lines of the 68th at the rear. The soldiers kept firing on us but none of us was killed, and only a few wounded. I believe that some of the soldiers were accidentally killed by their own comrades.

There followed nearly two months of minor skirmishes in the mountains before the British were able to gain revenge for their defeat at Gate Pa. On 21 June Colonel Greer, leading some 600 men from the 43rd (under Major Synge) and 68th Regiments (under Major Shuttleworth) along the ridge which extended south-east from Gate Pa (the present-day route of the Tauranga–Pye's Pa–Rotorua road), came across 500 Ngatirangi warriors who were busily engaged in the construction of a formidable new *pa* (fort) at Te Ranga, about 4 miles from the site of the earlier battle. After sending a request for additional men from Te Papa, Greer ordered his skirmishers forward and extended the 43rd Regiment and part of the 68th across the front and flanks of the pa and maintained a heavy rate of fire until his reinforcements arrived. Within two hours, 200 men arrived to support him, during which time futher Maoris were seen in the nearby woodland heading towards the pa. At 12.45pm, Greer ordered the advance of the 43rd Regiment, two companies of the 68th and a party of local militia. Both the British units were Light Infantry and adopted the tactics used by such regiments. The men of the 68th headed towards the left of the rifle pits. Charging forward into heavy enemy fire, the British troops closed with their enemy. As Ward wrote in his history of the Durham Light Infantry: 'the attack was carried out with irresistible dash and determination, and was received with equal determination and courage by the Maoris, who stood up in their pits without flinching ... The 43rd had a reputation to retrieve, the 68th a name to sustain, and the struggle was savage.' Leading the 68th charge, Captain Trent fell, severely wounded in the arm and Lieutenant Villiers-Stuart was bayoneted. Corporal John Byrne led his company into the rifle pit where he impaled one warrior with his bayonet. The warrior, however, was only severely wounded and, despite the bayonet embedded in his body, grabbed Byrne's rifle with one hand while trying to hit him with his war axe. It looked as if Byrne might have met his match. He could not break away as in doing so he would lose his rifle and leave himself exposed to the axe; if he remained in the struggle, he could not finish the fight and had to constantly avoid being hit by the axe. It was only the transfixed gun that was keeping the two men apart and Byrne alive. His predicament was spotted by Sergeant John Murray who had followed him into the rifle pit. The sergeant who had already taken on overwhelming numbers of the enemy (the official report states that it may have been as many as twelve) whom he had either killed or wounded with his bayonet when he worked his way up the trench, killed the warrior struggling with Byrne. The fighting seemed very evenly balanced until the supporting companies charged onto the right flank, breaking the Maori will to resist. During the intensive fighting the Maori leader, Rawiri, was killed as a result of which his men retreated and the position fell to the British. The British losses were 13 killed and 39 wounded while the Maori lost 120 killed and 27 wounded.

In Volume I (1845–64): *A History of the Maori Campaigns and the Pioneering Period,* James Cowan wrote:

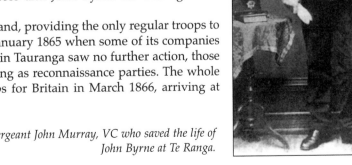

Colonel Greer in his report said they carried the rifle-pits 'in the most dashing manner.' They charged over the level glacis under a very heavy fire from the Kingite double-barrel guns, but the casualties were comparatively small, as most of the Maoris fired too high. The Ngai-te-Rangi and their allies fought like old heroes. They stood up to meet the bayonet charge unflinchingly, and as they had no time to reload they used gun-butt and tomahawk with desperate bravery. There were many hand-to-hand encounters. Even after being bayoneted some of the Maoris felled their foemen with their tomahawks. But the Kingite valour was of no avail before that rush with the bayonet. Scores of warriors went down under the steel, and the survivors broke for the cover of the gullies and swamps.

This defeat ended the Maori resistance in the north and the following month they surrendered their weapons. For his courage on this occasion, Sergeant Murray was awarded the Victoria Cross and John Byrne the Distinguished Conduct Medal.

The regiment remained in New Zealand, providing the only regular troops to garrison the Bay of Plenty area until January 1865 when some of its companies were sent to reinforce Taranaki. Those in Tauranga saw no further action, those further south saw little other than acting as reconnaissance parties. The whole regiment embarked aboard three ships for Britain in March 1866, arriving at Portsmouth in June and July.

Sergeant John Murray, VC who saved the life of
John Byrne at Te Ranga.

Byrne was promoted to sergeant in 1866 and served with the regiment in Aldershot and Manchester. It appears that when the 68th was ordered to Ireland in 1869, Byrne was discharged and served for a few weeks in the militia before re-joining the regiment as a sergeant, serving until 1872. During this time he would have been on home turf, including Kilkenny from July–September 1870. In February 1872, the regiment was posted to India but Byrne went, instead, to join the North Durham Militia, as did his fellow VC recipient, Sergeant Murray. Byrne's record for this period of his service seems to have been unblemished but then, after joining the North Durham Militia as a colour-sergeant, he was almost immediately dismissed '… for insubordination and highly improper conduct.' His fiery temperament had at last got the better of him. Perhaps his two gallantry awards had protected him whilst in the 68th Regiment but his new unit was not so impressed with his style of soldiering.

Records show that he intended residing in Durham after his discharge but the only extant comment on his post service life states that he lost all his possessions in a fire in the city of Cork in Ireland. Perhaps the fire also consumed his VC and DCM because neither have been seen since; only his New Zealand campaign medal appears to have survived. He next surfaced in Bristol in 1878, obtaining employment as a labourer with the Ordnance Survey. Sometime during the winter of 1878/9 he moved with his work to Newport in Monmouthshire where he took lodgings with Mrs Eliza Morgan at 7 Crown Street, Maindee. On 10 July, whilst working at Caerleon, he entered into an argument with a fellow worker named John Watts, a man of nineteen. During the course of the argument Watts is reported to have insulted the Victoria Cross (perhaps doubting that Byrne had the award, as he did not have the medal in his possession). Watts later reported:

He [Byrne] came on parade as usual at 8 o'clock and walked up to me with something in his hand. I held my shoulder up and I heard something go snap. His hand was about half a foot from my arm. I stood near him again. He turned his hand against me and I held up my arm to protect myself then he fired. I then ran away. I felt nothing until I had stopped running about 3 minutes then I felt pain. I saw a hole in my coat.

Byrne had fired a pistol, slightly wounding Watts. Later that day, a police officer called at Byrne's lodgings to question him about the incident. Byrne again lost his temper and drew out the revolver but, this time, instead of firing at the officer, put the gun in his own mouth and pulled the trigger. He died instantly. At the inquest held on 12 July his landlady stated that, although he liked a drink, she had never seen Byrne under the influence. The inquest returned a verdict of 'suicide whilst of unsound mind'. Byrne's lack of control and temper, which appears to have plagued him throughout his life, and which had no doubt played a significant part in the actions which resulted in the VC and the DCM, had finally proved fatal at the age of forty-six.

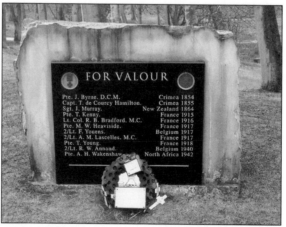

Memorial to the Durham Light Infantry VCs, DLI Museum, Durham.

HENRY RABY
Lieutenant
Naval Brigade

Henry Raby, VC, photographed during a vist to Homburg, Germany, c.1856.
[Mr Ralph Raby]

FULL NAME: Henry James Raby.

PLACE OF BIRTH: Boulogne, France, 26 September 1827. The Raby family were in some financial difficulties at this time and had no permanent address and were travelling to Germany. Previously, they had lived at Cae Mawr Cottage (also known as Plas Ucha), Llanelli, where Henry's father and grandfather (Alexander Raby) had various industrial interests. The house was destroyed by fire in 1824. A street in Llanelli was named after the family.

Father: Arthur Tournour Raby (died Homburg, Germany, 1856).

Mother: Henrietta Jane (née Smith), married in 1813. her family owned estates in the West Indies.

Father's Occupation: Industrialist (metal and coal industries), Llanelli, Carmarthenshire.

Education: Sherborne School, 1840–1. There is some strong circumstancial evidence that he was a pupil at Cowbridge Grammar School for some time before moving to Sherborne.

Service Record: Entered Royal Navy as a 1st class volunteer, HMS *Monarch*, 8th March 1842; paid off 28 October 1843; midshipman, HMS *Rodney*, 7 March 1848; sub-lieutenant, HMS *Ocean*, 30 March 1849; sub-lieutenant, HMS *Terrible*, 23 November 1849; lieutenant, 15 January 1850; discharged to half-pay (shore), 13 January 1850; lieutenant, HMS *Wasp*, West Africa Station, 2 October 1850; lieutenant, HMS *Wasp*, Circassia, in support of Turkish Army, January 1854; lieutenant, HMS *Diamond*, 24 October 1854; landed with the Naval Brigade in the Crimea, October 1854, present at Inkerman, 5 November 1854; served in the trenches before Sebastopol, 1854–5; second-in-command of ladder party during assault on the Redan, 18 June 1855; commander, 29 September 1855 (for services rendered during the siege of Sebastopol); CO, HMS *Medusa*, West Africa Station on anti-slavery operations, 1857; CO, HMS *Alecto*, West Africa Station, anti-slavery operation, 1859–62; took command of the squadron's boats at the capture of Porto Novo, April 1861 (wounded); promoted captain, 24 November 1862

Raby's campaign medals and decorations.
L–R: CB, Crimea Medal, Legion of Honour, VC (blue naval ribbon), Sardinian Crimea medal, Turkish Crimea Medal, Order of the Medjidie. Set of minatures below.
[Mr Ralph Raby, via Royal Naval Museum, Portsmouth].

(for services rendered in West Africa); CO, HMS *Adventurer*, China Station, 1868–71; retired from the service, 27 September 1877; rear-admiral (retired list), 21 March 1878.

Decorations, Medals and Rewards: Victoria Cross (for action during the assault on the Redan at Sebastopol, 18 June 1855); CB (1875); Crimean Medal (with clasps for Inkerman and Sebastopol); Legion of Honour, 3rd Class (1856); Order of the Medjidie, 4th Class (1856); Turkish Crimea Medal; Sardinian Crimea Medal; MinD (Crimea and West Africa); Reward for Distinguished Service.

Post-Service Employment: Retired rear-admiral. Committee member for the Royal Sailors' Home, Portsmouth and South Hampshire School & Home for the Blind.

Married: Judith, daughter of Thomas Watkin Foster of Holt Manor, Trowbridge, Wiltshire, 31 December 1863.

Children: Three sons (Montague, Arthur Reginald and Henry).

Died: 13 February 1907, at his home, 8 Clarence Parade, Southsea, Hampshire.

Buried: Highland Road Cemetery, Portsmouth.

Memorials: Highland Road Cemetery, Portsmouth. His name also appears on his wife's headstone at St Mary's Cemetery, Bath. Plaque in the entrance hall of Llanelli Town Hall.

Location of Victoria Cross: Royal Naval Museum, Portsmouth.

Citation for the Victoria Cross: *London Gazette*, 24 February 1857.
'On the 18th June 1855, immediately after the assault on Sebastopol, a soldier of the 57th Regiment, who had been shot through both legs, was observed sitting up and calling for assistance. Climbing over the breastwork of the advanced sap, Commander Raby and two seamen (John Taylor and Henry Curtis) proceeded upwards of 70 yards across open space towards the salient angle of the Redan, and in spite of the heavy fire which was still continuing, succeeded in carrying the wounded soldier to a place of safety, at imminent risk of their own lives.'

VC Investiture: By HM Queen Victoria at the first VC investiture held in Hyde Park, London, 26 June 1857.

Raby's wife, Judith, and their one-year old son, Arthur Reginald, 1870. [Mr Ralph Raby]

The grave of Henry Raby, Highland Road Cemetery.

8 Clarence Parade, Southsea; the house in the centre, with the two small balconies either side of a bay window, was the home of Henry Raby.

The Raby family originally hailed from Westminster in London where Alexander Raby (Henry's grandfather) was a member of the Drapers Company in the City and had business interests in an iron and copper works at Cobham in Surrey. According to Llanelli local historian Lyn John, Alexander came to the Welsh town after having financed two iron-founders, John Gevers and Thomas Ingham, who had run into difficulties with their iron furnace on the Stradey estate in 1791. Unable to recover his money, Raby foreclosed on them, took over the furnace in 1796 and then proceeded to turn Llanelli from a quiet backwater into a major centre of the industrial revolution in south Wales. He expanded the iron works and developed the settlement that became known as Furnace, even building his home there. His sons later worked with their father and the eldest, Alexander, lived at Bryn-môr (now the site of the Stradey Hotel) and Arthur at Plas Ucha (later the site of Cae Mawr Cottage). The business boomed during the Napoleonic Wars and the family expanded the works, built numerous cottages for their workers and developed a ship-building business for which Arthur later became primarily responsible. By 1806, however, the family business was in difficulties and for the next few years they walked a financial tightrope trying to keep everything going. In 1811, the company was restructured with Alexander Raby (senior) and Arthur Raby as the partners, but matters went from bad to worse, particularly after the restoration of peace in 1815. In 1823, Alexander Raby retired and Arthur assumed control of the failing business.

Rear-Admiral Henry Raby, VC, CB.

The following year Arthur's house was destroyed by fire and, twelve months later, their bankers, the Haynes Bank of Swansea, collapsed. The business failed and the family were forced to leave Britain, spending the next few years travelling in France and the Channel Islands. Arthur continued to dream of reviving the family's fortunes and, whilst en route to Germany (where his wife had property in Homburg), his son Henry was born at Boulogne.

One could speculate that Henry's career in the Royal Navy was the direct result of his family's business interests. His father had been a shipbuilder and there was therefore a strong link with the sea. If the business had not failed, then perhaps the third generation of Llanelli Rabys might have followed a career as a shipowner or even as master of his own ship. As events transpired, however, there was no career available in the family business and, instead, he joined the Royal Navy as a 1st class volunteer on HMS *Monarch* in 1842. For a young man with probably very society connections, he did quite well and progressed through the commissioned ranks, being promoted lieutenant by 1850. He served on the West Africa Station where the Royal Navy was concerned with the destruction of the slave trade. In January 1854 he was serving on HMS *Wasp* providing naval support to the Turkish forces against the the Russians in Circassia at the eastern end of the Black Sea.

The military operations in the Crimea necessitated the use of Royal Navy personnel to man some of the heavy artillery, to provide signallers for communications and additional men to supplement the relatively small numbers of British troops in the campaign. Raby landed with what was known as the Naval Brigade in the Crimea in October 1854 and served on land for the remainder of the conflict. The award of the Inkerman bar to his Crimean medal indicates that he served in that battle but it was during the seige of Sebastopol that he made his name.

In mid June the Naval Brigade was ordered to provide a number of sailors who were to form some of the ladder parties for the assault on Sebastopol, a joint Anglo-French attack which centred on two features, the Malakoff and the Redan. These men would be at the forefront of the British attacking force and would have to face the full brunt of the enemy's defensive fire. In earlier years such a party would have been known as the 'Forlorn Hope' and membership of it almost amounted to a death sentence. Henry Raby was given the invidious position of second-in-command of this group.

The Redan was a triangular, purpose-built fortification, with two faces looking out towards the British lines. Each face was 70-yards long and met at an angle of 65 degrees. In front was a 20-foot wide and 14-foot deep ditch. The flat faces of the Redan rose a further 15 feet above the ground level. Any attacking force would have to enter the ditch before attempting to scale the earthwork, by means of ladders — a climb of nearly 30 feet. In front of the ditch were approximately 450 yards of open ground (which was covered from every angle by Russian artillery and infantry fire) and a zone of tangled branches some eight feet in height. The third side of the Redan, following roughly the line of the main Russian perimeter earthwork, was protected by trenches manned by infantry and mounds of earth which shielded the gunners from anything but a direct hit by artillery. The plan envisaged the French attacking, and capturing, the Malakoff, followed shortly afterwards by the British assault on the Redan.

On 17 June 800 Allied guns opened fire on the Russian defences, possibly the greatest bombardment ever seen up to that date. The Russians returned the fire but, gradually, began to run short of ammunition and the advantage swung in favour of the Allies. Here and there, gaps began to appear in the Russian defences as the walls and parapets began to crumble under the unrelenting weight of artillery. The final assault was planned to take place two hours after dawn on the 18 June, the anniversary of Waterloo. Then, at the last minute, there was a change in the French command structure and the attack on the Malakoff was pushed back from 1.30am to dawn (3.30am). The British were not consulted until it was too late to do anything but conform.

From the start, the French assault failed to go according to plan. Even the start time went awry as General Mayran mistook the explosion of three artillery shells at 2.50am as the firework signal to commence the attack. As daylight came to the Crimea it became obvious that the French were not going to take their objective and, as everyone recognised, without the fall of the Malakoff the capture of the Redan was impossible. Raglan, in an ideal position to either delay or abort the British assault on the Redan, decided that honour insisted he order his troops into the attack, despite the fact that the chances of success were minimal. Shortly before the British commanders gave the order for the assault to begin, bugle calls from within Sebastopol signalled the deployment of 10,000 men in defence of the Redan — the British attacking force numbered less than 1500 men. At a time when the artillery should have been directed to hit the Redan with everything possible, the order was given for it to cease firing, just as the infantry climbed out of their trenches and began their dash across the 450-yard killing ground. Ahead of them, awaiting their arrival at the ditch, the Russian infantry lined the parapets four-deep.

The British skirmishers were massacred before they even reached the Redan's defences and the attackers began desperately to seek cover. The men of the Rifle and Naval Brigades took heavy casualties and the 57th Regiment lost its commanding officer. His replacement was in the British rear, in charge of the reserves so that, by the time a message had reached him and he had forced his way forward through the congested British trenches, it was too late and the men of his regiment had joined the others trying to gain cover behind anything that might protect them from the withering Russian fire. Within minutes the regiment had sustained 25% casualties and, unable to draw on support from the reserves, their new commanding officer ordered their withdrawal. Captain Fanshawe of the 33rd Regiment wrote:

> Our loss, I regret to say, was very considerable, having had 50 men killed or wounded. The loss our Division has sustained is frightful. The Rifle Brigade are almost annihiliated! Out of 130 men only 35 survive. The 23rd nearly cease to exist!

Behind them, still in the British trenches, Lieutenant Edward Hughes D'Eath (of HMS *Sidon*) spotted a private soldier of the 57th calling out for assistance, some 70 yards away in front of the Redan. The man, wounded in both legs, was

Impression of Lieutenant Raby's VC action, painted by Chevalier Louis Désanges and displayed in the Victoria Cross Gallery at Wantage until after the Second World War. The artist worked from life and, if one compares the painting with the photograph of Raby taken in Homburg, the similarity is quite striking. This therefore leads to the assumption that the portraits of the other two VCs, Taylor (wearing the peaked cap) and Curtis (right) are also reasonably accurate portrayals of the two men in question. Of interest is the inclusion of Raby wearing a monocle — a most unusual item to wear when 'in action'. The painting also lacks any portrayal of Lieutenant D'Eath, presumably because he did not survive the war and was not awarded the VC.
[Mr Philip Raby]

unable to move forward or back, nor take shelter until the fighting was over. Realising the man's chances of survival were minimal if left in the open, D'Eath asked Raby to assist him in bringing the soldier to safety. D'Eath then realised that the two of them would probably be unable to carry the soldier and called upon two seamen (Captain of the Forecastle (N° 601) John Taylor of HMS *London*, and Boatswain's Mate (N° 83) Henry Curtis of HMS *Rodney*) to volunteer to accompany them. The four men then 'climbed over the breastwork, went out, picked up the man, brought him in and handed him over to military surgeon. The soldier ... was lying I should judge about 60 or 70 yards in front of the sap and the fire was very

A photograph by Robertson of a group of Naval Brigade officers in the camp before Sebastopol. The figure seated in the centre is most probably Henry Raby. [Imperial War Museum Q 71154]

heavy at the time and apparently directed at us though we were all fortunate enough to escape without injury'. [Letter from Henry Raby to Rear Admiral Sir Stephen Lushington, 4 June 1856] For his gallantry on this occasion and for his services throughout the siege of Sebastopol, Raby was promoted to commander in September 1855. When Raby was nominated for the Victoria Cross for the same action, he was away 'on continental leave for a period of four months'. On his return, he wrote to Sir Stephen Lushington to try and correct what he thought was an injustice in his nomination.

I have only on my return to England become aware of your having already forwarded to Admiral Sir Edward Lyons, Commander in Chief of the Mediterranean Fleet, the names of such officers and men amongst those who had the honor of serving under your command in the Royal Naval Brigade who you consider to have deserved the distinction pf the 'Victoria Cross' by any special act of 'valour or devotion to their country' in the presence of the enemy during the late war.

Under these circumstances, I have the honor to request that you will allow me, in justice to the memory of my lamented comrade and brother officer the late Lieutenant Edward Hughes D'Eath, R.N. of Her Majesty's ship 'Sidon' to bring the following action to your notice —

On the 18th June 1855 Lieut D'Eath commanded the 4th party of seamen detailed to carry the scaling ladders to which party I had also the honor to be attached; in the morning soon after the repulse of the troops from the Redan, I was standing in the advanced sap in front of the Quarries when Lt D'Eath came to me and said that there was a soldier laying out in front of the sap badly wounded who he thought we might get in, and asked me if I would assist him to do, to which I agreed readily. Lieut D'Eath on again looking at the man considered that from his being wounded in the legs it would require more than ourselves to bring him in, he therefore asked John Taylor … and Henry Curtis … if they would volunteer to go with us, they immediately assented ….

As Lieut. D'Eath unfortunately fell a victim to cholera soon after this event, I as the survivor take the liberty of laying this simple statement of the facts before you trusting that should you consider it worthy of being classed with those 'deeds of valour &c' which are already known to you will be pleased to use your influence to procure the Honor of 'The Victoria Cross' for him and those others concerned, and I feel that by the family of my friend the late Lieut D'Eath nothing would be more highly prized than such a testimony to his bravery.

I have the honour to be, Sir, your very obedient humble servant

Henry J. Raby

* Perhaps it may not be superfluous for me here to state further that previously to this both Lt. D'Eath & myself had engaged in rendering what assistance we could to wounded officers and men & I was fortunate enough myself to be able to render great assistance to Captain Winkham [sic] of HM 33rd Regt & to send him in safety to where he could receive medical aid. [Wickham was badly wounded in the foot]

It would appear that, as a consequence of this letter, John Taylor and Henry Curtis were both awarded the Victoria Cross for the same action. Sadly, Taylor died on 24 February 1857, the very day that the citation appeared in the *London Gazette*. Lieutenant D'Eath, having contracted cholera, died on 7 August 1855 and was ineligible for nomination. Had he survived the war, it seems highly likely that he too would have been awarded the coveted honour. It is, however, rather unfortunate that his name was not mentioned in the citation for Raby's award.

As the most senior officer of the 'Senior Service' (the Royal Navy) to receive the award, Raby was the first in line to be decorated by Queen Victoria at the first investiture in Hyde Park on 26 June 1857, making him the first person to wear the

Boatswain's Mate, Henry Curtis VC.

new decoration. In later days, Raby used to proudly boast that he had survived the VC action unscathed only to be wounded by Queen Victoria when she pierced his chest with the pin of the Victoria Cross during the investiture.

After the end of the war, he returned to the West Africa Station and resumed operations against the slave trade. In April 1861 he was in command of the gunboats which captured and destroyed the major slave depot at Porto Novo on the Bight of Benin in West Africa. In the fighting which followed he was involved in the spiking of one of the guns when the gun exploded, slightly injuring him in the face. He was also responsible for setting up a treaty with the chiefs of the Old Calabar River in Nigeria.

CHARLES LUMLEY
Captain
97th (Earl of Ulster's) Regiment

Charles Lumley, VC.

The Officers Quarters, Brecon, where Lumley died. [Brian Best]

Charles Lumley's VC and medals displayed at Maidstone. L–R: VC; Crimean Medal; Turkish Crimea Medal; Legion of Honour. [Reproduced courtesy of the Queen's Own Royal West Kents Regimental Museum]

Full Name: Charles Henry Lumley.
Place of Birth: Kidbrooke, Kent. By 1851, after the death of his father, he was living with his maternal grandmother at 1 Shooters Hill, Eltham, Kent.
Date of Birth: *Circa* 1824.
Father: Robert Lumley.
Mother: Harriet Ellis (born Woolwich, Kent), the sister of Vice-Admiral William Ellis, RN.
Father's Occupation: Merchant.
Education: Royal Military Academy, Woolwich.
Service Record: Commissioned ensign, 97th Regiment of Foot, 30 August 1844; promoted lieutenant, 18 February 1848; promoted captain, 29 December 1854; served Crimean Campaign 1855–6 (siege of Sebastopol, second assault of the Redan, 8 September 1855, severely wounded in the head); brevet major, 2 November 1855; half-pay, 4 September 1857; major, 4 December 1857; unattached major, 1857–8; transferred to 2/23rd Regiment of Foot, 1858; OC, 2/23rd Regiment detachment at Brecon, 20 July 1858.
Decorations, Medals and Rewards: Victoria Cross (for action during the assault on the Redan, Sebastopol, 8 September 1855); Crimean Medal (clasp for Sebastopol); Turkish Crimea Medal; Legion of Honour.
Married: Letitia Beaulieu, daughter of William Clarke, gentleman, on 27 May 1852, at St Mary's Church, Marylebone. She was born (*c.*1830) in Woolwich. After her husband's death she lived with her husband's uncle, Vice-Admiral William Ellis, in Woolwich, and then Bath, where she died on 16 November 1890.
Children: None.
Died: Shot himself in the head at St Mary's Barracks, Brecon, 17 October 1858, and died a few hours later. An inquest which met eight days later gave a verdict of 'suicide due to temporary insanity'.
Buried: Brecon Cathedral churchyard, Brecon (north-east corner of the churchyard).

Memorials: Brecon Cathedral Churchyard, Brecon. His name appears on his wife's headstone in Bath Cemetery.

Location of Victoria Cross: Queen's Own Royal West Kent Regimental Museum at Maidstone in Kent.

Citation for the Victoria Cross: *London Gazette*, 24 February 1857.

'For having distinguished himself highly by his bravery at the assault on the Redan, 8th September 1855, being among the first inside the work, where he was immediately engaged with three Russian gunners reloading a field piece, who attacked him; he shot two of them with his revolver, when he was knocked down by a stone, which stunned him for a moment, but, on recovery, he drew his sword, and was in the act of cheering the men on, when he received a ball in the mouth, which wounded him most severely'

VC Investiture: By HM Queen Victoria at the first VC investiture held in Hyde Park, London, 26 June 1857.

The grave of Charles Lumley, Brecon Cathedral churchyard.

For many years it was erroneously believed that Charles Lumley was born at Forres House, Forres, Morayshire and, as a result, he has been claimed as a Scottish Victoria Cross winner. Lumley was in fact English, born in the parish of Kidbrook in Kent, possibly in the area of Shooters Hill near Woolwich. Extensive searches in the Scottish records have failed to show any link with Forres and similar searches in the Greenwich Record Office have failed to pinpoint his exact place of birth. He first appears in the 1841 Census as a gentleman cadet at the Royal Military Academy, Woolwich, aged 15 and then in the 1851 census as a 'soldier' living with his mother and grandmother at Shooters Hill, Woolwich. His marriage certificate of one year later shows him as a 'Lieutenant in the Army', the son of Robert Lumley, Merchant. He was commissioned by purchase into the 97th Regiment (Earl of Ulster's) which, since 1824 had been the 2nd Battalion of the 50th Regiment of Foot (Queen's Own Royal West Kent Regiment). In late 1854 the regiment was posted to the Crimea, arriving too late to take part in the great battles of the autumn and early winter, but in time for the hard slog of siege warfare endured throughout the terrible winter of 1854/5 as part of a British Army that was totally unprepared and ill-equipped to endure the conditions. Promoted to lieutenant he saw his first real taste of action on 8 September.

In August 1855, the Russians in Sebastopol made one last attempt to break out from the city and drive the Allies back into the sea. General Gortschakoff threw everything he had at the French end of the Allied line near the Tchernaya river. After some gains early in the day, the Russians were eventually driven back by the French and Sardinian armies and the time was rapidly approaching when either the allies would launch another assault or the Russians would withdraw across the harbour of Sebastopol to the northern side of the city. The Allied commanders would have found themselves in an embarrassing position should the latter have occurred first.

By now, the French army was three times the size of the British force in the Crimea and, as General Simpson pondered and did nothing, the French commander General Pélissier, took the initiative. The French would assault the Malakoff, which was only 25 yards from their forward trenches, while the British would again attempt to seize the Redan. Simpson failed to accurately judge the numbers of men required in the assaulting parties and the qualities that were required for success. It was to be the Light and 2nd Divisions who were to lead the attack. These divisions were suffering from nearly twelve months of continuous duty in the front line which meant that they were under-strength and 'trench happy', their men accustomed to seeking the protection of the trenches and parapets rather than drilled in open movement. In later conflicts it was realised that there was a maximum period that men could spend in the front line after which they lost efficiency. The replacements who had arrived now made up the majority of

Royal Military Academy, Woolwich.

the attacking force and the men who had survived the Alma and Inkerman were thin on the ground. Most had tried to cross the open ground in front of the Redan back in June and could well remember the dangers involved. On the toss of a coin, the Light Division had the dubious honour of providing the first storming party, commanded by Colonel Unett, closely followed by the men of Colonel Windham's 2nd Division. The attack was set for dawn on 8 September with the preliminary bombardment beginning three days earlier (during which 800 guns fired some 13,000 shells and 90,000 round shot at the Russian defences).

The storming party set off before the arranged time and the 23rd Regiment (Royal Welch Fusiliers), who were meant to be in close

Artist's impression of Charles Lumley's VC action.

support, were still some distance from the forward trenches. Some of the wounded were already back in the British trenches before the Fusiliers were able to begin climbing out. Lieutenant Boscawen Trevor Griffith of the 23rd recalled the events of the next few minutes:

Several officers we met coming back wounded said that they had been in the Redan and that supports were only wanted to complete the victory … We scrambled out of the trench on to open ground. That was a fearful moment. I rushed across the space … shot striking the ground all the way and men falling down on all sides. when I got to the ditch I found our men all mixed up in confusion but keeping up a steady fire against the enemy … we rushed over the next of the glacis into the ditch — here were lots of men of different regiments all huddled together — scaling ladders placed against the parapet crowded with our fellows. Radcliffe and I got hold of a ladder and went up it to the top of the parapet where we were stopped by the press — wounded and dead men kept tumbling down upon us. We could not get the men to come up the parapet in sufficient numbers.

The 97th Regiment formed part of the Light Division and one of the first officers into the Redan itself was Charles Lumley. Seeing three Russian gunners busy trying to reload a field gun ready to fire again at the assaulting British forces, he attacked them single-handed. The first two he shot with his revolver, just before being hit in the head by a stone (or, if the experience of others was repeated here, by small cannon shot thrown by hand). The blow knocked him to the ground where he took a few moments to gather himself. Drawing his sword he began to call his men forward when he was struck in the mouth by a musket ball. Fortunately, the wound, although severe, was not fatal and he was able to withdraw from inside the Redan along with the others as the assaulting wave petered out and began to ebb. Lieutenant Griffith continued his account:

Suddenly a panic seized our men and I grieve to say … they deserted their comrades inside and retreated in confusion towards out trenches. In vain we bellowed out to them and tried everything to rally them — it was no use and, after remaining as long as they were able, the officers were forced to follow their men.

Lumley's war was over, and he was invalided home on 29 September and, when sufficiently recovered from his wound, was promoted to major and placed on half-pay until he obtained a vacancy in the 2/23rd Regiment, Royal Welch Fusiliers, in 1858. He was the officer commanding a detachment of that regiment at Brecon when, on Sunday 17 October 1858, he shot himself, dying from the effects several hours later. At the inquest, one of Lumley's staff, Richard Davies stated:

I was in the service of Major Lumley. On Saturday evening, he appeared to be in very low spirits, and was

The interior of the Redan after the Russian withdrawal.

absent in his manner. He called me to his room three or four times and each time said there was nothing he wanted. I went to church on Sunday morning. Mrs Lumley also went to church and on coming back she went upstairs. Shortly after, Mrs Lumley came into the kitchen and asked me if I had seen the Major. I replied that I had not. She told me to go look for him as he had gone out with his pistol.

I went to the rear and found him in the water closet, lying on his left hand side on the ground with his pistol in his left hand. The door was shut but not fastened. I immediately ran for assistance and told Mr Stanley and Mr Hill, went to the rear and Mr Stanley then went for the doctor.

On Saturday, Major and Mrs Lumley intended to go out riding at half past 2, but the groom was out with the Major's horse and he could not go. He was in a great rage. He dined as usual on Saturday, but did not take tea as he generally did. When I took up the tea, the Major went to his dressing room and shortly afterwards came down and walked about the barrack square. He was walking there when I went to bed at 10 o'clock.

He got up between 8 and 9 o'clock on Sunday as usual. I noticed him going to the rear several times on Sunday morning and he was looking at me in a very strange manner. His look that morning frightened me.

Other witnesses described Lumley as having 'an absent manner' and behaving in an eccentric fashion during the Saturday and Sunday morning. A Mr Fitzroy recalled that Lumley had called out the guard on the Sunday morning, something that he had never before seen done since he had been in the service.

The post-mortem declared that Lumley had a single wound to the head, about two inches behind his right ear, made by a pistol ball which was recovered from the brain. The regimental surgeon declared that 'It was quite possible for the deceased to have inflicted the wound himself and it is my opinion it was the Major's own act'. If the newspaper report is accurate, then this statement is most peculiar as Davies had stated that he found Lumley with the pistol in his left hand, yet the entry point of the wound was 'two inches behind the right ear', a most difficult piece of contortion, but not impossible.

It appears that nobody was overly surprised at what had happened. Captain Reed described Lumley as 'absent in manner and hot tempered. He had lately been considerably worried by overwork, having to act as paymaster … and complained of not being able to attend to his duties as commanding officer'. The coroner found that Lumley had taken his own life 'whilst labouring under temporary insanity' (a verdict that would not be allowed today as it is held that a person cannot be 'temporarily insane' in much the same way as a leg cannot be 'temporarily broken'; it is either broken or not broken, and a person is either sane or insane).

He was buried with full military honours in the churchyard of Brecon Priory (now the Cathedral). His wife returned to Kent and went to live with her maternal uncle William Ellis, RN (who retired a vice-admiral) and moved with him to live in Bath where she died in 1890.

Dr Henry Sylvester.

Long Street, Devizes, the birthplace of Henry Sylvester. He was almost certainly born in the large house in the centre of the photograph.

HENRY SYLVESTER
Assistant Surgeon
23rd (Royal Welch Fusiliers) Regiment of Foot

FULL NAME: William Henry Thomas Sylvester (known as Henry).

PLACE OF BIRTH: Long Street, Devizes, Wiltshire.

Date of Birth: 19 April 1831.

Father: Charles Sylvester.

Mother: Elizabeth Sylvester.

Father's Occupation: Surgeon.

Education: Marischal College, Aberdeen (MB in 1853, and MD in 1855, this college merged with King's College to form the University of Aberdeen in 1860), Edinburgh University (LRCS in 1853, and LSA in 1869).

Service Record: Appointed assistant surgeon (staff), 3 March 1854; assistant surgeon, 23rd Regiment of Foot, Royal Welch Fusiliers, 22 September 1854; served Crimean Campaign (siege of Sebastopol); served Indian Mutiny 1857–8 (Relief of Lucknow); surgeon (Staff), 10 July 1860; retired from the army, 15 November 1861.

Decorations, Medals and Rewards: Victoria Cross (for action at the Redan, Sebastopol, 8 September 1855); Crimea Medal (clasp for Sebastopol); Indian Mutiny Medal (clasps for Relief of Lucknow and Lucknow); MinD (Crimea); Turkish Crimea Medal; Legion of Honour (5th Class).

Post-Service Employment: After leaving the army, Dr Sylvester was appointed a house surgeon at Swansea Hospital, Glamorgan. He later served as chief medical officer to Millbank Prison in London and had a private practice at 7 Bessborough Gardens, Westminster.

Married: Martha Elizabeth Watson, 7 May 1874 (she had been a nurse at Swansea Hospital). She died in 1934. At the time of his marriage he resided at 66, Bessborough Street, Westminster, London and later at 7 Bessborough Gardens.

Children: Reputedly two daughters, but only one, Alice Maud (born *c.*1877) can be identified.

Died: 13 March 1920, at his home 8, Beach Road, Paignton, Devon.

Buried: Paignton Cemetery, 18 March 1920, grave 2614.

Memorials: Paignton Cemetery, Devon.

The Sylvester display, including the brass bowl which he took with him on campaign.
[AMS Museum, Aldershot]

The VC, campaign medals and decorations of Surgeon Henry Sylvester.
L–R: VC, Crimea Medal, Indian Mutiny Medal, Legion of Honour, Turkish Crimea Medal. [AMS Museum, Aldershot]

Location of Victoria Cross: Army Medical Services Museum, Aldershot.

Citation for the Victoria Cross: *London Gazette*, 20 November 1857. 'For going out on 8th September 1855, under a heavy fire in front of the fifth parallel Right Attack, to a spot near the Redan, where Lieutenant and Adjutant Dyneley was lying mortally wounded and for dressing his wounds in that dangerous and exposed situation. N.B. This officer was mentioned in General Simpson's despatch of 18th September 1855, for going to the front under heavy fire to assist the wounded.'

VC Investiture: By HM Queen Victoria at the first VC investiture held in Hyde Park, London, on 26 June 1857.

See also Corporal Robert Shields, VC.

Dr Henry Sylvester, VC in old age.

The grave (foreground) of Dr Henry Sylvester in Paignton Cemetery.

Dr Henry Sylvester's home at Beach Road, Paignton.

Corporal Shields's VC action, painting by Chevalier Louis Désanges. [RWF Museum]

ROBERT SHIELDS
Corporal
23rd (Royal Welch Fusiliers) Regiment of Foot

FULL NAME: Robert Shields.
PLACE OF BIRTH: Hope and Anchor Inn, 41 St Mary's Street, Cardiff.
Date of Birth: Not known, but he was baptised on 26 August 1827.
Father: John Shields.
Mother: Anne Shields.
Father's Occupation: Mason, later a publican.
Education: —
Pre-Service Employment: Moulder.
Service Record: Enlisted in the 23rd Regiment of Foot, Royal Welch Fusiliers, 9 April 1847 (Service No. 2945); served in the Crimean Campaign 1854–6, present at the Battle of Inkerman and during the siege of Sebastopol; promoted corporal, 9 September 1855; bought his discharge for £15, 6 December 1856; served 17th (North) Middlesex Volunteers.
Decorations, Medals and Rewards: Victoria Cross (for action during the assault on the Redan, Sebastopol, 8 September 1855); Crimean Medal (clasps for Inkerman and Sebastopol); Legion of Honour; Turkish Crimean Medal; Cambrian Torque of Valour (presented to him at the Llangollen National Eisteddfod, 1858). He is also recorded as having been awarded the 'Beaufort Medal', details of which are unknown, but which may have been given by the parish of Beaufort, Monmouthshire, where Shields was living at the time of the Crimean War.
Post-Service Employment: Park Ranger *c.*1857 (possibly Regents Park, London); he is referred to as a 'Gate Keeper' in Queen Victoria's Journal for 2 June 1857. In 1864, he emigrated to Bombay, India, where he was employed as an overseer by the Back Bay Reclamation Company.
Married: Elizabeth Anne Crewe (schoolmistress) on 23 April 1857.
Children: None recorded.
Died: Bombay, India, 23 December 1864.
Buried: Location of grave is not known.
Memorials: St Thomas's Cathedral, Bombay.
Location of Victoria Cross: Not known. The last reference to the VC was in 1956 when the RWF discovered a report stating that it was in a strongroom at Wellingborough Urban Council offices. It had been placed there for safe-keeping in 1923 by a local hairdresser who had taken it as security on a £2 loan in 1911.
Citation for the Victoria Cross: *London Gazette,* 24 February 1857.
'For volunteering, on 8th September 1855, to go out to the front from the 5th parallel after the attack on the Redan, to bring in Lieutenant Dyneley, who was wounded and found afterwards to be mortally so.'
VC Investiture: By HM Queen Victoria at the first VC investiture in Hyde Park, London, on 26 June 1857.

See also Assistant Surgeon Henry Sylvester, VC.

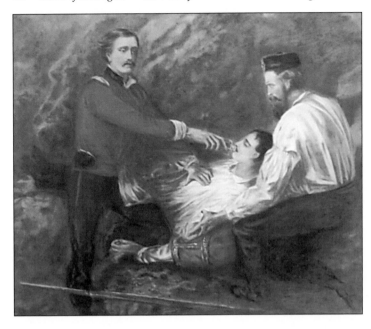

Painting by Chevalier Louis Désanges, depicting Henry Sylvester's VC action. For the purpose of identification, the figure on the right can be compared with the portrait of Shields by the same artist.
[AMS Museum, Aldershot]

The Allied bombardment of the Russian defences of Sebastopol began on 5 September 1855, a three day artillery barrage which was a forerunner of the style of warfare to come. At noon on 8 September, the French attacked the position known as the Malakoff which was occupied with very little loss as the assaulting troops began their assault whilst the Russian defenders were in the middle of changing duties and had withdrawn many of the troops from their first line of defence in order to allow the relief to move in without causing too much congestion and thereby providing a tempting target for the Allies. As soon as the Tricolor was seen flying above the Malakoff, the British forces launched their own attack on the Redan. Five companies of the Royal Welch Fusiliers, led by Colonel Daniel Lysons, were formed up in the Fifth Parallel (line of trenches) and eventually made their way across the sloping, open ground towards the Russian positions. The first wave of assaulting troops had been brought to a complete halt by the heavy defensive fire from the Redan and as the Royal Welchmen closed on their objective, they too were halted by the intense fire, the congestion of troops desperate to gain cover and those troops who were already beginning to fall back. As the British troops began to fall back a certain degree of panic appeared in the ranks, as Lieutenant Boscawen Griffiths of the Royal Welch wrote at the time:

> I grieve to say … they deserted their comrades inside and retreated in confusion towards our trenches. In vain we bellowed out to them and tried everything to rally them — it was no use and, after remaining as long as they were able, the officers were forced to follow their men.

Lysons, thirteen other officers and about 100 men had been wounded. Amongst these was 23-year old Lieutenant and Adjutant Douglas Dyneley who, having been hit in the head, had sought cover in a shallow cave under the Russian defences. The lieutenant was a popular figure with both the rank and file and his brother officers. Brief enquiries led to reports that some of the soldiers had seen him fall but had been unable to help him as their orders expressly forbade stopping to assist the wounded. The general feeling was that Dyneley had not been killed outright and might be lying wounded somewhere in front of the Russian positions.

The account of the Victoria Cross action which followed (published in *A History of the Royal Welsh Fusiliers*, Howell Harris, 1916) stated that Dr Sylvester, on hearing of Dyneley's situation, went out in search of him under heavy enemy fire. On reaching the officer, who was attended by Private Thomas Harris, he dressed his wound but, being unable to carry him unassisted, then returned to the British lines. Later, when the regiment was ordered to return to camp, Captain Drewe, accompanied by Corporal Robert Shields and Privates Michael Aherne (3420), James Tailor (2715), John Green (3645) and Thomas Kennedy (3909), asked leave to bring in Dyneley. They waited until dusk before venturing out into the open, still under fire, and brought him and Harris safely back. Sadly, Dyneley died in the early hours of the following morning.*

This account clearly requires further examination if a clearer picture is to be formed of what happened, as it conflicts with the citations of Sylvester and Shields which add no further information; in fact they provide even less as there is no mention made of any of the others involved in the treatment and rescue of Dyneley. If the facts were as stated in the regimental record, why was the Victoria Cross only awarded to Sylvester and Shields and not to the other six men involved? Perhaps there were simply too many men for them all to be nominated? If this were the case, might it be that nominations were made for two men, one officer and one NCO, to receive the award on behalf of them all? There is, however, no documented or recollected evidence to suggest that this was what happened. Were Sylvester and Shields selected simply because their actions stood out as meriting the award above those of their comrades?

Colonel Lysons wrote a letter in support of Shields's nomination for an award from the Llangollen Eisteddfod in 1858:

> On the 8th September 1855, he [Shields] was in the attack on the Redan; I observed him amongst the foremost; he was one

of the few who got into the ditch at the re-entering angle, and remained there till one of the last when our troops retired. After he had returned to the trenches, he heard that the Adjutant-Lieutenant Dyneley had been left out near the Russian works, dangerously wounded; he took off his coat and went out in search of that officer; he found him, and would have brought him in, but his wounds were too painful to permit of his being carried without a regular stretcher; he therefore returned to the trenches and obtained the services of Assistant-Surgeon Sylvester, who gallantly volunteered to accompany Corporal Shields to the place where Lieutenant Dyneley was lying, and dress his wounds; they went out under a heavy fire and accomplished their purpose; as soon as it was dark, Corporal Shields went out a third time, accompanied by Lieutenant, now Major, Drewe, and several other men; they succeeded then in bringing in their wounded comrade. The Russians fired at them as they went out, but desisted when they returned, apparently perceiving that they were carrying a wounded man. Poor Lieutenant Dyneley, one of the finest officers in the corps, died before the morning.

This is a most illuminating document which clearly shows that the part played by Shields in the rescue was far more significant than had previously been suggested; in fact, his was the dominant role and Sylvester's action had been prompted by him. The other participants were only involved at a much later stage in bringing the injured officer back on a stretcher. Far from only going out into what we would now term 'No-man's Land' on the one occasion, Shields went out three times.

There is one further source of evidence which supports the Colonel's version of the events and which both Sylvester and Shields would have been directly involved with. The artist Louis Désanges produced two paintings of this VC action, one each for Sylvester and Shields. What is significant about these is that Shields appears in both. In the Sylvester painting, the gallant doctor is depicted attending to the wounded Dyneley whilst the patient's head is supported by a soldier. Shields was of such a distinctive appearance that any comparison of this figure with the one in the Shields painting clearly shows it to be the same person. Shields was therefore present with Sylvester.

Yet again, the brevity of the citations for most of the early VC actions not only devalues them in comparison with future awards but, in doing so, fails to do justice to the individuals concerned. Sylvester's action compares favourably with those of his medical colleagues in the wars of the twentieth century while Shields would undoubtedly have been nominated for the VC in any conflict; to have gone out three times under fire to try to save a wounded officer is clearly deserving of the highest award.

This second assault on the Redan was, if anything, more of a disaster than the first.** The French, however, had taken the Malakoff and during the night of 8/9 September, realising that the south side of Sebastopol could no longer be held, the Russians withdrew across the harbour. To all intents and purposes the war was over. Although a peace treaty was not signed until the following April, the duties of the British troops in the Crimea were no longer combat but more those of garrison troops. There was to be no more killing or dying (except for those who died of wounds already received or of disease) and there were to be no more awards of the Victoria Cross on Russian soil until 1918.

Henry Sylvester served with the Royal Welch Fusiliers throughout the Indian Mutiny but was forced to retire in 1861. It would appear that he contracted some form of spinal disease whilst in India which resulted in a stooped back for the remainder of his life. Returning to Britain he was able to take up an appointment as a house surgeon at Swansea Hospital (where he first met his wife) before moving to London, where he set up in private practice in Westminster and served as the chief medical officer to Millbank Prison. This was London's largest prison built on the 'Pentonville style' which, in 1854, saw 2,659 new prisoners pass through its gates

Millbank Prison (Penitentiary) where Sylvester was Chief Medical Officer. Demolished in the 1890s. The Tate Gallery and Queen Alexandra Military Hospital were built on the site. Coincidentally, Sylvester's VC and medals were displayed at the RAMC Museum in this building until 1977.
[AMS Museum, Aldershot]

Bessborough Gardens, a few hundred yards from Millbank Prison, where Sylvester had a medical practice in the 1880s.

which resulted in 11,890 recorded cases of illness. The post of CMO at such an establishment was certainly no sinecure. The prison closed and was demolished in the 1890s. By 1901, Sylvester was in general practice in Lambeth and living at 66 Stockwell Park Road, where it is believed he remained until his retirement when he moved to live in Paignton, Devon. He is believed to have worked with Florence Nightingale at Scutari Hospital following the end of hostilities in the Crimean War.

Corporal Robert Shields was a native of Cardiff, who later lived at Beaufort, Monmouthshire, a small settlement to the north-east of Ebbw Vale. Although there is no known photograph of this man, his portrayal by Désanges matches descriptions that have survived of him and can be assumed to be reasonably accurate. He left the army shortly after the end of the Crimean War, taking up employment as a park keeper at Regent's Park, London.

An interesting footnote to the story of Robert Shields stems from the *Eisteddfod Fawr* (the Great Eisteddfod, forerunner of the National Eisteddfod of Wales) held at Llangollen in 1858. Amongst the prizes awarded was the Cambrian Gold Torque of Valour, 'given to the best soldier in the 23rd or 41st Regiment most highly recommended by his officers for courage and conduct in the field'. Letters had been sent to the two regiments, as a result of which, Corporal Robert Shields, VC was selected to receive the award. At the presentation, testimonials from a number of his former officers were read out, all extolling the courage and soldierly qualities of the recipient. Amongst these were the letter from Colonel Dysons which is quoted above, which added substantially to our knowledge of the circumstances surrounding the award. The regiment's assistant quartermaster general, Frederick Sayers, added:

> The act of gallantry for which he obtained the Victoria Cross entitles him to great consideration; his conduct on that occasion was fine in the extreme. With very many others I entertain the highest esteem for him, believing him to be a most gallant soldier, and peculiarly respectable man. I should be pleased to see him obtain any reward given for courage in the field.

When the torque was presented to Shields at Llangollen, the crowd called out (in Welsh) 'Is he a Welshman?' to which Shields replied (also in Welsh), 'I am a true Welshman in blood and language' and then addressed the crowd in his mother tongue. The press described him a 'a fine, manly, young fellow, with a superb beard, which falling downwards, conceals, in great measure, the torque from view'.

---

* Douglas Dyneley is buried in the Light Division Cemetery in the Crimea. His memorial reads: 'Sacred to the memory of Lieutenant Douglas Dyneley, 23rd Royal Welch Fusiliers, who fell mortally wounded before Sebastopol in the attack on the Redan, September 8th 1855. Born 19th December 1831. Died 9th September 1855'.

** For further details about the early part of this attack see the entry on Charles Lumley (above).

JAMES HILLS
2nd Lieutenant
Bengal Horse Artillery, East India Company Army

Brevet Major James Hills, VC, c.1868.
[National Library of Wales]

Full Name: James Hills (he adopted the surname Hills-Johnes, by royal licence, after his marriage in 1883).

Place of Birth: Neechindipore, Bengal, India. Moved to Edinburgh, Scotland 1837, where the family resided at Dean Bank House.

Date of Birth: 20 August 1833. He was the second son, a brother to Archibald Hills and Major-General Sir John Hills, RE, KCB, FRS.

Father: James Hills.

Mother: Charlotte Hills, daughter of Dr John Angelo Savi of Moisgunge, Bengal, India (originally of Elba). She was the grand-daughter of General Corderan, GOC French forces at Pondicherry.

Father's Occupation: Indigo planter. He was one of the largest landowners in Bengal.

Education: Edinburgh Academy, 1843–47; Royal Naval & Military College, Edinburgh; Addiscombe, 1851–3.

Service Record: Commissioned 2nd lieutenant, Bengal Artillery, 11 June 1853; 2nd lieutenant, Bengal Horse Artillery, 11 January 1856; lieutenant, Bengal Horse Artillery, 8 September 1857; served Indian Mutiny, 1857–8 (present at the actions at Hindun River, May 1857; Budlee-ke-serai, June 1857; occupation of Delhi Ridge, June 1857; Nujufghur, 25 August 1857; assault and capture of Delhi, September 1857 (severely wounded 9 July 1857); capture of Lucknow, Fort Rooiya, April 1858; Bareilly, May 1858; relief of Shahjehanpur, May 1858; and Mohmundee); ADC to Lord Canning, Governor General and Viceroy of India, 22 September 1859–10 March 1862; captain, 24 November 1860; assistant resident in Nepal, April 1862–March 1863; 2nd captain, Royal Horse Artillery, 1 March 1863–26 September 1864; brevet major, 19 January 1864; resigned from Royal Horse Artillery on appointment as brigade major to the inspector Royal Artillery, Northern Division, Bengal, 27 September 1864–27 October 1867; Eusofzai Expedition, 1863–4; joined 5/25th Royal Artillery for service with Abyssinian Expedition, 28 October 1867–24 June 1868 (present, as OC Mortars, at the capture of Magdala); reappointed brigade major to the inspector of Royal Artillery, 25 June 1868–8 October 1869; brevet lieutenant-colonel, 15 August 1868; OC Peshawar Mountain Battery, Punjab Frontier, 9 October 1869-4 July 1872; captain Royal Artillery, 28 August 1871; major Royal Artillery, 5 July 1872; OC Kohat District, February 1870–April 1871; served Lushai Expedition, 1871–2; major commanding 'C' Battery, 7th RHA, 5 September 1872–23 July 1875; appointed officiating assistant adjutant-general, Lahore Division, 24 July 1875–8 February 1876; brevet colonel, 14 February 1876; assistant adjutant-general, Lahore Division (permanent establishment) 19 July 1876–12 October 1878; assistant adjutant-general to General Stewart, Kandahar Field Force, 1878–80 (present at Patko Shano; defence of

The VC, campaign medals and decorations awarded to James Hills Johnes.
Top: KCB and Collar for GCB. Centre L–R: VC, Indian Mutiny Medal, Abyssinian War Medal, India General Service Medal, Second Afghan War medal. Bottom: Star of the GCB. [NLW Dolaucothi Papers]

Kandahar; Kurram Valley; Charasiah Sherpur; and the occupation of Kabul), MinD 24 June 1879 and 22 July 1879; major-general, 10 July 1879; joined Lieutenant-General Sir Frederick Roberts' Column, Kurrum Valley, September 1879 in the Commissariat Department (present at Charasiab and occupation of Kabul), MinD 20 November 1879; military governor of Kabul, 13 October 1879–17 January 1880 (post abolished), MinD and thanks of the Viceroy; unemployed, 18 January 1880–15 May 1880, but worked on various committees and assisting the Commissariat Department; GOC 3rd Division, Northern Afghanistan Field Force, 16 May–September 1880 (force dissolved), directed operations at Padoka Shana Logar Valley, 1 July 1880, MinD; lieutenant-general, 31 December 1883; retired, 1888; Honorary Colonel Carmarthenshire Artillery, 1891–1907; Honorary Colonel Pembrokeshire Volunteer Battalion; Honorary Colonel 4th Bn The Welsh Regiment, 1909.

Decorations, Medals and Rewards: Victoria Cross (for action during the siege of Delhi, 9 July 1857); Indian Mutiny Medal (clasps for Delhi and Lucknow); Abyssinian Medal, 1867–68; Indian General Service Medal, 1852–95 (clasp for Looshai); Second Afghan War Medal, 1878–80 (clasps for Charasia and Kabul); MinD (Indian Mutiny, Lushai Campaign and Abyssinian Campaign); received the thanks of the Governor General of India for his services in Kabul (1880); received the thanks of both Houses of Parliament for his services in Kabul, 1880 (5 May 1881); CB (*London Gazette*, 10 September 1872); KCB (*London Gazette*, 22 February 1881); GCB (*London Gazette*, 2 June 1893); Reward for Distinguished Service in India (1883); LL.D. (University of Wales, 1917); Freeman of the County and Borough of Carmarthen (1910).

Post-Service Employment: County councillor for Carmarthenshire; member of the Council of the University College of Wales, Aberystwyth; member of the University Court, Aberystwyth; treasurer of the University College of Wales, Aberystwyth; senior trustee and treasurer of Llandovery College; member National Council for Promoting the Civil Employment of Reserve and Discharged Soldiers; member of Committee of the West Wales

Lieutenant-General Sir James Hills-Johnes, VC, GCB, LLB.

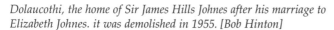

Dolaucothi, the home of Sir James Hills Johnes after his marriage to Elizabeth Johnes. it was demolished in 1955. [Bob Hinton]

Miss Elizabeth (Betha) Johnes of Dolaucothi, whom James Hills married in 1882.

Captain James Hills, in the full dress uniform of the Royal Horse Artillery.

Sanatorium; vice-president of the Tariff Reform League; member of the Finance Committee of the 1911 National Eisteddfod of Wales, Carmarthen; accompanied Field Marshal Lord Roberts, VC, to South Africa (in a civilian capacity) in April 1900 and served on the Staff during the Anglo-Boer War; in 1915, he visited the Western Front in Belgium; he was high sheriff of Carmarthenshire (1886); Deputy-Lieutenant of Carmarthenshire; Justice of the Peace.

Married: Elizabeth (Betha), daughter of John Johnes Esq., of Dolaucothi, Carmarthenshire, in the Henry VII Chapel, Westminster Abbey, London, 16 September 1882. She was born on 9 July 1834 and died 1927. The Dolaucothi estate then passed to her relative, Rev. Herbert Lloyd, MC, MA, rector of Croydon, Hertfordshire.

Children: None.

Died: At his home, Dolaucothi, Carmarthenshire, 3 January 1919, one of the millions of victims of the influenza pandemic.

Buried: Caio Churchyard, Carmarthenshire.

Memorials: Caio Church, Carmarthenshire, and portrait in Edinburgh Academy, Edinburgh. St John's Royal Garrison Church, Woolwich.

Location of Victoria Cross: Held, on loan, by the Royal Artillery Institution.

Citation for the Victoria Cross: *London Gazette,* 27 April 1858.

'For very gallant conduct on the part of Lieutenant Hills before Delhi, in defending the position assigned to him in case of alarm, and for noble behaviour on the part of Lieutenant-Colonel Tombs in twice coming to his subaltern's rescue, and on each time killing his man.'

VC Investiture: By Sir Cohn Campbell, C-in-C India, 1858.

The entrance to the Dolaucothi vault at Caio Church where Hills-Johnes is buried.

The inscription in the lychgate at Caio Church.

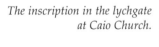

The memorial plaque to James Hills-Johnes, one of the most detailed to any VC recipient, is on the wall of Caio Church

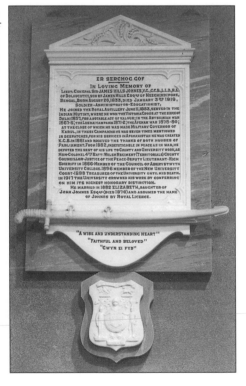

Lieutenant-Colonel James Hills, c.1870.

James Hills was half Scottish, half French by blood, an Indian by birth but a Welshman by adoption. His association with the sub-continent went back to his birth in Bengal, the son of James Hills, a Scottish indigo planter, and Charlotte, the daughter of Angelo Savi of Bengal. Educated in Edinburgh, he was commissioned into the Bengal Artillery in 1853, via the East India Army College at Addiscombe, Surrey, the training college for officers of the East India Company Army from 1809 to 1861. He arrived at the college twelve months after Frederick Sleigh Roberts (later Field Marshal Sir Frederick Roberts, VC) who was to become his life-long friend and colleague. The college was accommodated in a country house that had once been the home of the Earl of Liverpool and was run under a strict, physical and very demanding regime. Each day began with reveille at 6am, followed by chapel at 6.30 then an hour's work before breakfast at 8am. Students were back in the classroom between 9am and 1pm when they had one hour for lunch and recreation before continuing with work until 4pm. There followed a two hour break for tea and further recreation, then more work until 9pm when they again went to chapel before lights out one hour later. Cadets spent four terms at the college, known as 'Greens', 'Browns', 'Young Cadets' and 'Old Cadets'. Those who passed out top of their term were sent to the engineers, those coming below them to the artillery and the remainder to the infantry (unless they expressed a personal desire to join the cavalry). The 20-year old 2nd lieutenant Hills (known as 'Jemmie' to his friends) must have been one of the middling group and was appointed to the Bengal Artillery in June 1853.

Hills saw extensive action throughout the period of the Indian Mutiny and gained the Victoria Cross for his action during the siege of Delhi. In the case of many Victorian VCs, the official citations tell us little of the action which led to the award and it is often necessary to build a clearer picture from various other sources. This was certainly the case with James Hills whose citation is a model of brevity.

The operations grouped under the collective title of the 'Siege of Delhi' officially began on 14 May 1857 and ended on 14 September. The city, which was surrounded by high stone walls and several strategically defensive positions, would prove a tough nut to crack after its capture by the rebels on 11 May. Almost immediately, British forces from Simla, Umbala and Meerut were ordered to begin operations aimed at its recapture. When the mutineers and the British force (under the command of Colonel Archdale Wilson) met some 15 miles from the city, the former were soundly routed and the British, reinforced by a column under the command of Major-General Sir Henry Barnard, took the Delhi Ridge by mid June. At the height of the Indian summer, with temperatures reaching an incredible 140 degrees, the British defeated every attempt by the rebels to retake the ridge.

On 9 July, Hills was in command of a cavalry picket guarding two field guns at the Mound, an outpost on the right of the British camp, on the main trunk road leading to Delhi. At about 11am rumours began to spread that rebel cavalry were approaching. Hills moved his men into the pre-arranged position ready to repel any attack when, without warning, a large body of sepoys from the rebel army charged the unprepared field guns. He later recorded:

You must have seen accounts of their [the Mutineers] rush into our Camp on the 9th; it was a bold thing to do, so much so, that when they were in they were quite aback at their audacity. My guns were ridden over before I could get them into action, and I

was very nearly polished off — Tombs saving my life by potting a Pandy [*sepoy*] who was in the act of splitting my skull. I was down on the ground, regularly done up, without a single thing to defend myself with. I have got great 'kudos' for my conduct. This is it. The alarm went, and off I started with my two guns to a position laid down for them, when, to my astonishment, through the opening to my right, only fifty yards off, dashed a body of cavalry.

The soldiers under Hills' command immediately fled leaving

Addiscombe House, the home of the East India Army College in Surrey.

him alone to protect the gunners. Desperate situations called for desperate action.

Now I tried to get my guns into action; but only got one unlimbered when they were upon me. I thought that by charging them I might make a commotion and give the guns time to load, so in I went at the front rank, cut down the first fellow, slashed the next across the face as hard as I could, then two *sowars* charged me. Both their horses crashed into mine at the same moment, and, of course, both horse and myself were sent flying. We went down at such a pace that I escaped the cuts made at me, one of them giving my jacket an awful slice just below the left arm — it only, however, cut the jacket.

Well, I lay quite snug until all had passed over me, and then got up and looked about for my sword. I found it a full ten yards off. I had hardly got hold of it when these fellows returned, two on horseback. The first I wounded [using a pistol], and dropped him from his horse. The second charged at me with his lance. I put it aside [by catching the lance with his left hand], and caught him an awful gash on the head and face. I thought I had killed him. Apparently he must have clung to his horse, for he disappeared. The wounded man [whom he had shot] then came up, but got his skull split. Then came on the third man — a young, active fellow.

I found myself getting very weak from want of breath, the fall from my horse having pumped me considerably, and my cloak, somehow or other, had got tightly fixed round my throat, and was actually choking me. I went, however, at the fellow and cut him on the shoulder, but some '*kupra*' [cloth] on it apparently turned the blow. He managed to seize the hilt of my sword and twisted it out of my hand, and then we had a hand-to-hand fight, I punching his head with my fists, and he trying to cut me, but I was too close to him. Somehow or other I fell, and then was the time, fortunately for me, that Tombs came up and shot the fellow. I was so choked by my cloak, that move I could not until I got it loosened. By-the-bye, I forgot to say I fired at this chap twice, but the pistol snapped, and I was so enraged I drove it at the fellow's head, missing him, however. Then, when I got up, Tombs was so eager to get up to a mound near us, that I only picked up my sword and followed him.

After being there some time, we came down again to look after the unlimbered gun which was left behind. When we got down, I saw the very man Tombs had saved me from, moving off with my pistol (the brute had only been wounded, and shammed dead). I told Tombs, and we went at him. After a little slashing and guarding on both sides, I rushed at him and thrust; he cleverly jumped aside and cut me on the head, knocking me down, not, however, stunning me, for I warded his next cut when down. Tombs, following him up, made him a pass, and up I jumped and had a slash at him, cutting him on the left wrist, nearly severing it. This made him turn round, and then Tombs ran him through. He very nearly knocked over Tombs, for he cut through his cap and pagrie, but fortunately did not even cut the skin. I fancy I am indebted again to Tombs for my life, for, although I might have got up again and fought, still I was bleeding like a pig, and, of course, would have had a bad chance. One thing, however, if Tombs had not been there the second time I should have fought more carefully. It was the wish to polish off the fellow before Tombs could get up to him that made me rush at him in the way I did. I wanted awfully to pick up the swords of the men I had killed as trophies, but I was getting very faint, and had to come to my tent as fast as I could; but before I got the wound bound up, the swords had been looted off. I lost an awful lot of blood, as two veins were cut through; but I fancy it did me good, keeping off inflamation. The wound was a beautiful one, just as if it had been done with a razor. It was four inches long, and down to the skull, a line being left on it; so I had a narrow escape.

However, if I live to see the end of these mutinies, I shall have good reason to thank the 'sowars' for their courage — Tombs' name and mine having been sent up to the governor-general by the commander-in-chief, the latter recommending us 'worthy of the highest honour for distinguished bravery and gallantry'.

Major-General Sir Henry Tombs, VC, KCB.

Also present on that day was Hills' friend, Frederick Roberts, who later described the event in his autobiography *Forty-one Years in India*.

Stillman [lieutenant commanding 30 men of the Carabineers] and Hills were breakfasting together, when a *sowar* from the Native officers' party rode up and reported that a body of the enemy's Cavalry were in sight. Hills told the man to gallop to Headquarters with the report, and to warn Tombs as he passed his tent. Hills and Stillman then mounted their men, neither of them having the remotest idea that the news of the enemy's advance had been purposely delayed until there was not time to turn out the troops. They assumed that the *sowar* was acting in good faith and had given them sufficient notice, and while Hills moved his guns towards the position from which he could command the Trunk Road, Stillman proceeded to the top of the Mound in order to get a better view of the ground over which the enemy were said to be advancing. The troop of the Carabineers was thus left by itself to receive the first rush of the rebel Cavalry; it was composed of young soldiers, some of them quite untrained, who turned and broke.

The moment Hills saw the enemy he shouted, 'Action front!' and, in the hope of giving his men time to load and fire a round of grape, he gallantly charged the head of the column single-handed, cut down the leading man, struck the second, and then was ridden down himself. It had been raining heavily, so Hills wore his cloak; which probably saved his life, for it was cut through in many places, as were his jacket and even his shirt.

Lieutenant-General Sir James Hills-Johnes, c.1910.

For this action in defending the guns Hills was mentioned in the despatch of Lieutenant–Colonel Mackenzie, GOC 1st Brigade Horse Artillery, 10 July 1857 and subsequently awarded the VC. His saviour, Major Tombs,* received the same award for saving Hills' life.

Hills went on to have a very distinguished career in the Indian Army, taking part in several campaigns and rising to the rank of lieutenant-general before retiring, in circumstances that were unusual enough to merit mention. A careful study of his military record will show that his talents were regularly recognized, not only by being appointed to a variety of positions, both administrative and combat, but also by his rapid promotions. The British Army had a dual rank structure with officers being appointed to either a regiment (or a corps) in which they held a regular rank (which depended upon seniority) or being granted a brevet rank (in the army as a whole). This meant that a relatively junior regimental officer could be given an army brevet rank (usually as a reward for gallant or distinguished service) so that, in certain circumstances, such as a staff appointment, he outranked men who were senior to him in the regiment e.g. a captain in a regiment might be appointed a brevet lieutenant-colonel on a brigade staff and would therefore outrank his regimental major. In the case of James Hills, his artillery ranks and brevet ranks were as follows:

	Artillery/regimental rank	Brevet/army rank
1853	2nd-lieutenant	–
1857	lieutenant	–
1862	captain	–
1864	captain	major
1868	captain	lieutenant-colonel
1872	major	lieutenant-colonel
1876	major	colonel
1878	lieutenant-colonel	colonel
1879	lieutenant-colonel	major-general
1880	colonel	major-general
1883	–	lieutenant-general
1888	–	retired

This rate of brevet promotion meant that Hills was rapidly moving up the level of command whenever a field force was organised for operations in either India or (in the 1860s) Abyssinia and, as a consequence, his level of experience was outstripping those who were his regimental seniors. Matters came to a head when, after serving with the Northern Afghanistan Field Force in 1880, with the local rank of major-general, he anticipated promotion to a divisional command, with the rank of lieutenant-general. Due to the nature of the work he had carried out, he had not held the 'normal' army staff and regimental commands held by colonels, i.e. he had never commanded a regiment. As seniority for general officers was based upon the date of their appointment to the rank of colonel, Hills, despite having seen active service as a major-general, was low down on the list for promotion. By 1883, this was having an adverse effect upon his career and a memorial was sent on his behalf to the Secretary of State for India, the Earl of Kimberley:

… he [Hills] was certainly most rapidly promoted to the rank of Major-General, but the immediate results of this promotion were most adverse to his interests, in that not only had he to resign his Army Staff appointment (Assistant Adjutant-General) one and a half years before the term of his tenure was completed, but he also became ineligible for a Brigade Command, a command which he had every prospect not only of obtaining, but of holding for five years, if the rank of Major-General had come to him in the ordinary course of promotion. The counterbalancing recompense against these heavy losses would have been advancement in the List for Divisional Commands.

By the special decision of the Secretary of State for India … this right has been taken from him, and no provision made to save him from the evil effects … so that

* The Tombs Memorial Prize is awarded annually to the most outstanding cadet entering the Royal Artillery. In 1903 it was won by Cadet L. W. B. Rees who was later awarded the VC (vide Major Lionel Rees, VC).

1. He is neither allowed to have the rights of his present nor of his former rank.
2. He is superceded for Divisional Commands by officers junior to himself in army rank, several of whom have served for months in the field under his command.
3. By promotion to the rank of Lieutenant-General before his time for a command can come round … he may and probably will become ineligible for a Divisional Command.
4. He is rendered liable to summary removal to the Retired List after five years of non-employment.

All the above penalties are owing to his rapid promotion, which is solely due to services in the field … but for these field services, he would still be a Lieutenant-Colonel, and free from the above-mentioned disadvantages under which he now labours, he has to point out that he only obtained his Regimental Lieutenant-Colonelcy, on 31st December 1878, and that by regimental promotion he would not be a full Colonel till the 31st December next.

The memorial was to no avail and Hills's request that he be given special consideration with regard to the rules of promotion fell on deaf ears. In September, the Earl of Lytton, Viceroy of India, wrote:

Sir James Hills-Johnes, c.1910.

Lord Kimberley's decision appears to me not only a singularly hard and unjust one as regards Sir J. Hills, but also to say the least, *most* unfortunate from a more general point of view. I can conceive nothing more discouraging to spirit and efficiency in the higher ranks of the service than a decision which practically punishes an exceptionally distinguished officer for the distinction he has obtained in it. *Mais qui faire!* I know of no higher authority than that of the Secretary of State in Council to which appeal can be made from this decision. … as regards General Hills my sincere belief is that there are very few officers where deprivation from active command would involve a greater loss to our Indian Army.

Hills was eventually promoted to the rank of lieutenant-general in December 1883 but never again received an active command, devoting his working days to serving on various committees and preparing reports on behalf of the army. Five years later, in accordance with the rules of promotion and service, he was retired.

James Hills's youngest sister, Emelia, had married Sir Griffith Pugh Evans of Lovesgrove, Llanbadarn Fawr, who had been a member of the Viceroy of India's Legislative Council. On one social occasion, Major-General Hills met a west Wales neighbour of his brother-in-law, Miss Elizabeth (Betha) Johnes. A relationship quickly developed and they were married at Westminster Abbey in 1882, and he embarked on a new life as a Welsh country landowner. Contrary to the normal practice, but typical of Sir James, the betrothed couple had announced that their tenants were not to give them any form of wedding present but that, instead, they would make a gift to them of a 20 per cent rent reduction for the year of the marriage. With such acts of altruism the former career soldier endeared himself to the new society in which he was to play a prominent role for nearly 40 years.

Their marriage was a romantic success story which followed on from a period of great tragedy. Betha's father, Judge John Johnes of Dolaucothi, Carmarthenshire, had been a well-respected member of the local community, owning an estate of some 2,500 acres, which included the famous Dolaucothi gold mine, which dated back to the time of the Roman occupation of Britain. In 1874, Judge Johnes had a dispute with his butler, Irishman Henry Tremble, which resulted in the latter's dismissal. Shortly afterwards, Tremble confronted the judge in his house and shot him dead, then shot and seriously

Sir James and Lady Elizabeth Hills-Johnes, c.1910.
He is wearing the full robes of the Order of the Bath.

A group of Victoria Cross recipients at the Royal Hospital, Chelsea on the occasion of the 75th birthday of Sir George White, VC, 6 July 1910. L–R: Lieutenant-General Sir James Hills-Johnes, Major-General Sir Luke O'Connor, Field Marshal Sir Evelyn Wood, Field Marshal Lord Roberts, Field Marshal Sir George White, Colonel Sir Edward Thackeray.

wounded Charlotte Johnes, the judge's eldest daughter before turning the gun on himself. Such was the high esteem in which Judge Johnes was held that when news of his murder reached the National Eisteddfod of Wales at Wrexham, the entire audience stood in silence. In 1883, in compliance with the terms of the judge's will, Sir James Hills adopted the additional name of 'Johnes', and brought not only his bride, but her sister Charlotte, back to the house at Dolaucothi where they lived, 'radiantly happy', for the remainder of their lives.

Sir James threw himself wholeheartedly into the life of the community in both Carmarthenshire and Wales as a whole, earning the undying respect and admiration of the local people. Although not a Welshman, his activities in support of farming, the Welsh language, the National Eisteddfod and education (serving as a governor of the University College at Aberystwyth, treasurer of the University of Wales and treasurer of Llandovery College) earned him a very special place in nineteenth century Welsh society. He was described by Herbert Lloyd as 'a real, unfailing altruist'. When the explorer Sir Henry M. Stanley visited Dolaucothi, he described Sir James as having 'a very winning character, for he takes one's good-will and affection by storm. His heart is 'white and clean'. A most kind, straightforward soldier'.

Although retired, Sir James continued to play a role in the military affairs of the nation. In 1900, when his friend, Lord Roberts of Khandahar was appointed to command the British forces in South Africa, he accompanied him to the seat of war and, in an unofficial civilian capacity, gave valuable service. In September 1915, aged 82, he visited the Western

Two photographs taken when Sir James visited France in October 1915. Left: inspecting the Royal Naval Division armoured cars at Vinchem, Belgium. Right: Visiting Belgian trenches at Pervyse where he has exchanged his cap for that of a lower rank soldier in an effort to avoid becoming the target of a sniper. Later this day he came under artillery fire when only 800 yards from the German lines. [Dolaucothi photograph albums, NLW]

Front in Belgium, travelling as far as the front line and coming under direct artillery fire.

He is on record as having said that his greatest honour was the Victoria Cross and, having no children of his own, he must have been immensely proud of his sister Isabella's husband, William Cubitt, who was awarded the Victoria Cross for gallantry while serving with the 13th Bengal Native Infantry in June 1857, and of his nephew, Brigadier Lewis Pugh Evans, of Llanbadarn Fawr, who gained the Victoria Cross in Belgium in 1917.

A plaque to his memory in Caio Church is perhaps one of the most expansive and detailed to any VC in Wales and reads:

A newspaper photograph showing one of the oldest holders of the VC meeting the newest; Sir James Hills-Johnes, VC shaking hands with Sergeant Robert Bye, VC, Welsh Guards, 1917.

ER SERCHOG GOF
IN LOVING MEMORY OF
LIEUT. GENERAL SIR JAMES HILLS-JOHNES, V.C., G.C.B., L.L.B., R.A. OF DOLAUCOTHY, SON OF JAMES HILLS ESQRE OF NEECHINDIPORE, BENGAL, BORN AUGUST 29, 1833, DIED JANUARY 3RD 1919.
SOLDIER – ADMINISTRATOR – EDUCATIONALIST.
HE JOINED THE ROYAL ARTILLERY JUNE 11, 1853, SERVED IN THE INDIAN MUTINY, WHERE HE WON THE VICTORIA CROSS AT THE SEIGE OF DELHI 1857, FOR A NOTABLE ACT OF VALOUR; IN THE ABYSSINIAN WAR 1867–8; THE LUSHAI CAMPAIGN 1871–2; THE AFGHAN WAR 1878–80; AT THE CLOSE OF WHICH HE WAS MADE MILITARY GOVERNOR OF KABUL, IN THESE CAMPAIGNS HE WAS SEVEN TIMES MENTIONED IN DESPATCHES, FOR HIS SERVICES IN AFGHANISTAN HE WAS CREATED K.C.B. IN 1881 AND RECEIVED THE THANKS OF BOTH HOUSES OF PARLIAMENT. FROM 1882, INDEFATIGABLE IN PEACE AS IN WAR, HE DEVOTED THE REST OF HIS LIFE TO COUNTY AND UNIVERSITY WORK, AS HON-COLONEL 4TH BATT: WELSH REGIMENT (TERRITORIALS) COUNTY COUNCILLOR-JUSTICE OF THE PEACE-DEPUTY LIEUTENANT-HIGH SHERIFF IN 1886-MEMBER OF THE COUNCIL OF ABERYSTWYTH UNIVERSITY COLLEGE. 1898 MEMBER OF THE NEW UNIVERSITY COURT-1898 TREASURER OF THE UNIVERSITY UNTIL HIS DEATH. IN 1917 THE UNIVERSITY CROWNED HIS WORK BY CONFERRING ON HIM ITS HIGHEST HONORARY DISTINCTION.
HE MARRIED IN 1882 ELIZABETH, DAUGHTER OF JOHN JOHNES ESQRE (DIED 1878) AND ASSUMED THE NAME OF JOHNES BY ROYAL LICENCE.
'A WIDE AND UNDERSTANDING HEART'
'FAITHFUL AND BELOVED'
'GWYN EI FYD'

JACOB THOMAS
Bombardier
Bengal Artillery, East India Company Army

Full Name: Jacob Thomas.
Place of Birth: Coed-y-Bwddy, Llanwinio, Carmarthenshire.
Date of Birth: *Circa* February 1833.
Father: Jacob Thomas.
Mother: —
Father's Occupation: Farmer and carpenter.
Education: —
Pre-Service Employment: Fitter-up.
Service Record: Enlisted in the artillery at Cardiff for 12 years' service, 6 July 1853; sailed for Bengal for service with the East India Company Artillery, 1853; bombardier, 1 August 1857; served Indian Mutiny 1857–8 (present at the defence of Lucknow); corporal, 6 August 1858; sergeant, 29 March 1859; transferred to the Royal Artillery, 12 June 1861, served with the 16th Brigade RA in India; hospital sergeant, 1 February 1862; battery sergeant, 7 March 1863; quarter-master sergeant, 23 March 1863–14 November 1865; took his discharge (unfit for further service) at Darjeeling, India, 30 October 1866; granted a pension due to injuries sustained when a horse fell on him.
Decorations, Medals and Rewards: Victoria Cross (for action at Lucknow, 27 September 1857); Indian Mutiny Medal (clasps for Defence of Lucknow and Lucknow).
Post-Service Employment: There is some confusion regarding Thomas' life after he left the army. The records of two men, both named Jacob Thomas, would seem to fit him. The first joined the local police force and rose to become a police inspector in Darjeeling. The second was employed as a fitter at Hooghly. The evidence would seem to indicate that Jacob Thomas, VC, was the latter (he had been a fitter before joining the army).
Married: Margaret Hamilton (widow), daughter of Alexander Taggart at St James' Church, Delhi, 14 March 1859.

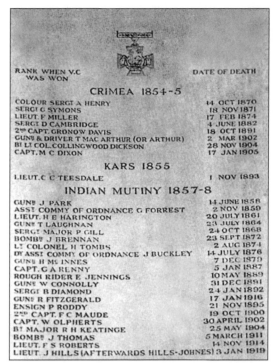

The Royal Artillery VC Memorial plaque bearing the name of Jacob Thomas (third from bottom) and Sir James Hills-Johnes (bottom).

One of the artillery pieces that decorate the grounds of the Residency ruins in Lucknow today.

St George's Royal Garrison Church, Woolwich was consecrated in 1863, damaged by enemy action in 1918 and severely damaged by a V-1 flying bomb on 13 July 1944. Among the few surviving features of the church is the Royal Artillery VC Memorial, an Italian mosaic of St George, flanked by marble tablets which are inscribed with the names of all the Royal Artillery VC recipients. The church has not been restored and is used for open-air services on Remembrance Sunday. The names of Jacob Thomas, James Hill-Johnes and Lionel Rees are recorded here.

Thomas's VC is owned by the 55th (The Residency) Field Battery, Royal Artillery. The whereabouts of his Indian Mutiny Medal is unknown.

Children: None recorded.
Died: 24 April 1896, at Hooghly, India (if the VC was the 'fitter' referred to above), or 3 March 1911, at Darjeeling (if he was the police inspector).
Buried: 24 April 1896, at Bandel Church, Hooghly, India (if the 'fitter' referred to above).
Memorials: Royal Artillery Victoria Cross Memorial, St George's Garrison Church, Woolwich.
Location of Victoria Cross: Royal Artillery Institution (on loan from the 55th (The Residency) Field Battery, Royal Artillery).
Citation for the Victoria Cross: *London Gazette*, 24 December 1858.
'For distinguished gallantry at Lucknow on 27th September 1857, in having brought off his own back, under a heavy fire, under circumstances of considerable difficulty, a wounded soldier of the Madras Fusiliers, when the party to which he was attached was returning to the Residency from a sortie, whereby he saved him from falling into the hands of the enemy.'
VC Investiture: By HM Queen Victoria at Windsor, 4 January 1860.

Bombardier Jacob Thomas has a fairly detailed background history but, unfortunately, its accuracy cannot be verified. Extensive searches through the census and tithe records for the parish of Llanwinio have failed to identify either a Thomas family that matches his details, or a farm named Coed-y-Bwddy. Checks for similar place names, making allowances for the possible inaccurate spelling of the farm name e.g. Coed y Beudy, Coed y Bwthyn, have also drawn a blank. A general search through the 1841 census for both Wales and England has failed to come up with a Jacob Thomas who matches the presumed known details. Contact with the descendants of Jacob's sister has enabled this researcher to get no further, but the search continues.

Jacob Thomas was a member of the only artillery company (then part of the Bengal Artillery, which today carries the title 55th (Residency) Battery, Royal Artillery) to be present throughout the siege of Lucknow during the Indian Mutiny. On 30 May 1857, most of the sepoys in Lucknow rebelled but were successfully dispersed by Sir Henry Lawrence and the force under his command. Despite this, Lawrence was forced to make preparations for a siege as the troops that were loyal to him were not in a position to fight their way out of the city, taking with them some 600 women and children and 600 non-combatants. The strength of the rebel forces has been variously estimated at between 6,000 and 10,000 fighting men against which Lawrence had a maximum of 1,700 soldiers. To have attempted a withdrawal would have been to court disaster and, indeed, on 30 June, when he led a force of 700 men out of the city, he was defeated with heavy losses (381 casualties) at Chinhat. On 1 July, realising that he could be trapped in Lucknow for some time before relief forces could arrive, Lawrence withdrew his garrison to the area around the Residency which stood on the highest spot in the city. For the following seven weeks, the Anglo-Indian force inside the Residency put up a strong defence against a much stronger, but badly led, enemy. Whenever a rebel artillery battery began to have a seriously adverse effect upon the defences, raiding parties were sent out to try and destroy the guns or the buildings in which they were positioned. When Sir Henry Havelock eventually fought his way through to the Residency at the end of August, he found a garrison that was, understandably, low in morale, but amply supplied with basic foodstuffs. His relief column, however, was too weak to be able to fight its way out of the city and back to Cawnpore, taking with it the many hundreds of European civilians. As a consequence, it was decided that the relief column would remain inside Lucknow to reinforce the existing garrison, and there await the arrival of a second relief column.

The policy of sending out raiding parties from the Residency was continued by Havelock. The first of these took place on 27 September with the intention of destroying a rebel battery sited in the grounds of a house to the south-east of the Cawnpore Battery, which was itself on the south-east of the defensive perimeter. The party, commanded by Major Stephenson, comprised a detachment of men from the 32nd Regiment and another from the Madras Fusiliers. They were accompanied by a small party of artillerymen (which included Jacob Thomas) who were to destroy any guns that might be captured.

The whole operation was badly handled from the start. There was a lack of discipline and planning, so that the men rushed forward and several became lost in the narrow lanes leading towards the battery. The first group managed to reach the guns without too much difficulty only to find that the artillerymen (and their explosives) had not managed to keep up. When the gunners did eventually arrive, they were unable to carry out their task. The usual methods of destroying captured cannon were to either spike the fuse-hole with a suitable nail or to blow up the gun by detonating a quantity of gunpower in the barrel which had been blocked off with clay. The first method was effective as a short-term solution, the latter made the gun permanently unusable. The day being particularly hot, the soldiers had drunk their water and failed to retain any for moistening the clay with which they were to block the mouths of the cannons. The guns, therefore, had to be abandoned and the party retired towards the Residency perimeter. By this time, the rebel defenders had been alerted to their presence and, pouring a hail of fire from the houses lining the escape route, took a heavy toll from the raiding party. One of the sepoys, hit and unable to continue, was picked up by Thomas and carried over his shoulder, still under heavy fire. Miraculously, they both made it to safety. Had the Fusilier been left, he would certainly have been killed; had Thomas been caught he would also have suffered a most unpleasant death.

Jacob Thomas survived to the end of the siege (which was eventually lifted by a column led by Sir Colin Campbell and the garrison was evacuated on 18 November) and remained in the army after the end of the Mutiny, serving in the Royal Artillery after the East India Company Army was absorbed into the British Army. At some time during the 1860s he was severely injured when a horse fell on him and was discharged as unfit for military service in 1866 and granted a pension.

Thomas was obviously taken with India and decided to remain there in civilian life. Once again, the details of his private life are somewhat confused. Careful searches through the records of the time show two men named Jacob Thomas working in India in the latter part of the nineteenth century, both of whom could have been Jacob Thomas, VC. The first lived in Hooghly where he was employed as a fitter, and died there in 1896. As Jacob Thomas, VC had been employed as a fitter before joining the army in 1853, there is a strong possibility that this is the same man. He would have been in his mid 60s, a good age for a European in India. The second 'candidate' is a Jacob Thomas who was employed as a police inspector at Darjeeling, who died in 1911. Thomas, VC's military background, and the fact that he had served as a senior NCO, would have made him a likely candidate for the police service where, as a European, promotion to inspector would not have been remarkable. If this man was the VC recipient, he would have been about 78 years of age when he died.

There is one further loose end which cannot be tied up. When Jacob Thomas, VC died, he left a substantial sum of money to his family back in Wales and his VC to the Residency Battery, Royal Artillery. There appears to have been some sort of legal wrangle with regard to this legacy which, if it can be untangled, could lead to some light being thrown on the true backgound and fate of the first Carmarthenshire-born Victoria Cross recipient.

Painting of the defence of the Residency, Lucknow. In the lower left of the picture is a representation of Thomas carrying a wounded soldier to safety. [55th (The Residency) Field Battery, Royal Artillery]

The Residency, Lucknow, 1858.

Augustus Anson.

THE HON. AUGUSTUS ANSON
Captain
2/84th Regiment

FULL NAME: Augustus Henry Archibald Anson.
PLACE OF BIRTH: Slebech Hall, Pembrokeshire.
Date of Birth: 5 March 1835.
Date of Birth: *Circa* February 1833.
Father: Thomas William Anson, 1st Earl of Lichfield, 2nd Viscount Anson, of Shugborough and Orgleave, Staffordshire.
Mother: Louisa Catherine Anson, daughter of Nathaniel Philips of Slebech Hall, Pembrokeshire.
Father's Occupation: Peer of the realm, landowner.
Education: —
Service Record: Commissioned as an ensign, Rifle Brigade, 27 May 1853; lieutenant, 8 December 1854; captain, 6 July 1855; served Crimean Campaign, 1855 (present at the fall of Sebastopol); transferred to 84th Regiment of Foot, 8 January 1856; served Indian Mutiny, 1857–8 (present at the siege and capture of Delhi; attached to the 9th Lancers, Bulandshahr; 2nd relief of Lucknow and Secundra Bagh; assault and capture of Lucknow, Koolsie and Baree); wounded at Delhi and Secundra Bagh; transferred to 10th Light Dragoons, 24 August 1858; transferred to 7th Light Dragoons, 7 December 1858; brevet major, 28 May 1859; served with Indian forces in China, 1860 (present at the capture of Peking, storming of the Northern Taku Forts); ADC to General Sir Hope Grant in China, 1860; unattached, 5 February 1861; major, 15 February 1861; brevet lieutenant-colonel, 20 July 1870; lieutenant-colonel, 23 July 1870; retired 31 July 1873; major, London Scottish Volunteers until shortly before his death.
Decorations, Medals and Rewards: Victoria Cross (for action at Bulandshahr, India, 28 September 1857); Crimea Medal (clasp for Sebastopol); Indian Mutiny Medal (clasps for Delhi, Relief of Lucknow and Lucknow); China Medal (clasps for Taku Forts 1860 and Pekin 1860); MinD (Indian Mutiny, 14 times); Turkish Crimea Medal; Turkish Order of the Medjidie, 5th Class.
Post-Service Employment: Member of Parliament for Lichfield, 1859–68 and Bewdley, 1869–74.
Married: Amelia Maria, daughter of Reverend Thomas Legh Claughton, Bishop of Rochester, 1 December 1863. After Anson's death, she married the 8th Duke of Argyll.

Shugborough Hall, the home of the Anson family.

Slebech Hall, the birthplace of Augustus Anson.

Children: None.

Died: Cannes, France, 17 November 1877. He was living in the south of France due to ill health.

Buried: Cimitière Protestant du Grand Jas, Avenue de Grasse, Cannes, France.

Memorials: Cimitière Protestant du Grand Jas, Cannes, France; Lichfield Cathedral, Staffordshire; Parish Church, Colwich, Staffordshire; Anson Memorial Sword presented to the cadet obtaining the highest mark in the written examination at RMA Sandhurst.

Location of Victoria Cross: Privately held.

Citation for the Victoria Cross: *London Gazette*, 24 December 1858. 'For conspicuous bravery at Bolundshahur on 28th September 1857. The 9th Light Dragoons had charged through the town and were reforming on the serai, the enemy attemped to close the entrance by drawing their carts across it, so as to shut in the cavalry and form a cover from which to fire upon them. Captain Anson, taking a lance, dashed out of the gateway and knocked the drivers off their carts. Owing to a wound in his left hand received at Delhi he could not stop his horse, and rode into the middle of the enemy who fired a volley at him, one ball passing through his coat. At Lucknow, at the assault of the Secundra Bagh, on 16th November 1857, he entered with a storming party on the gates being burst open. He had his horse killed and was himself slightly wounded. He has shown the greatest gallantry on every occasion and has slain many enemies in fight.'

VC Investiture: By HM Queen Victoria at a ball held at Buckingham Palace, 8 June 1859.

Anson, a photograph taken shortly before his death in 1877.

Anson's grave in Cannes, France.

Memorial in Lichfield Cathedral, Staffordshire

4·HARRIET·FRANCIS·MARIA·B·1827·
MARRIED·AUGUSTUS·6ᵀᴴ·BARON·VERNON·
D·1898·BURIED·AT·SUDBURY·DERBYSHIRE·
5·WILLIAM·VICTOR·HORATIO·B·1833·
LIEUT·R·N·
D·1856·BURIED·AT·HASLAR·HOSPITAL·CEMETERY·
6·AUGUSTUS·HENRY·ARCHIBALD·B·1835·
LIEUT·COLONEL·V·C·
D·1877·BURIED·AT·CANNES·S·FRANCE·

Memorial to Augustus Anson and his siblings in the Parish Church, Colwich.

Robert Blair's VC. The whereabouts of his Indian Mutiny Medal is unknown.
[QDG Museum, Cardiff]

Avontoun House, Linlithgow, the birthplace of Robert Blair. The house was demolished and the site developed for housing and light industry.
[West Lothian Council Libraries]

ROBERT BLAIR
Lieutenant
2nd Dragoon Guards (Queen's Bays)

Full Name: Robert Blair.

Place of Birth: Aventoun, Linlithgow, Scotland (demolished). The family also had a house in George Square, Edinburgh.

Date of Birth: 13 March 1834.

Father: William Blair.

Mother: Isabell Cornelia Blair, daughter of Colonel Charles Cragie Halkett of Lawshill, Fifeshire, Scotland.

Father's Occupation: Barrister. He later became a judge in the Ionian Islands and member of the Council of Corfu.

Education: Early education not known. Studied at the University of Glasgow 1849–51, gaining a number prizes including a second place in the Latin and Greek Black Stone Examinations for the Cowan Gold Medal. Read law at Balliol College, Oxford (Snell Exhibitioner) 13 May 1852–December 1853.

Service Record: Cornet, 9th Queen's Royal Lancers, 16 December 1853 (by purchase); lieutenant, 2nd November 1855 (by purchase); exchanged, 2nd Dragoon Guards, 20 December 1856; captain, 7 July 1858; served Indian Mutiny, 1857–8 (present at the assault on Delhi, where his horse was killed under him).

Decorations, Medals and Rewards: Victoria Cross (for action at Bulandshahr, Meerut, India, 28 September 1857); Indian Mutiny Medal (clasps for Lucknow and Delhi).

Married: Unmarried.

Died: Kanpur, India, 28 March 1859 of smallpox.

Buried: Old British Cemetery, Kanpur. Grave unmarked.

Location of Victoria Cross: Queen's Dragoon Guards Museum, Cardiff.

Citation for the Victoria Cross: *London Gazette,* 18 June 1858.
'A most gallant feat was here performed by Lieutenant Blair, who was ordered to take a party of one serjeant [sic] and twelve men and bring in a deserted ammunition wagon. As his party approached, a body of fifty or sixty of the enemy's horse came down upon him, from a village, where they had remained unobserved; without a moment's hestitation he formed up his men, and, regardless of the odds, gallantly led them on, dashing through

An artist's impression of Blair's VC action which, in reality was a clash with enemy cavalry and not artillery.

the rebels. He made good his retreat without losing a man, leaving nine of them dead on the field. Of these he killed four himself; but, to my regret, after having run a native officer through the body with his sword, he was severely wounded, the joint of his shoulder being nearly severed.' [The citation was taken from Major-General Sir James Hope Grant's despatch of 10 January 1858.]

VC Investiture: By HM Queen Victoria on Southsea Common, Hampshire, 3 August 1858.

Lord President Blair, the illustrious grandfather of Robert Blair, VC.

Robert Blair was descended from a distinguished Scottish ancestry which included the Reverend Robert Blair, chaplain to the King; the poet Robert Blair (1699–1746); and Robert Blair of Avontoun (1741–1811), a lawyer who served as Solicitor General for Scotland, Dean of the Faculty of Advocates and Lord President of the Court of Session (the senior Scottish officer of the law).

Robert was an academically gifted young man, gaining great honours at both the University of Glasgow and Balliol College, Oxford before opting for a career in the army. The lack of any previous military connections led to his father having to puchase a commission, and then a promotion, for him in the 9th Lancers with which regiment he served in India. His cousin, James Blair, VC, had a career which followed a similar route. Robert's decision to transfer from the 9th Lancers to the Queen's Bays was undoubtedly a step up the Army's social ladder. At the time of his exchange, the Queen's Bays were still in Britain but scheduled to be posted to India. Rather than make an unneccessary journey back to Britain, Blair opted to complete the transfer but remain in India, on attachment to the 9th Lancers.

On the outbreak of the Indian Mutiny the 9th Lancers were stationed at Ambala and its four squadrons were divided between the 1st and 2nd Brigades of the Delhi Field Force. When this joined up with the Meerut Brigade, it routed the mutineers at Badli-ki-Serai, and took control of Delhi Ridge where the 9th Lancers saw three months arduous service before Delhi fell on 21 September. The regiment was then detailed to join Colonel Greathed's Flying Column which, on the 24 September began to search the Gangetic Goab. At dawn on 28 September, the advanced units arrived at a crossroads near Bulandshahr where gunfire was exchanged with rebel skirmishers. It soon became evident that a strong enemy force was preparing to make a stand. As the British troops began their advance the enemy's artillery opened fire and their cavalry began to withdraw. The 75th Regiment captured two 9-pounder guns, and drove the enemy back from a strong position in front of the town. The British cavalry, made up of the 9th Lancers and detachments from the Punjab Cavalry overran a third gun. The horse artillery immediately opened fire but the infantry refused to move into the town. Captain Augustus Anson [see pp75–6 above), also attached to the 9th Lancers, wrote, 'They could not be got to look round a corner or to advance in any way.' The commanding officer of the 9th Lancers decided to seize the initiative and 'ordered them to charge through the main street. I went through with them myself. We passed through a shower of musketry from both sides of the houses. We met with no loss till we got to the other side of the city. There the enemy made a stand for a moment, but the head squadron charging, the rebels took flight.'

Anson's description of the action was brief and very understated, certainly as far as his own involvement was concerned. Having charged through the town, the 9th Lancers began to reform and were in danger of being trapped by the enemy who blocked their exit route by dragging a number of carts across a gateway. Anson, despite suffering from an injured hand, which made control of his horse difficult, immediately charged the enemy position and, with the use of a lance, drove the cart drivers off their vehicles. Unable to stop his horse, he then found himself in the middle of the enemy before he was able to turn around and return to the 9th Lancers.

During this action, Captain Drysdale, who was leading the charge, received a fractured collar bone when his horse, at full gallop, was shot from under him. Surrounded by the enemy, he would have been killed had his orderly Trumpeter Robert Kells and Private Henry Jordan not come to his rescue. Kells and Jordan held the enemy at bay until further assistance arrived. During the fighting, Private Jordan was severely wounded by a musket ball. Trumpeter Kells received the Victoria Cross for his gallantry. Drysdale was also nominated for the Victoria Cross but the award was not approved.

At this point, Robert Blair was ordered to bring in an ammunition wagon (possibly one of those charged by Anson), that appeared to have been abandoned by the enemy. Accompanied by a sergeant and twelve men he was approaching the wagon when a party of about 60 enemy cavalry suddenly appeared from behind a small group of huts and tried to cut off he and his party from the regiment. Disregarding the heavy odds against him, Blair formed up his men and charged through the enemy and rejoined the regiment, leaving a native officer and eight of the sowars dead on the field; four of them killed by Blair personally. During the fighting, Blair received a sabre cut which nearly severed his arm from his shoulder, very close to the joint. He was in great danger of being overcome when his life was saved by Private Patrick Donohoe of the 9th Lancers; the two of them successfully reaching the regimental lines. None of Blair's men were lost in the action.

Carried to the rear, Blair received the attention of the regimental surgeon who had no choice but to amputate the damaged arm. For their gallantry Blair and Donohoe were both awarded the Victoria Cross.

It appears that Anson was incorrect in his belief that the charge through the town was executed without loss as Farrier Stillman fell seriously wounded. Private James Reynolds Roberts, despite himself being wounded in the bridle hand, went to his assistance. Immediately the two soldiers were surrounded by sepoys but Roberts managed to defend their position long enough for more support to arrive. Stillman died of his injuries but Roberts survived and was awarded the Victoria Cross. Outside of the 9th Lancers and their attached officers, a further

Augustus Anson, VC.

two VCs were awarded to Sergeant Bernard Diamond and Gunner Richard Fitzgerald of the Bengal Horse Artillery.

Blair returned to Britain and was sufficiently recovered from his injuries to appear before Queen Victoria some eleven months later to receive the VC. Almost immediately, he returned to India where he died of smallpox the following March.

When the Victoria Cross was first established and news of it reached India, Blair and his close friend Lieutenant Alfred Stowell Jones (see Appendix) were on record as having decided to do everything possible to gain the award. They both achieved their ambition. Blair's cousin, Lieutenant James Blair also won the Victoria Cross during the Indian Mutiny. Robert Blair, because of his attachment to the 9th Lancers, was the only officer of the Queen's Bays to receive the clasp for Delhi on his Indian Mutiny Medal.

Anson went on to further distinguish himself at the Secundra Bagh in November where he was wounded. For these two actions he was awarded the Victoria Cross. The following summer, Major-General Sir Hope Grant wrote of Anson: 'He has shown the greatest gallantry on every occasion and has slain many enemies.'

THOMAS HACKETT
Lieutenant
23rd (Royal Welch Fusiliers) Regiment of Foot

Captain Thomas Hackett, VC.

Full Name: Thomas Bernard Hackett.

Place of Birth: Not known. The family resided at Moor Park, King's County (now Co. Offaly), Ireland and Riverstown House, Co. Tipperary, Ireland. He was one of several brothers who took up careers in the Army: Major-General Simpson Hackett (Gloucestershire Regiment); Lieutenant-Colonel Charles Hackett (5th Fusiliers); Colonel Robert Henry Hackett (90th Light Infantry).

Date of Birth: 15 June 1836.

Father: Thomas Hackett.

Mother: Jane Hackett (daughter of Mr Bernard Shaw of Monktown Castle, Co. Cork, Ireland).

Father's Occupation: Landowner, High Sheriff for King's County, 1844.

Education: —

Service Record: Commissioned ensign, 6th Regiment of Foot, 7 June 1854 (by purchase); transferred to 23rd Regiment of Foot (Royal Welch Fusiliers), 3 November 1854; lieutenant, 9 February 1855; served Crimean Campaign (present during the siege and fall of Sebastopol); served Indian Mutiny, 1857–8 (present during the relief and capture of Lucknow; defeat of the Gwalior Contingent and recapture of Cawnpore); captain, 26 January 1858 (by purchase); major, 3 September 1870; brevet lieutenant-colonel; served Ashanti War, 1873–4 (2nd RWF); lieutenant-colonel, 1 April 1874 on which date he retired from the army by selling his rank.

Decorations, Medals and Rewards: Victoria Cross (for action at the Secundra Bagh, 18 November 1857); Crimean Medal (clasp for Sebastopol); Indian Mutiny Medal (clasps for Relief of Lucknow and Lucknow); Ashantee Medal 1873–74; Turkish Crimea Medal.

Post-Service Employment: Landowner and Justice of the Peace, Co. Tipperary, Ireland. Resided at Arrabeg, Co. Tipperary.

Riverstown House, Co. Tipperary.
[Geoff & Ethel Lumb]

Major Hackett, seated in the centre, wearing his VC with fellow officers of the 2nd Battalion RWF at Windsor, September 1871.
[RWF Museum, Caernarfon]

The damaged headstone on the grave of Thomas Hackett VC. The centre of the cross shows a Victoria Cross in detail. The front kerbstone is inscribed: 'Thomas Bernard Hackett, VC'. [Geoff & Ethel Lumb]

Married: Josephine, daughter of Reverend Joseph Marshall of Barrone Court, Co. Tipperary, 1874.
Children: None recorded.
Died: 5 October 1880, of gunshot wounds at Arrabeg, Co. Tipperary. An inquest returned a verdict of accidental death.
Buried: 8 October 1880, Hackett family vault, Lockeen churchyard, Borrisokane, Co. Tipperary
Memorials: Grave and memorial window at Lockeen Church, Co. Tipperary.
LOCATION OF THE VC: Bought by a private collector at Sotheby's on 26 March 1997.
Citation for the Victoria Cross: *London Gazette,* 12 April 1859,
'For daring gallantry at Secundra Baugh, Lucknow, on the 18th November 1857, in having, with others, rescued a Corporal of the 23rd Regiment who was lying wounded and exposed to a very heavy fire. Also for conspicuous bravery in having, under a heavy fire, ascended the roof and cut the thatch of a Bungalow to prevent its being set on fire. This was a most important service at the time.'
VC Investiture: Believed to have been by Lord Clyde at Lucknow, India.

Anglo-Irishman Thomas Hackett served with the 23rd Regiment of Foot (Royal Welch Fusiliers) in the latter part of the Crimean campaign before embarking for China in 1857. The regiment never arrived at their intended destination, being diverted to India following the outbreak of the Indian Mutiny. Hackett was involved in the operations leading to the relief of Lucknow where the area of the British Residency contained some 2,000 European women and children who had been besieged by the mutineers since the outbreak of hostilities.

The Royal Welch formed part of the second Lucknow relief column under the command of General Sir Colin Campbell, a force comprised of some 5,000 men and 49 pieces of artillery. Heavily outnumbered, Campbell decided to evacuate the besieged Europeans without forcing a full-scale confrontation with the mutineers who were were strongly positioned behind prepared defences. On 18 November, the general's plan entailed a force being established at a bridgehead over the river Gumti at the Secundra Bagh which they would have to hold, come what may, until the evacuation had been completed. Part of this force was made up of the Royal Welch Fusiliers.

In the ensuing fighting, a corporal of the 82nd Regiment was shot and severely wounded. Unable to move, he lay close to Brigadier Russell's bungalow, outside the perimeter of the British held lines, near an intersection of roads where the enemy's musket fire was so intense that it caused all others in the vicinity to dash for cover. Lieutenant Hackett saw the man's predicament and called for volunteers to assist in bringing him in. He was immediately joined by three artillerymen (Lieutenant Hastings Edward Harrington and Gunners Ford and Williams) and the 17-year old Private George Monger (officially ranked as 'Acting Drummer' with the Royal Welch), who was serving as a medical orderly. The five men then left the security of the house in which they had been sheltering and crossed the road at which point they were exposed to heavy firing from the ranks of the mutineers. Reaching the wounded corporal, Monger straddled the man, acting as a shield whilst giving

Lieutenant-Colonel Thomas Hackett, VC, JP.

The Secundra Bagh, Lucknow, showing the damaged caused during the siege of 1857. [RWF Museum]

some basic medical attention to his wounds. The gallant rescuers then remained to protect the corporal until the area had been cleared when they then lifted him and carried him back to the British lines where he received further medical attention. Monger managed to carry with him the corporal's rifle to prevent it falling into the hands of the enemy. Both Hackett and Monger survived not only the gallant rescue, but also the Indian Mutiny. Lieutenant Harrington also received the Victoria Cross under Rule 13 of the Warrant whereby an officer could be elected to receive the award. He died at Agra in 1861.

The Royal Welch remained in India after the end of the Mutiny and Hackett became a company commander before transferring to the 2nd Bn Royal Welch Fusiliers where he saw further active service in the Ashanti War of 1873. He retired as a lieutenant-colonel the following year. He then returned to Ireland where he lived the life of a country gentleman.

On Monday, 4 October 1880, at 2pm, Hackett went out partridge shooting at Lismacrory, accompanied by Mr William Fayle of Parsonstown and a local boy named Thomas Carroll. About two and a half hours later the party split and Hackett moved off on his own across Arraghmore estate, but within calling distance of the others. Some minutes later, Fayle heard a gunshot and then Hackett's voice calling out 'Willie'. Fearing the worst, Fayle rushed over and found his shooting partner lying on the ground, close to losing consciousness, with blood pouring from his stomach area. Hackett told him that he had placed the double barrel shotgun on the ground whilst trying to get through a hedge and, when he stooped to pick it up, it had gone off very close to him. The full force of the charge in the left barrel had entered his right side, very close to the liver 'leaving a gaping wound some three inches in diameter, and so close was the muzzle to his body that the coat and shirt were burned.' When Mr Fayle examined the gun he discovered the second barrel still loaded and cocked, ready for shooting. Hackett had committed the cardinal sin of all shooters and failed to break the gun whilst walking and overcoming obstacles on his path. Help arrived and Hackett was carried to a nearby house where he received medical attention for several hours, during which time he remained conscious. The prognosis was not good and his wife and brother were called and remained at his bedside where, despite the obvious outcome and the pain he was in, 'he maintained a calm and tranquil spirit which characterised his whole life, and ever made him an object of admiration to all who had the privilege of knowing in any degree his military history or private character.' At 11.25pm on the following evening, he died. The coroner's jury returned a verdict of 'accidental death'.

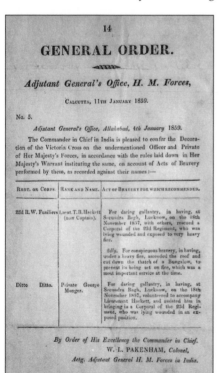

The local press were unusually generous in their eulogy: 'thousands … now mourn his untimely loss. But he will be remembered principally as the friend and kindly neighbour, ever the same, to rich and poor, the simplicity of whose nature and the total abrogation of self rendered him such a universal favourite and now invokes the widespread sorow amongst all classes.' On the day following the death, his brother, Colonel Robert Henry Hackett, received a telegram from Balmoral: 'I am commanded by the Queen to convey to you Her Majesty's deepest grief at the sad death of your gallant brother. The Queen is still more shocked at the thought of the irreparable loss that you must experience in him who seemed everything to you.'

General Order, dated 11 January 1859, relating to the award of the Victoria Cross to Lieutenant Hackett and Private Monger. [Geoff & Ethel Lumb]

Thomas Hackett's brother, Robert, is also of interest to any student of the Victoria Cross. Commissioned into the 19th Regiment of Foot in 1856, he later exchanged into the 90th Light Infantry with which regiment he saw service in South Africa in 1878 and 1879. At the action at Kambula on 29 March 1879 he was a brevet major commanding three companies. At a crucial point in the battle, the Zulus captured a cattle kraal some fifty yards from the perimeter of the main British laager. Colonel Evelyn Wood, VC, in overall command of the British troops, realised that a large enemy force could gather in the kraal and rush the British line without much chance of being stopped. A gap was quickly made in the main laager of wagons and Hackett led a counter-attack which charged the Zulus with bayonets, driving them out of the laager and back into a nearby ravine. Hackett then lined his men along the edge of the ravine and fired into the massed Zulus below. At this point the men of the 90th Regiment began to sustain heavy casualties from a heavy cross-fire from Zulus concealed in nearby huts. Realising that the position was untenable, Wood ordered them to withdraw back into the main laager. For Robert Hackett, the order came moments too late and he was hit by a bullet which passed right through his head. He was carried back to the British lines where it was assumed that it was only a matter of a short time before he died. However, despite the bullet having passed through his right temple and destroying the sight of both his eyes, before exiting on the left side of his head, he survived. Wood later wrote:

Thomas Hackett, VC (third from left, centre row)
with brother officers of the RWF.
[RWF Museum]

> Major Hackett, one of the ablest and bravest officers who, directing his men to take cover, himself walked erect amidst a hail of missiles, until one wounded him so cruelly.

Many felt that Robert Hackett should have been recommended for a Victoria Cross but it was not to be. Invalided home he was promoted to the rank of major, lieutenant-colonel and finally colonel, but retired from the service. He died in 1893, aged 54.

The Hackett family headstones in Lockeen churchyard.
The left hand plot includes: Thomas Hackett, VC;
Josephine Hackett; Colonel Robert Henry Hackett.
[Geoff & Ethel Lumb]

GEORGE MONGER
Private/ Acting Drummer
23rd (Royal Welch Fusiliers) Regiment of Foot

FULL NAME: George Monger.
PLACE OF BIRTH: Woodmancote, Basingstoke, Hampshire.
Date of Birth: 3 March 1840.
Father: Joseph Monger.
Mother: Jane Monger (née Carnmie).
Father's Occupation: Labourer.
Education: Not known.
Pre-Service Employment: Labourer.
Service Record: Enlisted 23rd Regiment of Foot, Royal Welch Fusiliers, at Winchester, 10 November 1855 (Service No. 5202) as a boy soldier; served Indian Mutiny 1857–8 (present at relief and capture of Lucknow) as a drummer; discharged at Walmer, 9 November 1868 (his intention being to reside at North Walton, Hampshire).
Decorations, Medals and Rewards: Victoria Cross (for action at the Secundra Bagh, Lucknow, 18 November 1857); Indian Mutiny Medal (clasps for relief of Lucknow and Lucknow).
Post-Service Employment: Builder's labourer and bricklayer.
Married: Mary Ann Love at Basingstoke, Hampshire, December 1869. She was originally from North Walsham, Hampshire and was ten years his junior.
Children: Nine (four of whom died at birth or shortly afterwards). In 1881 the census shows his then three children as being Leavina, Joseph William and Ernest John. In 1891 the census shows Mary as having two further daughters, Adelaide and Catherine.
Died: 9 August 1887, of consumption, at his home, 25 Tower Road, St Leonards on Sea, Sussex (in 1881 the family were living in 12 South Street, St Leonards).
Buried: Grave space E, section H, number E.18, Hastings Borough Cemetery, 13 August 1887. This was a common grave, but in 1889 it was purchased by a local resident and a headstone was erected.
Memorials: Borough Cemetery, Hastings; St James' Church, Woodmancote, Hampshire; blue plaque on his house in Tower Street, St Leonards; Monger Road, Wrexham.
Location of Victoria Cross: RWF Museum, Caernarfon Castle.

Private George Monger, c.1861. Aged only seventeen, Monger was one of the youngest recipients of the Victoria Cross.

The VC and Indian Mutiny medal of George Monger.
[RWF Museum, Caernarfon]

St James' Church, Woodmancote, the village where Monger was born. Inside there is a small, framed paper memorial to him.

Citation for the Victoria Cross: *London Gazette,* 12 April 1859.
'Private George Monger volunteered to accompany Lieutenant Hackett when he assisted in bringing in a corporal of the 23rd Regiment.'
VC Investiture: Believed to have been decorated with the VC by Lord Clyde at Lucknow, India.

George Monger is one of a small band of VC recipients to have the prefix 'Boy'. Having joined the Royal Welch Fusiliers as a boy soldier when aged only 15 years, the label has remained with him ever since, although at the time of his VC action he was 17 years of age.

George Monger, at the time of his award, the youngest man to receive the Victoria Cross, was a native of Hampshire who had probably joined the army as a route out of poverty. After the Indian Mutiny he never again saw action and was discharged in 1868. He married the following year but life as a civilian appears to have brought him very little happiness. He and his wife had nine children of whom four died in infancy and, in 1886, Monger himself developed the symptoms of what was then called consumption (today it is tuberculosis). Unable to work in the building trade, he faced poverty and pawned his Victoria Cross and Indian Mutiny medal and later had to rely upon charity until his death in 1887.

Monger's home at 25 Tower Road, Bohemia, St Leonards-on-Sea where he died of comsumption on 9 August 1887. The blue plaque above the door reads: 'George Monger 1840–1887 lived in this house. He was awarded the Victoria Cross, at the siege of Lucknow, aged 17.'

When Major-General Sherer heard of the family's poverty he wrote to the *Hastings Observer* and, as a consequence, the Duke of Cambridge arranged for payments to be made to them from the Woodman's Trust. In addition, the local population of Hastings donated £120 to the family shortly before Monger's death. His son was educated at the Duke of York's Royal Military School in Dover. As Monger had spent over three years in boy service he was only entitled to a pension for just under 10 years service.

Many a debate has focused on whether having the letters VC after a man's name has a beneficial or an adverse effect upon his life, a question to which there is no definitive answer: the effects of the VC have been as varied as the men who were awarded it. Whilst an officer might desire the VC with a view that it might further his career (see Robert Blair above, who set out to attain the coveted award), to a man in the ranks it could prove a millstone around his neck and, whilst giving him a period of his life when he was feted by his comrades (having his '15 minutes of fame' as coined by the American Andy Warhol), it could later prove an encumbrance. In the case of George Monger, the medal appears to have done him little good as after 1868, he never managed to do more than scrape a meagre living for himself and his family.

The grave of George Monger in Hastings Borough Cemetery. The inscription reads: 'In Memory of George Monger, VC, drummer & late private 23rd Regt R.W. Fusileers, who at the early age of 17, won the 'Victoria Cross' for an act of daring and gallantry at the siege & relief of Lucknow in the Indian Mutiny, November 1857. He died of consumption, at Bohemia, St Leonards on the 9th August 1887 after much patient suffering aged 47 years. 'Lord Jesu, King of Paradise, Receive me in Thy love, And guide me to that happy land, Of perfect rest above'.'

THOMAS MONAGHAN
Trumpeter
2nd Dragoon Guards (Queen's Bays)

Thomas Monaghan, VC.

Full Name: Thomas Monaghan.
Place of Birth: Abergavenny, Monmouthshire.
Date of Birth: 18 October 1833 (recorded in the Roman Catholic Registers of Abergavenny. His gravestone incorrectly records this as being April 1833).
Father: Thomas Monaghan.
Mother: Frances Monaghan (née McAdam).
Father's Occupation: Soldier (8th Hussars).
Education: No school certificate but he was able to sign his name well on enlistment.
Service Record: Attested 3rd Light Dragoons at Westminster, 6 July 1847 (his age being incorrectly given as 14 years and 3 months) (Service No. 1158); trumpeter, 6 March 1851; served in the Indian Mutiny (present at Lucknow) 1857–8; served for eleven months with the Osmandi Irregular Cavalry; re-engaged in India, 10 March 1863; reduced to private (date not known); trumpeter, 7 July 1868; reduced to private, 28 June 1870; private, 29 November 1871; discharged at Woolwich, 10 May 1873; later served with the 3rd Kent Position Artillery Band.
Decorations, Medals and Rewards: Victoria Cross (for action at Jamo, near Sandila, Oudh, India, 8 October 1858); Indian Mutiny Medal (clasp for Lucknow).
Post-Service Employment: Army Pensioner. Trade recorded on discharge papers as Groom. He resided at 38, Ogilby Street, Woolwich, *c.*1875.
Married: Margaret, *c.*1870.
Children: None recorded.
Died: 10 November 1895, at his home, 1 Pellipar Road, Woolwich.
Buried: 16 November 1895, section 33 (Roman Catholic), plot 826, an unmarked grave at Woolwich Cemetery.
Memorials: Headstone dedicated at his grave in Woolwich Cemetery, London, 15 October 1967.
Location of Victoria Cross: Queen's Dragoon Guards Museum, Cardiff.
Citation for the Victoria Cross: *London Gazette*, 11 November 1862. 'For saving the life of Lieutenant-Colonel Seymour, CB, commanding the regiment, in an attack made on him on 8th October 1858, by mutinous sepoys, in a dense jungle of sugar canes from which an attempt was made to dislodge them. The mutineers were between 30 and 40 in number. They suddenly opened fire on Lieutenant-Colonel Seymour and his party at a few yards' distance, and immediately rushed in upon them with drawn (native) swords. Pistolling a man, cutting at him and emptying with deadly effect at arm's length every barrel of his revolver, Lieutenant-Colonel Seymour was cut down by two sword cuts when the two men above recommended rushed to his rescue, and the Trumpeter shooting a man with his pistol in the act of cutting at him and both Trumpeter and Dragoon driving at the enemy with their swords, enabled him to rise and assist in defending himself again, when the whole of the enemy were despatched. The occurrence took place soon after the action near Sundeela Oudh on the date above

Thomas Monaghan's VC and Indian Mutiny medal as displayed at the old Queen's Dragoon Guards Museum in Shrewsbury.

Monaghan's grave in Woolwich Cemetery.

mentioned.'

VC Investiture: Believed to have been by General Sir Hugh Rose, GOC India, at Benares, March 1863.

The Dragoon mentioned in the citation was Private Charles Anderson, VC (see below).

The Roman Catholic register for Abergavenny records that Thomas Monaghan, an Irishman by blood but a Welshman by birth, was the subject of an emergency baptism by Blanche Ellis, the local 'handy woman' (midwife) as he was thought unlikely to survive long enough for the priest to be called. As it was, not only did he survive infancy, but became a healthy young man with sufficient physical strength to enlist under-age in 1847 and complete a total of 13 years and 5 months service in India and Turkey, stations which were breeding grounds for diseases which caused the death of many thousands of British servicemen. Not so with Monaghan, and, by the time of the Indian Mutiny, he was one of the regiment's old hands. His service career was somewhat erratic, with his being promoted several times and, each time, reduced to private soldier. He was eventually discharged from the army at Woolwich in 1873 and, as far as is known, spent the remainder of his life in that garrison town. When he died in 1895 he was buried in a private plot of the Roman Catholic section of Woolwich Cemetery but no headstone was erected. This discrepancy was corrected in 1967 when a Commonwealth War Graves Commission-style headstone was erected by the Queen's Dragoon Guards Old Comrades' Association.

They played the 'Last Post' for Tommy Monaghan on Sunday — for the hero everyone forgot. The notes echoed over the sun-lit Woolwich Cemetery, where Tommy has lain for 72 years. There has been no stone on his grave — nothing to say that here rested a holder of the Victoria Cross, not until the Army tracked down the old soldier who had served his country so bravely, and who had been buried in a common grave simply as an 'Army pensioner'.

But once all Britain knew about young Trumpeter Tommy Monaghan, when he was home from the wars with the ribbon of the country's highest award on his tunic. In a thousand barrack rooms they told the story of the man who saved the life of his commanding officer.

But at Woolwich on Sunday a little group of men stood to attention in memory of hero Tommy, and a stone telling of his bravery has been put up over his grave. Bdr James Reed played the 'Last Post' and the call of Tommy's old regiment, the one he must have sounded himself countless times.

Until this year no one realised that the humble grave at Woolwich was Tommy's. Then the Victoria Cross which Trumpeter Thomas Monaghan won as a man of 25 came up for sale. It was bought by an officer of the Regiment and the search began to trace where the hero was buried. The search led the Queen's Dragoon Guards Old Comrades' Association to the unmarked grave … Major Ronald Strutt told the *Mercury* 'We tried very hard to trace some relative of Monaghan, but we have so far been unsuccessful. It is amazing that he should have been buried without recognition.'

The South East London Mercury

CHARLES ANDERSON
Private
2nd Dragoon Guards (Queen's Bays)

Charles Anderson, VC.

Full Name: Charles Anderson.
Place of Birth: Liverpool.
Date of Birth: *Circa* 1827.
Father: —
Mother: —
Father's Occupation: —
Education: —
Pre-Service Employment: —
Service Record: Enlisted in 2nd Dragoon Guards at Dublin, 11 December 1845 (Service No. 875); promoted to corporal, *circa* 1858 (field promotion for gallantry); twice demoted from corporal; served Indian Mutiny, 1857–8; discharged as a corporal at Colchester, at his own request, 28 June 1870 (his intended place of residence was given as Dublin).
Decorations, Medals and Rewards: Victoria Cross (for action at Jamo, near Sandila, Oudh, India, 8 October 1858); Indian Mutiny Medal (clasp for Lucknow); received five Good Conduct Badges.
Post-Service Employment: Details not known but he could have been a coal miner (see details of his death below).
Married: No record of marriage.
Died: Confirmed details of his death are unknown. The last entry in the Army pension records shows a payment being made to Anderson, VC, at Dublin in 1877. There are no records of Anderson's death in that city at that time, or in the years following.
Buried: No confirmed details available. See memorials below.
Memorials: In 1989 a headstone was erected on the grave of a Charles Anderson at Princess Road Cemetery, Seaham Harbour, Sunderland, section A, grave 1271 by the Queen's Dragoon Guards.
Location of Victoria Cross: Queen's Dragoon Guards Museum, Cardiff.
Citation for the Victoria Cross: *London Gazette*, 11 November 1862. 'For saving the life of Lieutenant-Colonel Seymour, CB, commanding the regiment, in an attack made on him on 8th October 1858, by mutinous sepoys, in a dense jungle of sugar canes from which an attempt was made to dislodge them. The mutineers were between 30 and 40 in number. They suddenly opened fire on Lieutenant-Colonel Seymour and his party at a few yards' distance, and immediately rushed in upon them with drawn (native) swords. Pistolling a man, cutting at him and emptying with deadly effect at arm's length every barrel of his revolver, Lieutenant-Colonel Seymour was cut down by two sword cuts when the two men above recommended rushed to his rescue, and the Trumpeter shooting a man with his pistol in the act of cutting at him and both Trumpeter and Dragoon driving at the enemy with their swords, enabled him to rise and assist in defending himself again, when the whole of the enemy were despatched. The occurrence took place soon after the action near Sundeela Oudh on the date above mentioned.'
This was a shared citation with Trumpeter Thomas Monaghan. See Thomas Monaghan for details.
VC Investiture: Believed to have been by General Sir Hugh Rose, GOC India, at Benares, India, in March 1863.

The VC and Indian Mutiny Medal of Charles Anderson. The clasp for Lucknow appears to be missing. [QDGs Museum]

The 2nd Dragoon Guards (The Queen's Bays) were serving in Ireland when news reached Britain of the outbreak of the Indian Mutiny. The regiment was ordered to the sub-continent as part of the reinforcements necessary to help suppress the violence. Travelling via the Cape of Good Hope they arrived in Calcutta in November 1857 and saw action for the first time at Nusrutpore in January before joining the column under the command of Sir Colin Campbell which was to break the siege of Lucknow. On the 6 March, two squadrons of the regiment made a charge against the enemy force outside Lucknow and, following the recapture of the city some ten days later, took part in operations designed to pacify the surrounding region and clear it of rebel forces. Detachments from the regiment were involved in various minor actions throughout the early summer of 1858, when they suffered more from the effects of the climate and disease than from the assaults of the enemy. By mid June active operations were suspended during the height of the hot season and not resumed until September. In October, the regiment formed part of Brigadier-General Sir George Baker's column and it was whilst operating near Jamo in the area near Sandila in Oudh that the action took place for which Monaghan and Anderson were each awarded the Victoria Cross.

On 21 September, Major W. H. Seymour, the officer in command of the regiment, led a cavalry column in pursuit of the enemy who had just been defeated in an action at Jamo, Oudh. On their return to the British camp, finding the action to be virtually over, Seymour led his men to a grove of trees where they dismounted and were given the opportunity to rest and received a ration of rum. Whilst this was going on, a message arrived from Major Stapylton (2nd Dragoon Guards) who was with another cavalry unit in a nearby grove, stating that a party of mutineers from the 42nd Bengal Native Infantry were concealed in a thick sugar-cane plantation nearby. Seymour immediately decided to act and, assumed command over a unit of about 40 men from the 3rd Bn The Rifle Brigade, led by Lieutenants Green and Richards, which had just arrived at the scene. On foot they rushed into the sugar-cane and began 'beating about in the rain for some little time'. Suddenly, the mutineers, only a few yards away, but concealed by the dense foliage, opened fire then rushed at the infantry with drawn native swords. It was an accepted fact that native blades were far more effective than the government issue swords used by the British. Although the steel was probably of similar quality, they were carried in wooden scabbards and only drawn for cleaning and sharpening and for use. The British swords, however, were sheathed in steel scabbards and were regularly drawn for ceremonial purposes and for drill. As a consequence, the native weapons had a much sharper edge and, if not fatal, inflicted horrendous wounds.

Seymour and Lieutenant Green were the first to receive the attack, and the subaltern was immediately 'cut down and hacked on the ground in a fearful manner'. The Major desperately attempted to defend himself with both his sword and pistol, and later wrote: 'Pistolling a man, cutting at him and emptying with deadly effect at arms length every barrel of my revolver, I was myself cut down by two sword cuts, wounding me however but slightly.' Struggling on the ground, Seymour thought that his life was measured in seconds. Unknown to him, his orderly trumpeter, Thomas Monaghan, and Dragoon Charles Anderson, had decided to follow him from the grove and into the sugar-cane. Just as the mutineer was about to administer the *coup de grâce*, Monaghan shot him with his pistol. Then, with drawn swords, he and Anderson launched themselves at the enemy, driving them back from the prone Seymour who was given the opportunity to get back on his feet and continue defending himself. Within seconds, the sepoys withdrew into the jungle. Major Seymour wrote: 'I attribute the safety of my life on this occasion solely to the gallant

The charge of the Queen's Bays at Lucknow, 1858.
[QDGs Museum, Cardiff]

Lieutenant-Colonel W. H. Seymour, CB, whose life was saved by Monaghan and Anderson during their VC action. [QDGs Museum, Cardiff]

and timely assistance rendered me by these two men.'

In due course, delayed by the demands of active service, Seymour put forward the names of Monaghan and Anderson for the new 'distinction of the Victoria Cross'. On 23 February 1861, he wrote to Brigadier Sir George Baker, KCB, RA, who had been in overall command of the British forces at Jamo:

… I trust you will do me the favor of recommending the individuals of the Regiment under my Command in the Margin for that high and envied distinction the 'Victoria Cross' as I firmly and earnestly believe that by their daring gallantry alone my life was saved on this occasion as Major Commanding my Regiment.

When no official response was received to the recommendation and there was no sign of any decision being made about the awards to Monaghan and Anderson, Seymour (by now a lieutenant-colonel commanding the 2nd Dragoon Guards) wrote to make enquiries. It transpired that no recommendation had been received and, as a consequence, the two men's names were added to a short list of possible retrospective awards sent to General Sir Hugh Rose, GCB, Commander-in-Chief in India who in turn forwarded it on to the Horse Guards in London.* On 7 October 1861, a reply was sent:

With reference to the last named claims for Service performed during the Mutiny in India, HRH has also received the concurrence of the Secretary of State for War that no more applications should be taken into consideration, unless made by the Commander of the Forces or Commander of the Troops engaged within a short period of the Act of Valor having been performed — occasional exception however being made as in the grant of the Victoria Cross for the Crimean Campaign, should the causes of delay in bringing the case to notice be of a special nature and those for which the Oficer responsible for such recommendations had no control.

Seymour immediately upon receipt of this rejection of his recommendation took up the case on behalf of his two saviours, writing to HRH The Duke of Cambridge, Commander-in-Chief of the Army, via Major-General Forster of the Horse Guards.

The reason for the non bestowal of the decoration of the 'Victoria Cross' on the soldiers of the 2nd Dragoon Guards as per margin [No 875 Private Charles Anderson and No 1158 Trumpeter Thomas Monaghan both of the 2. Drag. Gds.] appears from the said extract (marked 'A') to be on account of 'no application having been made by the Commander in Chief of the Forces or Commander of the Troops engaged within a short period of the Act of Valor having been performed.'

I beg to be allowed to remark that this application <u>was</u> originally made at the time of the occurrence in the usual manner and such should have been stated in the renewed application only through the Officer Comg. the Column to which the 2nd Dragoon Guards under my Command were attached (Brigadier Sir George R. Barker Royal Arty.) but as this Column of Troops was daily and continually marching surrounded at times by the Enemy the postal communications were very insecure, instances occurring of post runners being killed or deserting and as <u>many</u> letters were at that period lost in this way, and as no answer was ever received by myself to the said application I presume that it miscarried.

Imagining that it had been forwarded home to England for approval, I made no enquiries at the time regarding it, and many months afterwards when I <u>did</u> enquire I could find no trace of it, even at the Divisional headquarters.

Guaranteeing to honor as I do the validity of the facts of this case as in the appended application the occurence having happened to <u>myself</u> and firmly believing that my life was saved on the occasion referred to therein by <u>these men</u> I trust HRH may deem me not intrusive in begging that the matter may meet with just re-consideration.

P.S. I may be permitted to remark that these cases have passed the 'Board of Officers' and have been recommended by His Ex. Sir H. Rose (the Comr. in Chief in India) as far back as August 1861.

A short time later, whilst making reference to all those on Sir Hugh Roses's short list of retrospective claims, the Horse Guards noted:

---

* The other names on this short list were: Crimean Campaign — Privates J. Burke, P. Callaghan and T. Catling (1st Bn 20th Foot and Sergeant W. Sudders, 2nd Bn The Rifle Brigade. Indian Mutiny — Colour Sergeant C. Coughlan (75th Foot) and Private D. Neill (83rd Foot). Of these, the recommendation of Cornelius Coughlan was subsequently approved and his award was gazetted on 11 November 1862, the same date as the awards to Monaghan and Anderson.

The GOC, in accordance with decisions already arrived at, declined to put forward the claims as too much time had elapsed, except in the case of 2 men of the 2nd Dragoon Guards — Anderson & Monaghan — the application on whose behalf was properly made at the time, but through some accident it did not reach its destination. These two men are recommended for saving the life of the Commanding Officer of the Regiment.

The reverse of Charles Anderson's Victoria Cross. [QDGs Museum, Cardiff]

Charles Anderson is one of the mystery men of the Victoria Cross. Virtually nothing is known of his life before he enlisted in the 2nd Dragoon Guards at Dublin in 1845. Like Monaghan, he was an old hand by the time the regiment arrived in India and he seemed equally as unable to retain any rank to which he was promoted. His post-service life is also a mystery and nothing can be stated with any degree of certainty although, remarkably, there is a good image of a man, in civilian dress, wearing the VC and the Indian Mutiny medal, who is generally accepted to be Charles Anderson. He was discharged at Colchester in 1870 and gave his intended place of residence as Dublin. This reference to Dublin, along with his place of enlistment and his probable place of birth (Liverpool) would seem to suggest a strong link with Ireland. Various studies of VC recipients have attempted to track Anderson's movements post 1870 with little success. A careful trawl through the General Register Office records for England and Wales bring up very few possible candidates, the most promising being a man named Charles Anderson who resided as a lodger at Swinbank Cottages, Seaham Harbour, near Sunderland. He was a coal miner who died of a fractured skull following an accident when he fell off the local cliffs on 19 April 1899. The press coverage of his death and funeral make no mention of his being the holder of the VC or an ex-soldier, rather an unusual oversight if he was in fact Charles Anderson, VC. The only link, other than the name, was the approximate age of the collier, which would indicate that he was born at the same time as Charles Anderson, VC. For nearly one hundred years the grave at Seaham remained unmarked and, when enquiries were made by the Queen's Dragoon Guards regarding the possibility of placing a headstone on the grave, a number of features appeared in the local media. As a result of this some descendants of Charles Anderson, VC's siblings contacted the regiment. They resided in the north-east of England and Scotland, thereby establishing, for the first time, a link between the Anderson family and the area.

In the late 1980s, the Queen's Dragoon Guards (the successor regiment to the Queen's Bays), in conjunction with Seaham Town Council, arranged for a headstone to be placed on Charles Anderson's grave in Princess Road Cemetery, Seaham. The headstone was dedicated at an official ceremony on 14 December 1989.

For many years, the Queen's Dragoon Guards held what they believed was the Victoria Cross awarded to Charles Anderson. In the mid 1960s, the regiment discovered that another VC to Charles Anderson was held by a museum in Edinburgh. Checks were made which verified that this was in fact the genuine Cross and it was acquired by the regiment in 1967.

A wreath is laid on the grave of Charles Anderson at Seaham, following the dedication of the headstone, 14 December 1989.

CAMPBELL DOUGLAS
Assistant Surgeon
2/24th (2nd Warwickshire) Regiment of Foot

FULL NAME: Campbell Mellis Douglas.

PLACE OF BIRTH: Grosse Isle, Quebec, Canada.

Date of Birth: 5 August 1840. He had one younger brother, Archibald Lucius, born 1842 (he became Admiral Sir Archibald Douglas, GCB, GCVO, LLD, JP).

Father: Dr George Mellis Douglas, MD.

Mother: Charlotte Saxton Douglas, daughter of Archibald Campbell, Queen's Notary, of Quebec, Canada. Married in 1832.

Father's Occupation: Superintendent of Gaspe Island/Grosse Isle Quarantine Station, Quebec (1836–64).

Education: St John's College; Laval University, Quebec, Canada; Edinburgh University (MD 1861, LRCS).

Service Record: Probationary assistant surgeon, Nova Scotia, 1 October 1862; assistant surgeon, attached 24th Regiment of Foot, Mauritius, 22 May 1863; medical officer with the Andaman Islands Expedition, 1867; transferred Royal Artillery, Nova Scotia, 31 August 1872; surgeon major, 28 April 1876; retired, 1 October 1882; honorary brigade surgeon with the rank of surgeon lieutenant-colonel; served as medical officer in charge of the field hospital for the 2nd Riel Expedition, Canada, 1885.

Decorations, Medals and Rewards: Victoria Cross (for action in the Andaman Islands, Indian Ocean, 7 May 1867); North West Canada Medal, 1885 (no clasp); Silver Medal of the Royal Humane Society (for action in the Andaman Islands, 7 May 1867).

Post-Service Employment: Private practice at Lakefield, Ontario, Canada. He later returned to Britain where he resided at Dunmore, Essex. He was appointed depôt medical officer at Berwick on Tweed and retired in 1897. Financial problems resulted in his appointment as depôt medical officer at Perth, a position which he held until his final retirement in 1902.

Married: Eleanor McMaster, widow of Valentine McMaster, VC, MD, daughter of Colonel Burmeister, RE, at Halifax, Canada, 10 August 1874.

Children: Two sons and one daughter. His wife also had two children by her first marriage.

The young Assistant Surgeon Campbell Douglas in the uniform of the 24th Regiment of Foot. [Late Mrs Frances Douglas]

Campbell Douglas (standing) with his brother, Archibald.
[Late Mrs Frances Douglas]

The grave of Campbell Douglas, VC, Wells Cemetery.

A dapper Campbell Douglas photograph probably taken shortly after his VC action.

Birdwood, Horrington, the home of his daughter Muriel, where Campbell Douglas, VC, died in 1909.

Campbell Douglas, VC (left) with his brother Admiral Sir Archibald Douglas. [Mrs Frances Douglas]

Died: 31 December 1909, at his daughter's home, Birdwood, Horrington, near Wells, Somerset.

Buried: Borough Cemetery, Wells, Somerset, grave M20, with his daughter, Muriel Constance Bigg-Wither.

Location of Victoria Cross: Canadian War Museum, Ottawa.

Citation for the Victoria Cross: *London Gazette* 17 December 1867

'For the very gallant and daring manner in which, on 7th May 1867, they risked their lives in manning a boat and proceeding through dangerous surf to the rescue of some of their comrades who formed part of an expedition which had been sent to the island of Little Andaman by the order of the Chief Commissioner of British Burmah, with the view of ascertaining the fate of the commander and seven of the crew of the ship *Assam Valley*, who had landed there and were supposed to have been murdered by the natives.

The officer who commanded the troops on the occasion reports, 'About an hour later in the day, Dr Douglas, 2nd Battn 24th Reg., and the four privates referred to, gallantly manned the second gig, made their way through the surf almost to the shore but finding their boat was half filled with water they retired. A second attempt made by Dr Douglas and party proved successful, five of us being safely passed through the surf to the boats outside. A third and last trip got the whole of the party left on shore safe to the boats.' It is stated that Dr Douglas accomplished these trips through surf to the shore by no ordinary exertion. He stood in the bows of the boat and worked her in an intrepid and seamanlike manner, cool to a degree, as if what he was doing was an ordinary act of everyday life. The four privates behaved in an equally cool and collected manner, rowing through the roughest surf when the slightest hesitation or want of pluck on the part of any one of them would have been attended by the gravest results. It is reported that seventeen officers and men were thus saved from what might have been a fearful risk, if not certainty, of death.'

This was a shared citation with Privates Bell, Murphy, Griffiths and Cooper.

VC Investiture: By Major-General Faunce, GOC Pegu Division, at Rangoon, Burma, 16 April 1868.

DAVID BELL
Private
2/24th (2nd Warwickshire) Regiment of Foot

Full Name: David Bell.
Place of Birth: County Down, Ireland.
Date of Birth: Commonly believed to have been *circa* 1845 but, if he gave the correct age on his enlistment, he was born *circa* 1842.
Father: —
Mother: —
Father's Occupation: —
Education: -
Pre-Service Employment: —
Service Record: Enlisted 24th Regiment of Foot at Lisburn, Ireland, 19 April 1860 (Service Nº 1348); served Mauritius, Rangoon and Secunderabad, 1863–73; served Andaman Islands Expedition, 1867; discharged at Warley, 26 May 1873; one extant document indicates that Bell may have been promoted to sergeant but there is no firm evidence to substantiate this.
Decorations, Medals and Rewards: Victoria Cross (for action in the Andaman Islands, Indian Ocean, 7 May 1867).
Post-Service Employment: Employed at a cement factory as a labourer. He was later employed as a skilled labourer at Nº 8 Machine Shop, Chatham Dockyard, Kent.
Married: Ann, who died on 27 October 1944 .
Children: None recorded.
Died: 7 March 1920, at his home 2 Unity Cottages, Gardiner Street, Gillingham, Kent.
Buried: 12 March 1920, grave CH782, Woodlands Cemetery, Gillingham, Kent.
Memorials: Woodlands Cemetery, Gillingham, Kent.
Location of Victoria Cross: RRW Museum, Brecon.
Citation for the Victoria Cross: *London Gazette* 17 December 1867. This was a shared citation with Assistant Surgeon Douglas and Privates Cooper, Murphy and Griffiths. See entry for Assistant Surgeon Douglas for details.
VC Investiture: By Major-General Robert N. Faunce, GOC Pegu Division, at Rangoon, Burma, 16 April 1868.

David Bell, VC.

Gardiner Street, Gillingham, where Bell VC lived immediately prior to his death.

David Bell's Victoria Cross.
[RRW Museum, Brecon]

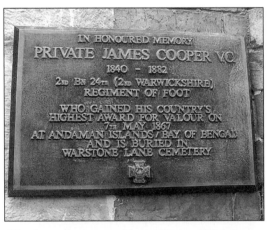

JAMES COOPER
Private
2/24th (2nd Warwickshire) Regiment of Foot

Full Name: James Cooper.

Place of Birth: Birmingham. In 1851, the family were lodging in Gerrard Street, Aston.

Date of Birth: *Circa* September 1841.

Father: William Cooper.

Mother: Elizabeth Cooper, employed as a stay maker.

Father's Occupation: Jeweller.

Education: Illiterate (unable to sign his name on his attestation papers).

Pre-Service Employment: Jeweller.

Service Record: Attested at Birmingham, 12 November 1858 (Service Nº 496); served overseas Mauritius and Burma; discharged at Sheffield, 31 December 1868; recalled to Army service, 2nd/6th Regiment of Foot, 13 April 1878; transferred to Army Reserve, 1 August 1878; discharged from the Army Reserve, 14 May 1881.

Decorations, Medals and Rewards: Victoria Cross (for action at Little Andaman Island, 7 May 1867); two Good Conduct Badges.

Post-Service Employment: Jeweller. In 1871 he resided at Aston's Buildings, Wheeler Street, Birmingham. In 1876 his address was Back Court, 4 New John Street, Birmingham.

Married: Maria Hampton, daughter of George Hampton, market gardener, at St Silas Church, Birmingham, 19 November 1871. His address at this date is given as Berners Street, Birmingham.

Children: None recorded.

Died: 9 October 1882, at his home, 43 Court Farm Street, Birmingham.

Buried: Warstone Lane Cemetery, Warstone, Hockley, Birmingham, grave 1428 (no headstone).

Memorials: A plaque in his memory was unveiled at Warstone Lane Cemetery on 30 November 2003 by the Shropshire War Memorial Association.

Location of Victoria Cross: Held by the Royal Warwickshire (TA) Regiment. This was originally part of a private collection belonging to Major T. Richards, 1st VB Royal Warwickshire Regiment.

Citation for the Victoria Cross: *London Gazette*, 17 December 1867. This was a shared citation with Assistant Surgeon Douglas and Privates Bell, Murphy and Griffiths. See entry for Assistant Surgeon Douglas for full details.

VC Investiture: By Major-General Faunce, GOC Pegu Division, Rangoon, Burma, 16 April 1868.

The plaque in memory of James Cooper, VC at the rear of the gatehouse at Warstone Lane Cemetery, Birmingham.

The unmarked grave of James Cooper (between the two kerbed graves in the foreground) at Warstone Lane Cemetery.

THOMAS MURPHY
Private
2/24th (2nd Warwickshire) Regiment of Foot

Full Name: Thomas Murphy.
Place of Birth: Co. Roscommon, Ireland.
Date of Birth: *Circa* 1839.
Father: —
Mother: —
Father's Occupation: —
Education: —
Pre-Service Employment: Cloth Dresser.
Service Record: Enlisted 24th Regiment at Leeds, Yorkshire, 25 April 1859 (Service Nº 1052); served Mauritius and Burma; discharged, time expired, at Preston, 17 November 1869.
Decorations, Medals and Rewards: Victoria Cross (for action at Little Andaman Island, 7 May 1867).
Married: —
Children: —
Post-Service Employment: Emigrated to the United States where he became an American citizen.
Died: Philadelphia, USA, 22 March 1900.
Buried: Laurel Hill Cemetery, Philadelphia, USA, plot Q, grave 361. David Harvey (in his book *Monuments to Courage*) states that Murphy was buried in a family plot (with Samuel N. Murphey and Sarah A. Murphey) and that the late date of burial may have been as a result of his body being 'given to medical science.'
Memorials: None known.
Location of Victoria Cross: Not known.
Citation for the Victoria Cross: *London Gazette,* , 17 December 1867. This was a shared citation with Assistant Surgeon Douglas and Privates Bell, Cooper and Griffiths. See entry for Assistant Surgeon Douglas for full details.
VC Investiture: By Major-General Faunce, GOC Pegu Division, Rangoon, Burma, 16 April 1868.

Thomas Murphy, VC.

Thomas Murphy was buried in Laurel Hill Cemetery in an unmarked grave. Other members of the family were later buried in the same plot and the above marker was placed there in 1924. [William Sweeney]

The entrance to Laurel Hill Cemetery, Philadelphia, one of America's oldest historic 'lawn' cemeteries, where Thomas Murphy was buried. [Mike Reed]

The VC of William Griffiths in the RRW Museum, Brecon. The location of his South Africa Medal is unknown.

The final stand at Isandlwana as portrayed by the London magazine The Graphic.

WILLIAM GRIFFITHS
Private
2/24th (2nd Warwickshire) Regiment of Foot

Full Name: William Griffiths.
Place of Birth: County Roscommon, Ireland.
Date of Birth: *Circa* 1841.
Father:
Mother: —
Father's Occupation: —
Education: —
Pre-Service Occupation: Collier.
Service Record: Enlisted 24th Regiment of Foot at Warwick, 11 April 1859 (Service N° 1056); served Mauritius and Burma; served Cape of Good Hope and Natal and Zululand, 1 October 1877–January 1879; served Zululand, January 1879.
Decorations, Medals and Rewards: Victoria Cross (for action at Little Andaman Island, 7 May 1867); South Africa Medal (clasp for 1877–8–9).
Married: No record of any marriage.
Children: None recorded.
Died: KinA at Isandlwana, Zululand, 22 January 1879.
Buried: Mass grave on the battlefield at Isandlwana, June 1879.
Memorials: Regimental Memorial, Isandlwana, Zululand; Brecon Cathedral (nave).
Location of Victoria Cross: RRW Museum, Brecon .
Citation for the Victoria Cross: *London Gazette,* 17 December 1867. This was a shared citation with Assistant Surgeon Douglas and Privates Bell, Cooper and Murphy. See entry for Assistant Surgeon Douglas for full details.
VC Investiture: By Major-General Faunce, GOC Pegu Division, Rangoon, Burma, 16 April 1868.

The award of the Victoria Cross to five members of the 24th Regiment in 1867 raised a debate about its validity that has continued for nearly 140 years. The wording of their joint citation has done little to dampen the flames of controversy which makes it worthwhile to study in greater detail their actions on the Little Andaman Islands on 7 May 1867.

The original 1856 Warrant had clearly specified in Clause 5 that 'the Cross shall only be awarded to those Officers and Men who have served Us in the presence of the Enemy and shall then have performed some signal act of valour or devotion to their Country'. When consideration was being given to the first batch of nominations for the new award, the courage shown by men of the 54th Regiment of Foot in extinguishing a major fire aboard the transport ship *Sarah Sands* was brought before the War Office. As a consequence of this, on 10 August 1858, a Royal Warrant was signed which directed that the Cross could be awarded in cases of 'conspicuous courage and bravery displayed under circumstances of danger but not before the enemy' where, 'through the courage and devotion displayed, life or public property may be saved'. Today, such an action, at the highest level, would undoubtedly merit the award of the George Cross, but in the mid-nineteenth century no such alternative award was available. The name of Private Walsh of the 54th Regiment was then put forward, but rejected, on the grounds that too long a period had elapsed between the action in question and the nomination for the Victoria Cross. Such a change in the criteria for which a VC could be awarded was quite radical but, for several years, no such awards were made. In 1860 the name of Ensign Bourke of the 1st West India Regiment was brought before the Horse Guards for consideration of the award of a Victoria Cross for his gallant actions during a fire at Fort Charlotte in the Bahamas. The application was turned down. Six years later, the Horse Guards received a nomination under the terms of the 1858 Warrant in the name of Private Timothy O'Hea who had displayed conspicuous gallantry in extinguishing a fire in an ammunition car at Danville Station in Canada. Some argued that although extremely brave, O'Hea's actions were simply those of a serviceman carrying out his expected duties under trying circumstances. The Board of Officers, however, felt that the action merited the VC and Queen Victoria confirmed the award to O'Hea, it being gazetted on New Year's Day, 1867. The most notable example of the award of Victoria Crosses for an action not in the face of the enemy is that of the five men of the 2/24th Regiment who saved the lives of their comrades off the coast of the Little Andaman Island in the Indian Ocean in 1867. Fortunately for the researcher, this incident is amongst the best documented in the history of the Victoria Cross and yet, despite this, there are still details which have been obscured, either by accident or design, which give a very different picture to the chain of events which led to the five awards.

Campbell Mellis Douglas was born in Quebec, the son of the Superintendent of the Grosse Isle Quarantine Station, Dr George Douglas. He was educated in Canada and Edinburgh and returned to his homeland to practise medicine in Nova Scotia. Aged 23, he was appointed assistant surgeon to the 24th Regiment at Mauritius, serving in the area of the Indian Ocean for nearly ten years. In addition to his medical employment, Douglas was also passionately interested in boats of every description, a pastime that perhaps began back in Quebec with the boats plying to and from Grosse Isle in the St Lawrence River. By the time he joined the army he was already an accomplished boatman and prepared a regimental boat for entry into a regatta in Burma. The crew that he trained was so strong that, after winning the first race, the boat was excluded from further competition in order that other boats might have some chance of winning a prize. The names of his crewmen have not been recorded, but it is possible that they were the same men that he led on 7 May 1867.

The background to the events of 7 May 1867 is worth recording as a whole series of circumstances combined to bring about near disaster for a large body of British soldiers and sailors, something which was only averted by the action of Douglas and his crew.

By 1867, the 24th Regiment was serving in Rangoon, Burma with a detachment on the Andaman Islands in the Bay of Bengal, a small archipelago comprised of four main islands: North Andaman, Middle Andaman, South Andaman and, some 60 kilometres further south, Little Andaman. In 1864, the administrative control of the islands had passed from India to Rangoon in Burma. There was a small settlement at Port Blair near the south of the South Andaman Island where a superintendent acted on behalf of the British Colonial Office. During the Indian Mutiny, large numbers of former mutineers were transported to, and incarcerated on, the Andaman Islands. The islands' indigenous population were subjected to the efforts of the British to 'civilise' them and there were constant rumours of barbarism and even cannibalism amongst the tribes on the more remote islands. The Superintendent, Major B. Ford was responsible for the civil administration of both the natives, the penal colony, the Andaman Homes (an organisation designed to civilise the native population, which, in 1867, was under the control of Mr Homfray) and the military forces (under the direct command of Captain W. J. Dakeyne) which comprised mainly of a detachment of about three officers and 100 men of the 2/24th Regiment, a smaller group of Naval Brigade officers and men, and a regiment of native infantry.

The *Assam Valley*, a merchant vessel operated by Messrs Bulloch Brothers, sailed from Bombay under the command of Captain Manley who had been appointed to replace the ship's captain, C. H. Hervey who had died. En route to

Rangoon, on 22 January 1867, the vessel came into some heavy weather during which she lost her main top-sail yard. Having reached Rangoon without further incident, the captain failed to obtain a replacement spar and, as he was required to sail forAkyab, decided to make a stop at Little Andaman Island where he believed there was ample timber which the ship's carpenter could fashion into a spar. On 21 March the *Assam Valley* dropped anchor some two miles off the coast of Little Andaman Island where, at 11.45am, the captain led a party of seven men ashore in the quarter boat (Captain Manley, 2nd Officer Edward Madden, Ship's Carpenter Robert Knowles, Seamen Owen Owens, James Farrell, William Moltes, Joseph Bowers and William Bishop). The landing party were equipped with all the ship's firearms namely two muskets and two pistols as well as five cutlasses and a quantity of powder and shot. They also took with them axes, saws and all the equipment needed to fell a tree and from it produce a spar which could then be brought back to the ship. The *Assam Valley* was left in the command of 1st Officer George Bruford who had with him the remaining sixteen crew. Due to a freshening wind from the north-east, Bruford had to up anchor and spend his time keeping the vessel heading to windward and, when necessary, tacking, in order to maintain some sort of position off the shore, eventually coming to within half-a-mile of the beach.

To attempt to land on the island from a small boat was difficult at any time due to the powerful surf which pounded the shore. Captain Manley and his men were seen to reach the beach safely where they dragged their boat out of the water before all disappearing into the dense undergrowth a few yards away. They were never seen again. About an hour later, at about 12.30pm, Bruford saw a group of about 30 people gathering on the beach. Through his telescope he could see that they were natives and that most came from the same area of jungle which he had seen the sailors enter. The natives seemed to be highly excited and were involved in what appeared to be dancing. Some two hours later they were observed to be taking the quarter boat from the beach.

The *Assam Valley* remained off-shore, watching, until about 5pm and, as the sun set, watches were arranged to keep an eye out for a blue light which Captain Manley had taken with him for use in an emergency. The night passed without incident and, the following morning, Bruford brought the ship close in to the shore to see if some men he could see were members of the landing party. When he was able to identify them as natives he drew the conclusion that the crew 'were either all murdered, or was prisoners'. Neither he nor any other crew member had heard any sound of gunfire during the whole time the party had been ashore. Believing that the natives were trying to lure more of the sailors ashore and, as they had no real means of defending themselves, Bruford felt that sending a search party would be dangerous in the extreme and maintained his position, hoping against hope that Manley and the other crewmen would reappear. Eventually, at 5pm on 24 March, having sailed part of the way along the west coast of the island, he decided to leave and set a course for Akyab, reaching that port on 5 April. A telegram was then sent to Rangoon describing the loss of the eight men.

On arriving at Port Blair, chief officer Bruford reported what had transpired to the authorities and the government survey vessel *Sylvia* was ordered to sail to Little Andaman to try and discover what had happened to the missing men. Commander Brooker sailed on 10 April but, on reaching Little Andaman, was unable to land due to the high surf. He did, however, manage to get close enough to the shore to see a sailor's blue cap and a piece of rope on the beach before returning to Port Blair. On 17 April the settlement steamer *Quantung* sailed for Little Andaman where two aborted attempts were made at landing from two cutters. Lieutenant F. Duncan, commanding the *Quantung,* then sailed some miles north, up the east coast, where he anchored in a more sheltered bay and on 21 April, two cutters (commanded by J. N. Homfray, assistant superintendent of the Andaman Home, and the Chief Engineer of the *Quantung* and Mr Beaumont) and a jolly boat were able to safely land a search party. A short time later, the party saw a group of local tribesmen who appeared to have hostile intentions and were trying to cut the sailors off from their boats. Discretion being the better part of valour, the party withdrew towards the boats where they came under attack from a shower of arrows fired from only 30 feet away. Two Settlement Brigade men were wounded, one through the leg and the other through the hand and their comrades, under the command of Petty Officer Cooper, opened fire to cover the retreat — 'had they not done so [they were under orders not to use violence against the natives] a number of our men might have been killed, as the aborigines knelt on the beach and took deliberate aim at them in the water, until routed by a volley.' No natives were believed to have been hit.

Campbell Douglas. [The late Mrs Frances Douglas]

The search party then re-embarked and returned to the *Quantung*.

On 6 May, the steamer *Arracan* sailed from Port Blair with a small force of soldiers from the 2/24th regiment aboard. Commanded by Lieutenant Much, two cutters and a gig were launched at 8.30 the next morning, under the overall command of acting first officer A. Dunn. Aboard the first cutter was a crew of thirteen, under the command of acting third officer Eastwood, plus a party of ten men from the 2/24th Regiment who were to act as a covering party for the men who were going ashore. Amongst these ten soldiers were Privates Murphy, Cooper, Griffiths and Bell. In the second cutter were Acting First Officer Dunn and a crew of thirteen, Lieutenant William Thomas Much, Petty Officer Alexander Wilson, six members of the Naval Brigade, *Jemadar* (Lieutenant) Mootien and four men from the Madras Sappers. In the gig, in addition to a crew of five, were J. N. Homfray, Lieutenant Glasford (9th Bengal Native Infantry, along for the ride), Dr Campbell Douglas, three sappers and four Andamanese. The second cutter manged to reach the beach and landed Lieutenant Much and his party safely but, in doing so, the boat's rudder was smashed and a new rudder was improvised from an oar. Homfray failed to get his gig through the surf but Lieutenant Glasford somehow managed to transfer to the damaged cutter while Douglas and four Andamanese swam to the shore.

The landing party immediately set about drying their equipment, particularly their ammunition, before commencing a search. They soon came across a European skull, which, according to Douglas, had been beaten in on one side 'as if with a club or an axe', as well as an ankle boot 'such as is worn by sailors' and some planking from a white painted boat. As they drew close to the edge of the beach they could see natives concealed low in the undergrowth, who began firing arrows as they approached and the soldiers were compelled to return fire.

At 11.30am, fearing that his men were running low on ammunition, Much ordered a withdrawal and signalled for Dunn's cutter to come ashore to pick them up. Unfortunately, the surf had now increased considerably and 15–20-foot high waves were hitting the beach. As the cutter approached the shore, stern first, it was capsized by the surf and Glasford was drowned.* The party then moved further along the beach in an effort to find a safer spot for the boats to come in. Douglas, however, plunged back into the sea and was able to swim out to the gig from which covering fire was being laid down by the men of the 2/24th. Three hundred yards further along the beach, Much's party discovered four bodies, partially covered by the sand with the heads protruding from the ground. Nearby was a seaman's blue cotton jacket. They naturally made the assumption that they had discovered the fate of the missing sailors. Lieutenant Much later recorded:

> … to these bodies I could not give more than a cursory glance, my whole attention being given to the critical position in which we were placed, from the want of ammunition, the apparent little chance of boats ever reaching us, and the knowledge that in our state, with the enemy down upon us in any number, our case was hopeless.

Sometime before 2pm, the boats off-shore signalled to the party to return to the original landing place where a raft managed to get through the surf and Much and three others got aboard and desperately tried to battle against the waves, but to no avail and they were swept back into the water. Sometime in the early afternoon, the cutter with the men of the 2/24th returned to the *Arracan* and Douglas, accompanied by four of the soldiers — Cooper, Murphy, Bell and Griffiths — and a native boatman named Toke, volunteered to take the boat back to try and effect a rescue of the beach party. At their first attempt, they were forced to withdraw when the boat began to fill with water. By this time, due to their struggles in the water, Much and his men had lost most of their weapons and what little ammunition they had remaining was wet. Shortly afterwards, Douglas and his men returned and five of the shore party were able to get through the surf and into the boat. After delivering them safely back to the *Arracan*, the boat returned for a third time and brought the remainder of the party to safety

* There is some secondary evidence (*Liverpool Gazette*) to suggest that Dr Douglas twice dived into the surf to save Much and Dunn when the latter's cutter was capsized. Douglas also may have tried to save Lieutenant Glasford but struck his head against a rock, becoming stunned and unable to make headway through the surf.

Painting of Campbell Douglas in the bow of the gig during the Andaman Islands VC action.

at about 5pm. Lieutenant Much later wrote in his report:

> I cannot speak too highly of the manner in which all of the party which proceeded on shore behaved; both officers and men of both services. To commence with Dr Douglas, who at the risk of his own life, gallantly made 3 trips through the surf to the shore with his soldier crew — This was accomplished by no ordinary exertion. He stood in the bows of the boat and worked her in an intrepid and seaman like manner, cool to a degree as if what he was then doing was an ordinary act of every day life. Privates Murphy, Cooper, Bell and Griffiths, his 4 gallant volunteers, behaved equally cool and collected, rowing through the roughest surf when the slightest hesitation or want of pluck on the part of any one of them, would have been attended with the gravest results, — not only to themselves, but also to the party on shore they were attempting to rescue. I can only express for myself and for those who were with me on shore, the deep sense of gratitude felt by all, for the services rendered on this occasion by Dr Douglas.
>
> I trust that no opportunity will be lost in bringing to the notice of Government, the name of one who to save the lives of others risked his own.
>
> I have great pleasure likewise in reporting the excellent manner and bearing of the Naval Brigade under Petty Officer Wilson, also of the Sappers under Jemadar Mootien, both of whom, under most trying circumstances, behaved with every degree of pluck; rendering to Mr Dunn and myself, when perfectly helpless in the surf, the greatest assistance, and helped us out to the boat, when Dr Douglas came to rescue us.

Throughout the extensive period of their foray ashore, the British party had been under regular attack. Petty Officer Alexander Wilson wrote in his report:

> The number of Andamanese killed, I can positively say, as counted by me, was 57. When Lieutenant Much and Mr Dunn and others were on the raft, we were attacked again by the natives, numbering, I should say, about 200, who retired on our firing at them. We advanced about 15 yards up the beach, and there appeared in the jungle at least a good hundred pits with bows and arrows lying alongside of them.

What had been a mercy mission had turned into a highly dangerous situation. Thanks to the actions of Douglas and his men, a potential disaster was averted, and the only life lost was that of Lieutenant Glasford.

It seemed obvious to those present that Douglas and his men were deserving of the highest award available for their gallantry on that day. Their action and the circumstances surrounding it seemed to fit perfectly the 1858 Warrant for the Victoria Cross and, accordingly their names were put forward for the award. By the time the nomination details had reached London, however, there were some in the Secretary of State for War's office who were doubting the justification in making the award.

> The Warrant of the 10th August 1858 … directs that the Cross may be bestowed in cases in which, through the courage and devotion displayed, life or public property may be saved. To establish the claim it must be clearly shown that this condition has been fulfilled in the present instance; but … although the risk incurred by Dr Douglas and the 4 soldiers was great, and their conduct most intrepid + praiseworthy, the several statements scarcely establish with certainty that the lives of their comrades would have been sacrificed if they had not been rescued. Before a decision is arrived at on the claim, it might be advisable to refer the claim to a Board of Officers who should be furnished with a copy of the Warrant, with a view to their opinion being obtained after a thorough investigation, whether the claim is established in accordance with its terms.

The matter was finally resolved by the Commander-in-Chief, HRH the Duke of Cambridge, whose department wrote:

> … the statements in this report … do establish with sufficient clearness that the lives of the party on the shore would have been sacrificed but for the intrepid action of Asst. Surgeon Douglas & the 4 men recommended …

The danger to the boatmen involved in the rescue cannot be doubted, which is highlighted by the death of Lieutenant Glasford. The threat to the men on the shore (and to those in the boat were they to be capsized) from the natives who had been attacking them for a period of several hours and the fate of the crew of the Assam Valley was clear evidence that the whole episode was fraught with danger. Of

An aged Campbell Douglas, VC, probably photographed at his daughter's home near Wells. [The late Mrs Frances Douglas]

Campbell Douglas VC in his canoe.
[The late Mrs Frances Douglas]

interest, however, is the convenient overlooking of Toke, a native Andaman islander, who was in the boat throughout the rescue but who appears to have received no recognition for his equal gallantry. Even the painting of Douglas and his men battling through the surf manages to omit him. If Douglas was on the prow of the boat, and the four privates were rowing, then Sekunie must have been in the stern, possibly handling the rudder. The various Victoria Cross warrants in 1867 did not make any provision for the award to be made to native soldiers or sailors. However, there was another older award, the Indian Order of Merit, which was bestowed upon Jamadar Mootien for his action on Little Andaman, but no such award was made to Toke.

It is significant that all reports of the events that followed described the boat which they used as a 'gig'. The *Oxford English Dictionary* definition of 'gig' is: 'Light narrow clinker-built ship's boat for oars or sails; rowing-boat chiefly used for racing'. This would suggest that this was the type of boat that Douglas had used in the recent regatta and the speed with which he was able to obtain volunteers for what was undoubtedly a hazardous and very skilled task, would suggest that Bell, Cooper, Griffiths and Murphy were in fact his original crew. The regimental history of the South Wales Borderers reinforces this theory in its description of what then transpired.

> The surf was running high and the boat was in constant danger of being swamped, but Assistant-Surgeon Douglas handled it with extraordinary coolness and skill and, being splendidly supported by the four men, who showed no signs of hesitation or uncertainty, keeping cool and collected, managed eventually to get through the surf …

Throughout the journey, Douglas stood in the bow of the boat and had given careful orders to his crew when to row, whilst shifting his own weight from side to side in an endeavour to maintain the boat's equilibrium. Despite having been involved in the activities off the coast for some nine hours and, in the case of Douglas, having swum through the surf twice, the men were not physically exhausted, another indication of the trained nature of the crew. Had the four oarsmen been a scratch crew, then it would have been sensible for Douglas to take on another team for the second journey. That he chose the same men suggests they were something special, not ordinary run-of-the-mill soldiers volunteering for an act of great danger.

With the benefit of hindsight, it would seem strange to us that, if Douglas could swim twice through the surf, why did the stranded beach party not do the same. In the 1860s, the ability to swim at all would have been an unusual talent for a private soldier to possess. Campbell Douglas' background and lifelong attachment to the water would have almost guaranteed that he was a strong swimmer. If half the men on the beach had been unable to swim, then for their comrades to leave them by swimming to boats off-shore would have been tantamount to condemning them to death. Whilst the party stayed together, as long as their ammunition held out, they could withstand the attacks of the natives.

If this scenario was repeated today, few would suggest that Douglas and his men did not warrant the award of the George Cross. When the Royal Humane Society heard of Douglas's actions, they awarded him the Silver Medal, the highest of their three awards.

Douglas remained in the army until 1882 when he retired to start a private medical practice in Canada. In 1885, when the Canadian authorities sent troops to quell the Metis uprising on the prairies he returned to military service and was appointed the first medical officer in charge of the 1st Canadian Field

Campbell Douglas, VC, on the beach at Dover after completing
his single-handed crossing of the English Channel
by canoe, June 1895. [The late Mrs Frances Douglas]

Hospital, one of two field hospitals despatched in support of the troops for the second expedition against Riel. Once again, he made a name for himself outside the world of medicine. When the arrival of the steamer *Northcote* at Saskatchewan landing was inexplicably delayed, he set off down the river in a 12-foot collapsable canoe, discovered the missing steamer (which had run aground on a sandbar) then carried on to Saskatoon, a journey of some 200 miles, where he resumed his medical duties. Returning to Britain, Douglas continued to serve in the army off and on until 1902.

He wrote several books on medical subjects and also on canoeing. As a canoeist, he achieved a number of remarkable journeys in a twelve-foot Canadian canoe, including a single-handed crossing of the English Channel in June 1895, and a single-handed voyage from New York to Boston in 1889. He also patented a modification to a folding boat which was later put into general use. He died in 1909.

Of Douglas's companions in 1867 little remains to be said. All four survived their tour of duty in Burma; Bell becoming a skilled machinist at Chatham Dockyard; Murphy emigrated to the United States where he died in 1900 and is buried in an unmarked grave; Cooper returned to his pre-army service occupation as a jeweller in Birmingham where he died in 1882 and was buried in an unmarked grave in Warstone Lane Cemetery, in the heart of Birmingham's jewellery and silver quarter. The fourth member of the boat crew, William Griffiths remained in the army and served in the various wars in the Cape Colony and Natal in 1877–8. He was a member of the fateful N° 3 Column that invaded Zululand in January 1879 and fought and died with so many of his comrades at Isandlwana on 22 January. He is buried on the battlefield in a communal grave.

David Bell, VC's grave in Woodlands Cemetery, Gillingham, Kent.

EDRIC GIFFORD
Lieutenant
2/24th (2nd Warwickshire) Regiment of Foot

Lord Gifford, VC.

Full Name: Edric Fredrick Gifford, 3rd Baron Gifford.

Place of Birth: Ropely House, Ropely, Hampshire.

Date of Birth: 5 July 1849. Baptized 11 August 1849, at Ropely.

Father: Robert Francis Gifford, 2nd Baron Gifford.

Mother: The Hon. Frederica Charlotte Fitzhardinge, daughter of Admiral Sir Maurice Fitzhardinge, 1st Baron Fitzhardinge, Member of Parliament for Gloucester.

Father's Occupation: Peer of the realm, landowner and lieutenant 6th Dragoons.

Education: Harrow School, April 1863–July 1867 (Moreton's House).

Service Record: Commissioned as ensign, 83rd Regiment of Foot, 17 April 1869; lieutenant, 30 November 1872; transferred to 24th Regiment of Foot, 26 February 1873; captain, 1 April 1874 (half-pay); ADC to GOC Ashanti, 8 February 1874–4 March 1874; Special Service officer Ashanti War, 1873–4 (present at repulse of Ashanti army at Abrakrampa, November 1873; OC scouting party from Prah to Kumasi); ADC to Sir Garnet Wolseley 1874; transferred to 57th Regiment of Foot, 31 May 1876; ADC to Major-General Sir Garnet Wolseley, GOC British troops Natal, 22 February 1875–20 October 1875; ADC to Major-General Sir Garnet Wolseley, High Commissioner for Cyprus, 10 August 1878–11 January 1879; served Anglo-Zulu War 1879 with the 57th Regiment of Foot (afterwards Mounted Infantry, present at the capture of the Zulu King, Cetewayo); ADC to Lieutenant-General Sir Garnet Wolseley, High Commissioner of Natal and GOC British troops South Africa, 7 July 1879–May 1880; brevet major, 1880; major, 24 July 1880; retired, 1882.

Decorations, Medals and Rewards: Victoria Cross (for action during the Ashanti War, 1873–4, particularly at Becquah); Ashantee War Medal (clasp for Coomassie); South Africa Medal (clasp for 1879); MinD (Ashanti and Anglo-Zulu Wars).

Post-Service Employment: Accepted the post of Colonial Secretary for Ceylon, April 1880, then offered, and accepted the post of Inspector General of Police, Mauritius; Colonial Secretary for Western Australia & senior member of Legislative Council, 1880–3; Colonial Secretary for Gibraltar, 1883–8; director of Chartered British South Africa Company, 1889 onwards.

Ampney Park, Cirencester, the childhood home of Edric Gifford. [Richard Harrow via Angela Scott]

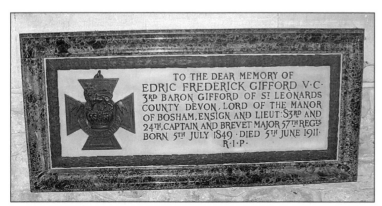

The memorial plaque to Lord Gifford, VC in Bosham Church, Sussex.

The grave of Lord Gifford, VC in Fairfield Road Cemetery, Bosham, Sussex. The gravestone is very mediaeval in style with an inscription in Latin.

Married: Sophie Catherine, daughter of General John Alfred Street, CB, 27 April 1880. She was an Honorary Serving Sister of the Order of St John of Jerusalem. She served with the Army Nursing Service in South Africa, 1900–02 and in the First World War as a hospital matron.

Children: None.

Died: 5 June 1911, at his home, Old Park, Chichester, Sussex.

Buried: 8 June 1911, at Bosham, Sussex.

Memorials: Speech Room, Harrow School; plaque in Bosham Parish Church, Sussex; gravestone in Fairfield Road Cemetery, Bosham (the original was destroyed by falling trees in October 1987 and replaced in 2001); there was a memorial to him in the Anglican Cathedral at Harare but this was removed during the 1990s; the shield and assegais of King Cetewayo were presented to Gifford.

Location of Victoria Cross: Private collection.

Citation for the Victoria Cross: *London Gazette*, 31 March 1874.
'For his gallant conduct during the operations and especially at the taking of Becquah. The Officer Commanding the Expeditionary Force reports that Lord Gifford was in charge of Scouts after the army crossed the Prah and it is no exaggeration to say that since the Adansi Hills were passed he daily carried his life in his hand in performance of his most dangerous duties. He hung upon the rear of the enemy, discovering their position and ferreting out their intentions. With no other white man with him he captured numerous prisoners; but Sir Garnet Wolseley brings him forward for this mark of Royal favour most especially for his conduct at the taking of Becquah, into which place he penetrated with his scouts before the troops carried it, when his gallantry and courage were most conspicuous.'

VC Investiture: By HM Queen Victoria at the Windsor Park Review, 30 March 1874.

Among the many 'small wars' of Queen Victoria's long reign, the Second Ashanti campaign of 1873–4 is now all but forgotten. At the time, the warriors of the Ashanti empire were regarded as a formidable enemy whose fame was only overshadowed by the rise of the Zulu nation and their success in the Anglo-Zulu War of 1879. Located in the Gold Coast (what is now Ghana) in west Africa, the Ashanti, led by King Kofi Karikari, were the most aggressive and feared tribe in the region and dominated a number of smaller groups. In 1872, the British who had controlled the coastal hinterland for many years, as a Crown territory, acquired the port of Elmina from the Dutch and refused to honour the established agreements with the Ashanti. King Kofi, who was already suffering from a declining income due to Britain's suppression of the slave trade, now feared that his last trade link with the coast was about to be severed. In June 1873, he sent an army to attack some of his neighbouring tribes and the port of Elmina. Although driven back by the small British garrison made up of 100 Royal Marines and the 2nd West India Regiment, the Ashanti refused to withdraw and regularly mounted raiding parties against the Fante tribe south-east of the river Prah. Eventually the government in London decided to send Major-General Sir Garnet Wolseley, accompanied by 35 officers, to Elmina with orders to drive the Ashanti away from the coast region and establish a long term peace. Amongst the officers on Wolseley's staff was Lieutenant the Lord Gifford.

Edric Gifford was born into a very comfortable upper class family. His grandfather, Sir Robert Gifford, having served as Solicitor-General (1817–9), Attorney-General (1819–24), Lord Chief Justice of Common Pleas (1824) and Master of the Rolls (1824–6), had been elevated to the peerage as Baron Gifford of St Leonards in Devon in 1824. Edric's father, Robert Francis Gifford, a former cavalry officer in the 6th Dragoon Guards, succeeded to the title in 1826 and the family appear to have bought Ropely House in 1844 but moved in the 1850s to Ampney Park, near Cirencester.

After completing his education at Harrow School, Edric was commissioned into the 83rd (County of Dublin) Regiment and transferred to the 24th Regiment (2nd Warwickshires) four years later. He was appointed a Special Service officer for the Second Ashanti War of 1873–4, which meant his being placed on half-pay from his regiment in

Lord Gifford, VC.

the hope that he could gain some distinction which would help to advance his future career. As this was his first active service appointment, there is every likelihood that someone had used their influence to enable an inexperienced junior officer to have the opportunity to make his name. His transfer to the 24th Regiment would appear to be a convenience rather than a carefully thought out long term career plan. Perhaps his original regiment was unable to release him for service elsewhere and exchanging into another regiment which was not quite so rigid was the only way to achieve his ambition.

Wolseley began his operations by inflicting a series of defeats on the Ashanti who were operating between the Prah and the coast. Brevet Major Baker Russell had been given command of a unit of locally enlisted men, usually referred to as 'Russell's Regiment' although its numbers fell far below the normal minimum requirement for a British regiment. Gifford was appointed Russell's adjutant. Wolseley and his staff, 250 marines and sailors, and Russell's Regiment left Cape Coast Castle for Assayboo, then moved on to Abrakrampa on 27 October where he prepared defences ready for the commencement of military operations. Russell's men then went forward towards Iscabio where they surprised a force of about 3,000 Ashanti whom they engaged and who fled into the dense forest. On 3 November, a column led by Lieutenant Gordon, made up of Hausas (from what is now northern Nigeria) and the Winnebah company of Russell's Regiment, commanded by Gifford who was anxious to join in the action. When the Winnebah made contact with the Ashanti they immediately broke and fled from the field, knocking over Gifford in their panic. The column returned to camp without seeing any further action.

At 4pm on 5 November, Gifford was present when the British camp at Abrakrampa was attacked from the west by a large Ashanti force. Fortunately, Wolseley had constructed a network of trenches and the gunfire had little effect on the defenders. The Ashanti had acquired poor quality gunpowder which meant that their musket balls had very little effect beyond about 50 yards. Even when they hit their target the effect was often little more than a bruise. The assault continued until darkness fell and then resumed the following morning. A message was sent to Wolseley who sent reinforcements who arrived at sunset. When another British column commanded by Brevet Lieutenant-Colonel Evelyn Wood, VC, attacked the Ashanti in the rear, they withdrew and retreated north.

Wolseley then offered the Ashanti a ceasefire but realised that he needed to take aggressive action into the heart of their territory if he was to bring an end to the unrest. Whilst negotiations were taking place he concentrated upon building a 12 foot wide road the 73 miles from Cape Coast Castle to the River Prah, which was carried over river and streams by an amazing 237 bridges and culverts and was carried over swamps by causeways. They also built staging camps, with roughly a day's march between them, which could accommodate 400 British soldiers and their officers as well as a regular garrison of 50 men. At Prahsu, a bridge was constructed across the 60 yard-wide Prah River.

By the end of November 1873 the region south of the Prah was peaceful and Wolseley bided his time awaiting the arrival of imperial troops to strengthen the small force already under his command.

Early in the new year, an expeditionary force was assembled of about 4,000 British troops drawn from the Black Watch, the 2nd Bn Royal Welch Fusiliers, the 2nd Bn Rifle Brigade, the 2nd West Indian Regiment, the Royal Marines, a detachment from the Royal Navy and a locally raised force of tribesmen. On 20 January 1874, the expeditionary force crossed the river Prah with the declared intention of capturing the Ashanti capital at Kumasi. Such an advance would mean Wolseley moving his force over more than 70 miles of undulating terrain, through dense tropical forest, scrubland and swampy valleys. The label the 'White Man's Graveyard' had been given to this part of Africa for good reason and Wolseley was aware that he had two enemies to contend with; the Ashanti and the tropical diseases that could render his army powerless. By the time the campaign was over, 71 per cent of the British troops had suffered from some form of tropical sickness, killing 50 of them and resulting in over 1,000 being

Garnet Wolseley: Gilbert and Sullivan's 'very model of a modern Major-General';
Gifford's mentor and commanding officer in Ashanti and South Africa.

invalided home.

From the start of the campaign, Russell's men were operating a day's march ahead of the main force. Gifford was placed in command of the forward scouting party, moving through a landscape totally unsuited to the European style of warfare that he would have spent his last few years practising, a duty which he seems to have revelled in. As Wolseley's column began their move from the River Prah, Gifford was approaching Essiaman. Moving on foot, his scouts (who had been raised by Major Redvers Buller from the Assin people, and included some Hausas, Kossos and a small number of West Indian soldiers who had proved themselves in battle) searched the landscape for information about the Ashanti army and selected the best routes forward. Each night he halted to allow elements of the main column to catch him up before moving on again at daybreak. His small command was the very tip of the British column and, as such, was in constant danger of being ambushed by the Ashanti.

When he reached Accrofoomu, Gifford ran into a large Ashanti force and had to be restrained from attacking by Baker Russell. By the following morning, when reinforced, he found the town deserted.

On 17 January, Gifford attacked a strong Ashanti defensive position on a hill overlooking the village of Moinsey, just north of the Parakoom River. Despite being greatly outnumbered, his small unit was able to outflank the position and the Ashanti withdrew without firing a shot. The following day the Army engineers caught him up and, once again, he moved off into the unknown, reaching the village of Quisah.

On 19 January, Gifford's scouts were placed under the command of Colonel McCleod who was spearheading the main British column. Moving towards the town of Fommanah, Gifford was given a clear signal of what faced him and his men were they to fall into the hands of the Ashanti. As he approached the town, he came across a wooden 'gun' in the middle of the road, with a number of knives stuck into it. Nearby was a dead man impaled on a stake. The body had been horribly mutilated and several parts cut off and hung around its neck. At the side of the road was a large pit which contained the remains of numerous victims of the Ashanti practice of human sacrifice.

By 24 January, Gifford had reached Dompoassie and sent a message to Wolseley (who had halted at Fommanah to allow his supplies to catch him up) that the main Ashanti force seemed to be retreating. Towards the end of the month as the main column approached the Dansaboo River, Gifford was across the other side entering the village of Egginassie, about a mile from Amoaful where Wolseley expected the Ashanti to make their stand. As the scouts entered the village, Ashanti guards gave the alarm and their warriors gathered in large numbers and opened fire, hitting three of the scouts and forcing Gifford to withdraw back across the river. He reported back that the Ashanti seemed ready to fight.

The following morning, 31 January, the British column moved out of its camp at daybreak, led by Gifford and 40 scouts, followed some time later by the Black Watch. Returning to the north side of the Dansaboo, they passed through the village of Quarman without hindrance. Just under a mile further on, near Egginassie, they came under heavy, but long-range musket fire from their front and their left. Undeterred, the scouts pushed on through the forward enemy line and took control of the valley. The amount of noise and smoke coming from the enemy's muskets was a clear indication that a very large Ashanti force was in position across the road and on their two flanks. It was obvious that Gifford's small force, having forced the enemy to reveal themselves, would not be able to move further and a halt was called to allow the infantry to pass through them and take up the main assault. It was impossible to get off the road and the Ashanti, for the first time firing from the dense bush at point blank range began to take a heavy toll. Lying down in the undergrowth, firing and then crawling away, they became difficult to locate and the British casualties mounted. Eventually, Egginassie was cleared and the engineers were called upon to cut paths through the undergrowth towards the upper slopes of the surrounding hills where the main Ashanti camps were believed to be located. Every small unit of soldiers was fighting for survival, even the war correspondents (who included H. M. Stanley, the man who found Dr Livingstone) were firing to stay alive. Eventually, the artillery was brought forward and, at a range of 50 yards, firing over open sights, proved lethal. After taking four hours to advance less than a mile, the column broke the Ashanti line and by 1.45pm the action was really all over. At 4pm, Gifford closely following the enemy reported that the centre and right were in full flight but on the left they were still posing a serious threat to the British supply lines. As night closed in, the fighting ended and the battle of Amoaful was over. The Black Watch alone had two men killed outright and nine officers and 104 men wounded. The Ashanti were later estimated to have had 2–3,000 casualties.

The following morning, Buller and Gifford scouted west beyond Amoaful, towards the town of Becquah, the highest point of the enemy's defensive line. There they discovered the Ashanti in occupation and a message was sent calling to infantry to assault and capture it. The attack was led by Gifford's scouts who advanced along a narrow native track, closed-in on both sides by dense bush. As he approached Becquah, he made contact with the Ashanti and was ordered 'to take it by storm'. In the intense fighting which followed, half the scouts became casualties but, supported by Gordon's Hausas, they managed to gain a foothold in the settlement which was held until members of the Naval Brigade arrived and the Ashanti withdrew.

Gifford's scouts entering Egginassie. This is probably a reasonably accurate portrayal as it was prepared for the Illustrated London News.

On 2 February, the column moved on with the advanced guard again made up of Gifford's scouts, Russell's Regiment and one company of the Rifle Brigade. At Jarbinah they came up against 1,000 Ashanti warriors in a strong position in a swamp but managed to drive them out. Time after time the modern Snider rifles had proved more than a match for the ancient ineffective muskets of the enemy and by nightfall they were in Adwabin. The next morning, after advancing for less than an hour, Gifford came up against another Ashanti force positioned on higher ground, deeply embedded in dense undergrowth, behind a small stream. Without a second thought, he launched into an attack but was too far ahead of any possible support as a consequence of which lost nearly 25 per cent of his men before Russell's men arrived. Later that day, they were ambushed several times but managed to reach the River Ordah, the last water barrier before Kumasi, by 2pm.

On 4 February the main column crossed the river and reached Ordashu, fighting for most of the time. There the artillery blasted a route through the main defensive position until the Ashanti eventually broke and fled. At 5.30pm, a little before nightfall, Wolseley's men entered Kumasi. The Ashanti king had fled and was unwilling to discuss terms. Fearing for his supplies and having achieved his objective, the Major-General ordered Buller to loot the Royal Palace and the Royal Engineers prepared it for demolition. As the British force began to withdraw at 6am, Kumasi was set ablaze.

The Ashanti forces, considering their limited resources, had fought well but, despite their superior numbers and experience of the terrain, they could not stand up to the modern military technology of the British. A peace treaty was signed at Fommanah which resulted in the collapse of the Ashanti empire, the deposition of Kofi Karikari, and the eventual destabilisation of the whole region. The bulk of the column was back at Cape Coast Castle by 20 February and the British regiments immediately began embarking for home. Wolseley had a few loose ends to tie up before sailing for Britain on 4 March.

As soon as peace had been established, Wolseley appointed Gifford as his ADC, by way of recognition for his services during the campaign. In addition, Gifford's name had been brought to the attention of Wolseley's chief of staff, Colonel Greaves, by Colonel J. M. McLeod of the Black Watch:

> I should desire specially to bring under the notice of the Major General the conspicuous good service rendered by Lieutenant the Lord Gifford, 24th Regt., in command of the scouts during the advance from the river Prah to the village of Ordasu.
>
> Ever in front of his men, he carried his life in his hand, feeling by day and by night for an enemy concealed, treacherous, cruel & crafty. In the execution of this duty, the most difficult and hazardous which could befall a British officer, he never spared himself and won my admiration by the unsparing endurance and the courageous self possession which he maintained under the most trying circumstances: often I felt the gravest apprehension for his safety and especially on the occasion at Inbubali [beyond Adwatin] where he was cut off from me for a moment and surrounded. His services exceptionally hazardous, & bravely carried out are deserving of marked recognition. I would recommend him for the Victoria Cross for his conspicuous good work in command of the scouts.

To this strong recommendation, Wolseley added his own support and submitted the recommendation to the War Office in London, the wording of which became, almost unchanged, the citation for Gifford's Victoria Cross.

The award is particularly worthy of note because it was not made for one single, courageous action, either rescuing a comrade or driving back an enemy attack. Instead, Gifford's VC is amongst the first for a continuous period of combat where the individual has displayed, on numerous occasions, a level of courage far and above the normal call of duty. Both Wolseley and McLeod emphasised the difficulties which he would have encountered, operating far ahead of the main British force in a landscape and against an enemy that would offer no mercy.

His actions in Ashanti made Gifford a very definite member of the so-called 'Ashanti Ring' (albeit at a lower level than others), a group of staff officers who enhanced their reputations serving under Wolseley, who were later to reappear alongside him in other campaigns, most noticeably in South Africa in 1879. Amongst the leading members were Evelyn Wood, VC, Redvers Buller (who was to earn the VC in the Zulu War), William Francis Butler, George Pomeroy-Colley, Archibald Alison and Baker Creed Russell. The latter had begun his army career in the 6th Dragoon Guards in 1855 and may well have been an associate of Gifford's father. That being the case, it may have been Russell who provided the introduction which the junior officer required to join Wolseley's staff in Ashanti.

Gifford remained with Wolseley in a staff capacity until 1879 when they both went to South Africa, the latter to take over command of the British forces from Lord Chelmsford after the disaster at Isandlwana. Wolseley did not meet up with Chelmsford until 7 July, three days after the Battle of Ulundi, and the war was over. All that remained was to establish the peace and capture the Zulu king Cetshwayo who had gone into hiding, moving from kraal to kraal to try and avoid the British forces. Gifford arrived on 13 July (coincidentally in the company of Baker Russell and George Pomeroy-Colley) and was given the task of hunting down Cetshwayo. Major Percy Barrow led a squadron of the 1st Dragoon Guards from Ulundi, guided by Cornelius Vijn, a Dutchman who had lived in Zululand for a number of years. Vijn had seen Cetshwayo but, by the time they reached their destination, the king had gone. Gifford joined this patrol, but left them on 15 July at the head of a small group, to scout the landscape ahead and search for clues that might lead them to the king, returning later that day with over 40 prisoners. The next morning he again set off ahead of the main party and by sunset had what seemed to be concrete evidence

Colonel John McLeod who recommended Gifford for the Victoria Cross.

about Cetshwayo's whereabouts. Barrow somehow managed to lose Gifford's trail and was forced to head back for Ulundi. That evening, Gifford questioned five prisoners. Two were flogged and later escaped and the other three refused to talk. Threatening to shoot them one at a time, he blindfolded all three and took one away before firing a gun into the air. The others then told him that they had seen the king that morning some fifteen miles away. Despite the fact that it was nearly midnight, Gifford ordered his men to mount up and began the pursuit. During the day he came across a number of clues that suggested he was on the right trail but, unknown to him, Cetshwayo knew he was coming and had watched him crossing the White Umfolozi river that morning. The king seemed to have vanished but Gifford, undaunted, spent days scouring the countryside and searching kraal after kraal.

Most of the Zulu chiefs had now surrendered and one of them, Mnyamana, was coerced by Wolseley into betraying his king who he said was hiding in the Ngome Forest. A second patrol, under the command of Colonel Clarke, left Ulundi on 23 July. Three days later, Wolseley dispatched Captain Maurice to join the hunt, followed the next day by Major Marter at the head of a squadron of the 1st Dragoon Guards, a company of the Natal Native Contingent, Lonsdale's Mounted Rifles and ten Mounted Infantry. Marter's guide was Martin Oftebro, a friend of Cetshwayo. A Zulu hinted at where the king might be and Marter headed along the trail. He then sent a message to Captain Maurice which was intercepted by Marter.

On 26 July Gifford found some of Cetshwayo's possessions in a kraal along with two Zulu boys. By again threatening to shoot one, he persuaded the other to lead him to the kraal where the king was. At dawn the following day, Gifford was shown a kraal at the foot of a steep cliff where he could just make out the figure of Cetshwayo moving around. He felt that to advance down the cliff with mounted men would be both extremely difficult and would give the Zulus ample warning of his approach. He decided to return to his campsite and wait until dark before making his move. Some time later, Marter also arrived at the cliff top, saw the kraal and decided to act at once. Removing anything that might make a noise his men began the descent leading their horses, reaching the bottom at 3am, where they remounted and charged the kraal. They caught the Zulus totally by surprise and captured Cetshwayo. That same morning they began the long walk back to Ulundi. Gifford, having heard that he had been pipped to the prize, headed for Ulundi with the news.

The Zulu king, Cetshwayo, photographed in London in 1882.

Although the king had been seized by Marter, Wolseley, ever loyal to his own 'chosen few', felt that the credit really belonged to Gifford who had spent two weeks carefully scouting and searching for his prey, slowly building up intelligence in the field. By way of a reward, Wolseley sent him to London with his dispatches; an acknowledged method of rewarding distinguished service as the 'messenger' was usually honoured in some way. In Gifford's case, he was given a grant of £300, a not inconsiderable sum in 1879.

Lord Gifford retired from the army as a major in 1882 and then commenced a distinguished career as a diplomat.

Edric Gifford was the uncle of Captain John Fitzhardinge Paul Butler, VC, DSO, King's Royal Rifle Corps, attached Pioneer Company, Gold Coast Regiment, who received the Victoria Cross for his gallantry in the Cameroons in 1914. He was also the uncle of Lieutenant-Colonel Claud Dansey, deputy chief of the British Secret Intelligence Service (MI6). Edric Gifford's younger brother, Maurice Raymond, raised a volunteer cavalry unit for service in Matabeleland in 1893 and 1896 for which service he was created a CMG. He led the Rhodesian Horse at Queen Victoria's Diamond Jubilee in 1897.

TEIGNMOUTH MELVILL
Lieutenant
1st/24th (2nd Warwickshire) Regiment of Foot

Full Name: Teignmouth Melvill.

Place of Birth: 4, Clarendon Place, London.

Date of Birth: 8 September 1842, one of ten children (eight girls and two boys).

Father: Philip Melvill, FRGS.

Mother: Eliza Melvill, daughter of Colonel Sandys of Lenarth, Helston, Cornwall.

Father's Occupation: Secretary to the Military Department of the East India Company.

Education: Harrow School, January 1856–March 1858; Cheltenham School; Trinity College, Cambridge (BA, February 1865).

Service Record: Commissioned ensign, lst/24th Regiment of Foot, 20 October 1865 (by purchase); lieutenant, 2 December 1868 (by purchase); adjutant, 7 March 1873; served Cape Colony, 1875–7; passed entrance examination for the Staff College, 1877; returned to England to attend Staff College, January 1878; returned to his regiment to serve in the Galeka War, February 1878; served Anglo-Zulu War, January 1879, with No. 3 Column (present at attack on Sirayo's Stadt, 13 January 1879, and Battle of Isandlwana, 22 January 1879).

Decorations, Medals and Rewards: Victoria Cross (for action following the Battle of Isandlwana, 22 January 1879); South Africa Medal (clasp for 1877–8–9), twice MinD; widow granted a £100 pension by Queen Victoria paid from the Civil List.

Married: Sarah Elizabeth, daughter of George Thomas Reed, Esq, of Port Elizabeth, South Africa, on 28 February 1876. She was born in Cape Colony. After her husband's death she lived in Bournemouth, England, with her sister-in-law, Elizabeth Melvill. She died at Johannesburg 14 January 1943.

Children: Two sons, Teignmouth Philip (born Cape Colony, 1877, died 1951); Charles William (born Cornwall, 1878, died New Zealand, 1925).

Died: KinA at Fugitive's Drift, Natal, 22 January 1879.

Buried: Isolated grave (with Lieutenant Coghill, VC), Buffalo River, near Fugitives' Drift, Natal, 4 February 1879. Re-interred 14 April

Teignmouth Melvill, c.1876, taken at about the time of his marriage. [Bryan H. Coode]

Teignmouth Melvill's VC and South Africa medal, displayed at the RRW Museum, Brecon.

Ethy, near Lostwithiel, Cornwall, the home of the Melvill family in the mid-nineteenth century. [Vanessa Leslie]

1879, service conducted by Padre George Smith of Rorke's Drift fame.

Memorials: Fugitives' Drift, Natal; Harrow School Chapel; Big Classical, Cheltenham School; St Winnow's Parish Church, Cornwall; Colour Pike, 24th Regiment of Foot; Harare Anglican Cathedral, Zimbabwe (believed removed 1990s).

Location of VC: RRW Museum, Brecon.

Citation for VC: *London Gazette*, 2 May 1879.

'Memorandum. Lieutenant Melvill, of the 1st Battalion, 24th Foot, on account of the gallant efforts made by him to save the Queen's Colour of his regiment after the disaster at Isandlwana; and also Lieutenant Coghill, 1st Battalion, 24th Foot, on account of his heroic conduct in endeavouring to save his brother officer's life, would have been recommended to Her Majesty for the Victoria Cross had they survived.'

The award of the first posthumous VCs during the Anglo-Boer War prompted the request to King Edward VII by Mrs Melvill that the award should be made retrospectively to her husband. The request was finally approved by the King and gazetted on 15 January 1907.

VC Investiture: The VC was sent to Lieutenant Melvill's widow in June 1907.

Philip Melvill, the father of Teignmouth Melvill. [Bryan H. Coode]

Bryan Coode, standing beside his great-great-uncle's grave [Bryan H. Coode]

Memorial window to Teignmouth Melvill in St Winnow's Parish Church.

Sarah Elizabeth Melvill, the wife of Teignmouth Melvill. [Bryan H. Coode]

Nevill Coghill, late 1878. He grew a beard shortly before the start of the operations in Zululand.

The Victoria Cross and South Africa Medal [RRW Museum (Brecon)].

NEVILL COGHILL
Lieutenant
1st/24th (2nd Warwickshire) Regiment of Foot

Full Name: Nevill Josiah Aylmer Coghill.

Place of Birth: Probably Belvidere House, Drumcondra, County Dublin, Ireland. The family also lived at: Simmon's Court, Donnybrook, Dublin; Castle Townshend, County Cork, Ireland; 3 Royal Marine Terrace, Bray, County Dublin, Ireland; 21 Bolton Studios, Redcliffe Road, London.

Date of Birth: 25 January 1852, eldest of 3 (possibly 4) boys and 4 girls.

Father: Sir Joscelyn Coghill, Bart, JP.

Mother: The Hon. Katherine Frances, daughter of John Span Plunket, QC, 2nd Baron Plunket, of Dublin. She died at Interlaken, Switzerland in 1881.

Father's Occupation: Landowner, Justice of the Peace and High Sheriff. He had served in the 59th Regiment.

Education: Haileybury School, 1865–69; RMC Sandhurst, 2nd February 1874–April 1874.

Service Record: Commissioned as supernumerary lieutenant Dublin County Militia, 13 May 1871; commissioned sub-lieutenant, 24th Regiment of Foot, 26th February 1873; lieutenant, 13 August 1875 (seniority backdated to 26 February 1873); served Cape Colony, 1877–8 as ADC to General Sir Arthur Cunynghame in the Galeka War; returned to England, 1878; returned to Cape Colony, 1879, as ADC to Sir Bartle Frere; granted six weeks leave to take part, with his regiment, in the invasion of Zululand, January 1879; ADC with Colonel Glyn's Column but, due to an injured leg, he was unable to accompany that officer when he later left the camp at Isandlwana, 22nd January 1879; present at the Battle of Isandlwana, 22nd January 1879.

Decorations, Medals and Rewards: Victoria Cross (for action following the Battle of Isandlwana, 22 January 1879); South Africa Medal (clasp for 1877–8–9); twice MinD.

Married: Unmarried.

Children: None. His brother, Egerton Bushe Coghill, named a son after him who became Professor Neville Coghill, the noted Fellow of Merton College, Oxford, translator of *The Canterbury Tales*, writer, lyricist and producer.

Died: KinA at the Fugitives' Drift, Natal, 22 January 1879.

Buried: Isolated grave (with Lieutenant Teignmouth Melvill, VC), Buffalo River, near Fugitives' Drift, Natal, 4 February 1879, service conducted by Padre George Smith of Rorke's Drift fame.

Memorials: Fugitives' Drift, Buffalo River, Natal; Colour Pike, 24th Regiment of Foot; plaque and window at Castle Townshend Parish Church, Co. Cork, Ireland; tablet Drumcondra Parish Church, Dublin; St Finbarre's Cathedral, Cork, Ireland; inscription on the war memorial and panel in the library at Haileybury School (there used to be a painting in the chapel but this was covered up in the 1930s); sword worn on parade by the Queen's Colour ensign, The Royal Welsh; *Whom the Gods Love — a memoir of Lieutenant Nevill Josiah Coghill, VC, The 24th Regiment 1852–1879*, compiled by his nephew Patrick Coghill.

Location of Victoria Cross: RRW Museum, Brecon.

Citation for the Victoria Cross: *London Gazette*, , 2 May 1879.
'Memorandum. Lieutenant Melvill, of the 1st Battalion, 24th Foot, on account of the gallant efforts made by him to save the Queen's Colour of his regiment after the disaster at Isandlwana; and also Lieutenant Coghill, 1st Battalion, 24th Foot, on account of his heroic conduct in endeavouring to save his brother officer's life, would have been recommended to Her Majesty for the Victoria Cross had they survived.'

This citation was shared with Lieutenant Teignmouth Melvill.

VC Investiture: The VC was sent to Sir E. B. Coghill, Bart, Lieutenant Coghill's brother on 6 February 1907.

*Sub-Lieutenant Nevill Coghill, c.1873.
[RRW (Brecon) Museum]*

*Belvidere House, Drumcondra, the probable birthplace of Nevill Coghill. Today this forms part of St Patrick's College of Education. The house was built in the seventeenth century and became the home of Sir John Coghill, Master in Chancery, and his son, Marmaduke, the Chancellor of the Exchequer. It eventually passed to John Cramer who assumed the name Coghill and was created 1st Baronet in 1778.
[St Patrick's College]*

Lieutenant Nevill Coghill.

The stone cross above the grave of Melvill and Coghill. This was damaged beyond repair and a new headstone now marks the grave. The headstone is inscribed: 'In memory of Lt and Adj. Teignmouth Melvill and Lt Nevill J. A. Coghill, 1st Batt. 24th Regt, who died on this spot 22nd Jany 1879, to save the Queen's Colour of their Regiment.'

Teignmouth Melvill came from a military background, his grandfather, Captain Philip Melvill, had served in India with the 73rd Highlanders and had been severely wounded and captured, remaining a prisoner for four years. Due to his disabilities, he was appointed Lieutenant-Governor of Pendennis Castle near Falmouth, thereby establishing the family's link with Cornwall. Teignmouth's father, Captain Melvill's fourth son, did not follow a career in the armed forces but became an administrator with the Honorable East India Company, eventually rising to Secretary to the Military Department before retiring to Ethy in Cornwall when the Company's Army was absorbed into the British Army following the Indian Mutiny. He married Eliza, daughter of Colonel William Sandys. Teignmouth was one of ten children, born fifteen years after his only brother, Philip. A bright boy, he graduated with a BA from Cambridge University, an unusual move for an army officer in the mid nineteenth century, which may suggest that the army was not his first choice of career. He was commissioned into the 24th Regiment in 1865 and had a fairly routine period of service until arriving in South Africa in 1875, where he was the adjutant to the 1st Battalion. Following his marriage in 1876, he travelled back to Britain on a 'long leave' the following year. Returning to Cape Colony on the *Windsor Castle* he, and the other passengers (which included his wife) and crew, were shipwrecked on 19 October 1878 on Dassen Island off the west coast of South Africa. At daybreak, Melvill and another volunteer were rowed to the mainland where they purchased a cart and horses and succeeded in

Lieutenant Teignmouth Melvill.
[Bryan H. Coode]

reaching Cape Town, some fifty miles away, by late evening where they reported the shipwreck and, the following morning, returned to Dassen Island aboard the SS *Florence*. The 160 passengers of the *Windsor Castle*, although cold and uncomfortable, were all rescued safely. Amongst them, was Sir Theophilus Shepstone, the Secretary for Native Affairs, who was to play such a key role in the forthcoming events in Natal.

No sooner was Melvill back at his post than he passed the examination for admission to the Staff College and again left for Britain on 4 December to try and secure a place on the next course. Reaching London, he undoubtedly used every contact that he had to assist him with his application but to no avail. He returned to the Cape aboard the *American*, arriving at East London on 9 March, to rejoin his battalion. During the following few months, he became deeply involved in trying to organise the various attempts to capture Sarhilli, Paramount Chief of the Xhosa people. As Philip Gon describes in his book *The Road to Isandlwana*:

> Melvill … had set his heart on capturing Sarhili. He followed up every clue to the chief's whereabouts with relentless vigour; with ten mounted men and a platoon of infantry he searched the Dwessa Forest, crossed the Bashee and scoured Bomvanaland. All his information pointed to a hide-away on the lower Bashee, but the Galeka chief stayed one jump ahead of his pursuers.

In the middle of August, Melvill again began to make preparations to return to England, and a place at the Staff College. His position as battalion adjutant seemed likely to pass to Nevill Coghill. Continuing trouble in the Transkei, however, meant that his trip was cancelled and, on 28 August, he left King William's Town, under orders from Colonel Glyn of the 1/24th Regiment, to assess the level of the trouble. He found a great deal of unrest amongst the native people, many thousands of whom were under arms and ready to take violent action against neighbouring tribes and, if necessary, the British and Boer settlers. He reported back directly to Sir Bartle Frere, stating that the situation was critical and no preparations had been made to protect the white population should the unrest turn to actual violence.

At the time of the invasion of Zululand, Melvill was with his battalion as it crossed the Buffalo river and took part in the first action, the storming of Sihayo's stronghold in the Bashee Valley on 12 January 1879 before making his way to the camp at Isandlwana.

Nevill Coghill, the son of an Irish baronet, had been one of the first to be commissioned into the army after the abolition of purchased commissions. In 1870 he sat, and passed, the entrance examination, albeit with a very low score, as a consequence of which he was obliged to serve in the Dublin Militia as a supernumerary lieutenant before being commissioned as a sub-lieutenant in the 24th Regiment of Foot. When the regiment was posted to Cape Colony from Gibraltar, he was posted back to the regimental depot at Brecon 'for further instruction', passing with exceptionally high marks and being promoted to lieutenant, with seniority backdated to 26 February 1873, the date of his original commission as a sub-lieutenant. He travelled to re-join his regiment at the Cape aboard the *European*, arriving at Cape Town on 10 February 1876. He was an ambitious young man who immediately set his sights on being appointed ADC

Sir Bartle Frere (seated centre) with members of his staff, 1878. Seated on the ground, on the left, is Lieutenant Nevill Coghill.
[RRW Museum (Brecon)]

to Lieutenant-General Cunynghame, which he attained in late August. This was an administrative post which carried duties far less onerous than those of a subaltern in a line regiment. Also, by being in close proximity to the GOC of the forces in the region, he had ample opportunity to be noticed by everyone who might be useful for his further promotion. He accompanied the general on a tour of the eastern frontier during September and October, then spent a number of weeks in the busy whirl of society life in the colony. In May 1877, he accompanied the general on a trip by sea to Durban and then overland to Pietermaritzburg, Newcastle, Standerton, Pretoria and Kimberley before news reached them of conflict breaking out between the native tribes on Cape Colony's eastern frontier. In the fighting which followed Coghill saw no direct action, describing his duties as 'work day and night combining the duties of ADC, deputy assistant adjutant-general, assistant quartermaster-general and private secretary'. His only recorded presence at an action is the small battle at Nyumaga on 13 January, where he was an observer. In March 1878, when Cunynghame was replaced as GOC Cape Colony, Coghill returned with him to Britain where he very nearly got married before sailing from Portsmouth aboard the *Tyne* on 31 July, bound, once again, for Cape Colony, arriving in Cape Town on 12 September. On his arrival he was immediately appointed ADC to the Governor, Sir Bartle Frere, just as plans were being put in motion for war with the Zulus. In a letter to his mother he wrote 'I think I can smell sulpher [sic] …' As the likelihood of war increased, Coghill asked Colonel Glyn of the 1/24th Regiment whether he could find him a place on his staff if he could persuade Frere to release him from his duties as ADC. The Colonel agreed and Coghill was appointed orderly officer for the battalion shortly after Christmas.

Coghill joined the column that crossed the Buffalo River on 12 January and, like Melvill, was present at the action against Sirhayo the following day.

The British column, under the direct command of Lord Chelmsford, encamped at the foot of Isandlwana on the evening of 20 January, some seven miles from the Buffalo River crossing at Rorke's Drift. Believing the main Zulu army to be a long way to the south, Chelmsford led a reconnaissance out from the camp during the afternoon of 21 January. One member of this group was Nevill Coghill who, whilst returning to the camp in the evening, attempted to catch some chickens; in the chase that followed he fell and badly wrenched his knee, so that he was barely able to walk and spent most of the following day confined to his tent.

On the morning of 21 January, Chelmsford ordered roughly one third of his column to carry out a reconnaissance in force of the region south-east of Isandlwana. At this time, the general had no notion that the main Zulu army was anywhere in the vicinity. By the time he returned, reports were coming into the camp of large formations of Zulus gathering within a few miles of Isandlwana, messages which Chelmsford chose to ignore. At dawn on the fateful morning of 23 January, Chelmsford led a large force south-east from Isandlwana, leaving the camp under the command of Lieutenant-Colonel Henry Pulleine of the 1/24th Regiment. Having covered some twelve miles Chelmsford's column spotted Zulu units scattering and began to follow them. At 9.30am he received a message from Pulleine which read: 'Report just come in that the Zulus are advancing in force from the left front of the camp (8.5am).' Chelmsford, failing to treat the message with the seriousness it deserved, continued with his breakfast.

A cavalry vedette sent out from Isandlwana, spotted sizeable Zulu forces moving towards the camp and delivered a report to Lieutenant Coghill who was on duty at the column headquarters. This prompted Pulleine to send his message to Chelmsford, failing to mention that the Zulu forces in the area amounted to several thousand warriors. Those in the camp, despite their lack of preparation for a full scale attack, felt confident that they had sufficient men (in excess of 1700) and firepower to repel anything the Zulus might send against them. Over the next few hours, sporadic fighting broke out between Zulus and various units sent out to act as scouts from the main camp. Towards noon, as the men in the camp began to prepare for their lunch, they were interrupted by a dramatic increase in the sound of gunfire from the surrounding area as the pickets began to encounter the advance units of the Zulu army. Within minutes, the entire British force was engaged and, as a result of the rapid firing that was taking place, it was not long before the defenders began to run low on ammunition. When the re-supply began to break down, individuals started to panic as, despite having executed great slaughter amongst the attacking Zulus, more warriors were still attacking, and breaking through the British line. Facing certain death if they remained where they were, some of the defenders tried to flee back towards the Buffalo River, several miles away. For those on horseback there was a chance of out-riding the pursuing Zulus; for those on foot, the chances of escape were almost nil.

Throughout the fighting, Lieutenant Melvill had been with Pulleine in the centre of the camp. When it became obvious that all was lost, he rode over to the 1/24th Regiment's headquarters tent knowing that the Queen's Colour was stored there and determined to try and prevent it falling into the hands of the Zulus. Fortunately, the colour, affixed to its 8-foot long pole, was secure inside its leather case. Picking it up he placed it across the front of his saddle and headed away from the camp. Coghill, likewise, remained in the centre of the camp until the last moment, then turned his horse towards the west, fighting off attempts by other, panic-stricken, fugitives to mount his horse. It was now a case of every man for himself. It is likely that his wearing of a blue patrol jacket (rather than the usual red jacket of the 24th Regiment) enabled him to pass through the attacking Zulus uninjured as Cetshwayo had given orders to kill the men in red coats. Reaching a deep gully, where other riders had dismounted to slowly lead their horses down the slope, Coghill rode down the steep slope and up the other side. Apart from the need for speed, his leg injury gave him little alternative, and he reached the top without any major problem. Shortly afterwards he caught up with Melvill and together they reached the slope leading down to the Buffalo River. Pushing and stumbling their way through the dense bush, they made it to the river bank and put their horses into the fast flowing, swollen river. Coghill made the crossing successfully but Melvill, undoubtedly encumbered by the Queen's Colour, was swept off his horse and carried towards a large boulder in mid stream. Lieutenant Higginson of the Natal Native Contingient was already clinging to the rock and Melvill called out for him to grab the colour pole. In trying to do so, Higginson lost his grip and both men were swept down stream. Zulus on the bank and on the slope above the river were now firing at the two men in the water. Observing all this from the west bank, Coghill plunged his horse back into the water and, in doing so, attracted some of the rifle fire away from the two men in midstream. Despite his horse being shot, he eventually reached them and the three were carried to the bank. In the diffcult conditions, Melvill had lost his grip on the colour pole and the Queen's Colour was washed away downstream.

By this time, some Zulus were already on the Natal side of the river and the details of the subsequent events are based upon the report later made by Lieutenant Higginson. As the three men scrambled up the slope, two Zulus were seen coming towards them. At a range of about thirty yards, Melvill shot, and killed, both. The trio then continued up the slope until both Melvill and Coghill declared themselves to be exhausted and unable to continue — the latter's injured knee was certainly a great impediment. Higginson then left them, saying he would go and find some horses. In his report to Lord Chelmsford, Higginson said he did manage to find mounts and returned to try to locate Melvill and Coghill only to discover them surrounded by Zulus and, carrying no weapons, he was unable to assist them. According to another survivor, Trooper Barker of the Natal Carbineers, Higginson approached him and asked for help. Barker helped him onto his horse at which point the lieutenant rode away, leaving the trooper to his fate. When questioned about

An artistic impression, by Charles Frith, of Coghill making a final stand above the body of Melvill.

The Wreath of Immortals presented to the 24th Regiment by Queen Victoria. Now preserved in the Havard Chapel, Brecon Cathedral.

the horse by Barker's comrades, Higginson said he had found it abandoned. Barker was later found, exhausted, having been chased on foot by Zulus for nearly three miles.

Whatever the truth was of the circumstances, the outcome for both Melvill and Coghill was the same. Sometime around 2.30pm they were both killed.

On 3 February, a patrol led by Major Black (which included Lieutenant Higginson) searched the area of the riverbank where the fugitives from Isandlwana had crossed. On the right of the steep path used by those trying to escape, they discovered the bodies of Melvill and Coghill; 'Both were lying on their backs about a yard from each other … Melvill at right angles to the path and Coghill parallel to it, a little above Melvill with his head up-hill. Both had been assegaied, but otherwise their bodies had been left untouched.' The following day, Captain Henry Harford found the lost Queen's Colour in the Buffalo River.

In a recent book some unfounded suggestions were made about the motivation behind Melvill's attempt to save the Queen's Colour. Suggesting that there was no evidence of Pulleine ever having given Melvill an order to save the Colour, the author implies that the latter took the Colour in order 'to provide himself with an excuse for leaving the battlefield … he appears to have been the only officer of the 24th who chose to abandon his men'. There is no first-hand evidence to support such a damning suggestion. If Melvill had been concerned with simply saving his own life, would he have gone to the headquarters tent to retrieve the Colour and then carry such an unwieldy object for several miles under the constant threat of attack from, not only Zulus, but also British soldiers desperate to obtain a horse to enable them to flee to safety? Even when he reached the river and lost his horse, and had witnesses to that fact, he continued to cling on to the colour pole until the power of the water took it away from him.

On 2 May 1879, the *London Gazette* carried a notice, prefaced by the word 'Memorandum' to the effect that both Melvill's and Coghill's names would have been submitted to HM Queen Victoria for the award of the Victoria Cross, had they survived. This type of citation, now generally referred to as the 'memorandum procedure' had been used for some potential VC recipients during the Indian Mutiny. General Sir Hastings Doyle approached Sir John Coghill, father of Nevill, by 'influential request' to state that the War Office authorities 'required to ascertain in what manner it would be most agreeable to him to have his son's conduct recognised'. Sir John replied, 'send the parent the Victoria Cross so nobly earned by these officers.' The request was refused with the remark that 'it was impossible, that the Cross was for the breast of a living man and not a dead one, and that to do so would be acting in contravention of the Victoria Cross Warrant' [Letter to R. B. Haldane, Secretary of State for War]. However, in 1858, Victoria Crosses had been delivered to the relatives of Lieutenants Home and Salkeld and Cornet Bankes, all of whom had been killed in action; a precedent had arguably therefore been set. On 15 May 1879, a recommendation was made by the authorities in India for a Victoria Cross to be awarded to Lieutenant Walter Hamilton for his actions on 2 April. Unfortunately, Lieutenant Hamilton was killed on 3 September, *before* any decision had been made in London. The subsequent submission to Queen Victoria was deliberately dated 1 September in order to avoid 'an awkward precedent in giving the decoration after death'. The award was gazetted on 7 October and the Cross sent to Hamilton's father.

In the cases of Melvill and Coghill, a number of other factors played their part in the awards not being made.

1. Both officers had been killed in the action for which the Victoria Cross would have been awarded.
2. The senior officer in South Africa, Sir Garnet

The slopes above Fugitives Drift on the Buffalo River (middle left) with the graves of Teignmouth Melvill and Nevill Coghill in the centre foreground.

Wolseley, had not made any recommendations for the award. His attitude towards a number of VC awards in the Zulu War would suggest that he had a strong feeling against making any awards that might strengthen the position of his predecessor, Lord Chlemsford.

3. The senior officer of the 1/24th Regiment, Colonel Glyn, whilst praising the two officers concerned, had not made a specific recommendation for the award.

4. The suggestion that Melvill and Coghill should receive a 'Memorandum'-style citation came from the C-in-C, the Duke of Cambridge himself, a man who had no direct involvement with the war in South Africa.

5. An unwritten fifth factor was the feeling amongst some senior officers that Melvill and Coghill were fleeing from a disastrous battle at the time of the events described, and were therefore undeserving of the highest award.

In the end, the matter was quietly allowed to disappear as the focus of the Horse Guards and the British public shifted away from Zululand and on those military events occurring in Afghanistan and in the Transvaal.

In 1897, further 'Memoradum' applications were made, following the decision 'The Victoria Cross cannot be forwarded to the relatives of a soldier unless he has been recommended for it or it had been provisionally conferred upon him whilst alive'. Two years later, however, Lieutenant The Hon. Frederick Roberts, son of Field-Marshal Earl Roberts, VC of Kandahar, was given a 'Memorandum' recommendation for the Victoria Cross as he had died of his wounds on 17 December 1899, two days after the action. Despite this, the award was gazetted on 2 February 1900, and the Cross was presented to his father by Queen Victoria herself. If Lieutenant Roberts had fulfilled the criteria of being alive at the time of the recommendation, he had only just scraped in. Unfortunately for the student of the VC, the documentation for this award has not survived. This decision led to a number of questions being asked about posthumous awards, although it would appear that no further award was made during the Anglo-Boer War that raised any doubt that the regulations were being strictly adhered to. In the case of Lieutenant F. N. Parsons, Lord Roberts himself intervened to try and have the award made but the C-in-C, Lord Wolseley, insisted that the ruling could not be changed.

By 1902, with Lord Roberts as C-in-C of the British Army, the situation changed. Whilst those in senior military positions were in favour of maintaining the unchanged ruling, Roberts tended towards the views of the families of men who, had they survived, would have been recommended for the Victoria Cross. The ageing field-marshal was, after all, not only the recipient of a Victoria Cross, but the father of a son who had died in a VC action. A list was drawn up of men who fitted into the debated category who had died during the recent conflict in South Africa and, on 8 August 1902, six names were gazetted under the wording 'The King has been graciously pleased to approve the decoration of the Victoria Cross being delivered to the relatives of the undermentioned officers, NCOs and men who fell during the recent operations in South Africa in the performance of Acts of Valour which would, in the opinion of the C-in-C of the forces in the Field, have entitled them to be recommended for that distinction had they survived.' This immediately raised the question of similar awards being made to 'Memorandum' cases from before the Anglo-Boer War, including Lieutenants Melvill and Coghill. The general fear in the War Office was that they had opened the flood gates to numerous cases dating back to the Crimean War. In reality, the number of claims was small — six — being restricted to those 'Memorandum' cases which had not already been awarded the VC. King Edward VII was stringently opposed to the making of such awards, but letters of support came from many quarters (including the then historian of the Victoria Cross, Philip Wilkins). Mrs Melvill herself wrote on 1 December 1906:

It is my most earnest wish that the VC should be in my possession to hand to my sons, one an officer in His Majesty's Army, as an heirloom in order to keep in memory of the deed performed at Isandula,[sic] Zululand 1879. I feel sure when His Majesty has been made acquainted with the facts of the case he will give ear to my petition and will graciously sanction the issue of this much prized decoration, the gaining of which cost my husband his life in the Service of His Queen and in defence of the Colours of his Regt. The VC has I know been given to relatives of deceased officers and I venture to hope that it may be given to us.

After lengthy deliberations it was decided that such an award would be made to the six men — Private Edward Spence (Indian Mutiny, 1858); Ensign Everard Aloysius Lisle Phillips (Indian Mutiny, 1857), Trooper Frank Baxter (Mashonaland, 1896); Lieutenant Hector McLean (Tirah, India, 1897); Lieutenant Teignmouth Melvill; and Lieutenant Nevill Coghill (Anglo-Zulu War, 1879).

2nd Lieutenant Teignmouth Philip Melvill, the eldest son of Teignmouth Melvill, VC. [Bryan H. Coode]

2nd Lieutenant Charles William Melvill, the second son of Teignmouth Melvill, VC. [Bryan H. Coode]

The debate about how deserved Melvill and Coghill's awards were is one for which there can never be a definitive answer. Those raising such doubts do so after a very lengthy passage of time, without any new evidence. We can therefore only look at the two cases in the light of hard, factual knowledge. Amidst all the doubt, the confusion of war, and the real lack of solid evidence, certain facts remain undisputed:

1. Melvill *did carry* the Queen's Colour away from Isandlwana and prevented its capture by the enemy.
2. Coghill, despite his injured knee and inability to function without a horse, *did return* to the Buffalo River in an effort to save the lives of Lieutenants Melvill and Higginson and, at the same time, bring the Queen's Colour to the relative safety of the Natal bank.
3. Both men died as a result of their endeavours when either, or both, could have survived had they not been encumbered with the Queen's Colour or by assisting each other.

On this basis, in the eyes of their contemporaries, both men merited the Victoria Cross.

Teignmouth Melvill's sons both followed him into the army. The eldest, Teignmouth Philip Melvill, known as 'Shabash', was commissioned into the South Wales Borderers but, because of a passion for polo, transferred into the 17th Lancers. He saw active service on the Western Front throughout the First World War, eventually rising to the rank of colonel and gaining the DSO. He was a member of the Great Britain polo team that won the Gold Medal at the 1920 Olympic Games in Antwerp. He died in 1951. Charles William Melvill served with the South Lancashire Regiment in India before emigrating to New Zealand where he joined the New Zealand Staff Corps. He served in the First World War and commanded the 1st NZ Infantry Brigade (1917) and later became GOC New Zealand Forces. He was awarded the DSO and the Croix de Guerre, and was created a CMG, CB and an officer of the Ordre de la Couronne (Belgium). He died in 1925.

Outline of the Defence of Rorke's drift, 22/23 January, 1879

On 21 January 1879, 'B' Company, 2/24th Regiment was stationed at Rorke's Drift Mission Station on the Natal side of the Buffalo River, a short distance from the point at which No 3 Column had crossed into Zululand. The previous day, Lord Chelmsford had led the column away from the river towards its fateful encounter with the Zulus at Isandlwana. Also at Rorke's Drift were small detachments of Royal Engineers (OC Lieutenant John Chard), medics (OC Surgeon Major Reynolds), a commissariat unit (OC Assistant Commissary Walter Dunn), members of the Natal Native Contingent (OC Captain Stevenson) and Acting Army Chaplain, the Reverend George Smith, vicar of Estcourt, Natal. In addition there were a number of men in the hospital suffering from various complaints, some of whom were later able to defend themselves whilst about 20 others were totally defenceless. The whole garrison was under the command of Brevet Major Henry Spalding. There was no reason for those at the post to be concerned, the main army was heading into enemy territory with Chelmsford's avowed intention of bringing the main Zulu army to battle as soon as possible. The thought that victory might go to the Zulus did not enter the minds of anyone.

On 22 January, the Royal Engineers, led by Chard, moved out of the post to join the main British force at Isandlwana where, upon arrival, Chard was told to leave his men and return to Rorke's Drift, where he found Spalding about to leave for Helpmekaar to hurry along the movement of Captain Rainforth's company of the 2/24th, which should already have arrived at the Buffalo River. As RE officers were commissioned directly into the rank of lieutenant, Chard, despite having served for a year less than Bromhead, was technically the senior officer and consequently Spalding placed him in command of the post.

Shortly after lunch, fugitives from the British camp at Isandlwana began arriving at Rorke's Drift with the news of the disaster that was taking place only a few miles away. Most thought that the mission station would be attacked and overwhelmed in a short period of time and rode on further into Natal. Lieutenant Adendorff of Lonsdale's Regiment, Natal Native Contingent decided to remain at the post, and Lieutenant Bromhead and Assistant Commissary Dalton began to prepare defensive positions linking together the hospital and store buildings.

At about 4.20pm, some firing was heard behind a large hill which overlooked the drift and Captain Stevenson and his men decided that discretion was the better part of valour and left for Helpmekaar. As the men rode away, the men of B Company, furious at being left understrength, opened fire on them. One man, Corporal Bill Anderson, was hit in the head and killed (quite possibly by Private Fred Hitch).

Some ten minutes later, the first Zulus were spotted coming around the hill to the south of the post and the fighting commenced. Contrary to the general perception of the battle for Rorke's Drift, the Zulus did not hurl themselves lemming-like into the massed fire-power of the ranks of defending British soldiers. Far from it, their attacks were well thought out and moved from one part of the defence to another, testing the relative strengths and weaknesses of the defenders and their positions. The ground around the mission station was well covered with scrub and intersected with ditches and stone walls. All gave ample cover for the Zulus who could not be fired upon until they were very close to the defensive positions. The defenders now numbered only 154 men who were spread very thinly around the perimeter. The main Zulu force arrived a few minutes after the vanguard and it is estimated that their total strength was somewhere in the region of 4,000 warriors. Some Zulus were equipped with firearms and some of these positioned themselves on the hill overlooking the post and began a sustained harassing fire into the rear of the British position whilst they were defending the northern and western perimeter.

The early assaults were made from the north/north-west against the hospital building and that corner of the defensive wall. Gradually, they moved along until, by 6pm, they were attacking the entire northern side of the post. Fearing that the Zulus would overwhelm the northern wall, Chard decided to reduce the area which had to be defended by falling back to an inner wall which had been constructed of biscuit boxes running from the north-west corner of the store to the northern wall. In doing this, Chard realised he was effectively abandoning those men fighting inside the hospital. Now, able to shelter behind the abandoned walls in the north-east area of the post, the Zulus managed to set light to the thatch on the roof of the hospital and there a desperate struggle began as men fought from room to room to save not only themselves but also the disabled patients.

Chard then ordered the construction of a raised redoubt of mealie bags inside the new perimeter defences which gave the defenders a field of fire of about 270°. As darkness fell after 7pm, the Zulu attacks moved eastwards, completely surrounding the beleaguered garrison who were beginning to realise that their ammunition might run out if the fighting did not ease up. Bromhead, who may not have had a dazzling career up to this date, was a good infantry

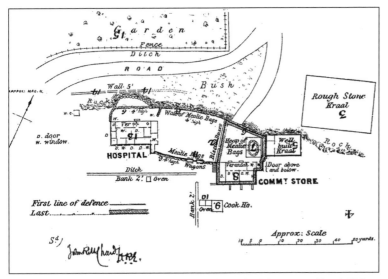

Sketch plan of the station at Rorke's Drift, drawn by Lieutenant Chard, VC.

officer, popular with his men, with an excellent understanding of how a company operated and, most importantly, he was fully conversant with the use and effect of the Martini-Henry breech-loading rifle, probably the most effective small-arms weapon of its time. He maintained a calming influence on his men, advising them to make every round count. In the words of historian Lieutenant-Colonel Snook: 'Hearing their company commander's voice did them a power of good. It exerted a steadying effect. B Company calmed itself, steeled itself and shot straighter.'

The Zulu assaults then began to peter out, but until midnight, they kept up a heavy fire from behind the cover of the walls and the darkness. During the early hours of the morning, as Chard later recorded, 'although they kept us constantly on the alert, by feigning as before, to come on at different points, the fire was of a desultry character. Our men were careful, and only fired when they could see a fair chance … a few shots from the Zulus, replied to by our men — again silence, broken only by the same thing repreatedly happening.'

At daybreak, the defenders peered into the grey light and saw nothing; the Zulus had withdrawn to the south-west. Chard and Bromhead reorganised their defences, strengthened the barricades and removed the thatch from the roof of the store in anticipation of the renewal of the attacks. At 7am, a large Zulu force was seen on the hills to the south-west but, unbeknown to the defenders, they were not returning. Far from it, the Zulus had seen the forward units of Lord Chelmsford's column coming from the direction of Isandlwana and were shortly to start withdrawing back across the river into Zululand.

At 8am, the British column came into view and the last Zulus disappeared. A detachment of mounted men led by Major Cecil Russell, forded the river and rode up to the mission station. The following day, the British buried 351 Zulu bodies for the loss of fourteen men (plus Corporal Anderson and two further men who later died of their wounds). Six men were severely wounded, nine were slightly wounded. It was a remarkable feat of arms and all ranks were to be commended for their action during the evening and night of 22/23 January in what was to become the most famous small force action of the Victorian period. Amongst the dead was Private Joseph Williams (1398) of Monmouthshire who, had he not been killed in the defence of the hospital, would almost certainly have been added to the list of names recommended for the Victoria Cross. He had fought alongside John Williams who had broken through the wall into the next room and dragged the patients through, whilst Joseph Williams kept the Zulus at bay. John Williams last saw him fighting desperately at the external door, unable to make a dash for the comparative safety of the next room. Had he tried to save himself, the Zulus would have been through the door. The following morning, fourteen dead Zulus were discovered outside his position. Somewhere outside the building, Joseph Williams was overwhelmed and killed.

In the days which followed, eleven of the defenders of Rorke's Drift were nominated and awarded the Victoria Cross. A further five were nominated for the Distinguished Conduct Medal (only four were awarded (to Colour-Sergeant Frank Bourne, 2/24th; Corporal Francis Attwood, Army Service Corps; Private William Roy, 1/24th; and Wheeler John Cantwell, Royal Artillery), the fifth (to Corporal Michael McMahon, Army Hospital Corps) was withdrawn for misconduct.

Lieutenant Gonville Bromhead.

Brevet Major Gonville Bromhead, VC, c.1880.

The VC, South Africa medal and Burma medal displayed at the RRW Museum (Brecon).

GONVILLE BROMHEAD
Lieutenant
2nd/24th (2nd Warwickshire) Regiment of Foot

Full Name: Gonville Bromhead.

Place of Birth: Versailles, France. The family home was at Thurlby Hall, Newark, Lincolnshire.

Date of Birth: 29 August 1845 (or 1844). He was the youngest son. His brothers were: Captain Edward Bromhead (died Burma, 1869); Colonel Sir Benjamin Parnell Bromhead, CB; Colonel Charles James Bromhead. His sisters were: Frances Judith; Helen Morrison; Alice Margaret; Janetta Gonville; Victoria Gonville; Elizabeth Frances.

Father: Sir Edmund de Gonville Bromhead, 3rd Bart (1791–1870).

Mother: Judith Coristine Cahill Bromhead, daughter of James Wood of Woodville, Co. Sligo, Ireland (1798–1873).

Father's Occupation: Retired major, landowner. As a lieutenant in the 54th Regiment, he served in the Waterloo campaign and was present as part of a British brigade at Hal, blocking any attempt by the French to sweep around to the north of the main Allied army at Waterloo. He was the son of Lieutenant-General Sir Gonville Bromhead who served at Quebec with Wolfe.

Education: Magnus Grammar School, Newark-on-Trent, 1859–64.

Service Record: Commissioned ensign 2nd/24th Regiment of Foot, 20 April 1867 (by purchase); lieutenant, 28 October 1871; 1st Class Certificate, School of Musketry, Hythe, 4 December 1875; served in Eastern Cape (1878), Natal (1878–9) and Zululand (1879, present at the defence of Rorke's Drift, 22/23 January 1879); captain and brevet major, 23 January 1879; major, 4 April 1883; served India, 1880–82; School of Musketry, Hythe, 1882 (First Class Extra Certificate); served in Burma, 1886–8.

Decorations, Medals and Rewards: Victoria Cross (for action at Rorke's Drift, Natal, 22/23 January 1879); South Africa Medal (clasp for 1877–8–9); India General Service Medal (clasps for Burma

1885–7 and Burma 1887–9); brevet major (for action at Rorke's Drift, Natal, 22/23 January 1879); MinD (Natal, 1879); Sword of Honour from the City of Lincoln; presented with a revolver by the tenants of Thurlby Hall.

Married: Unmarried.

Children: None.

Died: 9 February 1891, at Camp Dabhaura, Allahabad, India (of enteric fever).

Buried: New Cantonment Cemetery, Allahabad, India.

Memorials: Magnus Church of England School, Newark-on-Trent (where there is a Bromhead House and a permanent exhibition about his life); stained-glass window in St Germain's Church, Thurlby; New Cantonment Cemetery, Allahabad, India; Havard Chapel, Brecon Cathedral. *Honour the Brave*, a grand slow march for pianoforte, by J. Riviere with words by H. Hersee, dedicated to the heroes of Rorke's Drift, 1879.

Location of Victoria Cross: RRW Museum, Brecon.

Citation for the Victoria Cross: *London Gazette*, , 2 May 1879.

'For their (Bromhead and Lt M. Chard who commanded the defenders at Rorke's Drift) gallant conduct at the defence of Rorke's Drift, on the occasion of the attack by the Zulus on the 22nd and 23rd January 1879.

'The Lieutenant-General Commanding the troops reports that, had it not been for the fine example and excellent behaviour of these two Officers, under the most trying circumstances, the defence of Rorke's Drift post would not have been conducted with that intelligence and tenacity which so essentially characterised it.

'The Lieutenant-General adds that its success must, in a great degree, be attributable to the two young Officers who exercised the Chief Command on the occasion in question.'

VC Investiture: By Lieutenant-General Sir Garnet Wolseley, GCMG, KCB, High Commissioner and GOC British Troops South Africa, at Utrecht, Transvaal, 11 September 1879.

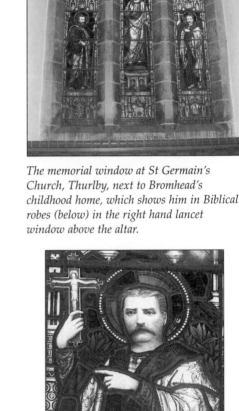

The memorial window at St Germain's Church, Thurlby, next to Bromhead's childhood home, which shows him in Biblical robes (below) in the right hand lancet window above the altar.

The grave of Gonville Bromhead (white cross) at the New Cantonment Cemetery, Allahabad, India. The large dark cross next to it is the memorial to the soldiers and families of the 2/24th Regiment who died whilst the regiment was serving in India. Bromhead's name also appears on this memorial, a total of 101 names, most of whom died of disease. [Martin Everitt]

Lieutenant Bromhead, born at Versailles, France in 1844, was christened Gonville — as had nearly all family members (both male and female) — in recognition of their descent from Edmund Gonville, the founder of Gonville and Caius College, Cambridge. The Bromheads had a military pedigree going back for several generations: his grandfather had served with Wolfe and in the American War of Independence and his father in the Waterloo campaign. Gonville's eldest brother, Edward, was commissioned into the 4th Regiment of Foot, saw active service in the Crimea, and died in Burma in 1869. His second brother, Benjamin Bromhead, served with the Indian Army (his daughter, Janetta Hope Gonville Bromhead, was the wife of Field Marshal Lord Birdwood of ANZAC). His third brother, Charles James, of the 24th Regiment, saw active

The old Magnus School buildings, Newark.

service in the Ashanti and Anglo-Zulu Wars and was the officer selected to present the Queen's Colour of the 1/24th Regiment to Queen Victoria following its recovery from the Buffalo River in 1879.

Gonville's childhood mostly slipped by without record and it is likely that he spent much of it in Ireland with his uncle, Sir Edward Thomas ffrench. The first documented reference to him appears in the admissions register of the Magnus Grammar School, where he was admitted as a boarding pupil, aged 15 years, for the mid-summer term of 1859. He remained a pupil at the school until Christmas 1864 (a note alongside this entry records 'Hero of Rorke's Drift, RIP'). There are no surviving academic records of his period at the school (which was housed in a Tudor/Georgian building in the centre of Newark) although there is a brief description of his talents on the cricket ground. The school's 1st XI, coached by leading local professionals, was noted even in a 'cricket mad' county such as Nottinghamshire. Gonville Bromhead was a left-handed, medium pace bowler and he appears in the only known photograph of the team, dressed in scarlet shirts and caps, taken in 1863. Unfortunately, he appears to be the only member to have moved during the session and, therefore, his image is the least clear. He was twenty years of age before he left the school and details of the following three years, until he was commissioned into the 2/24th Regiment, are a blank.

His first period of active service began in 1878 when his regiment was posted to Cape Colony. In April of that year, Captain Goodwin-Austen, OC B Company, was accidentally shot and wounded in the back, as a consequence of which, Bromhead was given command of the company. He is remembered by the Bromhead family as a somewhat quiet, unassuming man which seems to fit in well with the image that has survived of him as an army officer. He appears to have suffered from a profound hearing defect which made it difficult for him to react to orders on the parade ground and this may have been the cause of his somewhat retiring personality. It is likely that this handicap had manifested itself after his entry into the army and was unknown to those not in direct contact with him. There is a possibility that it did not exist before the action at Rorke's Drift or was at least intensified by the continual percussive noise of the guns during the fighting there. When Sir Garnet Wolseley decorated both Bromhead and Lieutenant Chard with the Victoria Cross in September 1879, he disparagingly remarked: 'I have now given away these decorations to both the officers who took part in the defence of Rorke's Drift, and two duller, more stupid, more uninteresting even or less like Gentlemen it has not been my luck to meet for a long time.' At the same time, Major Francis Clery, a staff officer, wrote: 'Chard and Bromhead … are almost typical in their separate corps of what could be termed the very dull class. Bromhead is a great favourite in his

The Magnus School Cricket XI; Gonville Bromhead is standing on the extreme right.
[Magnus School, Newark]

Artist's impression of Gonville Bromhead, VC.

regiment and a capital fellow at everything except soldiering. So little was he held to be qualified in this way from unconquerable indolence that he had to be reported confidentially as hopeless. This is confidential as I was told it by his CO.' Whilst in no way complimentary, these descriptions of Bromhead can be seen in a different light if one bears in mind his hearing problem. Whatever the reason, Bromhead's company was chosen to remain behind at Rorke's Drift whilst the remainder of the central column crossed into Zululand in January 1879, Major Henry Spalding of the 104th Regiment, one of Lord Chelmsford's staff officers, had been placed in command of the mission station, with Lieutenant Bromhead in charge of defence.

On the morning of 22 January, Spalding decided to leave Rorke's Drift and ride to the town of Helpmakaar to expedite the movement of additional infantry to guard the river crossing. Before leaving, he appointed Chard to take command of the post in his absence. Although Bromhead had been commissioned in 1867 and Chard in 1868, the latter had always held the rank of lieutenant whereas Bromhead had only been promoted to lieutenant in 1871. Shortly after Spalding's departure, reports began to arrive of the Zulus' successful attack on the main camp at Isandlwana. Initially, the two officers thought that their best option was to abandon the post and withdraw their men towards Helpmakaar. Acting Assistant Commissary Dalton quickly pointed out to them that such a move would be suicidal, that the rapidly moving Zulu forces would quickly overhaul them and attack the slow moving force in the open. The decision was then made to prepare the mission station to withstand a Zulu attack.

Utilising the large supply of mealie sacks, the two stone buildings were linked together and a second line of defence was built using biscuit tins. By the time the Zulu forces reached the post, the defenders had been reduced to 104 men and 35 hospitalised soldiers, some of whom were able to play their part in the defence, but others were totally unable to fight, suffering as they were from various debilitating illnesses.

As Chard was in command of the post, it was he who wrote the official report and Bromhead left nothing by way of any personal memories of the events of 22/23 January 1879. A naturally shy man, he spent very little time back in Britain before leaving for service in Burma and India, where he died. Undoubtedly, had he lived to old age, the Victorian media would have pressed him to obtain his account of the events at Rorke's Drift. His movements can, however, be pieced together from the report prepared by Chard for Queen Victoria in February 1880.

Lieut Adendorff of Lonsdale's Regiment, Natal Native Contingent, asking if I [Chard] was an officer, jumped off his horse … and told me that the camp [Isandlwana] was in the hands of the Zulus and the army destroyed. … I had the saddle put on my horse, and while I was talking to Lieut Adendorff, a messenger arrived from Lieut Bromhead, who was with his Company at his little camp near the Commissariat Stores, to ask me to come up at once.

I galloped up at once to the Commisariat Stores and found that a pencil note had been sent from the 3rd Column by Capt. Allen Gardner to state that the enemy were advancing in force against our post — Lieut Bromhead had, with the assistance of Mr Dalton, Dr Reynolds and the other officers present, commenced barricading and loopholing the store building and the Missionary's house, which was used as a Hospital, and connecting the defence of the two buildings by walls of mealie bags, and two wagons that were on the ground.

I held a consultation with Lieut Bromhead, and with Mr Dalton, whose energy, intelligence and gallantry were of the greatest service to us, and whom I said in my report at the time, and I am sure Bromhead would unite with me in saying again now, I cannot sufficiently thank for his services.

About 4.20pm the sound of firing was heard behind the Oscarberg. The officer of Durnford's returned, reporting the enemy close upon us, and that his men would not obey his orders but were going off to Helpmakaar, and I saw them, about 100 in number, going off in that direction. … About the same time Capt. Stephenson's detachment of Natal Native Contingent left us — probably most fortunately for us. I am sorry to say that their officer, who had been doing good service in getting his men to work, also deserted us. We seemed very few, now all these people had gone, and I saw that our line of defence was too extended, and at once commenced a retrenchment of biscuit boxes, so as to get a place we could fall back upon if we could not hold the whole.

Private Hitch, 24th, was on the top of the thatch roof of the Commissariat Store keeping a look-out … We had not completed the wall two boxes high when, about 4.30pm, Hitch cried out that the enemy was in sight, and he saw them, apparently 500 or 600 in number come around the hill to our south (the Oscarberg) and advance at a run against our wall.

We opened fire on them, between five and six hundred yards, but only for a short time … The men were quite steady, and the Zulus began to fall very thick. However it did not seem to stop them at all, although they took advantage of cover and ran with their faces near the ground. it seemed as if nothing would stop them, and they rushed on in spite of their heavy

The members of 'B' Company, a photograph taken shortly after the events of 22/23 January 1879. Amongst those who can be identified are: Colour Sergeant Bourne (extreme left A), Lt Bromhead VC (front row left B), Pte John Williams (second row, centre C), Pte Henry Hook (third row, extreme right, D), Pte William Jones (back row, centre, E). [RRW Museum, Brecon]

losses to within 50 yards of the wall, when they were taken in flank by the fire from the end wall of the store building, and met with such a heavy direct fire from the mealie wall, and the Hospital at the same time, that they were checked as if by magic.

They occupied the Cook-house ovens, banks and other cover, but the greater number, without stopping, moved to their left around the Hospital, and made a rush at the end of the Hospital, and at our north-west line of mealie bags. There was a short but desperate struggle during which Mr Dalton shot a Zulu who was in the act of assegaing a corporal of the Army Hospital Corps, the muzzle of whose rifle he had siezed, and with Lieut Bromhead and many of the men behaved with great gallantry. The Zulus forced us back from that part of the wall immediately in front of the Hospital, but after suffering very severely in the struggle were driven back into the bush around our position.

Coporal John Lyons recorded that at this stage Lieutenant Bromhead '… was on the right face, firing over the mealies with a Martini-Henry. Mr Chard was also very busy, I only turned round once to see this, and in that brief interval I saw Private Cole shot, and he fell dead.' Hitch noted that:

It was then about when Mr Dalton was shot and Mr Dunn. We had to fall back to the second line of defence, and when the Zulus took possession of the Hospital, Bromhead and myself and five others took up the position on the right of the second line of defence which we were exposed to the cross fire. Bromhead took the centre and was the only one that did not get

wounded, myself was the last of the six shot. Bromhead and myself had it to ourselves about an hour and a half, Bromhead using his rifle and revolver with deadly aim. Bromhead kept telling the men not to waste one round. About this time all was pressed very much, Bromhead was using his revolver with deadly aim. They seemed determined to remove Bromhead and myself. We were so busy that one had [got] inside and was in the act of assegaiing Bromhead. Bromhead not knowing he was there, I put my rifle on him knowing at the same time it was empty, instead of him delivering the assegai, which no doubt would have been fatal, he dodged down and hopped out of the laager.

Rorke's Drift today. The building on the right is the rebuilt hospital.

Punch cartoon showing the eponymous character dressed as a field marshal, greeting two of the heroes of Rorke's Drift, Lieutenants Chard and Bromhead.

Later, having been wounded, Hitch was unable to use his rifle.

I tried to keep my feet, but could not, he could have assegaiied me had not Bromhead shot him with his revolver. ... I was able to make another stand, getting Bromhead's revolver, and with his assistance in loading it I managed very well with it. At this time we were fighting by the aid from the burning hospital, which was much to our advantage.

Chard's report continued:

Our fire at the time of these rushes of the Zulus [on the hospital] was very rapid — Mr Dalton dropping a man each time he fired his rifle, while Bromhead and myself used our revolvers. The fire from the rocks and caves on the hill behind us was kept up all this time and took us completely in reverse, and although very badly directed, many shots came among us and caused us some loss — and at about 6.00 pm the enemy extending their attack further to their left, I feared seriously would get in over our wall behind the biscuit boxes. I ran back with 2 or 3 men to this part of the wall and was immediately joined by Bromhead with 2 or 3 more. The enemy stuck to this assault most tenaciously, and on their repulse, and retiring into the bush, I called all the men inside our retrenchment — and the enemy immediately occupied the wall we had abandoned and used it as a breastwork to fire over.

All this time the enemy had been attempting to fire the hospital and had at length set fire to its roof and got in at the far end. ... The garrison of the Hospital defended it with the greatest gallantry, room by room, bringing out all the sick that could be moved, and breaking through some of the partitions while the Zulus were in the building with them. Privates Williams, Hook, R. Jones and W. Jones being the last to leave and holding the doorway with the bayonet, their ammunition being expended. ... Surgeon Reynolds carried his arms full of ammunition to the Hospital, a bullet striking his helmet as he did so. But we were too busily engaged outside to do much, and with the Hospital on fire, and no free communication, nothing could have saved it.*

Corporal Schiess, Natal Native Contingent, who was a patient in the Hospital with a wound in the foot, which caused him great pain, behaved with the greatest coolness and gallantry throughout the attack, and at this time creeping out a short distance along the wall we had abandoned, and slowly raising himself to get a shot at some of the enemy who had been particularly annoying, his hat was blown off by a shot from a Zulu the other side of the wall. He immediately jumped up, bayoneted the Zulu and shot a second, and bayoneted a third who came to their assistance, and then returned to his place.

As darkness came we were completely surrounded. ... and [they] kept up a heavy fire from all sides until about 12 o'clock, they did not actually charge up in a body to get over our wall after about 9 or 10 o'clock. After this time it became very dark, although the Hospital roof was still burning — it was impossible from below to see what was going on, and Bromhead and myself getting up on the mealy sack redoubt, kept an anxious watch on all sides.

About midnight or a little after, the fire slackened, and after that, although they kept us constantly on the alert, by feigning, as before, to come on at different points, the fire was of a desultory character. Our men were careful, and only fired when they could see a fair chance. ... This sort of thing went on

* At about this time, according to Padre George Smith in his diary, Bromhead led several bayonet charges against the Zulus and each time succeeded in driving them back.

Major Gonville Bromhead, VC (seated centre) with the 2nd Bn SWB Instructors of Musketry, Burma, 1886. He had not long returned from a course of musketry at Hythe and his marksmanship at Rorke's Drift had been noted by Chard in his report.
[RRW Museum (Brecon)]

until about 4 am and we were anxiously waiting for daybreak and the renewal of the attack, which their comparative, and at length complete silence, led us to expect. But at daybreak the enemy were out of sight, over the hill to our south-west.

I have already, in my report, said how gallantly all behaved, from Lieutenant Bromhead downwards, and I also mentioned those whom I had particularly noticed to have distinguished themselves.

On their return to Britain, both Chard and Bromhead were invited to attend on Queen Victoria at Balmoral. Chard received the invitation and went to meet his sovereign, but Bromhead had already slipped away to his relatives in Ireland, probably to escape the attention of the press and the public. He was, however, later feted by the people of Lincolnshire and the tenants of his family estate at Thurlby and eventually meet the Queen.

In 1881, he rejoined the 2/24th (now the 2nd Bn South Wales Borderers) at Gibraltar from where, in August 1881, he embarked for India, forming part of the reinforcements being sent out in light of the disaster at Maiwand in Afghanistan. He was back in Britain in 1882 where he completed a musketry course before rejoining the battalion in Secunderabad and was promoted to major on 4 April 1883. After service at various stations in the sub-continent, the battalion arrived at Rangoon in May 1886 to quell the unrest in Burma following the overthrow of King Theebaw and the annexation of the country by Britain. Here Gonville Bromhead had the unusual experience of serving under the command of his brother Lieutenant-Colonel Charles Bromhead, with most of the activity involving small columns searching the jungle for enemy forces. The battalion returned to India in November 1888. On 31 January 1891, they moved to Allahabad and Charles Bromhead handed over command to Colonel Penn Symons. Less than a week later, Gonville Bromhead died of enteric fever (typhoid).

See also the entry on Lieutenant John Chard in the Appendix (page 220).

WILLIAM ALLEN
Corporal
2nd/24th (2nd Warwickshire) Regiment of Foot

Sergeant William Allen, VC

Full Name: William Wilson Allen (his surname was incorrectly spelled on his Army papers and should have been recorded as Allan).

Place of Birth: Kyloe, Northumberland (south-east of Berwick on Tweed).

Date of Birth: *Circa* 1844. He was the Allan's first child and later had three sisters and three brothers.

Father: Thomas Allan (born in Scotland).

Mother: Ellen Allan (born in Scotland).

Father's Occupation: Agricultural labourer.

Education: 2nd Class Certificate of Education (in latter years he was an assistant schoolmaster at the SWB Depot, Brecon).

Pre-Service Employment: —

Service Record: Attested at York, 27 October 1859, 2nd/24th Regiment of Foot (Service Nº 1240); lance corporal, 18 May 1876; served as assistant schoolmaster, Regimental Depot, Brecon, *circa* 1876; corporal, 6 July 1877; lance sergeant, 22 May 1878; reverted to Corporal, 21 October 1878; served Cape Colony and Natal, 1878–9 (present at the defence of Rorke's Drift, 22/23 January 1879, where he was wounded in the left shoulder and partly disabled for the remainder of his life); provisional lance sergeant, 11 November 1879, whilst serving with the Royal South Wales Borderers (Militia) at Brecon; sergeant, 16 June 1880; colour sergeant; sergeant instructor of musketry, 4th Volunteer Battalion, South Wales Borderers.

Decorations, Medals and Rewards: Victoria Cross (for action at Rorke's Drift, Natal, 22/23 January 1879); South Africa Medal (clasp for 1877–8–9); Good Shooting and Judging Distance Prize, 1878; gold watch from Brecon Borough Council.

Married: Sarah Ann Reeves at the Register Office, Brecon, 16 August 1876. Her father, Richard Reeves, was a staff sergeant in the Militia. Sarah was born *circa* 1858 and died in 1906. Her sister Mary married Private William Partridge who was also at Rorke's Drift.

Children: Full details not known but records exist for: Helen Letitia (1877), Elizabeth Alice (1878), H. E. (daughter, *circa* 1879), Llewellyn Glendower (son, *c.*1880), Margaret Mary (1882), William Roy (1882), Grace (*c.*1883), Gwladys Alice (*c.*1884), Gwyldo (1885), Jessie (*circa* 1887, died 1888), Olive (*c.*1888), Syble Jean (*c.*1889).

Died: 12 March 1890, at his home, 85 Monnow Street, Monmouth.

Buried: Monmouth Cemetery, Monmouth, section B, grave 25 (this is in the upper part of the cemetery, alongside the main path). Buried with him are his wife and infant daughter, Jessie.

Memorials: Monmouth Cemetery, Monmouth. *Honour the Brave*, a grand slow march for pianoforte, by J. Riviere with words by H. Hersee, dedicated to the heroes of Rorke's Drift, 1879.

Location of Victoria Cross: RRW Museum, Brecon.

Citation for the Victoria Cross: *London Gazette,* 2 May 1879.

'It was chiefly due to the courageous conduct of these men that communication with the hospital was kept up at all. Holding together at all costs a most dangerous post, raked in reverse by the enemy's fire from the hill, they were both severely wounded, but

The VC and South Africa Medal on display at the SWB Museum, Brecon.

Sergeant Instructor William Allan, VC.

their determined conduct enabled the patients to be withdrawn from the hospital, and when incapacitated by their wounds from fighting, they continued, as soon as their wounds had been dressed, to serve out ammunition to their comrades during the night.'

This citation was shared with Private Frederick Hitch.

VC Investiture: By HM Queen Victoria at Windsor Castle, 9 December 1879.

William Allan, VC's grave and (below) the inscription.

William Allan signed his attestation papers as 'William Allen' and thereafter his military records show this spelling of his name. All other references to him and his family show the spelling 'Allan', including his headstone in Monmouth Cemetery. He recorded in the 1881 census that he was born in Newcastle-upon-Tyne (not Yorkshire as suggested in a recent publication) but evidence would now indicate that he was actually born in Kyloe, south-east of Berwick on Tweed, Northumberland, his parents having moved there from Scotland. He enlisted in the 24th Regiment of Foot at York on 27 October 1859, and served with the battalion in Mauritius during the 1860s. His early military career does not appear to have been exemplary, having been confined to the cells October–November 1860; July–September 1861; January–March 1861; July, August and September 1864; October–November 1864. One can only assume that these were for minor misdemeanours, possibly for being drunk, a common problem at the time. When his period of service expired in 1873 he was re-engaged and posted to the Regimental Depot. There followed a period of promotion and demotion. At this time, the army was operating a system of compulsory education for the lower ranks, all recruits having to attend classes for at least five hours each week thus enabling soldiers to obtain one of four levels of certificate: 1st Class — eligible for consideration for a commission from the ranks; 2nd Class — eligible for promotion to senior NCO; 3rd Class — eligible for promotion to junior NCO; 4th Class — able to complete very basic arithmetic and writing. William Allen passed the 2nd Class Certificate, a clear indication of ability. During his second period of service he seems to have settled down a great deal, perhaps as a result of his marriage in 1876 and he served as an assistant schoolmaster at the barracks in Brecon. By the time he arrived at Rorke's Drift in 1879, he was a corporal, and the longest serving of all the men awarded the Victoria Cross for their actions on 22/23 January. His particular skill was in the field of marksmanship, having been awarded the good shooting and judging distance prize in 1878.

His private life seems to have been very stable and he and his wife had a number of children. Sadly, as was so often the case in Victorian Britain, not all survived infancy. His eldest child was born in 1877, followed by others in 1878, 1880 and twins in 1882. The twins died in about 1883. Another child, a daughter named Jessie, died in 1888 before her second

Sergeant William Allan, VC's home in Monmouth.

birthday, and is buried with her parents. Whilst serving in South Africa, Allen appears to have regularly sent his wife a monthly allowance of £3.

During the fighting at Rorke's Drift, Allen, the senior corporal in the company, accompanied by Private Hitch, provided covering fire to allow the patients and soldiers who had been trapped in the hospital building to cross the open ground and gain shelter behind the wall of biscuit tins. This meant that they had to position themselves in open ground in order to fire at the attacking Zulus. Whilst this was going on, they were themselves under fire from Zulus positioned on the hill above the mission station. Allen was hit by a bullet in the shoulder but remained at his post, using his skills as a marksman to the full then later, serving ammunition to his comrades throughout the night. When the fighting was over, he was nominated for the VC by Lieutenant Bromhead.

On 4 February he wrote to his wife:

I am getting the better of my wound, more rapidly than could be expected. We got here (that is the sick and wounded) on the 26th of January, and have been waiting an ambulance to convey us down the country, which is expected every day. My arm is mending quickly, though I am sorry I cannot say the same for the other wounded men, who appear to be making no progress towards recovery. We are in a strongly entrenched fort here with two companies of the 1/24th, three of the 2/24th, detachment of the 13th, part of a company of the Royal Engineers, and a battery of Artillery.

Smith is still at Rorke's Drift, where the whole of the regiment and part of the 1/24th are assembled. Everything is quiet, and we don't expect any fighting till the arrival of troops from home. My dear wife, I trust you will feel too thankful to God for having preserved my life, to fret over what might have been a great deal worse. I feel very thankful to God for leaving me in the land of the living. Give my respects to your relatives and love to yourself and the children, from your loving husband.

Returning to Britain, William Allen was fit enough to appear before Queen Victoria at Windsor Castle in December where he was presented with the Victoria Cross. He never fully recovered from his wound, however, and was never again posted overseas, spending the remainder of his military life in administrative and training posts at the depot in Brecon (with the 3rd Militia Battalion, a post previously held by his father-in-law) and, later, with 4th (Volunteer) Battalion in Monmouth. He lived at 85 Monnow Street, Monmouth, where he died of influenza in 1890. A charitable fund was established to assist his widow and children who, by 1891, were living at 87 Monnow Street where Sarah was employed as a grocer. By 1901, she is recorded as living at 56 Cinderhill Street where she was employed as a 'sick nurse'.

*Private Frederick Hitch, 1879.
His arm is in a sling following the severe
wound to the shoulder which he received at
Rorke's Drift.*

FREDERICK HITCH
Private
2nd/24th (2nd Warwickshire) Regiment of Foot

FULL NAME: Frederick Hitch.

PLACE OF BIRTH: Southgate, Middlesex.

Date of Birth: 29 November 1856. He was one of fourteen children.

Father: John Hitch (originally from Hull, born *c*.1797).

Mother: Sarah Hitch (née Champness, born in Epping, 1817).

Father's Occupation: Journeyman boot and shoe maker.

Education: Unable to sign his name on the attestation papers, but was able to write after joining the army.

Pre-Service Employment: Farm labourer and bricklayer's labourer.

Service Record: Attested Westminster Police Court, 7 March 1877; private, 2nd/24th Regiment of Foot, 9 March 1877 (Service Nº 1362); served Galeka War, Cape Colony and Natal, 1878; served Anglo-Zulu War, 1879 (present at the defence of Rorke's Drift, 22/23 January 1879, severely wounded in the right shoulder by a roughly made Zulu bullet which shattered the bone and permanently disabled him); patient at Netley Hospital, 1 June–25 August 1879; discharged as unfit for military service, Netley, 25 August 1879.

Decorations, Medals and Rewards: Victoria Cross (for action at Rorke's Drift, Natal, 22/23 January 1879); South Africa Medal (clasp for 1877–8–9).

Post-Service Employment: His discharge papers give his proposed employment as labourer. He was, for a time, employed in the Corps of Commissionaires at the Imperial Institute, London, and later at the Royal United Services Institute, Whitehall. He then became a London cab driver in which occupation he remained until his death.

Married: Emily Matilda Meurisse, daughter of Louis and Matilda Susan Meurisse (née Evanson), 5 July 1881 (born Petersham, Surrey,

*62 Cranbrook Road, Chiswick, where Fred
Hitch died in 1913.*

*The VC and South Africa medal awarded to Fred
Hitch, now on display at the RRW Museum, Brecon.*

27 September 1864) at St Matthew's Church, St Petersburg Place, London, W2. The marriage eventually broke down and by 1911 they were living apart.

Children: A total of eleven children: Frederick (1882-1928) a police constable; Charles Frederick (1884–1955); Louisa (1886–?); Emily Matilda (1887–88); William (1888–?); Florence (1891–93); Victoria Maud (1893–?); Winifred (1894–?); Courtney (1897–1906); Dorothy May (1901–?); Selina (1903–?).

Died: 6 January 1913, at his home, 62 Cranbook Road, Chiswick, Middlesex, of 'syncope due to pleuro-pneumonia and heart failure'.

Buried: Grave 17, block P, Old Chiswick Cemetery, Corney Road, London, 11 January 1913. In addition to the family and the military representatives it was estimated that over 1,500 London cabbies attended the funeral.

Memorials: Old Chiswick Cemetery, Corney Road, London (the grave was vandalised in 1994 then restored and rededicated on 22 January 1999, paid for by the Company of Hackney Carriage Drivers); Hitch Award for Bravery presented by The Company of Hackney Carriage Drivers; blue plaque, 62 Cranbrook Road, London, unveiled 25 January 2004. *Honour the Brave*, a grand slow march for pianoforte, by J. Riviere with words by H. Hersee, dedicated to the heroes of Rorke's Drift, 1879.

Location of Victoria Cross: His VC was stolen from his coat whilst he was a commissionaire. A replacement was produced by order of King Edward VII which he received in 1908. The original is still missing. The replacement is held by the RRW Museum, Brecon.

Citation for the Victoria Cross: *London Gazette,* 2 May 1879.

'It was chiefly due to the courageous conduct of these men that communication with the hospital was kept up at all. Holding together at all costs a most dangerous post, raked in reverse by the enemy's fire from the hill, they were both severely wounded, but their determined conduct enabled the patients to be withdrawn from the hospital, and when incapacitated by their wounds from fighting, they continued, as soon as their wounds had been dressed, to serve out ammunition to their comrades during the night.'

This was a shared citation with Corporal William Allen.

VC Investiture: By HM Queen Victoria at Netley Hospital, Hampshire, 12 August 1879.

Frederick Hitch, VC in the uniform of the Corps of Commissionaires.

Frederick Hitch's monolithic headstone at St Nicholas's Churchyard, Chiswick. The top of the stone is decorated with a Union flag and a helmet of the type worn in 1879. On the right is a wreath, palm frond and a representation of the VC.

Frederick Hitch was born in Southgate, Middlesex, in 1856, the tenth of fourteen children of John and Sarah Hitch. In 1861, the family were living at Chase Side, Southgate, Winchmore Hill, when the five year old Fred is recorded as a 'scholar'. He does not, however, appear to have pursued any formal education for any length of time as, he was unable to sign his name on his attestation papers. His father was a qualified boot and shoe maker but the young Fred does not appear to have followed him into the trade and his first recorded employment is as a farm labourer at East Pole Farm, Edmonton, in 1871. By the time he joined the army, he was employed as a bricklayer's labourer. His papers show him to have been 5' 8³/4" tall, with fresh complexion, hazel eyes and brown hair. His first posting after completing his basic training was to Cape Colony, South Africa.

Fred Hitch, VC.

There have been several versions of Private Hitch's account of the defence of Rorke's Drift published in various journals. Only one, however, appears to have been recorded without having been edited and corrected. This account, first published in the *South African Military History Society Journal* in December 1973, was full of spelling and gramatical errors; punctuation was almost non-existent. It is this evidence of originality that makes this version particularly interesting. When one recalls Hitch's inability to sign his own name on entering the army, the account is evidence that he did receive some education in basic reading and writing. The opening sentences have been left unaltered but the remainder of the account has been corrected for the sake of ease of reading and understanding.

As I have been asked many times to give my Illustration of Rorke's Drift I cannot Say it is A Pleasure for me to do so and to think Back on that treable night of 22 Jan 1879. It was about 3.30 o'clock noon that we heard of that fatal Disaster at Isandlwana. I was Cooking the tea for the Company. I tryed to get it Done before the zulus attacked the little Post Rorke's Drift, which I managed taken the tea and my rifle and ammunition and four Kettles tea. [Account corrected from this point]

I just got into the fort when Bromhead asked me to try and get on to the top of the house. I at once mounted it [and] as soon as I got on the top I could see that Zulus had got as near to us as they could without us seeing them. I told Bromhead that they were at the other side of the rise and were extending for [the] attack. Mr Bromhead asked me how many there were. I told him that I thought they numbered from 4 to 6,000. A voice from below [said] 'Is that all? We can managed that lot very well.' For a few seconds there were different opinions.

I stayed on the house watching the black mass extending into their fighting line, [at] the same time a number of them creeping along under the rocks and taking up cover in the caves and [they] kept trying to dismount me from the top of the house. Their direction was good, but their elevation bad. A few minutes later one appeared on top of the mountain from the other side; he could see us in the laager plain enough to count us. I put myself in a lying position but my shot fell short of him. He then moved steadily to the right and signalled with his arm [and] the main body at once began to advance. I told Mr Bromhead that they would be all round us in [a] very short time. He at once told the company to take up their posts. The enemy, making a right wheel, attacked us in [the] shape of a bullock's horns and in a few minutes were all round us.

I found, as they got close to the laager, [that] I was out of the fighting, so I slid down the thatched roof, dropping into the laager. Fixing my bayonet as I ran across the laager, [I] took up my position on an open space which we had not time to complete. [A reference to a gap in the unfinished defensive wall.] The deadly work now commenced.

The Zulus, pushing right up to the point, it was not until the bayonet was freely used that they flinched the least bit. Had the Zulus taken the bayonet as freely as they took the bullets, we could not have stood more than fifteen minutes — they pushed right on top of us and not only got up to the laager, but got in with us. But they seemed to have a great dread of the bayonet which stood to us from beginning to end. During the struggle there was a fine big Zulu [who] saw me shoot his mate down. He sprang forward, dropping his rifle and assegais, seizing hold of the muzzle of my rifle with his left hand and his right hand the bayonet, thinking to disarm me. He pulled and tried hard to get the rifle from me but I had a firm hold of the small of the butt of my rifle with my left hand. My cartridges [were] on top of the mealy bag, which enabled me to load my rifle and shoot the poor wretch whilst holding on to his grasp. For some moments they dropped back into the garden which served [as] a great protection for them. Had it not been for the garden and dead [ground behind the] wall, they could not have prolonged the engagement for thirteen hours as they did. Their next objective was to get possession of the hospital [where] the Zulus had burst open the doors and killed them in their beds. Whilst doing this I noticed it was with great difficulty [that] they were kept back. They kept up a very heavy fire from [both our] front and rear from which we suffered very much. It was about then when Mr Dalton was shot, and Mr Dunn. Mr Dalton was very active up until he was wounded. We had to fall back to the second line of defence.

When the Zulus took possession of the hospital, Bromhead and myself and five others took up a position on the right of the second line of defence, where we were exposed to three cross-fires. Bromhead took the centre, and was the only one that did not get wounded. There were four killed and two wounded, myself being the last of the six — one shot. Bromhead and myself had it to our two selves [for] an hour and a half, Bromhead using his rifle and revolver with deadly aim. Bromhead

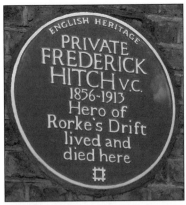

The blue plaque on Hitch's home in Chiswick.

kept telling the men not to waste one round. About this time we were pressed very much. Bromhead was using his revolver with deadly aim, they seemed determined to move Bromhead and myself. We were so busy that one got inside and was in the act of assegaiing Bromhead (Bromhead not knowing he was there). I put my rifle on him, knowing at the same time [that] it was empty. Instead of him delivering the assegai, which no doubt would have been fatal, he dodged down and hopped out of the laager.

Again, (this was just before they tried to fire the other building) they seemed to me as if they [had] made up their minds to take Rorke's Drift with this rush. They rushed up madly, notwithstanding the heavy loss they had suffered. It was in this struggle that I was shot. They pressed us very hard, several of them mounting the barricade. I knew this one had got his rifle presented at me but, at the same time, I had got my hands full in front and I was at the present when he shot me through the right shoulder-blade and [the bullet] passed through my shoulder which splintered the shoulder bone very much as I have had in all 38 pieces of broken bone taken from my shoulder. I tried to keep my feet, but could not. He could have assegaied me had not Bromhead shot him with his revolver. Bromhead seemed very sorry to see me down bleeding so freely saying, 'Mate, I am very sorry to see you down.' I was not down for more than a few minutes, stripped in my shirt sleeves, with my waist-belt on and valise straps, I put my wounded arm under my waist-belt, I was able to make another stand. Getting Bromhead's revolver and with his assistance in loading it, I managed very well with it. At this time we were fighting by the aid [of the light] from the burning hospital, which was very much to our advantage. Bromhead at this time was keeping a strict eye on the ammunition and telling the men not to waste one round as we were getting short. I was serving out ammunition myself when I became thirsty and faint. I got worse. A chum tore out the linen out of Mr Dunn's coat and tied it round my shoulder. I got so thirsty that I could not do much, in fact we were all exhausted and the ammunition was beginning to be counted. Deakin [Deacon], a comrade, said to me as I was leaning back against biscuit boxes: 'Fred, when it comes to the last, shall I shoot you?' I declined, 'No, they have very near done for me and they can finish me right out when it comes to the last.' I don't remember much after that.

When I came to myself again, Lord Chelmsford had relieved us of our task. Bromhead brought his lordship to me and his lordship spoke very kindly to me and the doctor dressed my wound. Bromhead was my principal visitor and nurse while I was at the Drift.

Bromhead nominated Hitch for the Victoria Cross.

Due to his serious injury, Hitch was treated at Rorke's Drift by Surgeon Reynolds before being moved to Helpmekaar where he arrived on 26 January and was treated by Surgeon Blair Brown who recorded: 'Pte F. Hitch of the 2/24th was hit during the defence of Rorke's Drift in the right shoulder. There was great swelling of the whole shoulder (when seen by me on 26/1/1879) and ecchymosis [bruising]. The tract of the wound was sloughing [dead tissue on the surface of a wound]. Poultices and cold water sufficed to allay this and the case did well.' His next move took him to Durban from where he was invalided back to Britain at the first opportunity aboard the troopship HMS *Tamar*. Hitch was admitted to the Royal Victoria Military Hospital at Netley, Hampshire, on 10 June. Despite the best endeavours of the medical staff, Hitch's wound was to become a permanent disability; the rough bullet had pierced his right shoulder. As he had his rifle at the 'present' at the time of the injury, presumably aiming to fire at one of the attacking Zulus, the bullet may have entered from below his arm, close to his armpit, and slightly to the side, hitting the scapula before exiting from the back. Hitch stated that 38 pieces of bone were removed from his wound which would suggest that the damage was beyond repair. Amazingly, although the injury was undoubtedly a handicap for the remainder of his life, it was not disabling. The detached pieces were probably small and may have come from one relatively small part of the shoulder blade. If, however, the scapula was badly damaged, it would still not have been totally debilitating as, even without a scapula, a person could have the full use of their arm up to shoulder level. Lifting the arm above that height would, however, be impossible without the added support of the shoulder blade. The fact that Hitch appeared before a medical board on 28 July and was invalided from the service on 25 August, would suggest that the scapula was indeed badly damaged, if not destroyed. The best prognosis would be a partial lack of articulation of his right arm which would have made

Frederick Hitch, VC in later life, still seeming to suffer from the shoulder wound received at Rorke's Drift.

Frederick Hitch, c.1905, wearing the ribbon of the VC and his South Africa Medal.
This photograph was obviously taken after the theft of his Victoria Cross.

him unfit for military service. If, however, the shoulder blade had been only partly damaged there would have been the possibility of his regaining full use of the arm and it is likely that the decision to discharge him from the service would have been delayed to allow time for a more accurate prognosis to be made.

Less than two weeks before being discharged, whilst still at Netley, Hitch was decorated with the VC by Queen Victoria, who described their meeting in her journal: 'He is a tall good looking young man, with a very determined expression, but very modest & bears a high character … . He could not say a word & I fear afterwards fainted'. Fred was not exceptionally tall for the period but to the Queen, who was only 5' $^1/4$", he must have seemed to be so. Later, when viewing the unfinsihed painting of Rorke's drift by Lady Butler, the Queen said 'The figure of Private Hitch is the most finished and wonderfully like.'

On his discharge papers he gave his intended place of residence as Southgate but, by 1881, having recovered sufficiently from his wound, he was residing at 44 Bedford Street, London and was, according to the census return of that year, employed as a 'Commissionaire and Chelsea Pensioner'. On 5 July 1881, he was married to Emily Matilda Meurisse at St Matthew's Church, St Petersburg Place, London. Despite claims that her father, a German immigrant named Louis Meurisse, was the manager of the Café Royal in Regent Street, there is no evidence to suggest that he ever rose above the position of waiter, or that he ever worked at the Café Royal. At the time of their marriage, Emily was working as a servant at the Langham Hotel, Portland Place.

Hitch spent many years moving from one job to another and, consequently, from one house to another, mostly in central London. His disability meant that he was restricted in the type of job that he could take up but, gradually he would have re-gained much of the use of his right arm although he would probably have difficulty lifting heavy weights to any great height. Despite this, by 1886, he was employed as a railway porter and was living in Pimlico which would suggest that he was working at Victoria Station. How long this employment lasted is unrecorded but by 1891 he was back working as a commissionaire, probably at the Imperial Institute off Queen's Gate where he was certainly working two years later. In 1894, he became the licensee of the Durweston Arms, a public house in a genteel area of Marylebone, whilst continuing with his employment at the Imperial Institute. This foray into the licensed trade may well have been on behalf of his wife who, with some background in the hotel trade, could well have carried out the day-to-day running of the pub. The scheme evidently did not work out as planned and he gave up the licence the following year by which time he is recorded as being a cab proprietor (although there is little evidence that he was a cab driver, as he did not hold a hackney carriage licence), probably renting out the vehicle as a source of extra income.

In the years which followed, the ever-expanding Hitch family moved regularly, mostly in the area of Fulham. In 1901 he become a licensed cab driver/proprietor (driving a 2-horse vehicle) and, if Philip Wilkins (author of *The History of the Victoria Cross*, published in 1904) is to be believed, made a comfortable living. There then followed a period of relative stability until 1906 when they moved to Southall, which coincided with Hitch giving up the proprietorship of his own cab and taking up employment as a driver of a motorised vehicle with the General Motor Cab Co. Ltd of Brixton Road. The following year the family moved to live in Chiswick, by which time there were problems in the Hitch marriage and by 1911 Fred had moved out of the marital home and into lodgings with a family friend, Mrs Wiley, a few streets away at Cranbrook Road.

In February 1901, whilst working as a commissionaire at the Royal United Services Institute in Whitehall, his Victoria Cross was stolen from his jacket. In September 1908, his son wrote to enquire whether it might be possible for him to obtain a replacement. The War Office agreed to the request on condition that Hitch paid £1-3s-0d (£1.15) and signed a declaration to the effect that, should the original ever be recovered, he would return the replacement Cross to the authorities. There is no evidence to support the rumour that his new VC was presented by either the King or by Field-Marshal Lord Roberts, VC; the truth of the matter is that it probably arrived in the post. The original VC has never been recovered.

The winter of 1912/13 saw discontent spread amongst the London motorised cab drivers following an increase in the duty on petrol. This culminated in a strike on 1 January when Fred Hitch offered his services on the picket line. The weather, however, was not kind to him and on 5 January, after a visit to friends in Epsom, he returned to his lodgings, complaining to his landlady, that he had a pain in his side. Overnight, his condition deteriorated and by 6pm on the

A retouched newspaper photograph of Fred Hitch in his uniform as a London cab driver.

evening of 6 January he was dead; according to the doctor who signed the death certificate, of heart failure and pleuro-pneumonia. Newspaper reports estimated that large numbers of cab drivers would be attending his funeral. As it transpired, over 1,500 London cabbies turned up and his own motor cab was decked with floral tributes and towed by a team of drivers. Less than three months later, his widow married William George Rainbow. Two of the witnesses to this ceremony were Hitch's friends, Mr & Mrs Joseph John Farmer, VC (ex-Corps of Commissionaires).

Hitch's grave in St Nicholas' Churchyard, Chiswick, very close to the Thames, is surmounted by an enormous decorated stone block which was paid for by 'Public Subscription'. A blue plaque, now adorns the house in Cranbrook Road.

With the passing of the years, Hitch was not forgotten by the London cabbies who, in the early 1990s, via the Worshipful Company of Hackney Carriage Drivers, established an award for bravery which is known as 'The Hitch Award'. To date (2006) there have been three recipients.

London cab drivers, pulling Hitch's flower decorated cab, stop outside his home at Cranbrook Road on the day of his funeral.

Private William Jones, VC, 1879.

WILLIAM JONES
Private
2nd/24th (2nd Warwickshire) Regiment of Foot

Full Name: William Jones.

Place of Birth: Bristol (possibly at 5 Lucas Street).

Date of Birth: 16 August 1839. He had an older half-brother, Thomas, and a younger brother James.

Father: William Jones (born in Monmouthshire).

Mother: Mary Ann Lancastle (she may have been his second wife).

Father's Occupation: Builder's labourer.

Education: None recorded but his promotion to corporal in 1859 would suggest that he must have satisfied the minimum educational requirements.

Pre-Service Employment: Boot closer.

Service Record: Attested at Birmingham, 21 December 1858, for 2nd/24th Regiment of Foot (Service N° 593); corporal, 1st September 1859; reduced to private, 5 September 1860; served Mauritius and Burma; re-engaged at Rangoon, 10 January 1868; served India; served Cape Colony and Natal (Galeka and Anglo-Zulu Wars, 1877–9, present at the defence of Rorke's Drift, 22/23 January 1879); discharged at Netley Hospital, 2 February 1880, due to chronic rheumatism.

Decorations, Medals and Rewards: Victoria Cross (for action at Rorke's Drift, 22/23 January 1879); South Africa Medal (clasp for 1879); Long Service and Good Conduct Medal 1 July 1879; three Good Conduct Badges.

Post-Service Employment: Jones was unable to obtain regular employment after his discharge despite an attempt to return to his trade in the boot industry. He is known to have worked in the theatre re-enacting the defence of Rorke's Drift. He also toured with Buffalo Bill's Wild West Show in the 1880s. In later life he was employed as a labourer. After discharge, he resided in Lupin Street, Birmingham, but later moved, with his second wife, to Rutland Street, Chorlton, Lancashire.

Private William Jones, VC, 1879, wearing his VC, Long Service & Good Conduct Medal (left) and South Africa Medal (right).

Right: The VC and South Africa medal awarded to William Jones. [RRW Museum (Brecon)]

Far right: William Jones' Long Service & Good Conduct Medal. [Mr & Mrs William Dodd]

Married: 1) Elizabeth, daughter of Charles Goddard, tailor, of Aldershot, 12 May 1875 at Farnham, Surrey. She died in 1878. (2) Elizabeth Frodsham, née Walters, at St Augustine's Church, Newton Heath, Manchester, July 1901.

Children: One son, William, by his first marriage (born 1876, at Dover and sent to his grandparents in Farnham, probably as both his parents went to South Africa shortly after his birth). He also had seven stepchildren by his second marriage.

Died: At his step-daughter's home, 6 Brampton Street, Ardwick, Manchester, 15 April 1913 (now demolished).

Buried: Philips Park Cemetery (Bradford Ward), Manchester, 21 April 1913. Public subscription grave, D887.

Memorials: Philips Park Cemetery, Manchester, CofE Common Ground. The grave did not originally record that he was a VC but simply read: 'William Jones who died 15 April 1913, aged 73'. The word 'who' has now been deleted and 'VC' added. There is also a plaque on the external wall of the CofE Chapel at Philips Park Cemetery. *Honour the Brave*, a grand slow march for pianoforte, by J. Riviere with words by H. Hersee, dedicated to the heroes of Rorke's Drift, 1879.

Location of Victoria Cross: Jones pawned the VC in his later years and was unable to redeem it. Now held by the RRW Museum (Brecon).

Citation for the Victoria Cross: *London Gazette*, 2 May 1879.

'In another ward, facing the hill, Private William Jones and Private Robert Jones defended the post to the last, until six out of the seven patients it contained had been removed. The seventh, Sergeant Maxfield, 2nd Battalion, 24th Regiment, was delirious from fever. Although they had previously dressed him they were unable to induce him to move. When Private Robert Jones returned to endeavour to carry him away, he found him being stabbed by the Zulus as he lay in bed.'

This is a shared citation with Private Robert Jones.

VC Investiture: By HM Queen Victoria at Osborne House, 13 January 1880.

William Jones, VC, wearing what appears to be a cut-out copy of the VC, having pawned the actual medal. [Mr & Mrs William Dodd]

William Jones' grave in Philips Park Cemetery after the inscription was changed.

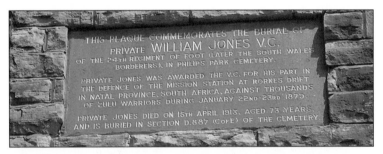

William Jones' memorial plaque in Philips Park Cemetery which reads: 'This plaque commemorates the burial of Private William Jones, VC of the 24th Regiment of Foot (later the South Wales Borderers), in Philips Park Cemetery. Private Jones was awarded the VC for his part in the defence of the mission station at Rorkes Drift in Natal province, South Africa, against thousands of Zulu warriors during January 22nd 23rd 1879. Private Jones died on 15th April 1913, aged 73 years and is buried in Section D.887 (CofE) of the cemetery'.

The Victoria Crosses awarded to the men of the 2/24th Regiment for their gallantry at Rorke's Drift cannot be said to have brought with them great happiness or success. With the possible exception of John Williams, their lives seem to have been blighted by the events of that evening and night in Natal. William Allan and Fred Hitch suffered from the effects of their wounds for the remainder of their lives, and neither was able to live a full, active life. William Jones, although surviving the battle without any physical wounds, discovered that, by September 1879, he was no longer fit for military service 'due to chronic rheumatism of the joints' a condition undoubtedly aggravated by his service in South Africa which, at best, had meant spending lengthy periods living under canvas or at worst, in the open. After the fighting at Rorke's Drift, the men of B Company were privileged to be allowed to sleep in the roof space of the mission station house with a tarpaulin draped over the rafters to keep out the rain. Outside, the men had to endure the smell of rotting corpses, flies, rain and the scorching sun. Little wonder that many became ill with various fevers and dysentery. Some, like 934, Private John Williams, died. A medical board, convened at Pietermaritzburg on 3 September, ordered William Jones home to Britain where he was admitted to Netley Military Hospital from where he was discharged on 2 February 1880.

Trained as a shoemaker before enlisting at Birmingham in 1858, William Jones' attestation papers show that he was 5' 5" tall, of sallow complexion, brown eyes and brown hair. He served in Mauritius and the East Indies, was promoted to corporal and later reduced to private. When his initial period of service expired at Rangoon in 1868, he re-enlisted with the intention of completing twenty-one years service. He married Elizabeth Goddard in 1875 and she went with him to South Africa as one of the wives allowed on the strength of the regiment. In Durban, she was taken ill and died of 'phthisis pulmmonatis' (tuberculois) on 11 October 1878, aged 21 (although the Register of Deaths shows 24).

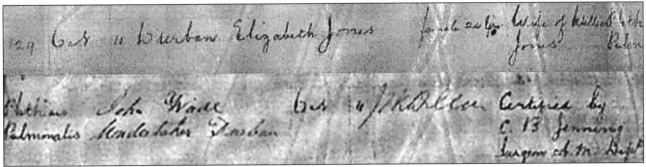

The entry in the Register of Deaths for Elizabeth Jones, the first wife of William Jones. Of interest is the fact that the death was certified by C. B. Jennings, Surgeon, Army Medical Department. [Tony Jones]

According to the *Natal Mercury* of 18 June 1879, 'When he [William Jones] came here with his regiment his wife was with him, but after he had been at the front some time she became dangerously ill, and he obtained leave of absence to come down to attend to her. Jones took a little room in a house facing the St George's Hotel Tap, and there by working night and day repairing boots and shoes he managed to earn many comforts for his then dying wife. He was a steady, plodding fellow, but his wife was beyond recovery, and he remained with her until she died. The next day he buried her remains, and at once started off to join his regiment, but he did not succeed in reaching it. He was nearly broken-hearted at the loss he had sustained, and cared perhaps little for his own life, which, however, as circumstances occurred, proved a most valuable one. He stayed at Rorke's Drift, and had not been there long when the memorable attack and defence were made. On this occasion Jones distinguished himself in a most heroic manner, having rescued a number of invalids from the burning hospital. For this gallant service Jones received the Victoria Cross, and is now with his regiment, a steady good soldier, as he always has been.'

William Jones' heavily edited account of the defence of Rorke's Drift, was published in *Strand Magazine* in 1891.

William Jones in old age, at his step-daughter's home in Manchester.
[Mr & Mrs William Dodd]

The Defence of Rorke's Drift by W. A. Dugan. [RRW Museum (Brecon)]

About half past three o'clock in the afternoon of the 22nd January 1879, a mounted man came galloping into our little encampment and told us that the Zulus had taken the Camp at Isandhlwana, and were making their way towards us at Rorke's Drift. We at once set to work, and with such material as we had at hand formed a slight barricade around us; this was formed of sacks of mealies (Indian corn), boxes of sea biscuits, etc., of which we had a good supply. We also loopholed the walls of the two buildings. We had scarcely completed our work when the Zulus were down upon us.

The Hospital being the first building in their line of attack, they surrounded. Having twenty-three sick men in the rooms, our Officer, Lieutenant Bromhead, ordered six men into the Hospital, myself being one of the number, to defend and rescue the sick from it. We had scarcely taken our post in the hospital when two of our number were killed in the front of our verandah, leaving four of us to hold the place and get out the sick. This was done by two (viz., Privates Hook and Williams) carrying the sick and passing them into the barricade through a small window, whilst myself (William Jones) and my comrade (Robert Jones) contended each door at the point of the bayonet, our ammunition being expended. The Zulus, finding they could not force us from the doors, now set fire to the thatched roof. This was the most horrifying time. What with the bloodthirsty yells of the Zulus, the cries of the sick that remained, and the burning thatch falling about our heads, it was sickening. Still we kept them at bay until twenty of the twenty-three sick men were passed into the barricade under the fire of our own men; the other three which I have every reason to believe must have wandered back into one of the rooms we had cleared, as they were men suffering from fever at that time. By this time the whole of the Hospital was in flames, and we could not stay in it any longer, we had to make our own escape into the barricade, by the window through which the sick had been passed. This we did, thank God, with our lives.

On leaving the army, Jones lived for a time in Birmingham before moving to Chorlton, Manchester. Sometime in the late 1880s/early 1890s, he fell on hard times and had to pawn his Victoria Cross and South Africa Medal which he was never able to redeem. According to his family, this was around the time that he took up employment with Buffalo Bill's Wild West Show when it was touring Britain in the early 1890s and with Hamilton's Pansterorama (where was involved in a re-enactment of the defence of Rorke's Drift). In his final years, the events of January 1879, came back to haunt him causing regular nightmares, imagining that the Zulus were coming for him and he would wake up screaming and terrified. He eventually reached a state where he was no longer able to care for himself and went to live with his step-daughter in Ardwick, Manchester. In 1910 he was admitted to New Bridge Street Workhouse, Manchester, for one night, having been found wandering the streets — a regular occurrence as he would awake in the night and flee the house, believing that he was back in South Africa and that the Zulus were about to attack. He was even known to have taken his small granddaughter from her bed before leaving the house in an attempt to save her from the imagined Zulu warriors. He died in 1913 and was buried in a public grave in Philips Park Cemetery. A gravestone was placed in the area of his burial and his name included as one of a number of paupers buried in the plot. In recent years the stone has been amended and the letters 'VC' added after his name.

Private Robert Jones, VC, 1879.

ROBERT JONES
Private
2nd/24th (2nd Warwickshire) Regiment of Foot

Full Name: Robert Jones.

Place of Birth: Tŷ Canol, Penrhos, Raglan. The family later lived at Tŷ Newydd Issa (Lower), Clytha, near Raglan, Monmouthshire. Robert was the fourth son.

Date of Birth: 19 August 1857.

Father: Robert Jones (born Treadem, Llantilio Crossenny, Monmouthshire. Died 1899).

Mother: Hannah Jones (daughter of Richard and Ann Fryer, born Overton, Arlingham, Gloucestershire; at the time of her marriage she was living in Blaenafon. She was living in Livingstone Place, Newport in 1901).

Father's Occupation: Farmer, owning 33 acres. He was at one time a self-employed haulier.

Education: 4th Class Certificate of Education.

Pre-Service Employment: Agricultural labourer at Drybridge Farm, Monmouth (1871).

Service Record: Attested at Monmouth, 2nd/24th Regiment of Foot, 10 January 1876; joined the regiment 28 January 1876 (Service N° 716); served Cape Colony and Natal, 1878–9 (present at the defence of Rorke's Drift, Natal, 22/23 January 1879, slightly wounded); served India 1880–81; returned to Britain 25 November 1881; transferred to the Army Reserve, 26 January 1882; recalled for service with South Wales Borderers, 2 August 1882; transferred to the Army Reserve, 7 February 1883; discharged from the Army Reserve, 26 January 1888.

Decorations, Medals and Rewards: Victoria Cross (for action at Rorke's Drift, Natal, 22/23 January 1879); South Africa Medal (clasp for 1877–8–9).

Post-Service Employment: He seems to have been employed as a farm labourer for most of his post-service life.

Married: Elizabeth, daughter of Richard Hopkins, at Llantilio, Monmouthshire, 7 January 1885 (born in Bridgewater, Somerset). After Robert's death, she married William Tilbury with whom she had a second family (Frank, William, Ethel and Beatrice). After

The headstone and grave of Robert Jones, VC in St Peter's churchyard, Peterchurch.

Robert Jones and his wife Elizabeth (née Hopkins). [Mrs Gillian Evans]

Elizabeth's death, Tilbury remarried and had two further sons. She is buried in St Margaret's Vowchurch, Herefordshire.

Children: One son, Robert (*c*.1892) and four daughters, Margaret Alice (1886), Lilly Rose (*c*.1896), Edith Emily (*c*.1885) and Elin (1898).

Died: Shot himself at Crossway House, Peterchurch, 6 September 1898. A coronor's inquest returned a verdict of suicide 'being of unsound mind'.

Buried: 8 September 1898 at Peterchurch, Herefordshire.

Memorials: Headstone at Peterchurch, Herefordshire. *Honour the Brave*, a grand slow march for pianoforté, by J. Riviere with words by H. Hersee, dedicated to the heroes of Rorke's Drift, 1879.

Location of Victoria Cross: It was sold to an itinerant 'dealer' by his widow, then resold at Sotheby's in December 1946. It was owned by Charles H. Lovell of Cirencester before being sold at auction by Glendining's in the 1950s for £98. Latterly it was owned by a collector in Somerset, before being sold by Dix Noonan Webb, London, on 11 June 1996 to a private collector for £80,000.

Citation for the Victoria Cross: *London Gazette*, 2 May 1879.

'In another ward, facing the hill, Private William Jones and Private Robert Jones defended the post to the last, until six out of the seven patients it contained had been removed. The seventh, Sergeant Maxfield, 2nd Battalion, 24th Regiment, was delirious from fever. Although they had previously dressed him they were unable to induce him to move. When Private Robert Jones returned to endeavour to carry him away, he found him being stabbed by the Zulus as he lay in bed.'

This citation was shared with Private William Jones.

VC Investiture: By Lieutenant-General Sir Garnet Wolseley, High Commissioner and GOC British Troops South Africa at Utrecht, Transvaal, 11 September 1879.

The events in the life of Robert Jones, VC are possibly the most tragic of all those who received the coveted decoration for their gallantry at Rorke's Drift, on 22/23 January 1879.

The Jones family were descended from William and Ann Jones, of Llantilio Crossenny who, in 1851, are shown on the census as farming 200 acres and employing a number of servants. His son, Robert (the father of Robert Jones, VC), was employed as a haulier, living at Coed Cae at the time of his marriage to Hannah Fryer of Blaenafon, on 12 June 1848. Hannah was born in Overton, near Arlingham, Gloucestershire, where her parents, Richard and Ann Fryer, were also farmers. By 1851, Robert and Hannah were living at Tŷ Canol, Penrhos, near Raglan, where he was farming 21 acres and where Robert (junior) was born. By 1861, William Jones had died and the family were living at Tŷ Newydd [Isaf], a farm of 33 acres at Clytha near Raglan where Robert (senior) is shown as a 'landed proprietor'. Today, the buildings at Tŷ Newydd farm have changed quite considerably (the present-day farmhouse was probably built in the 1890s or early 1900s) although the western end of the old farm building is unusual and shows evidence of having once been plastered, suggesting that this may once have been the farmhouse. The tradition amongst nineteenth century farming families was for sons to follow fathers into the business, first as agricultural labourers and then, in time, to inherit the farm and become farmers in their own right. By the time Robert (junior) was born in 1857, the family already included three sons and two daughters, so the prospects of his inheriting a substantial area of land to farm himself must have seemed very unlikely. By 1871, when he was aged 14, Robert (junior) was working as an indoor farm servant for Anthony Balenger at Drybridge Farm, Monmouth (very close to where the family of Hook VC was living during the 1870s). Like so many other young recruits, despite having such close links with agriculture, Robert Jones enlisted at Monmouth in January 1876. Whether he enlisted in an attempt to show his independence and to seek some adventure, or because life in rural Monmouthshire gave little indication of any prospects for the future, we shall never know. The family holds the belief that his decision to enlist resulted in a rift between him and his parents which was never bridged. At the time of Robert's death, not a single member of the Jones family came into contact with his widow and children, and there has been no contact since. The attraction of a military life appears to have been a strong one within the family as, eventually, four of his brothers ended up serving the Crown: Thomas, Philip, Charles Edgar and John

James. There is a belief within the family that Robert's brother, Thomas, may have been one of the soldiers of that name killed at Isandlwana.

Robert had his first overseas posting when the battalion went to Cape Colony in 1878. He made a brief record of his memories of the defence of Rorke's Drift, an edited account of which was published in *The Strand Magazine* in 1891.

On the 22nd January 1879, the Zulus attacked us, we being only a small band of English [sic] soldiers and they in very strong and overwhelming numbers. On commencing fighting, I was one of the soldiers who were in the Hospital to protect it. I and another soldier of the name of William Jones were on duty at the back of the hospital, trying to defeat and drive back the rebels, and doing our endeavours to convey the wounded and sick soldiers out through a hole in the wall, so that they might reach in safety the small band of men in the square. On retiring from one room into another, after taking a wounded man by the name of Mayer belonging to the volunteers, to join William Jones, I found a crowd in front of the Hospital and coming into the doorway, I said to my companion 'they are on top of us', and sprang to one side of the doorway. There we crossed our bayonets, and as fast as they came up to the doorway we bayoneted them, until the doorway was nearly filled with dead and wounded Zulus.

In the meantime, I had three assegai wounds, two in the right side and one in the left of my body. We did not know of anyone being in the Hospital, only the Zulus, and then after a long time of fighting at the door we made them retire, and then we made our escape out of the building. Just as I got outside, the roof fell in — a complete mass of flames and fire. I had to cross a space of about twenty or thirty yards from the ruins of the Hospital to the beleagured company where they were keeping the enemy at bay. While I was crossing the front of the square, the bullets were whishing past me from every direction. When I got in, the enemy came on closer and closer, until they were close to the outer side of our laager, which was made up of boxes of biscuits on sacks of Indian corn. The fighting lasted about thirteen hours, or better.

As to my feelings at that time, they were that I was certain that if we did not kill them they would kill us, and after a few minutes fighting I did not mind it more than at the present time; my thought was only to fight as an English soldier ought to for his most gracious Sovereign, Queen Victoria, and for the benefit of old England.

After the battle, Jones, along with his comrades of the 2/24th Regiment, remained at Rorke's Drift until mid April when B Company was ordered to Kopje Alleine for line of communications duties before being ordered to Gibraltar aboard the transport *Orontes* where they remained until posted to India.

After leaving the army, Robert returned to his home area on the borders of Monmouthshire and Herefordshire where, in 1885, he married Elizabeth Hopkins. During the late 1880s/early 1890s, if the birth records of his children are a suitable guide, he appears to have moved on a regular basis: Margaret Alice being born in Llanferin in 1886 and Edith Emily at Upper Nag's Head, Peterchurch in 1888. In 1891, he was living at The Lodge, Dorstone in Herefordshire, where he is recorded as being an agricultural labourer and there is also a claim that he lived at Kingstone Almshouses, although there does not appear to be evidence to support this. By 1898, Robert and his family were living in Rose Cottage, Peterchurch where he was employed as a farm labourer by Major de la Hay at Cross House, and where his last child, Elin was born. During that summer he began to complain of feeling unwell, suffering from headaches which culminated in a form of convulsion. Whether this was an after-effect of his military service, the advent of an illness or the after effects of alcohol we shall never know. What the headaches were not, were the consequences of wounds to his

head inflicted by the Zulus at Rorke's Drift. His own words, quoted above, show that, whilst wounded three times during the fighting, all the wounds were to his torso and not to his head. Robert's behaviour during the summer of 1898 certainly appears to have been unusual, perhaps caused by his health problems, and early in September 1898 the local police constable had ordered him to leave the Boughton Arms public house.

Right: Robert Jones's eldest child, Margaret Alice, photographed during the First World War.
[Mrs Elizabeth Griffiths]

Far right: Robert Jones's daughter Edith Emily, on her wedding day during the First World War.
[Mrs Elizabeth Griffiths]

On 6 September, Jones got up after a good night's sleep but, according to his wife, was 'very wild in appearance, and said he was fit to do anything'. Despite her trying to keep him at home, he managed to slip out through the back door. Mrs Jones followed him but he told her to go home. About half-an-hour later he returned, drank two cups of tea, got changed and went out again. He was not in the habit of returning home during the morning and certainly did not change his clothes. By about 7.30am he had arrived at his employer's home where he greeted Louis Wellers, the laundrymaid, with a 'Good morning' and borrowed his gun to go and shoot some crows. Almost immediately, she heard a shot from the garden, but no one paid it any heed. Some time later, Louis went out into the garden, saw Jones's hat, then came across his body. Major de la Hay then went out to the garden and saw Jones lying face down on top of the gun. He had apparently shot himself. When the village police officer arrived he noted that Jones was clutching the gun with his left hand 'close to the muzzle and the right near the trigger' The doctor examined the body and concluded that Jones had shot himself in the mouth and that there 'was no mark of powder on his face.' Jones was 'a big man, long-armed, and would have no difficulty in firing the gun in such a position.'

With what would appear to us in the twenty-first century to have been almost unseemly haste, an inquest was held the next day at the nearby Boughton Arms. Those involved would have still been suffering from the trauma of the previous day and should not have been subjected to the ordeal of an inquest. Confusion and shock would have been the main sensations felt by all concerned, not the best circumstances in which to reach a balanced, clear opinion of what had transpired the previous day. The coroner's papers have not survived but a detailed, ostensibly verbatim, report in the *Hereford Times* on 10 September 1898, gives a clear picture of the events. Those who knew Robert Jones said that he had never hinted at being suicidal although witnesses stated that he had suffered from nightmares about the struggle on that distant night in South Africa. Strangely, although Jones makes no mention of receiving a head wound at Rorke's Drift, his widow mentioned that he had been wounded 'close to the eye'. Based upon the evidence presented before them, particularly that of the doctor, the jury concluded that Robert Jones had committed suicide whilst 'temporarily insane'. As mentioned in the entry for Charles Lumley (page 56) no verdict of temporary insanity could be given by a modern jury.

Later, suggestions were made that the shooting was a tragic accident, that the gun which he used was a box-lock shotgun which could easily have gone off had it sustained any sudden knock. In the 1890s, people were less 'health and safety' conscious and often walked about without 'breaking' a shotgun. If Jones had tripped, or dropped the gun, it could easily have gone off by itself. The evidence of PC Bowen and Dr McMichan clearly ruled this out. Jones had seemed happy enough in the hours immediately before the shooting. His greeting to the laundrymaid made no suggestion that he was preoccupied or distressed, although it is not uncommon for suicides to develop a contented demeanour shortly before taking their own life. There are also reports that Jones was shot twice; there is no evidence to support this claim. One historian claims to have seen written testimony from Major de la Hay to the effect that the gun in question was known to go off 'at the slightest knock' but the Major did not appear to have given any such evidence at the inquest.

A sad feature of Robert Jones's death is that the headstone on his grave was positioned facing west, the opposite direction to all the others in the same row in Peterchurch churchyard. This once normal, but heartless, tradition when marking the grave of suicides, has now, thankfully, ceased. Today, suicide is seen as the tragic outcome of a medical condition and not as a crime.

In early 1900, a widow with four young children, Elizabeth Jones married William Tilbury, a farmer of Rose Farm, Peterchurch. By 1901, she had another child but her second husband seems to have cared for her other children as lovingly as he did his own.

One of the more unusual items of VC memorabilia, a poster depicting Robert Jones, VC produced by the Wye Valley Brewery to celebrate their 'Victory Ale'.

HENRY HOOK
Private
2nd/24th (2nd Warwickshire) Regiment of Foot

Pte Henry Hook, VC, 1879

Full Name: Alfred Henry Hook. It would appear that he was baptised as 'Alfred Hook', the name by which he was known in his youth. He later adopted his father's name, Henry, and became known as Harry in adult life.

Place of Birth: Birdwood, Churcham, Gloucestershire. His family moved to Drybridge Street, Monmouth in the 1870s.

Date of Birth: 6 August 1850. He was the eldest child.

Father: Henry Hook.

Mother: Eleanor (Ellen) Hook (née Higgs) of Birdwood, Churcham, Gloucestershire.

Father's Occupation: Agricultural labourer and woodman.

Education: Basic formal education. As late as the 1880s he is recorded as being 'unable to read or write with any facility'.

Pre-Service Employment: Farm labourer in Huntley, seven miles north-west of Gloucester, and woodman.

Service Record: Served for five years in the Royal Monmouthshire Militia (Service N⁰· 4454), he first appears in the records on 10 May 1869; attested at Monmouth, 13 March 1877, and posted to 2nd/24th Regiment of Foot, 11 May 1877 (Service N⁰· 1373); served Cape Colony and Natal, 1878–9 (present at the defence of Rorke's Drift, 22/23 January 1879, received a scalp wound from a Zulu assegai which, in later years, caused him some discomfort); purchased his discharge, 25 June 1880 (for £18); February 1882 joined the Bloomsbury Rifle Volunteers (19th Middlesex), promoted to corporal, resigned 24 January 1887; joined 17th (North) Middlesex Volunteers 26 January 1887 as a private, lance corporal March 1887, corporal, resigned 1 November 1880; applied to become a Yeoman of the Guard but was turned down as not meeting the statutory requirement of having been a sergeant in the Army and having served twenty-one years; joined 1st Volunteer Battalion Royal Fusiliers 20 April 1896 in which he was promoted to sergeant instructor of musketry; discharged 23 January 1905 on the grounds of ill health.

Decorations, Medals and Rewards: Victoria Cross (for action at Rorke's Drift, Natal, 22/23 January 1879); South Africa Medal (clasp for 1877–8–9); Good Conduct Badge; Marksman Badge.

Post-Service Employment: On his discharge he was employed as a groom in Monmouth before moving to London where he resided at Sydenham Hill and was employed as a labourer at the British Museum from 26 December 1881. He later became a duster, then a cloakroom attendant at the same museum, a post which he held until ill-health forced him to retire on 31 December 1904 (receiving a Treasury gratuity for his service). Whilst in London he resided at 89 Patshull Road, Kentish Town, 23 Lesly Street, Holloway and 4 Cumberland Street, Pimlico. He was a member of the Loyal St James Lodge of the Oddfellows. After retiring he returned to Gloucestershire.

Married: (1) Comfort Jones of Kilcot, Gloucestershire, at Aston Ingham Church, Herefordshire, 26 December 1870. (2) He married Ada Letitia, daughter of William Frederick Taylor, goldsmith of the City of London, at St Andrew's Church, Islington, 10 April 1897.

The VC and South Africa medal of Henry Hook, now displayed at the RRW Museum, Brecon.

Children: One son and two daughters by his marriage to Comfort Jones. Two daughters by his marriage to Ada Taylor.

Died: 12 March 1905, at his home, 2 Osborne Villas, Roseberry Avenue, Gloucester (now demolished), of pulmonary consumption. His health had always been poor since his return from South Africa.

Buried: Churcham, Gloucestershire, 18 March 1905. Amongst the mourners was Frederick Hitch, VC.

Memorials: Churcham, Gloucestershire; Havard Chapel, Brecon Cathedral, Brecon. *Hook of Rorke's Drift*, a biography by Barry C. Johnson, was published by Bartletts Press in 2004. The same author had previously published an article in *Colonnade* (British Museum staff magazine) in 1967 and *Rorke's Drift and the British Museum: The Life of Henry Hook, VC*, in 1986. *Honour the Brave*, a grand slow march for pianoforté, by J. Riviere with words by H. Hersee, dedicated to the heroes of Rorke's Drift, 1879; Hook Close, Monmouth.

Location of Victoria Cross: RRW Museum, Brecon.

Citation for the Victoria Cross: *London Gazette*, 2 May 1879.

'Private John Williams was posted with Private Joseph Williams and Private William Horrigan, 1st Battalion 24th Regiment, in a distant room of the hospital, which they held for more than an hour, so long as they had a round of ammunition left; as communication was for the time cut off, the Zulus were able to advance and burst open the door; they dragged out Private Joseph Williams and two of the patients, and assegaied them. Whilst the Zulus were occupied with the slaughter of these men a lull took place, during which Private John Williams who, with two of the patients, were the only men now left alive in this ward, succeeded in knocking a hole in the partition, and in taking the two patients into the next ward, where he found Private Hook.

These two men together, one man working whilst the other fought and held the enemy at bay with his bayonet, broke through three more partitions, and were thus enabled to bring eight patients through a small window into the inner line of defence.'

This was a shared citation with Private John Williams (Fielding).

VC Investiture: By Lieutenant-General Sir Garnet Wolseley, High Commissioner and GOC British Troops, South Africa, 3 August 1879, at Fort Melvill, Rorke's Drift, Natal. He was the only one of the Rorke's Drift VCs to be decorated at the scene of the VC action.

Pte Henry Hook, VC, 1879 with another soldier, almost certainly his brother. [Mrs Jean Furness]

The Hook family. Top, Henry Hook, probably his wedding photograph. Right: Ada Hook, his second wife. Far right: Victoria Catherine (named to give her the initials 'VC'), wearing her father's miniature medals, and Letitia Jean, Hook's daughters by his second marriage. [all pictures courtesy of Mrs Jean Furness]

Henry Hook has become one of the most celebrated recipients of the Victoria Cross and, at the time of his death, his funeral in Gloucester was possibly the largest ever held in the city. Why he should have been so fêted is unclear and, perversely, his name was again brought to the fore by his total misrepresentation in the classic film *Zulu*, released in 1964. While his comrades-in-arms enjoyed brief fame immediately after 1879, before slipping back into relative obscurity, Hook remained in the public eye and has been the subject of a full biography, *Hook of Rorke's Drift* by Barry C. Johnson (2004) which has cleared-up much of the ambiguity and misrepresentation. It is not my intention to reiterate here the facts uncovered by Mr Johnson, but merely to clarify those details which were previously wrongly reported.

Alfred Hook (which was his registered name) was born in Gloucestershire in 1850, and became known as Henry (or Harry) after his father. It was common, particularly in Wales, and perhaps also along the border area, for all sons to be given their father's name even if it was not shown on their baptism or birth certificates. There is no doubt, therefore, that Hook was an Englishman by birth, although the family later moved to live in Monmouth.

Henry first sampled military service in the Royal Monmouthshire Militia which he joined in 1869, when his particulars were recorded as N° 4454, height 5′ 6″, occupation labourer, aged 18 years and 9 months. On Boxing Day 1870 he married Comfort Jones at Aston Ingham Church and the couple had three children: Raymond John (1871), Henrietta (1873) and Julia Ann (1876). It would appear that the marriage was not a happy one and that, by the time of Julia Ann's birth, Henry had left the family and may have been living in London, where there is some evidence that he may have joined the Bloomsbury Rifles, a volunteer unit (his service with the militia having expired in 1874). Within a short time, however, he was back in Monmouth where, on 13 March 1877, he enlisted in the 2nd Warwickshire Regiment (24th Regiment of Foot), a unit which had been allocated the 24th District in 1871 with a depot at Brecon. At this point, another inconsistency appears with regards to Hook's early life. His age, according to his attestation papers, is given as 23 years and 8 months

Sgt Henry Hook, VC of the Royal Fusiliers, inscribed 'Dadie'. [Mrs Jean Furness]

which gives him a birth date of the summer of 1853 — three years later than his actual birthday. Had he revealed his real age of 26 years and 7 months he would have been too old to enlist, the upper age limit then being 25 years.

After early service in the south-east of England, at Dover and Chatham, he embarked with his regiment at Portsmouth in February 1878 aboard the troopship *Himalaya* and arrived at East London, Cape Colony on 9 March. There is no evidence that during this early period of his regular army service that Henry Hook had any contact with his wife and family in Gloucestershire.

The regiment served in the Frontier War of 1878 and formed part of the force assembled by Lieutenant-General Lord Chelmsford for the invasion of Zululand in January 1879. As a member of B Company, Hook was posted to the former mission station at Rorke's Drift. In later years, he made his own record of the events of 22/23 November 1879. Assisted and edited by Walter Wood, the account appeared in *The Royal Magazine*, February 1905.

Everything was perfectly quiet at Rorke's Drift after the column (Durnford's force) had left, and every officer and man was going about his business as usual. Not a soul suspected that only a dozen miles away the very men that we had said 'Goodbye' and 'Good Luck' to were either dead or standing back-to-back in a last fierce fight with the Zulus. Our garrison consisted of B Company of the 2/24th under Lieutenant Bromhead, and details which brought the total number of us up to 139. Besides these, we had about 300 men of the Natal Native Contingent; but they didn't count, as they bolted in a body when the fight began. We were all knocking about, and I was making tea for the sick, as I was hospital cook at the time.

Suddenly there was a commotion in the camp, and we saw two men galloping towards us from the other side of the river, which was Zululand. Lieutenant Chard of the Engineers was protecting the ponts over the river and, as senior officer, was in command at the drift. The ponts were very simple affairs, one of them being supported on big barrels, and the other on boats. Lieutenant Bromhead was in the camp itself. The horsemen shouted and were brought across the river, and then we knew what had happened to our comrades. They had been butchered to a man. That was awful enough news, but worse was to follow, for we were told that the Zulus were coming straight on from Isandhlwana to attack us. At the same time, a note was received by Lieutenant Bromhead from the Column to say that the enemy was coming on and that the post was to be held at all costs.

For some little time we were all stunned, then everything changed from perfect quietness to intense excitement and energy. There was a general feeling that the only safe thing was to retire and try to join the troops at Helpmakaar. The horsemen had said that the Zulus would be up in two or three minutes; but luckily for us they did not show themselves for more than an hour.

Henry Hook's miniature VC and South Africa Medal.
[Mrs Jean Furness]

Lieutenant Chard rushed up from the river, about a quarter of a mile away, and saw Lieutenant Bromhead. Orders were given to strike the camp and make ready to go, and we actually loaded up two wagons. Then Mr Dalton, of the Commissariat Department, came up and said that if we left the drift every man was certain to be killed. He had formerly been a sergeant-major in a line regiment and was one of the bravest men that ever lived. Lieutenants Chard and Bromhead held a consultation, short and earnest, and orders were given that we were to get the hospital and storehouse ready for defence, and that we were never to say die or surrender.

Not a minute was lost. Lieutenant Bromhead superintended the loopholing and barricading of the hospital and storehouse, and the making of a connection of the defences between the two buildings with walls of mealie bags and wagons. The mealie-bags were good, big, heavy things, weighing about 200 pounds each, and during the fight many of them were burst open by assegais and bullets, and the mealies (Indian corn) were thickly spread about the ground.

The biscuit boxes contained ordinary biscuit. They were big, square wooden boxes, weighing about a hundredweight each. The meat boxes, too, were very heavy, as they contained tinned meat. They were smaller than the biscuit boxes. While these precautions were being made, Lieutenant Chard went down to the river and brought in the pont guard of a sergeant and half-a-dozen men, with the wagons and gear. The two officers saw that every soldier was at his post, then we were ready for the Zulus when they cared to come.

They were not long. Just before half past four we heard firing behind the conical hill at the back of the drift, called Oskarsberg Hill, and suddenly about five or six hundred Zulus swept around, coming for us at a run. Instantly the natives — Kaffirs who had been very useful in making the barricade of wagons, mealie-bags and biscuit boxes around the camp — bolted towards Helpmakaar, and what was worse, their officer and a European sergeant went with them. To see them deserting like that was too much for some of us, and we fired after them. The sergeant [sic] was struck and killed. Half-a-dozen of us were stationed in the hospital, with orders to hold it and guard the sick. The ends of the building were of stone, the side walls of ordinary bricks, and the inside walls or partitions of sun-dried bricks of mud. These shoddy inside bricks proved our salvation, as you will see. It was a queer little one-storeyed building, which it is almost impossible to describe; but we were pinned like rats in a hole; because all the doorways except one had been barricaded with mealie-bags, and we had done the same with the windows. The interior was divided by means of partition walls into which were fitted some very slight doors. The patients' beds were simple, rough affairs of boards, raised only about half a foot above the floor. To talk of hospital and beds gives the idea of a big building, but as a matter of fact this hospital was a mere little shed or bungalow, divided up into rooms so small that you could hardly swing a bayonet in them. There were about nine men who could not move, but altogether there were about thirty. Most of these, however, could help to defend themselves.

As soon as our Kaffirs bolted, it was seen that the fort as we had first made it was too big to be held, so Lieutenant Chard instantly reduced the space by having a row of biscuit-boxes drawn across the middle, about four feet high. This was our inner entrenchment, and proved very valuable. The Zulus came on at a wild rush, and although many of them were shot down, they got to within about fifty yards of our south wall of mealie-bags and biscuit boxes and wagons. They were caught between two fires, that from the hospital and that from the storehouse, and were checked; but they gained the shelter of the cookhouse and ovens, and gave us many heavy volleys. During the fight they took advantage of every bit of cover there was, anthills, a tract of bush that we had not had time to clear away, a garden or sort of orchard which was near us, and

Henry Hook's VC pension certificate.
[Mrs Jean Furness]

a ledge of rock and some caves (on the Oscarsberg) which were only about a hundred yards away. They neglected nothing, and while they went on firing large bodies kept hurling themselves against our slender breastworks.

But it was the hospital they assaulted most fiercely. I had charge with a man that we called Old King Cole of a small room with only one patient in it. Cole kept with me for some time after the fight began, then he said he was not going to stay. He went outside and was instantly killed by the Zulus, so that I was left alone with the patient, a native whose leg was broken and who kept crying out, 'Take my bandage off, so that I can come.' But it was impossible to do anything except fight, and I blazed away as hard as I could. By this time I was the only defender of my room. Poor Old King Cole was lying dead outside.

Then there was the whizz and rip of the assegais, of which I had experience during the Kaffir Campaign of 1877–8. We had plenty of ammunition, but we were told to save it and so we took careful aim at every shot, and hardly a cartridge was wasted. One of my comrades, Private Dunbar, shot no fewer than nine Zulus, one of them being a chief.

From the very first the enemy tried to rush the hospital, and at last they managed to set fire to the thick grass which formed the roof. This put us in a terrible plight, because it meant that we were either to be massacred or burned alive, or get out of the building. To get out seemed impossible; for if we left the hospital by the only door which had been left open, we should instantly fall into the midst of the Zulus. Besides, there were the helpless sick and wounded, and we could not leave them. My own little room communicated with another by means of a frail door like a bedroom door. Fire and dense choking smoke forced me to get out and go into the other room. It was impossible to take the native patient with me, and I had to leave him to an awful fate. But his death was, at any rate, a merciful one. I heard the Zulus asking him questions, and he tried to tear off his bandages and escape.

In the room where I now was there were nine sick men, and I alone to look after them for some time, still firing away, with the hospital burning. Suddenly in the thick smoke I saw John Williams, and above the din of battle and the cries of the wounded, I heard him shout, 'The Zulus are swarming all over the place. They've dragged Joseph Williams out and killed him.' John Williams had held the other room with Private William Horrigan for more than an hour, until they had not a cartridge left. The Zulus then burst in and dragged out Joseph Williams and two of the patients, and assegaied them. It was only because they were so busy with this slaughtering that John Williams and two of the patients were able to knock a hole in the partition and get into the room where I was posted. Horrigan was killed. What were we to do? We were pinned like rats in a hole. Already the Zulus were fiercely trying to burst in through the doorway. The only way of escape was the wall itself, by making a hole big enough for a man to crawl through into an adjoining room, and so on until we got to our inmost entrenchment outside. Williams worked desperately at the wall with the navvy's pick, which I had been using to make some of the loopholes with.

All this time the Zulus were trying to get into the room. Their assegais kept whizzing towards us, and one struck me in front of the helmet. We were wearing the white tropical helmets then. But the helmet tilted back under the blow and made the spear lose its power so that I escaped with a scalp wound which did not trouble me much then, although it has often caused me illness since. Only one man at a time could get in at the door. A big Zulu sprang forward and seized my rifle, but I tore it free and, slipping a cartridge in, I shot him point-blank. Time after time the Zulus gripped the muzzle and tried to tear the rifle from my grasp, and time after time I wrenched it back, because I had a better grip than they had. All this time Williams was getting the sick through the hole into the next room, all except one, a soldier of the 24th named Conley, who could not move because of a broken leg. Watching for my chance, I dashed from the doorway and, grabbing Conley, I pulled him after me through the hole. His leg got broken again, but there was no help for it. As soon as we left the room the Zulus burst in with furious cries of disappointment and rage.

Now there was a repetition of the work of holding the doorway, except that I had to stand by a hole instead of a door, while Williams picked away at the tar wall to make an opening for escape into the next room. There was more desperate and almost hopeless fighting, as it seemed, but most of the poor fellows were got through the hole. Again I had to drag Conley through, a terrific task because he was a very heavy man. We were now all in a little room that gave upon the inner line of defence which had been made. We (Williams and Robert Jones and William Jones and myself) were the last men to leave the hospital, after most of the poor fellows were got through the hole. Again the small window and away from the burning building; but it was impossible to save a few of them, and they were butchered. Privates William Jones and Robert Jones during all this time were doing magnificent work in another ward which faced the hill. They kept at it with bullet and bayonet until six of the seven patients had been removed. They would have got the seventh, Sergeant Maxfield, out safely, but he was delirious with fever and, although they managed to dress him, he refused to move. Robert Jones made a last rush to try and get him away like the rest, but when he got back into the room he saw that Maxfield was being stabbed by the Zulus as he lay on his bed. Corporal Allen and Private Hitch helped greatly in keeping up communications with the hospital. They were both badly wounded, but when they could not fight any longer they served out ammunition to their comrades throughout the night.

As we got the sick and wounded out they were taken to a verandah in front of the storehouse, and Dr Reynolds under a heavy fire and clouds of assegais, did

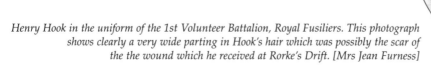

Henry Hook in the uniform of the 1st Volunteer Battalion, Royal Fusiliers. This photograph shows clearly a very wide parting in Hook's hair which was possibly the scar of the the wound which he received at Rorke's Drift. [Mrs Jean Furness]

Avove and below left: Henry Hook's funeral cortège passes through Gloucester. This is believed to have been the largest funeral ever seen in the city. When one considers that Hook had only lived in Gloucester for a few weeks before his death, the size of the crowd attending is quite staggering.
[Mrs Jean Furness]

Right: The funeral reaches the church at Churcham. If this photograph is typical, then the enormous crowd in attendance seems to have followed the cortège all the way from Gloucester.
[Mrs Jean Furness]

Henry Hook's brass memorial plaque in the Havard Chapel, Brecon Cathedral. He is the only private soldier to be commemorated on an individual plaque.

everything he could for them. All this time, of course, the storehouse was being valiantly defended by the rest of the garrison. When we got into the inner fort, I took my post at a place where two men had been shot. While I was there another man was shot in the neck, I think by a bullet which came through the space between two biscuit boxes that were not quite close together. This was at about six o'clock in the evening, nearly two hours after the opening shot of the battle had been fired. Every now and then the Zulus would make a rush for it and get in. We had to charge them out. By this time it was dark, and the hospital was all in flames, but this gave us a splendid light to fight by. I believe it was this light that saved us. We could see them coming, and they could not rush us and take us by surprise from any point. They could not get at us, and so they went away and had ten or fifteen minutes of a war-dance. This roused them up again, and their excitement was so intense that the ground fairly seemed to shake. Then, when they were goaded to the highest pitch, they would hurl themselves at us again.

I need hardly say that we were using Martinis, and fine rifles they were, too. But we did so much firing that they became hot, and the brass of the cartridges softened, the result being that the barrels got very foul and the cartridge chamber jammed. My own rifle was jammed several times, and I had to work away with the ramrod 'til I cleared it. We used the old three-sided bayonet, and the long, thin blade we called the 'lung' bayonet. They were very fine weapons, too, but some were very poor in quality, and either twisted or bent badly. Several were like that after the fight; but some terrible thrusts were given, and I saw dead Zulus who had been pinned to the ground by the bayonets going through them.

All this time the sick and wounded were crying for water. We had the water-cart full of water, but it was just by the deserted hospital and we could not hope to get it until the day broke, when the Zulus might begin to lose heart and to stop in their mad rushes. But we could not bear the cries any longer, and three or four of us jumped over the boxes and ran and fetched some water in.

The long night passed and the day broke. Then we looked around us to see what had happened, and there was not a living soul who was not thankful to find that the Zulus had had enough of it and were disappearing over the hill to the south-west. Orders were given to patrol the ground, collect the arms of the dead blacks, and make our position as strong as possible in case of fresh attacks.

One of the first things I did was to go up to the man who was still looking over our breastworks with his rifle presented to the spot where so many of the Zulus had been. I went up to him, and saw that he did not move, and that he looked very quiet. I went nearer and said 'Hello, what are you doing here?' He made no answer, and did not stir. I went still closer, and something in his appearance made me tilt his helmet back, as you sometimes tilt back a hat when you want to look closely into a face. As I did so I saw a bullet-mark in his forehead, and knew that he was dead.

I went away, and was walking up the dry bed of a little stream near the drift with my own rifle in my right hand and a bunch of assegais over my left shoulder. Suddenly I came across an unarmed Zulu lying on the ground, apparently dead but bleeding from the leg. Thinking it strange that a dead man should bleed, I hesitated, and wondered whether I should go on, as other Zulus

Hook Close, Monmouth.

Unveiling the memorial on Hook's grave at Churcham.

might be lurking about. But I resumed my task. Just as I was passing, the supposed dead man seized the butt of my rifle and tried to drag it away. The bunch of assegais rattled to earth.

The Zulu suddenly released his grasp of the rifle with one hand, and with the other fiercely endeavoured to drag me down. The fight was short and sharp; but it ended by the Zulu being struck in the chest with the butt and knocked to the ground. The rest was quickly over. After that we were not allowed to go on with our task except in twos and threes. When we had done this work we went back to the inner line of defence, sad enough, even the most cheerful of us. But we had no time to dwell on the awful scenes about us. We did not know how soon another assault might be made, but we did know that if the Zulus kept on attacking us it was only a question of time before we were cut to pieces, as our comrades a dozen miles away had been destroyed.

The roof of the hospital had fallen in by this time, and only the storehouse was standing. We were ordered to put ropes through the loopholes of the wall of the hospital and pull them down. This we did, and the walls, which had already been weakened by our picks, partially collapsed. Then we tore away the thatch from the storehouse so that the Zulus could not, even if they wished, set fire to it, as they had fired the hospital. With the ruins of the walls we strengthened our little fort, and again waited for the Zulus — if they cared to come. But they had finished their attack.

We looked about us everywhere for signs of relief, but saw nothing, and our hearts sank. Then came an awful time of suspense. Two of our men had been on the roof of the storehouse signalling with flags when the Zulus meant to attack us. This gave us time to make ready for them. The signallers were still able to stand above the ground, so that they could be seen at a good distance. We saw their flags going wildly. What was it? Everbody was mad with anxiety to know whether it could be friends to relieve us, or more Zulus to destroy us. We watched the flags flapping, and then learnt that signals were being made in reply. We knew we were safe and that friends were marching up to us.

We broke into roar after roar of cheering, waving red coats and white helmets, and we cheered again and again when, at about six o'clock in the morning, Colonel Russell rode up with some mounted infantry. We saw them come in, and at the same time we saw that the Zulus had once more got ready to sweep around the mountain to attack us. But it was too late, and on seeing that we were reinforced they turned silently away, and only their dead and a few wounded were left with us.

Lord Chelmsford and what was left of the 3rd Column came up to Rorke's Drift soon after. There was no time to sit down and mope.

Hook survived the battle relatively unscathed and assisted in the burial of the fifteen white men who had died in the fighting. He was then appointed servant to Scotsman Major (Brevet Lieutenant-Colonel) Wilsone Black, the officer who organised the search and recovery of the Queen's Colour of the 1/24th Regiment, and accompanied him to the field of Isandlwana on 21 May, where he is reputed to have recovered a Bible now on display at the Regimental Museum in Brecon. It was during this expedition that a start was made on burying the dead.

Hook was nominated for the Victoria Cross in Bromhead's letter to Lord Chelmsford of 15 February:

No 1395 Private John Williams … No 1373 Private Henry Hook. These two men together, one man working whilst the other fought & held the enemy at bay with his bayonet, broke through three more petitions, & were thus

The grave of Henry Hook, VC in Churcham, Gloucestershire.

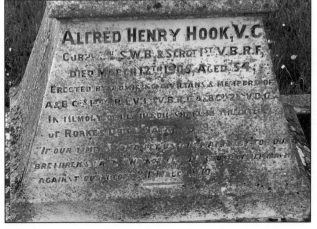

The inscription on the grave of Henry Hook, VC is now deteriorating rapidly. It reads:

ALFRED HENRY HOOK, V.C.
CORPL 2ND S.W.B. & SERGT 1st V.B.R.F.,
DIED MARCH 12th 1905, AGED 54,
Erected by admiring civilians & members of
A & B Coys 1st C. R. L. V. 1st V.B. R.F., A & B Co 2nd V.B.G.H.
In memory of his heroic share in the defence of Rorke's Drift, Natal, 1879.
'If our time is come, let us die manfully for our brethren's sake and not leave a cause of reproach against our glory' I Macc. IX.10.

Hook was never a corporal in the 24th Regiment.

Drybridge Street, Monmouth, the home of the Hook family during the 1870s.

enabled to bring eight patients through a small window into our inner line of defence …

— word for word the phrasing of the final citation. The presentation of the VC was arranged for 3 August, the day after the arrival of Sir Garnet Wolseley at Rorke's Drift (by now renamed Fort Melvill). He was the only one of the defenders to be decorated on the site of the action.

In October Hook accompanied Major Black to Gibraltar, ahead of the battalion, where he first exhibited signs of the ill health that was to plague his later years. Despite this, and his gallant action in Natal, when he decided to obtain his discharge from the Army, Hook was required to pay £18 compensation and sufficient money to pay for his transporation back to Britain. His discharge papers show that 'His conduct has been very good … He is in possession of one Good Conduct Badge.' His intended place of residence was his parent's home in Monmouth, not the home of his wife and children at Mount Pleasant, Newent in Gloucestershire.

Without work, Hook declared himself willing to turn his hand to almost anything and obtained a position as a groom with Dr Willis in Glendower Street. The following year his father died, and the Hook family moved away from Monmouth, his mother to Cardiff and Henry to London. His first job in the capital seems to have been as a labourer with William Cubitt & Co who placed him, on contract, in the general cleaning department of the British Museum. At the end of 1882 he was appointed to a permanent position on the staff of the British Museum, employed as a duster in the Library.

In 1897, Hook obtained a divorce from his wife Comfort on the grounds of her adultery. Three months later, he married Ada Taylor and the couple had two daughters, Victoria Catherine (1899) and Letitia Jean (1902). He remained at the Museum until forced to retire because of his health in January 1905 and immediately moved the family, in much reduced circumstances, to Gloucester. Following an application by Hook himself, his VC pension was increased from the standard £10 per annum, to £50. The efforts to improve his living conditions were to no avail and he died of consumption on 12 March.

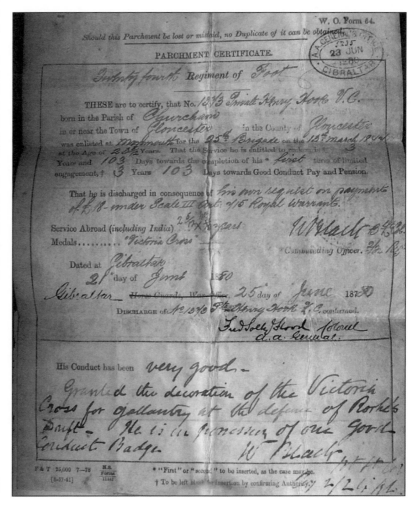

Hook's Army discharge certificate, 1880.
[Mrs Jean Furness]

JOHN WILLIAMS
Private
2nd/24th (2nd Warwickshire) Regiment of Foot

John Williams, VC, 1879

Full Name: John Fielding (Williams was a pseudonym).
Place of Birth: Merthyr Road, Abergavenny, Monmouthshire. The family moved to live in Cwmbran, Monmouthshire when he was aged about 5 years.
Date of Birth: 24 May 1857. He was one of ten children, the second eldest, and the second son. His brother Denis also joined the Army and served in the Sudan, the Boer War and the Great War.
Father: Michael Fielding (born Ireland, died 1914).
Mother: Margaret Fielding (née Godsil).
Father's Occupation: Gardener/labourer.
Education: No evidence of any formal education prior to his military service.
Pre-Service Employment: Employed aged 8 years by the Patent Nut & Bolt Works, Cwmbran.
Service Record: Enlisted in the Monmouthshire Militia, February 1877; attested at Monmouth, 24th Regiment of Foot, 27 May 1877 (Service N° 1395); joined 2nd/24th Regiment of Foot at Chatham, June 1877; served Cape Colony and Natal, 1877–9 (present at the defence of Rorke's Drift, 22/23 January 1879); Gibraltar 1879–80; served India, 1880–83; transferred to the Army Reserve, 1883; discharged from the Reserve, 22 May 1893; served as a sergeant in the 3rd Volunteer Battalion, South Wales Borderers; volunteered for service during the Great War and served with the SWB at Brecon Barracks (Service N° 15277), 4 December 1914–23 May 1920.
Decorations, Medals and Rewards: Victoria Cross (for action at Rorke's Drift, Natal, 22/23 January 1879); South Africa Medal (clasp for 1877–8–9).
Post-Service Employment: Employed in a nut and bolt factory.
Married: Elizabeth, daughter of Thomas Murphy, St Albans RC Church, Pontypool, 15 April 1884; she was of Irish extraction but born in Llantarnam, Monmouthshire. She died in 1914.
Children: Three sons: Thomas (born 1885, KinA with the SWB (Service N° 8391) during the Battle of the Aisne, 26 September 1914), William (born 1889), John (born 1895, served Dorsetshire Regiment in the First World War); two daughters: Margaret Ellen (born 1888) and Catherine (born 1892, also known as Kathleen and Kath); one step-daughter (Ann Murphy, born 1878, died 1901 of tuberculosis).
Died: 25 November 1932 at his daughter Kath's home, Tŷcoch, Cwmbran, Monmouthshire. He lived at the time with his daughter Margaret, at 28 Cocker Avenue, Cwmbran. He was the last surviving Rorke's Drift VC.
Buried: With full military honours in Llanfihangel churchyard, Llantarnam, Monmouthshire, 29 November 1932. Prior to the funeral, his coffin had lain-in-state, with a military guard of honour of the South Wales Borderers, in Our Lady of the Angels Church, Wesley Street, Cwmbran. The funeral was recorded by Pathé News and shown in cinemas across the country.
Memorials: Llanfihangel Churchyard, Llantarnam, Monmouthshire; John Fielding House (residential home for the mentally handicapped, opened 4 June 1973, closed *circa* 2001 and, at the time of writing, awaiting demolition), Llantarnam, Monmouthshire;

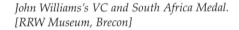

John Williams's VC and South Africa Medal. [RRW Museum, Brecon]

John Williams, VC, (centre) with his parents. [Mrs Aileen Johnston]

'John Fielding' public house, Cwmbran, Monmouthshire; John Williams VC, TA Centre, Cwmbran (opened 1999). *Honour the Brave*, a grand slow march for pianoforté, by J. Riviere with words by H. Hersee, dedicated to the heroes of Rorke's Drift, 1879.

Location of Victoria Cross: RRW Museum, Brecon.

Citation for the Victoria Cross: *London Gazette*, 2 May 1879.

'Private John Williams was posted with Private Joseph Williams and Private William Horrigan, 1st Battalion 24th Regiment, in a distant room of the hospital, which they held for more than an hour, so long as they had a round of ammunition left; as communication was for the time cut off, the Zulus were able to advance and burst open the door; they dragged out Private Joseph Williams and two of the patients, and assegaied them. Whilst the Zulus were occupied with the slaughter of these men a lull took place, during which Private John Williams who, with two of the patients, were the only men now left alive in this ward, succeeded in knocking a hole in the partition, and in taking the two patients into the next ward, where he found Private Hook.

These two men together, one man working whilst the other fought and held the enemy at bay with his bayonet, broke through three more partitions, and were thus enabled to bring eight patients through a small window into the inner line of defence.'

This was a shared citation with Private Henry Hook.

VC Investiture: By Major-General Anderson, GOC Gibraltar at Alameda Parade Ground, Gibraltar, 1 March 1880.

The regiment is formed up at Gibraltar for the presentation of the Victoria Cross to John Williams, St David's Day, 1880.

The headstone of John Williams, VC, in Llanfihangel churchyard, Llantarnam.

The John Fielding public house, Cwmbran.

John Williams, VC, a studio portrait taken during the Great War. [Cwmbran and District Ex-Service Association]

Close to the churchyard gate at Llanfihangel, Llantarnam in Cwmbran, fittingly in the shadow of a nearby pub sign bearing the word 'Courage', lies buried local man John Fielding, who is better known as John Williams, VC of Rorke's Drift.

John's father was of Irish extraction, having arrived in Wales sometime during the mid nineteenth century, probably to escape the great Irish famine. Michael Fielding had settled in Llanthewy Rhytherch near Abergavenny, Monmouthshire where he met Margaret Godsil, the daughter of a local schoolmaster. They were married in the Roman Catholic Chapel at Abergavenny on 31 January 1855. Rather surprisingly, when one considers the stated occupation of Margaret's father, the bride seems to have been unable to sign the marriage licence. Later that year their first son, Thomas, was born, followed by John in May 1857 (by which time the family appears to have been living in Merthyr Road, Abergavenny and the father was employed as a gardener). These two boys were then followed by seven more boys and one girl, spread over a period of twenty-five years. The family had moved from Abergavenny to the nearby village of Llanvetherine by 1861, and were in Cwmbran two years later. By 1871 they were living at 3 Pen-y-wain [Pen-y-Waun] Cottages in Llantarnam where, unfortunately for the historian, the census enumerator completed the form incorrectly and omitted to indicate whether John was in employment.

His military career began on 29 January 1877 when he enlisted (No 6621) as a private in the Royal Monmouth Regiment of Militia, following in the footsteps of Henry Hook VC, who had joined the same unit in 1869. What is of interest with Fielding's enlistment is that he joined under the assumed name of Williams. Speculation has been rife over many years as to why he assumed the surname Williams but, in terms of hard fact, there is no evidence to support any of the theories. It is possible, however, to disprove the most commonly held belief, that John Fielding assumed the name Williams to prevent his father from finding him in the army. The militia was a part-time military force and John Fielding continued to live at home with his parents whilst he served with the Royal Monmouths, a fact which he is unlikely to have been able to conceal from his father. Although the enrolment register shows his address as 'near Holly Bush Inn, Cwmbran' this is not an attempt to hide his home as 3 Pen-y-wain Cottages were located very close to this beer house. The medical officer examining him gave his age as 18 years (when in fact he was 19 years 8 months and his height as 5' 5$\frac{3}{4}$", chest measurement 34$\frac{1}{2}$", and occupation 'puddler' (at this time he was working at the Patent Nut & Bolt Works in Cwmbran). The militia was an old military force which could trace its origins back to the Anglo Saxon fyrd, an organisation which was made up of all able-bodied men in society who, in addition to their everyday occupations, were required to train in the use of weapons and who could be called upon for local or national defence. By the nineteenth century this organisation had evolved into the militia whose local head was the lord lieutenant of each county. Until the Militia Act of 1852, the force had been raised by compulsion via the Militia Ballot whereby the names of all able-bodied men in a county were balloted and those chosen were obliged to serve in the militia. After this date, the compulsory element of militia service was replaced by voluntary enlistment for a period of five years. Recruits were given a cash bounty for their service and were obliged to attend an annual period of training with their local regiment. During this time, every encouragement was given to the militiamen to persuade them to transfer their service to the regular Army. In 1871, the Cardwell army reforms transferred control of the militia from the lords lieutenant of each county to the Crown, and henceforth militiamen were paid and clothed in the same way as the regular soldiers. The enrolment register shows that John Williams's 'Bringer' [recruiter] was a Sergeant Harris, and it may very well have been that the potential young recruit gave a false name and age in the hope of avoiding the consequences of his dalliance with the sergeant, perhaps in a local public house, believing that the enlistment might all go away in the light of day. But, it did not go away and, whatever the actual reason for John Fielding's deception of the authorities, as far as the military were concerned, the young recruit was an 18-year old named John Williams, and as such he would remain for the remainder of his service. As for the choice of name 'Williams', it was probably nothing more than the first name that came to mind.

John Fielding appears to have taken to military life, so much so, that in less than four months, he decided to volunteer for service with the regular Army and proceeded to obtain his discharge from the Royal Monmouthshire Militia. His discharge was granted on 22 May, conditional upon his enlisting and, the following day, he took the oath of attestation at Monmouth and became a private soldier in the 24th Regiment of Foot. Once he had given false information about his name and age he was obliged to maintain the deceit and, on the attestation papers, his name was again given as 'Williams' and his age as 18 years 6 months. One further inaccuracy appears on this form —the Roman Catholic John Fielding had become the Anglican John Williams.

After basic training at the brigade depot at Brecon, Private John Williams joined the 2/24th Regiment at Chatham in June where he was posted to B Company and, the following year, sailed for Cape Colony where he saw service in the Frontier War of 1878 and the Anglo-Zulu War of 1879. Despite being the longest living of the Rorke's Drift VCs, he does not appear to have given his version of the events of 22/23 January 1879 until a very brief account appeared in the *Western Mail* on 22 January 1929:

I was born in Abergavenny in 1858 [sic] and 'listed on January 22, 1877 — two years to the day before the fight at Rorke's Drift. We got to South Africa in the beginning of 1878, and after remaining at Bailey's Post for some time were sent up country. While there, by the way, Capt. A. G. Godwin-Austen (whose brother was killed at Isandhlwana), was our captain and Lieut Bromhead was our lieutenant. We had a brush with the Kaffirs, and Capt. Austen was wounded and went home. He was shot in the loins by a Hottentot who was up a tree [sic]. We very soon settled accounts with him. We had him out of that tree like one o'clock. Well, we moved up to Pietermaritzburg, and thence to Rorke's Drift.

This, of course, was a mission station, and consisted of a few low buildings. The first of the regiment crossed on January 11th to the Bashi Valley and soon had an encounter with the Zulus, and then they moved on to Isandhlwana, and you know what happened there. My company was left at Rorke's Drift in charge of the hospital there, as well as the commissariat.

We first heard of the great disaster from Col Groom, who told us about Lieuts Melvill and Coghill. We had it, too, from the chaplain, the Rev. W. [sic] Smith. He is still living, I believe, but in any case I would like to say what a fine man he was, a true hero, who during the night that followed rendered magnificent service.

I can see it all now as clearly as I saw it on that day. There were 95 of us at that post, and we knew that 3,000 Zulus, flushed with victory and mad for more slaughter, would soon be upon us. We had just time. It was 3.30 in the afternoon when we saw them round the hill, and never did an enemy seem to have an easier prey. We had had no more time to improvise barricades with biscuit tins and mealie bags, and now they were upon us.

What did I feel? I don't know that I felt anymore than all the others felt. In his ordinary life a man often contemplates some possibility and feels he would be unable to face it, but when it does happen he does face it. He finds himself up against it and goes through with it. That is just about what happened to all of us.

We knew the seriousness of the affair, but we had no time to sit down and think about it. And now there was the Zulus, and there was one watchword for all of us — we must keep the enemy at bay. I heard that many times during the night that followed.

Besides, when the enemy appeared we had precious little time for thinking. The attack started at 3.30 [sic] in the afternoon, and for the next eighteen hours we knew all about it.

Yes, it was a terrible time. All we were concerned with was to keep the enemy at bay and to save the patients if we could. While they were killing poor Joe Williams and Horrigan I was as busy as I could be knocking that hole in the partition.

His closing comment to the newspaper reporter was that 'when his share in the fighting was ended he had just two rounds of ammunition left'. Such a brief and honest account of the defence seems typical of John Williams, and matches up with his shy, unassuming personality.

From Natal, John Williams went with his battalion to Gibraltar and from there in June 1882, aboard HM Troopship *Orontes* to India, arriving at Secunderabad in September from where he returned to Britain in October 1883

Depot Staff, South Wales Borderers, Brecon during the First World War. Sergeant John Williams, VC is wearing the darker uniform in the centre of the middle row. Due to a shortage of khaki uniforms, new members of staff were temporarily issued with police uniforms. [Mike Wilson]

Private Thomas Fielding (8391), South Wales Borderers, John Fielding's eldest son. He enlisted at Cwmbran on 9 March 1904, aged 19, for three years service with nine years on the Reserve. He was killed serving with the 1st Bn on 26 September 1914, during the Battle of the Aisne, when the regiment lost over 400 men. He has no known grave, but his name is recorded on the La Ferte-Sous-Jouarre Memorial, France.
[Mrs Monica Foster/Mrs Jayne Roper]

John Williams, VC, (centre) with his daughters.
[Mrs Aileen Johnston]

John Williams, VC with his son, John.
[Mrs Aileen Johnston]

and, having completed six years with the Colours, was transferred to the Army Reserve. He then joined C Coy 3rd (Volunteer) Battalion, South Wales Borderers in which he served until 1904, reaching the rank of sergeant.

Almost immediately upon his return to Llantarnam, John Fielding married local girl Elizabeth (Eliza) Murphy, a dressmaker, whose family had originally come from Ireland, and who lived on the same road as the Fieldings. Eliza had a daughter, Ann, born in early 1878. There is a strong possibility that Ann was John's natural daughter and the reason he had enlisted in the 2/24th Regiment. On one census return she is actually recorded as his daughter.

John resumed his pre-service employment at the Patent Nut & Bolt Works, first as a general labourer, then as a 'nut cutter', remaining there until 4 December 1914 when, aged 57, he re-enlisted in the South Wales Borderers at Brecon, with the rank of private (No 15277). Whether this was the result of a genuine desire to serve his country or a reaction to the death of his eldest son, Thomas, killed serving with the 1st Bn South Wales Borderers, is unrecorded. Serving in the Depot at Brecon, John Fielding was promoted to sergeant and was almost certainly used as a recruiting icon. Just as newly decorated VCs of the First World War were paraded around the country to aid recruiting, so the ageing hero of Rorke's Drift was held up as a model to prospective new recruits to the South Wales Borderers. He remained with the regiment until 1920 when he was discharged, given an Army Disablement Pension for 'chronic and recurring bronchitis', and returned to his old firm which was now part of Guest, Keen & Nettlefolds where he was employed as a machine operator until retiring in 1922, aged 65.

During the 1920s, John Fielding's status as a local celebrity was greatly enhanced and he was a regular visitor to the SWB barracks at Brecon and attended various VC reunions, including the Garden Party at Buckingham Palace on 26 June 1920, and the Reunion Dinner at the House Lords, on 9 November 1929. With the death of Dr James Reynolds, VC in March 1932, Fielding became the last surviving VC from the defence of Rorke's Drift. Living with his daughter, Margaret Pratley, at 28 Cocker Avenue, Cwmbran, he regularly walked along the canal bank to his other daughter

Catherine Jones's home at 7 Tŷcoch and it was whilst on such a walk, on 24 November 1932, that he was taken ill. Catherine called the doctor, but to no avail and he died the following morning. The Llantarnam *Parish Magazine* noted that his 'military bearing, geniality and smiling courtesy will be much missed amongst us.'

His funeral service was one of the most notable in the area's history with many thousands lining the route to the churchyard at Llantarnam. The event was covered by Pathé News and shown in cinemas throughout the country. Strangely, this Roman Catholic lies buried in an Anglican churchyard which, although closed for burials in 1906, was specially re-opened for the village's most famous son.

John Williams, VC, (centre) helping out with the harvesting, Llantarnam.
[Mrs Aileen Johnston]

John H. Williams, VC, DCM, MM and Bar
with John Williams, VC at Brecon, late 1920s.

The Union Flag-draped coffin of John Fielding is carried from the gun carriage into the churchyard at Llantarnam, 29 November 1932.

EDWARD BROWNE
Lieutenant
1st/24th (2nd Warwickshire) Regiment of Foot

Full Name: Edward Stevenson Browne.
Place of Birth: Park Terrace, St Andrew the Great, Cambridge.
Date of Birth: 23 December 1852, the eldest of four children, the others being Edward, Henry and Louisa.
Father: Salwey Browne, BA. Originally from Hatfield, Broad Oak, Essex. He died in 1859, at which time he was residing at Oakleaze, Almondbury, Gloucestershire.
Mother: Elizabeth Browne, daughter of William Stevenson, Esq, of Quebec, at Quebec, 11 May 1848. After her husband's death she lived at 13 Regent Street, Teignmouth, with her two sons and one daughter.
Father's Occupation: Captain, 68th (Durham) Regiment. He was a student at Cambridge University at the time of his son's birth.
Education: Early details unknown; RMC Sandhurst, 2 August 1869–31 December 1870.
Service Record: Commissioned as an ensign, 1st/24th Regiment of Foot, 23 September 1871; lieutenant, 28 October 1871; served Malta, 1872, Gibraltar, 1872, Cape Colony, 1875–7 (expedition to Griqualand West, 1875), Natal, Transvaal and Zululand 1877–9 (OC 1st Squadron Mounted Infantry, present at battles of Kambula and Ulundi); served 2nd campaign against Sekukuni, 1879; captain, 19 May 1880; adjutant, 4th Volunteer Battalion South Wales Borderers, 19 September 1881–18 September 1886; major, 2 November 1885; lieutenant-colonel, 2nd South Wales Borderers, 8 April 1893; DAAG, Musketry, Bengal, 3 November 1891–7 July 1892; colonel, 8 April 1897; CO Regimental District, Brecon, 8 April 1897; AAG North East District, 4 March 1900–6 September 1902; temporary brigadier-general, 7 September 1902; GOC 5th Army Corps, York, 1902; brigadier-general, 11th Brigade (later redesignated 6th Brigade), 2nd Army Corps, Southern Command, 10 November 1903–9th November 1906; retired, 10 November 1906; Colonel 2nd

Captain Edward Browne, VC, 1880.
[Brigadier M. E. Browne]

Browne at Hlobane, 28 March 1879. Painting by Stanley L. Wood. The citation for his VC incorrectly shows this action as being that for which he was awarded the Victoria Cross.

The VC, CB, Diamond Jubilee Medal and South Africa Medal of Edward Browne. [RRW Museum, Brecon]

Memorial plaque to Edward Browne, VC, Garrison Church, Portsmouth. [Courtesy of the Webmaster at www.memorials.inportsmouth.co.uk]

Volunteer Battalion, West Yorkshire Regiment, 3 December 1902 until his death.

Decorations, Medals and Rewards: Victoria Cross (for action at Khambula, Zululand, 29 March 1879); CB (*L.G.* 24 June 1904); South Africa Medal (clasp for 1878–9); MinD (twice); Diamond Jubilee Medal (1897).

Post-Service Employment: Retired general officer, residing at Gun House, Hampshire Terrace, Southsea.

Married: Annie Wright, at Edinburgh, 6 November 1879.

Children: Two sons (Colonel Maurice Browne, MC, DL, was Colonel of the Middlesex Regiment from 1942–52 and Major Edward Browne, OBE) and two daughters.

Died: Montreux, Switzerland, 16 July 1907.

Buried: Section 149, Commune de Chatelard, Clarens, Switzerland. The grave was re-used in 1991.

Memorials: The headstone at Clarens Cemetery, Commune de Chatland, Switzerland, was removed and the plot grassed over in 1962. Plaque in the Garrison Church, Portsmouth and Brecon Cathedral.

Location of Victoria Cross: RRW Museum, Brecon.

Citation for the Victoria Cross: *London Gazette,* 17 June 1879.

'For his gallant conduct on 29th March 1879, when the Mounted Infantry were being driven in by the enemy at Inholbana [sic], in galloping back and twice assisting on his horse (under heavy fire and within a few yards of the enemy) one of the mounted men who must otherwise have fallen into enemy hands.'

The citation is incorrect as the VC was awarded for the action at Khambula and not Inholbana.

VC Investiture: By Colonel R. T. Glynn, CB, at a brigade parade, at Pine Tree Camp, Durban, Natal, 22 August 1879. Surgeon Reynolds of Rorke's Drift was also decorated with his VC at the same parade.

Edward Stevenson Browne arrived in Cape Colony on New Year's Day 1875, a subaltern in the 1/24th Regiment of Foot. In May, the regiment formed part of an expeditionary force sent to Griqualand West to quell unrest amongst the local tribes. In May 1878, 47 men of the regiment were selected for training as mounted infantry under the command of Lieutenants Fred Carrington, John Dickinson and Edward Browne, the officers being chosen particularly for their skills as horsemen. The force was joined shortly afterwards by other detachments and trained at a camp near Newcastle. These were the forerunners of the mounted infantry units that played such a significant part in the Anglo-Boer War just over twenty years later. Known locally as Carrington's Horse, this unit was officially named the Transvaal Mounted Infantry.

Within days of the British annexation of the Transvaal in 1878, Browne was escorting the British Administrator Sir Theophilus Shepstone on a tour of the eastern Transvaal. He was ordered to lead a detachment as an escort to Henrique Shepstone, the Transvaal Secretary for Native Affairs, to the western boundary of the annexed territory to facilitate discussions with the native tribes and to try and persuade them to come under the protection of the British authorities. No sooner had the small column arrived at Christiana on 8 July than Browne was ordered to hand over to Lieutenant Newnham-Davies and proceed himself to Pretoria where he was to take command of the Mounted Infantry for the advance against the Pedi chief Sekukuni in the north-eastern Transvaal. This operation, under the overall command of Colonel Hugh Rowlands, VC (see page 37) was an utter failure. Before the column had even moved off, Rowlands had pointed out to Lord Chelmsford that the lack of manpower and resources, coupled with the advent of horse sickness, made the mission all but impossible. The Colonel's worse fears were to be realised and the column was forced to withdraw. Towards the end of 1878, command of the Transvaal Mounted Infantry was given to Chelmsford's favourite, Lieutenant-Colonel Charles Russell, with Browne as second-in-command, much to the indignation of all the men serving in the unit. The Mounted Infantry formed part of No. 3 Column for the invasion of Zululand and, the day before Isandlwana, Browne was ordered to take four men and scout the area behind the Siphezi looking for the main Zulu impi. As he was returning, his small party was attacked by more than 30 Zulus who were moving north. Shots were exchanged and one Zulu was killed and one wounded, but Browne and his men escaped unharmed, failing to realise that they had run into one of the forward scout groups of the Zulu army. The following morning the Mounted Infantry left the camp at Isandlwana at the head of Chelmsford's column, determined to seek out the Zulu army to the south. Although that decision was to have disastrous consqeuences for the men left at Isandlwana, it was one that probably saved the lives of Browne and his men; when they returned later that day, the camp had been destroyed and its defenders slaughtered.

While Chelmsford's No. 3 Column licked its near fatal wounds after the action at Isandlwana, the focus of activity moved onto Colonel Evelyn Wood, VCs No. 4 Column, operating in the Disputed Territories between Zululand and the Transvaal. Colonel Rowlands, VC had already tried and failed to wrest the native forces out of mountainous positions and learned the folly of such an action. By March 1879, Major Buller was pressing Wood to launch an assault on the abaQulusi forces located in a commanding position on top of Hlobane Mountain. To Buller it was a relatively straightforward matter, European courage and technology against native courage and weapons. Such arrogance clearly shows that he had learned nothing from either his own experiences when serving under Colonel Rowlands, or from those of Lord Chelmsford at Isandlwana. What transpired was almost a rehearsal for events in South Africa twenty years later.

Despite having misgivings about an assault on Hlobane, Wood wanted to advance further into Zululand and feared the consequences of leaving a large enemy force to his rear. If, as he hoped, he was to meet up with the main Zulu army which was reportedly moving north, he could have found himself trapped between the two forces. Chelmsford, meanwhile, wanted to move to relieve the British forces besieged at Eshowe and asked Wood to cause a distraction. Despite reports from scouts that the main Zulu army was indeed heading towards Wood's column, Chelmsford failed to change his plans and made no recommendation that No. 4 Column should remain inside its prepared positions at Kambula to await the arrival of the Zulus. Wood therefore decided to launch an assault against the abaQulusi on Hlobane Mountain and proceeded to compound the potential danger by dividing his force. One section, comprising the bulk of the infantry, would remain at Kambula while the mounted units and auxiliaries would attack in two formations. Buller commanded 408 mounted men and 280 auxiliaries, while Russell led 206 cavalry (including 82 men of the Mounted Infantry under the command of Browne) and 440 auxiliaries. Buller's men would assault the mountain from the east and Russell's men from the west. The commanders understanding of the terrain was poor, the 1500 ft high mountain being '… strongly protected by krantzes and terraces, huge masses of boulders and scrub, intersected with stone walls, backed up by caves and fissures in the mountain itself, accessible only by footpaths from the plains below'. The top of the mountain comprised a plateau some three miles long and one mile wide. The abaQulusi defenders probably numbered over 5,000 men, possibly as many as 10,000.

Buller moved his force out of the Kambula camp on the 27 March, and half a day behind him came Russell's column, both fully visible to the abaQulusi on the heights. The two assaults were to be timed to co-incide with each other, with Buller's main force taking the leading role in driving the enemy forces into the waiting men from Russell's column.

At 3.30am on 28 March, Buller began his advance, unaware that the main Zulu army, over 20,000 strong, was less than five miles behind him and in direct communication with the forces on Hlobane. The watching abaQulusi found it incredulous that Buller had failed to spot the approaching Zulus and began to play a delaying, waiting game. As Buller's men reached the main plateau they came under fire from above but, despite serious losses, reached the summit by 6am. At the same time, Russell's men were moving towards the western end of the mountain where they intended to seize the lower plateau then advance up a short 150 foot slope to the summit. Inadequate reconnaissance meant that they did not realise that this slope was totally unsuited for a mounted assault as it was covered in large boulders and almost impassable to horses, except at the very slowest pace; the slightest misjudgement would mean a fall, a broken limb for the horses and possible death for their riders. So treacherous was this slope that it was named 'The Devil's Pass'. At the last moment Russell realised that this pass was unsuitable for his mounted troops and ordered most of them to scour the lower plateau in search of enemy cattle. He then sent Browne and 20 men up the pass on foot to attempt to contact Buller. The sound of distant firing clearly indicating that the latter had engaged with the enemy.

Despite serious casualties, Buller was gradually driving the enemy back. To ensure that he was not cut off, he secured the only two possible lines of retreat — the route they had just ascended and Intyeutika Nek, about 400 yards to the north-west. The abaQulusi were like ghosts, refusing to stand and fight, disappearing behind the natural cover of the terrain. In reality, they were fighting a delaying action, waiting for the main Zulu force to close on the British from the rear. Due to the weather conditions, Buller was still unaware of the approaching Zulu army.

At 6.45am, Browne reached the top of the Devil's Pass where he awaited the arrival of Buller's men who were slowly picking their way through the boulder-strewn grassland while their rearguard protected the eastern escape routes. As they advanced, Buller's men herded before them a vast number of cattle and, they hoped, the bulk of the abaQulusi warriors. When the first members of this force reached the pass they immediately decided that it could not be negotiated by either the horsemen or the cattle and began to turn back the way they had come.

By mid morning, Russell, who was still on the lower plateau, spotted the advancing Zulu army closing on Hlobane — the trap was rapidly closing on the British as Wood had, inexplicably, failed to post scouts to the south, an unforgivable blunder. Russell immediately sent a message to Wood, who, simply acting as an observer, was wandering about on the mountain accompanied by a small party of staff officers. The messenger failed to find the colonel and, instead, delivered the message to Buller who had just been informed that the abaQulusi had blocked off the escape route via Intyentika Nek. To continue his withdrawal according to the original plan would result in a massacre, and he ordered his men, once again, to head for the western end of the plateau and the Devil's Pass. At the eastern end, the rearguard began to collapse and suddenly an organised withdrawal turned into a potential rout. Wood, by now aware of the approaching Zulu army, sent a badly worded message to Russell who was thrown into confusion and began to move his force away from Hlobane towards Kambula.

Lieutenant-Colonel J. Charles Russell (12th Lancers), CO Transvaal Mounted Infantry, whose life was saved by Browne.

As Buller and some 500 of his men began to make their descent of the Devil's Pass, discipline collapsed and the withdrawal became a case of every man for himself. The abaQulusi saw their chance and charged the near defenceless soldiers, but were held up by a rearguard made up of Browne, Commandant Raaf, Lieutenant Everitt and a few others. Protected behind the cover of some rocks, they checked the enemy's advance. Suddenly, one of their number, thinking that they were shooting at some of Wood's Irregulars, shouted for them to cease firing. In the seconds which followed this mistaken identity, the abaQulusi rushed forward into the rearguard, dashing the last chance of an organised retreat. As men and horses scrambled down the slope all semblance of order vanished. A few individuals carried out acts of great valour, placing themselves in mortal danger whilst trying to rescue some of their comrades by turning their horses to ride back to pick up men who were on foot — not least amongst these was Buller himself, who later received the Victoria Cross for his gallantry. Gradually, the fleeing soldiery reached the foot of the slope and tried to link up with Russell's force which was already some distance away. Eventually reaching Kambula, the badly mauled British forces prepared to fend off a full scale Zulu attack but it did not come that night and the defences were manned and recriminations began to fly about who was to blame for what was an unmitigated disaster. Somehow, both Buller and Wood managed to shift responsibility onto Russell who, although relatively incompetent, was only reacting to the bungled actions of the other two. He was accused of having fled the field of battle without putting up any resistance or cover for the beleaguered men on the mountain, and with losing the captured cattle. Browne, unaware of the confused messages which Russell had received, and undoubtedly supported by other members of the Mounted Infantry who had never taken to the appointment of Russell as their commanding officer, joined in the attacks on his superior officer and declared that he would resign rather than serve again under Russell's command.

As night fell, all activity at Kambula was centred on preparing the camp for the inevitable assault which would come the next day. Their situation, whilst precarious, was far better than that of the men at Isandlwana two months previously. Kambula was a well-positioned site with ample supplies and well-prepared defences. The soldiers inside were experienced, trained Imperial infantry, supported by colonial volunteers.

At 11am the following morning, some 21,000 Zulu warriors began to advance against the camp which they reached shortly after 1pm. In an effort to force the enemy's hand before he was ready to commit his forces, Buller led some cavalry out of the camp to challenge the Zulu right wing regiment. Calling a halt some 300 yards from the Zulus, the order was given to dismount and commence firing in volleys. The Zulus immediately charged forward and the cavalry re-mounted and began to make their way back towards the camp. Some of the horsemen, however, found themselves in difficulty as their mounts were not battle-hardened and many bolted leaving their riders behind.

Colonel Russell was part of this action and found himself unable to re-mount his panic-stricken horse. Suddenly, Troop Sergeant Major Learda, a Basuto of the Natal Native Horse, brought some of his men forward and formed a protective ring around him. Edward Browne, seeing what was happening, galloped in and held the struggling horse allowing Russell to mount. Unfortunately, the colonel compounded his difficulties by failing to find either his stirrups or his reins before the horse bolted, heading straight across the front of the oncoming Zulus. Browne immediately rode after him, grabbed the reins and brought both horse and rider back to the comparative safety of the camp.

In the ensuing battle, the British troops volley-fired into the massed Zulu ranks, cutting through them like a scythe, but still they came on. While at one time the battle appeared poised to go either way, the discipline and firepower of the British eventually carried the day, and by 5.30pm the Zulu army was withdrawing. Wood then released his cavalry

L–R, standing: Robert Jones, Henry Hook, William Jones. Sitting: David Bell, Edward Browne, Frederick Hitch, John Williams. [H. E. R. Bunting]

and turned the retreat into a rout. The disaster of Hlobane had been turned into a success and the reputations of Wood and Buller salvaged.

In the honours that followed, Troop Sergeant Major Learda became the first black soldier to be awarded the DCM, his citation reading:

… at Kambula, when Lieutenant-Colonel Russell was dismounted and unable to mount through the restlessness of his horse he rallied a few men within a few yards of the Zulus who were moving to attack in large numbers thus enabling Captain E. S. Browne, commanding the Mounted Infantry, to save Lieutenant-Colonel Russell's life.

When the award of the Victoria Cross to Browne was announced the citation simply said that he had 'saved a man's life' — there was no mention of Russell, perhaps tactful, in view of Browne's opinion of his superior officer.

N.B. Brigadier-General Browne, VC, decorated Sergeant W. B. Trayner with the Victoria Cross at York on 2 July 1902.

John Doogan, VC.

JOHN DOOGAN
Private
1st Dragoon Guards (The King's)

Full Name: John Doogan.

Place of Birth: Augrim, County Galway, Ireland.

Date of Birth: There is considerable confusion about this date. Doogan himself insisted that he was born in March 1860 (which would have meant he had enlisted aged 13) while his army records show his birth date as March 1857 (which would indicate that he may have given a false date of birth as he was 16). His gravestone, however, suggests that he was born in either March 1853 or March 1854.

Father: William Doogan.

Mother: —

Father's Occupation: Builder and contractor/mason.

Education: None recorded although he was literate and is on record as having said that 'he often played truant to follow the hounds'.

Pre-Service Employment: —

Service Record: Enlisted 1st Dragoon Guards, 1873 (Service No. 1401); served South Africa, 1879, during the Anglo-Zulu War (may have been present at Ulundi); served Anglo-Boer War, 1881 (present at Laing's Nek, 28 January 1881, severely injured with gunshot wounds) as servant to Major Brownlow; treated at Ingoga Hospital, South Africa; returned to Britain on the *Tamar* April–May 1881; hospitalised at Netley Hospital, May–June 1881; discharged from the army, unfit for military service, 28 June 1881; enlisted for service in the First World War as a recruiting sergeant, Shropshire, 1915.

Decorations, Medals and Rewards: Victoria Cross (for action at Laing's Nek, South Africa, 28 January 1881); South Africa Medal (clasp for 1879); Long Service & Good Conduct Medal (for six years service); Coronation Medal, 1937. He received a private pension of £20 per annum in the will of Major Brownlow, commencing in 1926. There are reports which show he was awarded the British War Medal 1914–20, the Allied Victory Medal 1914–19 and the Territorial Force War Medal. These are almost certainly the medals awarded to John Joseph Doogan, John Doogan VC's son, who was killed in 1918; they are held by the Tank Museum, Dorset.

The Black Lion, Ravens Square, Welshpool, the pub where John Doogan was landlord in the 1880s. William Waring, VC's home was situated behind this building.

John Doogan's VC, South Africa Medal and Coronation Medal. His LSGC Medal appears to be missing.
[QDG Museum, Cardiff]

Post-Service Employment: Coachman; lodgeman; constable, Royal Irish Constabulary (there is no extant service record of this); licensee Black Lion Inn, Welshpool (*c*.1887); Royal Mail van driver (1891) living at Mill Place, Welshpool; farmer of a small-holding at Cause Mountain, Westbury, Shropshire and, after the First World War, at Stapely Hill, Mitchell's Ford, Shropshire. He was also a butler. As well as the above mentioned addresses, he also resided at: Church Cottage, Shinfield East, Berkshire; Cheriton, Folkestone, Kent; 5 Folly Road, Folkestone, Kent (later 1930s).

Married: 1) Mary Evans of Montgomeryshire, at Toxteth Park, Liverpool, 1882. They had met in Bury, Lancashire, where she was employed as a nurse. She died in 1924 and is recorded on his headstone at Shorncliffe, although she is almost certainly buried elsewhere. 2) Martha Maria Roberts, at Welshpool, 16 September 1929. This marriage was dissolved at Shropshire Assizes on 20 February 1930 as she was already married. 3) Bessie, daughter of Mrs W. Evans of Ysgyborgoch, Welshpool, 1933 (she was then aged in her 20s).

Children: Five sons (John Joseph, William, Albert George, Richard Lumley and Henry) and seven daughters (Mary W., Sarah E., Alice M., Fanny, Ada Elizabeth, Margaret Louisa and Jenny). John, a corporal in the 10th KSLI (Shropshire & Cheshire Yeomanry), died on 19 September 1918, and Richard died of tuberculosis as a result of his war service. John Doogan is reported to have received an extra 17/6d pension for the loss of his two sons on military service (WO 97/11731).

Died: At 5 Folly Road, Folkestone, Kent, 24 January 1940, of bronchitis.

Buried: Military Cemetery, Shorncliffe, Kent.

Memorials: Military Cemetery, Shorncliffe, Kent. The grave was restored by his regimental association in September 2000.

Location of Victoria Cross: He bequeathed it to the 1st Dragoon Guards in his will. It was loaned to the VC Centenary Exhibition in 1956 after which it disappeared for over forty years, eventually being discovered in a bank vault where it had been placed for safe keeping. Now displayed at the Queen's Dragoon Guards Museum in Cardiff Castle.

Citation for the Victoria Cross: *London Gazette*, 14 March 1882. 'For gallant conduct during the action of Laing's Nek on the 28 January 1881. During the charge of the mounted men Private Doogan, servant to Major Brownlow, 1st Dragoon Guards, seeing that officer (whose horse had been shot) dismounted and among the Boers, rode up and (though himself severely wounded) dismounted and pressed Major Brownlow to take his horse, receiving another wound while trying to induce him to accept it.'

VC Investiture: By the Superintendent of Pensions at Cork, Ireland, in May 1882. It had been intended that he should be decorated by HM Queen Victoria at Windsor, 13 May 1882, but his address was not known to the authorities and he was not therefore contacted in time.

Church Cottage, Shinfield East, Berkshire, the home of John Doogan and his family in 1901.

5 Folly Road, Folkestone, the home of John Doogan at the time of his death.

The grave of John Doogan in Shorncliffe Military Cemetery, Folkestone.

John Doogan appears to have led the most restless, unsettled of lives. Born in Ireland, his early details are unknown until he enlisted in the 1st Dragoon Guards in 1873, aged about 20. The only photograph of him in his youth shows a well-dressed, good-looking young man. He seems to have had the so-called Irish gift of the gab as, on returning to civilian life, he embarked upon a series of jobs in varied locations, and was married three times. All of his employments were positions of responsibility, although none seems to have lasted any great length of time. Despite moving around the country, he appears to have been drawn to Montgomeryshire as all three of his wives hailed from the Welshpool area, the last, Bessie Evans, being over 50 years his junior!

His regiment was posted to South Africa on 12 February 1879, forming part of the reinforcements sent from Britain following the disaster at Isandlwana on 22 January. They arrived at Durban on 8 April and moved to Pietermaritzburg and then, via Rorke's Drift, to Isandlwana where, on 21 May, they were involved with the burial of some of the bodies which had lain there in the open for four months. The regiment was involved in the final stages of the campaign against the Zulus.

Not long after peace had been restored to Zululand, trouble broke out further north in the Transvaal. In 1878 the British had annexed the independent Boer state of the Transvaal, totally against the wishes of the Boer population. While fighting persisted in Zululand, Colonel Hugh Rowlands, VC, (see above) had been given the responsibility of containing the unrest amongst the Boers, a duty which he had carried out admirably well before passing the mantle on to Colonel Owen Lanyon. Discontent continued as the Boers refused to consider becoming part of a proposed South African Federation, a political structure under British control. At the end of 1880 they proclaimed the Republic of the Transvaal and, when the British began to mass troops in South Africa in readiness to force the issue in their favour, the Boers invaded Natal. On 19 December, Major Brownlow, OC the Depot Troop, 1st King's Dragoon Guards, at Pietermartizburg awaiting orders to return to Britain, was directed to form a mounted force (to be made up from the Depot Troop KDGs, No 7 Company Army Service Corps and volunteers from the 58th Regiment and the 60th Rifles) which was to join what was termed the Natal Field Force, then forming up at Newcastle.

The first major action of this brief but disastrous war (from the British perspective) occured at Bronkhorst Spruit where, on 20 December, the 94th Regiment was given a taste of what was to come when British imperial troops clashed with Boer irregulars. General Sir George Colley, fearing that the British citizens and troops in the towns of the Transvaal would be cut off and overwhelmed, and that settlements in Natal would be subjected to raids from across the border, felt compelled to act before the arrival of any reinforcements from Britain or India. In late December, British troops headed towards the border, with their commanders exuding confidence in their ability to more than match the Boer forces that they might come across.

Colley ordered the Boer forces to disperse but, when he received no reply, ordered his small army of 1200 men to advance towards the enemy on 24 January. The general estimated that the Boer forces numbered 5–7,000 men but that the discrepancy between the two sides was more than made up for by the presence in the British column of six artillery pieces. The Boer commander, Piet Joubert, ordered his men to occupy the high ground around Laing's Nek, a narrow pass in the Drakensburg mountains. When the first clash occurred, the Boers had only 250 men in position, protected by the natural features of the landscape. The advancing British were forced to move across an undulating grassy plateau before attempting to climb a steep slope without any form of cover.

Colley attacked shortly after 7am on 28 January. The artillery opened the action by bombarding the heights but to little avail as the Boer forces were scattered and shielded by boulders and trenches. Had the barrage continued for any length of time then it might have had a major effect upon the Boers but, after twenty minutes, Colley ordered his infantry to advance, in the classic line with bayonets fixed, quite the wrong tactics to use against concealed sharpshooters. Two subalterns unfurled the colours and the line surged forward in close formation, just as British infantry had done since the days of Marlborough. On the left flank of the British line, Major Brownlow, of the 1st Dragoon Guards, led the mounted troops in two lines toward the Boers. In 1882, Brownlow recorded his feelings about the handling of the battle:

Artist's impression of John Doogan's VC action.

Major (later General) W. V. Brownlow,
whose life was saved by John Doogan
during his VC action.
[QDGs Museum, Cardiff]

The first mistake now occurred, the guns and rockets had only been engaged for about twenty minutes, had not long got the enemy's range, and were beginning to make them feel uncomfortable, when in place of waiting till the Artillery had done its work more effectively, the wing of the 58th proceeded to storm a position called Table Hill, and the Mounted Squadron were ordered to take possession of a neck of land, connecting Table Hill and another hill on the right of our attack, and to 'charge the enemy no matter what their strength and to clear the rear and flanks of the 58th'. I may here point out two other mistakes, the command of the wing of the 58th was given to Colonel Deane, a Staff Officer, unknown to the men, though they had their Major and a full compliment of their own Officers; the other mistake was that Sir George Colley gave distinct orders to the Officer commanding the assaulting party to go up the connecting neck where I went, in advance of my Squadron, in place of which they actually did go half a mile to my left; if Colonel Deane had followed the directions he received it would have been a far easier ascent for his troops and it would have made all the difference to me. Owing to the impracticable nature of the ground and the faulty leading of Colonel Deane, the attack of the 58th failed and they retired, losing Colonel Deane, several Staff and Regimental Officers, and a large number of rank and file.

I proceeded at the same time to carry out my instructions, which as may well be imagined would have been a difficult task for a highly trained and disciplined body of cavalry, much more so for my small party composed of such a mixed lot; we were protected for a time while ascending the hill by our own guns firing over our heads, but when we got to the top we were exposed to such a heavy fire that though we soon gained the advantage of the falling ground and though the enemy had actually received the order to retreat, my men not concious of this, and (with the exception of a few Dragoons) utterly unaccustomed to their position, could not long stand the heavy fire, and broke; both attacks had now failed and after a little desultory Artillery fire we all retired to the camp at Mount Prospect.

The loss of the Mounted Squadron on that day was 4 killed, 15 wounded, 1 prisoner. 29 horses killed and missing, 5 wounded. Of these casualties, the following belonged to the King's Dragoon Guards: Sergt Major Lunny and Corporal Stephens killed. Myself slightly wounded, Corporal Clarke and Pte Doogan severely, Pte Venables prisoner.

Brownlow then completed this report by stating: 'The Squadron and the 58th were thanked by Sir George Colley in a speech that afternoon, and also in General Orders; and mention was also made in despatches of Sergt Major Lunny, Pte Doogan and myself, and Doogan has since received the Victoria Cross for his gallant conduct on that occasion.' Strangely, Brownlow failed to mention that Doogan's VC had been awarded for saving his life.

It may be of value at this point to reconstruct the events of that morning in Natal, based upon other reports of the battle, as it may throw some light on the full facts of the matter. No sooner had the infantry begun their advance than, suddenly, Brownlow wheeled his mounted force to the right and, at full gallop, with swords drawn, charged the enemy line. As both infantry and cavalry began to reach the top of the ridge, they came into full view of the waiting Boers whose independent rapid fire brought down scores of the charging troops. Brownlow's horse was shot from under him and the Major was thrown to the ground, shaken and bruised, but otherwise uninjured. Around him, the first line of cavalry was checked by the Boer firing, and those who were still unscathed tried to re-form as part of the second line but fared no better. The slope in front of the Boer positions became a killing ground and only one British cavalryman was reported to have breached the enemy line — Sergeant Major Lunny got amongst the Boers, killed one and wounded another, before being killed himself. When his body was later recovered, it had been hit six times, such was the intensity of the firing.

John Doogan, as Brownlow's servant, had stuck close to his officer and, during the charge, whilst riding alongside the major, had already been hit by rifle fire. He saw Brownlow attempting to get up after his horse had been killed, and saw the Boers approaching to either kill him or take him prisoner. Undaunted, Doogan immediately rode to his assistance, dismounted in full view of the enemy, and demanded that the Major take his horse and escape. Brownlow refused and, as the two argued the case, Doogan was hit again. Up to this point, all accounts are in basic agreement and are supported by the Victoria Cross citation. There appears to have been a veil drawn over what happened next. Did the Major take the horse and leave Doogan to make his own way back? Did the two men manage to make it back on the one horse? The official accounts give us no information. Was this an oversight? — it is strange that all the parties involved missed the same important fact — or was there an attempt to conceal something? No information seems to have been available from any source and neither Brownlow nor Doogan appear to have spoken publicly about the action. Careful research into every possible source, however, can provide some answers but, at the same time, may raise many more new questions.

Returning to the Battle of Laing's Nek — after thirty minutes of sustaining murderous fire, the British troops were ordered to retreat, which was done in a disciplined and orderly manner and, with the support of the artillery, the Boers were dissuaded from pursuing. It was reported that Major Brownlow was so shocked by the events of that morning that he was unable to speak to his men for several days. Laing's Nek was the first defeat of British troops by a European enemy since the failed assault on the Redan at Sebastopol in 1855. Brownlow, however, received a Mention in Despatches for his actions at Laing's Nek and, in early February, took part in the fighting at Ingogo River for which he received another Mention, and eventually returned to Britain, rising to the rank of general before his death in 1926. In his will, he bequeathed Doogan a pension of £20 per annum for life.

Obverse of John Doogan's VC.
[QDGs Museum, Cardiff]

As regards Doogan, Laing's Nek was his last military action and the gunshot wounds to his arm and thigh were deemed so severe that he was invalided from the Army in June 1881, deemed 'unfit for military service'. He was now aged about 27, with a VC pension of £10 per annum, a small wound pension, and little else by way of prospects. Within days of leaving Netley Hospital, he was in Liverpool where, in July, he married Mary Evans. On his marriage certificate he gave his occupation as 'Gentleman', omitting to mention his military career. A photograph of him taken shortly after this time, shows a good-looking, smart man, dressed in a three-piece suit with a cravat and tie-pin, every bit the gentleman of means. If Doogan did have some money behind him, he certainly did not get it as a direct result of his military service. Perhaps his father had died and left him some money — certainly, in 1882 when his VC was gazetted and he was scheduled to appear at Windsor to be decorated by Queen Victoria herself, Doogan was in the south-west of Ireland and missed out on the royal investiture. Might he have gone to Ireland to collect his inheritance? It may be that his new wife came from a monied background, although there is no evidence to support this but, later in life, after Mary's death, Doogan's finances seem to have become more strained. It may be, however, that his money came from another source. His financial security was evidently not sufficient to keep him in comfort for the remainder of his life, but seems to have been enough to enable him to become the landlord of a small public house in Welshpool (his wife's home town) then, some years later, the owner of a smallholding in Shropshire. Did he perhaps receive a financial reward from his officer for having saved his life? Major Brownlow himself came into a sizeable inheritance in 1881 when his father died and left him the family estate at Monaghan in Ireland (his elder brother having been killed in action the previous year). This is all supposition, and the matter does not become any clearer until 1933 when Doogan's third marriage was reported in the *County Times*:

ZULU WAR SURVIVOR MARRIED
Elderly VC Weds Local Farmer's Daughter

Reverse of Doogan's VC
[QDGs Museum, Cardiff]

Sergeant John Doogan VC, Stapely Hill, Middleton, near Chirbury, who claims to have possessed the Victoria Cross longer than any man in Great Britain, was on Friday of last week, married to Miss Bessie Evans, eldest daughter of Mrs W. Evans, Ysguborgoch, Golfa, near Welshpool. The ceremony took place at Middleton Parish Church … The bridegroom is about 70 years of age and the bride is in her twenties.

Describing how he won the VC, he said, 'I was among the troops, under the command of Major W. V. Brownlow, formed as an escort at the fighting line for General Colley. In the thick of the fight I saw that Major Brownlow's horse had been shot from under him. I rode up to him, dismounted, and lifted him onto my horse.

Up to this point, Doogan's account is little different from those given in 1881. From this point onwards, however, the account becomes not only markedly different, but reveals a sequence of events which had previously been unrecorded.

There were about seven Boers in a trench below, and they kept up a steady fire. I stood on the parapet over them with the reins over my left arm, a revolver in my left hand, and a sword in my right. They were down there below me, firing away, but I'm d—d if they could hit me. When I was in the act of lifting the Major into the saddle and fixing his boots into the stirrup, the Boers at last hit me and I fell. The Major, thinking I was dead, galloped away. But I was not dead, and for 48 hours I lay there on the African veldt without food or drink, bleeding and weakened by wounds, with lips parched and throat

John Doogan attending the Regimental Mounted Sports at Tidworth c.1938. The medals on his right breast are almost certainly those awarded to his son, John, for his service with the Yeomanry during the First World War.
[QDGs Museum, Cardiff]

Close-up of John Doogan's headstone showing the names of his first wife, Mary, and two of their sons.

swollen. The only survivors in that part of the battle were Major Brownlow, Sergeant Lunny and myself. Of the 500 men in the detachment, only 40 survived.

This last sentence is obviously incorrect as Lunny had been killed in the charge into the Boer positions but, in the light of his following statement, this error could easily be explained.

Eventually, we wounded were found, and I was among 25 men who were sent in an ambulance across to Ingoga. Before we had gone far, however, the Boers came down on us and captured us. They took the mules away and left us in the ambulance, with a threat that if one of us moved we should all be killed. For some time we lay there under the heat of the African sun, nearly suffocated with the heat and the foul smell of dried blood, and with our lips and throats parched. One of the hospital orderlies named Palmer at last became so desperate that he took a white flag and went over to General Joubert, who was commanding the Boers. While holding up the flag of truce, he was shot through his right arm, but he pluckily transferred the flag to his left hand and carried on. With the aid of an interpreter, Palmer explained the position to General Joubert, who apologised for the conduct of his men and sent us with an escort of blacks down to Newcastle. At last we reached Pietermaritzburg and from there we were sent in a cattle truck to Durban where we embarked for Southampton. We had rough weather, and the crossing took 84 days.

This account, if accurate, explains the absence of the final part of Doogan's citation — there was no mention of how Brownlow and Doogan got back to the British lines because the truth could prove embarrassing. Doogan, having come to the assistance of Brownlow, had been abandoned on the battlefield and, like the proverbial bad penny, had turned up amongst the wounded. Although Doogan had only been hit in the arm and the thigh, there is no reason to think that Brownlow had thought anything other than that Doogan had been killed as, in the heat of battle, there is little time to make an accurate assessment of any situation. To publicise such a fact in an official report or citation, would certainly cause tongues to start wagging and it was easier to omit all mention of what happened.

Whatever the truth of the matter was, it does not take away from Doogan's gallant action at Laing's Nek where he came close to losing his own life in order to save that of his officer.

*Samuel Vickery, VC, 1898. This photograph
shows him as a lance-corporal.*

*Peterhays Cottages, Yarcombe, the home of
the Vickery family in the 1880s.*

SAMUEL VICKERY
Private
1st Dorsetshire Regiment

Full Name: Samuel Vickery.
Place of Birth: Wambrook, near Chard, Somerset. In 1881 the family was living at 1 Peterhays Cottages, Yarcombe, Devon.
Date of Birth: 6 February 1873.
Father: Simon Vickery.
Mother: Sarah Vickery (née Singleton).
Father's Occupation: Farm labourer.
Education: —
Pre-Service Employment: Labourer.
Service Record: Enlisted 1st Dorset Regiment, at Cardiff Barracks, 26 July 1893 (Service N° 3937); transferred to 2nd Dorset Regiment, Belfast, 1895; transferred to 1st Dorset Regiment, Wellington, India, 1896; served Tirah Campaign 1897–8 (wounded by a severe sword cut across the foot, 16 November 1897); invalided to Britain, 1898, treated at Netley Hospital; transferred to 2nd Dorset Regiment; served South Africa, 1899–1901; captured by Boers but escaped after four days; severely wounded at Nooitgedacht, 13 December 1900 (present at Wittebergen, Diamond Hill, capture of Johannesburg, Driefontein, Paardeberg, Relief of Kimberley); invalided out of the army, unfit for military service, 31 August 1901; enlisted 6th Dorset Regiment, 17 September 1914 (Service N° 11601); served France, 1915, promoted to corporal; declared unfit for further service in the line and transferred to PoW camp guard duties, France, 1916; transferred to Labour Corps, 15 July 1918 (Service N° 56966); discharged, 31 March 1920.
Decorations, Medals and Rewards: Victoria Cross (for action at Dargai, Tirah, 20 October 1897 and Warah Valley, Tirah, 16 November 1897); India General Service Medal (clasps for Punjab Frontier, 1897–98 and Tirah, 1897–98); Queen's South Africa Medal (clasps for South Africa, 1901, Wittebergen, Diamond Hill, Johannesburg, Driefontein, Paardeberg, Relief of Kimberley); 1914–15 Star; British War Medal; Victory Medal; Coronation Medal (1937).

Samuel Vickery, VC (front row, extreme right) with various other VCs and ex-servicemen at a meeting with the Prince of Wales who had been to see the rugby international between Wales and Scotland. To the left of Vickery are Stokey Lewis,VC and John H. Williams, VC. Also standing in the front row, immediately behind the chair, is John Williams (Fielding), VC.

Post-Service Employment: Male nurse, Whitchurch Hospital, Cardiff (pre 1914); commissionaire, GPO, Cardiff, until he retired in 1946.

Married: Catherine Ann Green, seamstress, at Whitchurch Hospital, Cardiff, *c*.1907.

Children: None recorded.

Died: St David's Hospital, Cardiff, 20 June 1952. His home address at this time was 33 Romilly Crescent, Cardiff.

Buried: Cremated at Glyntaff Crematorium, Pontypridd, 25 June 1952.

Memorials: —

Location of Victoria Cross: Dorset Military Museum, Dorchester, Dorset.

Citation for the Victoria Cross: *London Gazette*, 20 May 1898.

'During the attack on the Dargai Heights on the 20th October 1897, Private Vickery ran down the slope and rescued a wounded comrade under heavy fire, bringing him back to cover. He subsequently distinguished himself with Brigadier-General Kempster's Column in the Warran Valley, killing three of the enemy who attacked him when separated from his Company.'

VC Investiture: By HM Queen Victoria at Netley Hospital, 14 May 1898, six days before the announcement appeared in the *London Gazette*.

Samuel Vickery, VC's home at 33 Romilly Crescent, Canton, Cardiff.

The growth and development of the British Empire in India during the early and mid ninetenth century brought with it additional problems which resulted in numerous military actions involving British troops in territories which had previously seemed both unattractive and economically of little value. As far as the Empire was concerned, the large Indian land mass was fortunate in being bounded by the ocean on two sides and by the Himalayan mountain range for much of the third side of the triangle. The one area of weakness was the north-west frontier, where the Punjab bordered on the independent state of Afghanistan, where the Hindu Kush mountain range could be penetrated by a number of passes leading directly into the plains of northern India. On the far side of Afghanistan lay the southern boundary of the Russian empire and the perceived threat that it implied to the security of the Raj. The best way to protect British India was to protect the Hindu Kush, a policy that resulted in a series of attempts to occupy the region, all met by near fanatical resistance by a tribal people determined to maintain their independence. These people, collectively known to the British as the Pathans (if on the Indian side of the mountains) or Afghans (if on the Afghanistan side) are renowned for their ability to resist even the most powerful of enemies, be they the British (in the nineteenth and early twentieth centuries), the Russians (in the late twentieth century) or the UN forces (in the twenty-first century). The obvious military strength of their enemies meant nothing to them. Mountstuart Elphinstone wrote that they were a people 'whose vices are revenge, envy, avarice, rapacity and obstinacy' who were also 'fond of liberty, faithful to their friends, kind to their dependents, hospitable, brave, hardy, frugal, laborious and prudent'. The main routeway from India to Afghanistan lay through the Khyber region which was accessed via the frontier garrison town of Peshawar. Nearby was the region known as the Tirah, a land which was almost totally unknown to outsiders, surrounded by mountains, whose people, the Afridis, had a fanatical distrust of all people, even their own.

In 1897, a holy war (*jihad*) was called for amongst all the tribes in the region resulting in an attack on a British agent and the death of an army officer. In the punitive attacks which followed, British troops killed over 2,000 tribesmen for the loss of five soldiers. Not surprisingly, the unrest continued and the Afridis and their near neighbours the Orakzais closed the Khyber Pass and wiped out a small British garrison at Saragarhi Fort. Such an affront to British power could not go unpunished and two divisions, a total of 35,000 men, set out in October 1897 to subdue the tribes in the Tirah. The majority of the troops were from the Indian Army but there several British infantry battalions, including the 1st Bn Dorset Regiment, part of the 3rd Brigade of the 2nd Division.

The British troops were marching into an unknown territory, most of which had not even been mapped and the first major action of the campaign occurred at Dargai where the enemy controlled the heights above a strategically important pass into the Chagra valley. On 20 October the attack began with an artillery bombardment, following which the infantry of the 2nd Division assaulted the heights but were initially repelled by rapid, accurate fire from the tribesmen concealed behind the rocks above. The first wave of Gurkhas suffered heavy casualties and were pinned down below a cliff. The Devon and Dorset regiments were then pushed into the attack but were also soon pinned down. The next assault was carried out by the Gordon Highlanders, who, led by their pipers, sustained heavy casualties before reaching the summit where, followed by the Gurkhas and the Devons and the Dorsets, they began to clear the ridge.

As F Company of the Dorsets charged over the ridge under very heavy rifle fire, Private Samuel Vickery tripped over a stone and fell. As he picked himself up Private Smyth ran past him and was immediately shot, rolling some 30 yards down the side of the hill. Vickery knew what would happen to the wounded Smyth if he were to be captured; the Afridis were renowned for torturing and mutilating their prisoners before killing them. Without hesitation, Vickery ran down the slope after Smyth, picked him up and carried him back to cover, the whole time under constant enemy fire. Having got Smyth back to some form of safety, Vickery then prepared to go out a second time to rescue another wounded man but was physically restrained from doing so by his colleagues. Kipling had summed up the feelings of the soldiers about the posibility of being taken prisoner:

> When you're wounded and left on Afghanistan's plains
> And the women come out to cut up what remains,
> Just roll to your rifle and blow out your brains
> And go to your Gawd like a soldier.

For his conspicuous gallantry on the Dargai heights, Vickery's name was passed forward to the GOC by Lieutenant-Colonel J. Piercy, CO 1st Dorset Regiment.

The British column then moved on to face further strong resistance at the SamPagha Pass on 29 October and the Arhanga Pass two days later, before entering the Tirah Valley itself, the first European troops to ever do so. The valley, or Tirah Maiden, was a 'wide, well-watered land … fairly timbered with apricot and walnut trees about the houses, which are very numerous and well built. A great deal is under cultivation, the fields are carefully terraced and signs of plenty and comfort are abundant' land that was 'extensive, fertile, highly cultivated and capable of much developemnt under a selected Government'. The villages were abandoned, their occupants having fled into the mountains from where they mounted guerrilla attacks against the British. The Field Force commander, General Sir William Lockhart decided to mount a scorched earth policy to try and force the Afridis to the negotiating table. Farms and houses were either burned or blown up, crops destroyed and wells filled with sand. The troops were allowed to loot whatever took their fancy. On 9 November, a column which included the 1st Dorsets stormed the Saran Sar ridge from which enemy marksmen had been firing down at the British. Clambering up the slope under heavy rifle fire, the troops reached the summit only to find the Afridi gone. This seemed to be the pattern whenever the invading columns tried to force their enemy into a fight in the open. These were tactics the Pathans had used for generations beforehand and which their descendants continue to use today.

On 13 November Brigadier-General Kempster led the 3rd Brigade into the Waran valley, marching through the Tseri Kandao Pass. The advance met with very little opposition and a number of deserted villages were destroyed before the column commenced its withdrawal on the 16th. During the return march, the rearguard was hotly engaged and took some significant casualties. Private Harris of the 1st Dorsets described one of the incidents:

> In the retirement of the 16th instant I was with Pte Vickery, and we were separated from the remainder of the Company who were retiring, being attacked by a large number of the enemy at close quarters; Pte Vickery was unable to walk very fast having been wounded by a sword cut across his foot, the enemy must have been kept back by the fire of some of our men, as we were able to get away down a deep nullah which we had to cross. I was in front of Pte Vickery and was climbing up the other side of the nullah, when I heard a shout, and looking back saw a few of the enemy running along the nullah. Pte Vickery was trying to climb the nullah, but three of the enemy were close to him. I could not fire as they were so close. I saw one fall, shot I think by Pte Vickery, and then another rushed at him from the front, this man he struck with his bayonet and before he could pull his rifle back, the last one struck at him with a sword, or something like a sword. I saw Pte Vickery knock him down with his fist, and then brain him with the butt end of his rifle, all this happened in so short a space of time that although I was only about 40 yards away I could not help him. I then got down to him and helped him up the side of the nullah as the blood was streaming over his face from the blow or fall he got in the struggle. By this time our Company was not to be seen, as it was nearly dark, but we came across a few men and got into a village which we held for the night, and returned to camp in the morning.

Vickery was given treatment for his two wounds and on the 18 November was evacuated to the Base Hospital and from there, to England where he was admitted to Netley Hospital in Hampshire.

When Lieutenant-Colonel Piercy heard of Vickery's action he immediately investigated the details and wrote:

> I saw the rifle of Pte Vickery myself on the morning he returned to camp and the barrel and butt was covered with blood, and bore every appearance of having been used for the purpose stated [by Private Harris], also that the bayonet of Pte Vickery is

missing, and it may be presumed the bayonet was lost in the struggle.

I cannot speak too highly of the way in which Pte Vickery has conducted himself during the present expedition. In addition to the two cases already reported, his general behaviour has been courageous on all occasions. ... I have already recommended [him] for the Victoria Cross for his bravery at Dargai on the 20th October 1897.

The letter has a footnote appended by Brigadier-General F. Kempster: 'I think this mans conduct most worthy of consideration as to VC, being 2nd occasion in which he behaved most gallantly.'

The recommendation for the Victoria Cross to Vickery was approved. On the 13 May a telegram was sent to the War Office from Windsor Castle asking;

Please let me know if any of the wounded at present at Netley have been granted the Victoria Cross. If so Queen would wish to confer the decoration when she visits the hospital Saturday afternoon.

Vickery, along with Piper Findlater of the Gordon Highlanders, was therefore decorated with the Victoria Cross by Queen Victoria at Netley Hospital on 14 May 1898, six days before the award was gazetted. After recovering from his wounds, Vickery resumed his military career, joining the 2nd Bn The Dorset Regiment in time for active service in South Africa where he was present at numerous actions before being captured by the Boers. Within four days he had escaped and rejoined his battalion only to be severely wounded at Nooitgedacht on 13 December 1900, during the early stages of the guerrilla war, and invalided out of the Army. Photographic evidence would seem to suggest that, at some stage after the VC award, Vickery was promoted to lance-corporal, although this does not appear in this surviving military papers. He joined the 6th Bn The Dorset Regiment in the First World War and saw active service on the Western Front before, in 1916, being posted to serve in a prisoner-of-war camp in France. He was demobilised in 1919.

The monolithic Royal Victoria Hospital, facing Southampton Water at Netley. The foundation stone (of Welsh granite) was laid by Queen Victoria in 1856, over a copper casket containing the hospital plans, a Crimea medal (with four bars), coins of the realm and the first Victoria Cross (now displayed at the Army Medical Services Museum, Aldershot). The building was completed in 1863. Until 1900, patients generally arrived by sea disembarking from ships at a 170 metre pier. The hospital was used during both World Wars and closed in 1958. The main building was demolished in 1966. The psychiatric hospital remained open until 1978. Today, all that remains in the Royal Victoria Country Park is the Royal Chapel and the Officers Mess (which has been converted into apartments). [Mick Crumplin]

NEVILL SMYTH
Captain
2nd Dragoon Guards (Queen's Bays)

Lieutenant Nevill Smyth.

Inverness Terrace, Paddington, where the Smyth family lived at Nos 5 and 96.

The decorations, medals and awards of Sir Nevill Smyth, VC. The Gallipoli Medallion appears top left with the Gallipoli Star top right. Between these medals are Sir Nevill's minatures. The medal on the extreme right of each group is the Khedives Sudan Medal (1896–1908) issued in 1899, with eight bars.
[Commodore Dacre Smyth]

Full Name: Nevill Maskelyne Smyth.

Place of Birth: 13 Victoria Street, Westminster, London. The family later lived at 96 and 5 Inverness Terrace in Paddington, London and had a holiday home West Cliff, Marazion, Cornwall.

Date of Birth: 14 August 1868. He had one brother, Herbert Warington, CMG, BA, LLB, FGS (born 1867), a barrister, mining engineer, travel writer and lieutenant RNVR.

Father: Sir Warington Wilkinson Smyth, the son of Admiral William Smyth, FRS, and the elder brother of Charles Paiazzi Smyth (astronomer) and General Sir Henry Augustus Smyth, KCMG, (Governor of Malta). Married 1864.

Mother: Lady Anna Maria Antonia Storey-Maskelyne, daughter of A. S. Maskelyne of Basset Down, Wiltshire (born c.1828). Her brother was Professor M. H. N. Storey-Maskelyne, FRS and MP for Cricklade.

Father's Occupation: Geologist, mining engineer, lecturer at the Royal School of Mines, Chief Inspector of Mines for the Crown and Duchy of Cornwall.

Education: The Orchard School, Mortlake, Surrey; Westminster School, London; RMA Sandhurst, graduated with honours, August 1888.

Service Record: Commissioned, 2nd lieutenant, 2nd Dragoon Guards, 22 August 1888 (he joined the regiment in India); lieutenant, 26 April 1895; served on detachment to the Royal Engineers (to carry out a railway survey) on the staff during the Zhob Valley Expedition, Afghan Frontier, 1890; Special Service officer, Egypt, 24 March 1896–8 October 1896; served with the Egyptian Army, 9 October 1896–8 January 1902; captain, 8 December 1897; served with the Dongola Expedition, Sudan, 1896, as orderly officer to the GOC Mounted Forces (present at the Battle of Firket and the pursuit of Suarda, MinD); staff officer to the Chief of Staff at the battle of Hafir and occupation of Dongola; staff officer, Camel Corps; served Sudan Campaign, 1897, as staff officer to GOC Dongola Province; DAAG and OC advanced posts at Atbara; OC infantry and machine-guns at bombardment of Metemmeh; served aboard Commander Beatty's gunboat, January 1898; present at battles of Atbara and Omdurman as intelligence officer to General Sir Archibald Hunter (severely wounded); served Sudan Campaign of 1899 which suppressed Khalifa Sherif's rising; present at Gedid, Abu Aadel and Om Debreikat; acting governor and military commander of the Blue Nile District (assisted in the survey of the Sudan and the Blue Nile from Wadi Halfa to Abyssinia); served Boer War January 1902 as APM and DAAG to Major Lawley's column; brevet major, 28 August 1902; major, 28 October 1903; transferred to 6th Dragoon Guards (Carabiniers), 1903; lieutenant-colonel, 6th Dragoon Guards, 1 May 1909; colonel, December 1912; half pay, 1 May 1913; gained aviator's certificate, 1913; CO Khartoum District, Sudan, 1913–4 where he was active in surpressing the slave trade; brigadier-general commanding 1st Australian Infantry Brigade, Dardanelles, 20 May–20 December 1915 (including assault on Lone Pine, 6 August); OC 1st Australian Infantry Brigade, Egypt, 21 December 1915–18 March 1916 and France March–December 1916; major-general December 1916; GOC 2nd Australian Division, Western Front, 1916–8; GOC 58th (London) Division, 1918; GOC 59th Division (including Portuguese artillery and infantry), 1918–9; GOC 47th (2nd London) Division (Territorial Army) 1919–24; Colonel, 3/6th Dragoon Guards (Carabiniers), 1st October 1920–5; Honorary Colonel Natal Carbineers; Honorary Colonel 37/39 Battalion Australian Army, 1926; retired, 1924; discharged from the Reserve of Officers, 13 August 1935.

Decorations, Medals and Rewards: Victoria Cross (for action at Khartoum, 2 September 1898); CB (*L.G.* 1916); KCB (*L.G.* 9 June 1919); Khedive's Sudan Medal (clasps for Hafir, Firket, Sudan 1897, The Atbara, Khartoum, Gedaref, Sudan 1899, Gedid); Queen's Sudan Medal; Queen's South Africa Medal; 1914–15 Star; British War Medal; British Victory Medal (MinD); MinD for Dongola Expedition, Atbara and Khartoum; Order of the Medjidie (4th Class); Order of Osmanieh (4th Class), 1900; Legion of Honour (France); Commander of the Order of Leopold; Croix de Guerre (Belgium); received eleven MinDs. Along with all other Gallipoli veterans and descendants, the Australian government presented the Smyth family with the 50th anniversary Gallipoli medal in 1967 and the Australian Gallipoli Star, designed in 1915, was privately produced for the 75th anniversary in 1990.

Post-Service Employment: Retired general officer. The family lived at Thurloe Lodge, Thurloe Square, London and in Cornwall before emigrating to Melbourne, Australia in January 1925, settling at Kongbool Homestead, near Balmoral, Victoria. He stood as a Nationalist Party candidate for the Victoria Senate in 1931.

Married: Evelyn Olwen, daughter of Sir A. Osmond Williams, Bart, Liberal MP for Merioneth, Lord-lieutenant of Merionethshire, of

Captain Nevill Smyth, VC wearing the Order of the Medjidie and the Khedive's Sudan Medal, c.1897. [QDGs Museum, Cardiff]

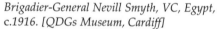

Brigadier-General Nevill Smyth, VC, Egypt, c.1916. [QDGs Museum, Cardiff]

Major-General Sir Nevill Smyth, VC, with his three children, 1923. [Commodore Dacre Smyth]

Castell Deudraeth and Borthwen, Merionethshire, at Holy Trinity Church, Chelsea 23 July 1918. She died 29 September 1960. Her father died in Australia whilst visiting her in 1927.

Children: Two sons, Dacre Henry Deudraeth (Commodore, Royal Australian Navy, Order of Australia, Legion of Honour) and Osmond Nevill (drowned Formosa, 1952) and one daughter, Olwen Annarella (Section Officer, WAAF).

Died: At his home, Kongbool Homestead, near Balmoral, Victoria, Australia, 21 July 1941.

Buried: Balmoral Cemetery, Victoria, Australia.

Memorials: Balmoral Cemetery, Victoria, Australia; portrait in the Australian War Memorial, Canberra; St Mary's Anglican Church, Balmoral.

Location of Victoria Cross: Held by his family.

Citation for the Victoria Cross: *London Gazette*, 15 November 1898. 'At the Battle of Khartoum on the 2nd September 1898, Captain Smyth galloped forward and attacked an Arab who had run amok among some Camp Followers. Captain Smyth received the Arab's charge, and killed him, being wounded with a spear in the arm in so doing. He thus saved the life of at least one of the Camp Followers.'

VC Investiture: By HM Queen Victoria at Osborne House, Isle of Wight, 6 January 1899.

The grave of Major-General Sir Nevill Smyth, VC in Balmoral Cemetery, Victoria. [Ian Marr, Balmoral Cemetery]

The inscription on the grave of Major-General Sir Nevill Smyth. [Ian Marr, Balmoral Cemetery]

Kongbool, near Balmoral, Victoria, home of Major-General Sir Nevill Smyth. Painting by his son, Commodore Dacre Smyth. [Commodore Dacre Smyth]

Captain Neville Smyth, VC, c.1899.
[QDG Museum, Cardiff]

Nevill Smyth was descended from a socially and financially comfortable background (his maternal great-grandfather, after whom he was named, had been the 5th Astronomer Royal). His father's sister, Henrietta Grace, was the mother of Robert Baden-Powell, the future defender of Mafeking and founder of the Boy Scout movement. He was the epitome of the professional British officer, and appears to have decided on a military career quite early on in life, perhaps influenced by his father's brother, General Sir Henry Augustus Smyth, KCMG, who, in 1887–8, whilst Commander-in-Chief of the British forces in South Africa, led the forces which ended the rebellion by Dinuzulu.

Passing out of Sandhurst with honours, Smyth was commissioned into the 2nd Dragoon Guards, one of the most prestigious cavalry regiments, and then saw service in India, on the North-West Frontier and in Africa, serving on detachment with the Royal Engineers and even, for a short time, with the Royal Navy. He was a staff officer, a Special Service officer and, with his own small independent commands, gained valuable experience of both military and civil administration, the whole time building up a network of contacts and experience which would stand him in good stead in the future. At a time when the British Army was involved in almost continual active service somewhere in the world, Smyth went out of his way to seek action and gain experience and responsibility. By the late 1890s, he was a widely experienced officer with a great deal of first-hand knowledge of service, particularly in north Africa.

In the summer of 1896, General Sir Herbert Kitchener, Sidar of Egypt, led an Egyptian army into the Sudan to try and destroy the power of the Khalifa Abdullahi, successor of the Mahdi who, with his Dervish army, had captured the Sudanese city of Khartoum and killed General Charles Gordon in 1884. The first assault on the Dervish forces came at Firket on 7 June 1896. Kitchener had divided his force into two columns, one under his own command, centred around the infantry brigade, was to launch the main assault against the enemy (via the river road), whilst the other, commanded by Major Burn-Murdoch, was to occupy the hills to the south-east of Firket to await developments. As soon as Kitchener's force had broken the Dervish line, Burn-Murdoch's Camel Corps and cavalry were launched in pursuit and to capture Koyeka and Suarda where the retreating Dervish commander, Osman Azrak, was believed to be heading. The fighting went according to plan and Kitchener quite rightly claimed a significant victory in which his enemy had sustained nearly 2,000 casualties with one British officer wounded and 20 native soldiers killed and a further 83 wounded. Smyth, who took part in the pursuit to Suarda received his first of many Mentions in Despatches. There was then a lengthy delay whilst steps were taken for the construction of a railway line across the desert from Wadi Halfa to Kosheh from where a small fleet of gunboats moved south to protect the supply lines and provide a mobile artillery platform for the advancing land force.

During this time, Kitchener's relationship with the war correspondents who were accompanying the expedition was deteriorating. Several were sending reports back to Britain that raised questions as to the Sirdar's ability as a field force commander which, when added to the various delays such as bad weather and the outbreak of cholera, resulted in a very bad press at home. As Winston Churchill, himself acting as a war correspondent, recorded in *The River War*, his account of the campaign: 'All the croakers were ready. 'A Jingo Government' — 'An incapable general'— 'Another disaster in the Soudan [sic]'— such were the whispers. A check would be the signal for an outcry.'

By mid September, the Anglo-Egyptian force was closing in on the forward units of the Dervish army. Smyth was serving as a staff officer to the Chief of Staff and was present at the battle of Hafir and the subsequent occupation of the town of Dongola which brought operations to an end for 1896.

The troops then settled into camp for what turned out to be nearly a whole year. In July 1897, Major-General Hunter was given command of a flying column to advance some 146 miles and capture the town of Abu Hamed which was achieved on 7 August. One month later he received orders to advance to Berber, which fell two days later. Once again, matters were halted whilst the railway line was extended as far south as this town and British reinforcements were despatched to join the expedition for the final push to the Dervish capital at Omdurman. During this period Smyth served in a variety of staff appointments including, in January 1898, aboard Lieutenant David Beatty's gunboat and, in April, commanded the advanced posts after the battle of the River Atbara when the Anglo-Egyptian army went into camp for the summer.

By August, the army was concentrated at Wad Hamed from where, on 24 August, they started to move south, for the last stage of the assault on the Dervish army. Smyth was appointed an intelligence officer with General Sir Archibald

Hunter's Egyptian Division. The army advanced in stages, on a broad front over one mile wide, along the west bank of the Nile. On 31st they took up their fighting formation with the British on the left (closest to the river) and the Egyptians on the right.

The Khalifa was sensibly of the opinion that his best chance of victory lay in fighting in the streets of Omdurman where the British artillery could not be brought to play on poorly armed but very numerous forces and where every house and street would become the scene of a struggle between individual groups of soldiers. If weight of numbers was to have any effect, this was were the Dervishes would have the best advantage, outnumbering their enemy by two or three to one.

On 1 August, at 1.30pm, the British gunboats commenced the bombardment of the city of Omdurman and so effective were they that the Khalifa foolishly ordered his army out of the city. In a dream he had seen that the place of victory was the plain of Kerreri (the death place of the infidels), just where Kitchener had positioned his army. This movement of the Dervish army caused Kitchener some concern as he feared a night or pre-dawn attack and, consequently, the searchlights aboard the gunboats were left on all night.

At 6am, the Dervish army was seen to be advancing on a four-mile front and twenty-five minutes later, in response to some under-ranged Dervish artillery fire, the British artillery opened fire. Not only were the Dervish guns out of range but their army had been broken up. Instead of throwing the mass of his force against the main concentration of the Anglo-Egyptian army, the Khalifa ordered a large force of over 20,000 north towards the Kerreri Hills against greatly inferior numbers of the Camel Corps and the Egyptian cavalry under the command of Colonel Broadwood, while only 8,000 men were sent against the main British position facing west with its back to the river, protected by the gunboats. The bulk of his army was held back behind the Jebel Surgham. His only real hope of success was to close the gap between the two armies as quickly as possible, thereby negating the artillery advantage of the British, and closing for hand-to-hand combat where his superior numbers would tell. As it was, the force which the Khalifa sent was too few in number and the British and Egyptian infantry carried out great execution amongst the Dervish warriors who provided them with a perfect target as they tried to cross the open plain. By 7.30am the Khalifa's troops were starting to waver.

Broadwood, on the other hand, had little option other than to order his cavalry to carry out a fighting withdrawal north,

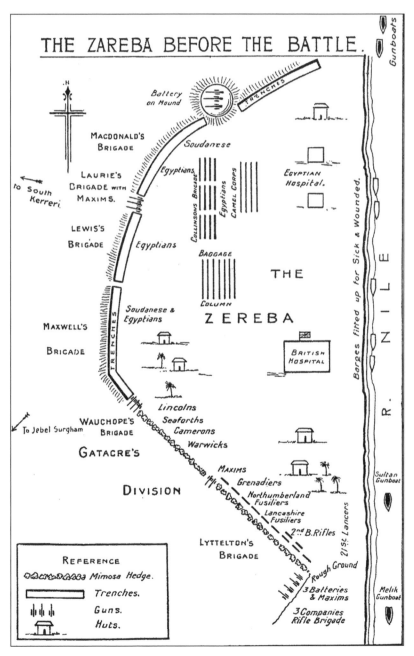

Map of the main Anglo-Egyptian dispositions at the commencement of the Battle of Omdurman. Colonel Broadwood's horse artillery, cavalry and Camel Corps units were on the south Kerreri. The site of Smyth's VC action was some 300 yards in front of Maxwell's Brigade. Map produced by Bennet Burleigh.

Painting, by W. T. Maud of Captain Smyth winning the VC.

leading the Dervish away from the weak Egyptian Brigade. In doing so, the Horse Artillery was partially overrun and lost two guns. The Camel Corps managed to withdraw towards the main British position where they were saved by a covering barrage from the gunboats.

By 8.30am the Dervish army had withdrawn and fighting ceased, bringing an end to the first phase of the battle. Large numbers of wounded Dervishes began to make their way, unmolested, towards the west. Shortly afterwards, some of the British camp followers left the defensive zariba (a barricade made of wood and thorns) in search of plunder and souvenirs. One of the British war correspondents, Bennett Sandford went out to survey the scene and was joined by two others, including Bennett Burleigh, the correspondent of the *Daily Telegraph*. One of the apparently wounded Dervishes then rose up, spear in hand, and attacked the camp followers who immediately ran for the shelter of the zereba, accompanied by one of the correspondents. Burleigh then described what happened next:

I was yet over 200 yards away, and so rode forward. One of the men attacked by the dervish was a native non-commissioned officer. He had followed the others out. Dropping upon his knee he aimed at the dervish, but his Martini-Henry missed fire. He fired again and missed, then the dervish being very near him, ran for the zereba. Mr Bennett Stanford, who was splendidly mounted, with a cocked four-barrelled Lancaster pistol aimed deliberately at the dervish, who turned towards him. Waiting till the jibbeh-clad warrior was but a score of paces or so off, Mr Stanford fired, and appeared to miss also, for the dervish without halt rushed at him, whereupon he easily avoided him, riding off. Then the dervish turned to the soldier who, encumbered with his rifle, did not run swiftly. By that time I had drawn up so as to interpose between them, passing beyond the dervish. I pulled up my rather sorry nag — my best was for carrying despatches— and took deliberate aim. The dervish turned upon me as I wished. I fired and believe hit him, and as my horse was jibbing about fired a second shot from my revolver with less success, then easily got out of the dervish's reach. He had a very heavy spear and showed no sign of throwing it as I rode away, keeping well out of his reach. The camp followers by then were all safe, and so was the native soldier, Mr Dervish having the field very much to himself. Thereupon an ADC, Lieutenant Smyth, came galloping out and riding hard past, fired at the fellow but missed. Checking his horse, Lieutenant Smyth wheeled it about, and he and the dervish collided. The man, who by this time appeared somewhat weak, grabbed the Lieutenant and strove to drive his lance into him. With great hardihood Lieutenant Smyth fired his revolver in the dervish's face, killing him instantly. It was a wonderous escape for the Lieutenant. The instant afterwards I asked him if he had been badly wounded, but he declared that he was untouched, a statement I could scarcely credit, and so repeated my question in another form, to receive a similar answer. In the excitement of the moment he no doubt did not feel the slight spear wound he actually received upon the arm, which saved him from the thrust aimed at his body. An examination of the dead dervish showed he had received four bullet wounds.

At 8.45am, the 21st Lancers, who had been positioned behind the left wing of the Anglo-Egyptian position, close to the river, were ordered to advance towards Omdurman to try and cut off the retreating Dervish warriors. When they came under fire from what they thought were a few hundred skirmishers, they formed into line abreast and commenced a full-blown charge. By the time they had realised that a much larger enemy force lay ahead of them, concealed in a dry river bed, it was too late and they had to fight their way through in what was to be the British Army's last cavalry charge.

The bulk of the Dervish army had still not been drawn into action and it is even likely that Kitchener was unaware of its presence behind the Jebel Surgham.

Bennett Burleigh, the Daily Telegraph *correspondent.*

Unwittingly, therefore, at 9am, he ordered his troops to advance from behind their defensive position and head straight towards the waiting Dervish. When the enemy finally appeared, the high standard of discipline amongst the Anglo-Egyptian troops enabled them to stand firm and the Dervishes were mown down with rapid rifle fire which, when supported by Maxim guns, proved decisive. Despite exhibiting raw courage of the highest degree, the enemy were unable to penetrate the steady lines of advancing infantry who were quickly outflanking them. Finally, in a suicidal charge, about 400 Dervish horsemen, headed straight for the 1st Brigade of the Egyptian Division. They rode to certain death without flinching, few making it to within 20 yards of the disciplined troops. The Anglo-Egyptians then advanced with fixed bayonets and drove the remaining Dervish troops off the field. At 11.30am, Kitchener ordered the army to march into Omdurman. As Winston Churchill wrote:

> Thus ended the battle of Omdurman— the most signal triumph ever gained by the arms of science over barbarians. Within the space of five hours the strongest and best-armed savage army yet arrayed against a modern European Power had been destroyed and dispersed, with hardly any difficulty, comparatively small risk, and insignificant loss to the victors.

Major-General Sir Nevill Smyth, VC. [Dacre Smyth]

With regard to Smyth's action in saving the life of the war correspondent, Major-General Hunter wrote to Sir Herbert Kitchener on 26 October:

> I beg to submit to you the particulars of the gallant behaviour of Capt Neville [sic] M. Smyth, the Queen's Bays (2nd Dragoon Guards) at the battle of the 2nd Sept 1898 which I witnessed and which I feel is worthy of the bestowal on him of the Victoria Cross.
>   Captain Smyth performed a singular act of valour. The troops, till then in a defensive position, were ordered to form to their left in echelon of brigades and to advance. The ground up to within 300 yards of the front of Maxwell's brigade, in its old position, was littered with dead. As the battalions were forming to their left and marching to their places two mounted British correspondents and several native civilians went forward some distance from the close support of the troops to plunder the dead. Thereupon a tall powerful Baggara, with a shovel spear, not wounded, and who had shammed dead, sprang up and ran amôk amongst these plunderers, who indiscriminately fled. The Baggara was gaining on the slowest, when Captain Smyth galloped forward and gallantly placing himself between the hindmost of the pursued and the Baggara, received the latter's charge & killed him, receiving a spear wound in the arm in so doing.
>   For this brave act of saving the life of one or possibly many of even our meanest camp followers I have the honour to submit that I think the name of Capain Smyth is highly worthy of being considered for the distinction of the Vcitoria Cross.

Nevill Smyth was awarded the Victoria Cross. The use of the term 'camp follower' in the citation, with no mention of the two war correspondents, was probably the deliberate choice of Major-General Kitchener, whose opinion of the latter had not improved as the campaign had progressed.

Smyth remained in the Sudan for some months, seeing further action in August 1899 when there was a Mahdist uprising on the Blue Nile. It was Smyth, as acting governor and military commander of the district, who had responsibility for suppressing the uprising and he commanded the force which captured the leader, Khalifa Muhammad al-Sharif, and two of the Mahdi's sons. He later presided over the summary court martial and execution of the three men.

In 1900, Kitchener was keen to see Smyth transferred to South Africa as a member of his staff but the captain was engaged as part of a team surveying the cataracts of the Blue Nile from Wadi Halfa to Abyssinia and it was not until January 1902 that he rejoined his regiment (then serving as part of Major Lawley's Column) for active service against the Boers in South Africa.

On 3 April, some 284 men of the 2nd Dragoon Guards made a night march to catch a Boer commando unawares at Enkeldebosch and Steenkilpruit in the Transvaal. Moving off at 1.30am, the regiment's scouts found some Boer horses hobbled near a laager. B Squadron was sent to surround the Boer camp and the remaining two squadrons attacked, catching the enemy completely off their guard. One of the Boer prisoners reported that there was a larger camp further up the stream and the force moved on to launch a second attack. This time, the tables were turned and it was the Queen's Bays that came under surprise attack by a large enemy force. In moments the troopers were forced to seek cover and had to beat off several determined attacks during the remaining hours of darkness. As dawn broke, Colonel Fanshawe ordered his men to retire to a point some three miles away where he felt they had a better chance of surviving until reinforcements arrived. As the mounted men withdrew, they left behind them their dead and wounded and Nevill Smyth, Sergeants Foweracker and Clerk, Corporals Day and Webb and four troopers, who had all lost their horses to enemy fire. Situated in a hollow, they continued to harass the enemy for some 20 minutes before they were all wounded, with the exception of Smyth. When the Boers called on them to surrender, Smyth managed to crawl away into the long grass and sometime later catch a horse, reputedly belonging to the Boer General Albrecht, which carried him back to the regiment. It was later discovered that the laager the Bays had stumbled across was a concentration of up to ten commandos, numbering as many as 1,200 Boers.

Smyth returned to Africa in 1913 when he was appointed to command the Khartoum District of the Sudan and saw distinguished service in the First World War when his old commanding officer, Kitchener, sent him to Gallipoli to command Australian troops. His handling of the 1st Australian Infantry Brigade at Lone Pine in August 1915 earned him the respect and trust of his men who admired his coolness under fire. Later, in France, he led the brigade at Pozieres and Mouquet Farm on the Somme before being promoted to major-general and taking command of the 2nd Australian Division. At the 2nd Battle of Bullecourt in May 1917, he became the target for considerable criticism over the failure of his division to capture its objective. His last major action commanding Australian troops was 3rd Ypres (Passchendaele) in 1917. He ended the war in command of the 58th Division at the liberation of Lille and, after the Armistice, was given command of the area around the Channel ports. He was probably unique amongst general officers in putting his skills as a pilot to unusual use by personally flying his own reconnaissance missions over enemy lines.

He thought highly of his Australian troops. On leaving the 2nd Australian Division he said: 'The fortune of war has indeed treated me kindly in enabling me to have the honour of being associated with your historic force.' His opinion of Australian soldiers was that they were the finest he had ever served with. The feelings were reciprocated, Major-General Sir Brudenell White said: 'He is so sphinx-like,* silent and imperturbable. But there is a quality that stands out in Smyth — his intense thoroughness. That was his great characteristic.' Major-General Sir Charles Rosenthal wrote: 'Among the soldiers he was recognized as an officer of wise moderation and calm courage, a strict disciplinarian'. His troops remembered him for 'his ability, fair-mindedness and sterling military qualities.'

His active military career drawing to a close, Smyth, aged 50, decided to settle down and in 1918 married and had

three children. On retiring from the British Army in 1924 he went to live in Cornwall before visiting Australia where he decided to settle, buying a farm in Balmoral, Victoria.

* Smyth's nickname during the First World War was 'The Sphinx', perhaps because of his service in Egypt and his rather 'sphinx-like' features.

Nevill Smyth's son, Commodore Dacre Smyth, who served in the Royal Australian Navy 1940–78. He was awarded the Legion of Honour by France in 2004 in recognition of his services at the D-day landings in June 1944 and created an Officer of the Order of Australia.

CONWYN MANSEL-JONES
Captain
West Yorkshire Regiment

Full Name: Conwyn Mansel-Jones (known as 'Mon').
Place of Birth: Beddington, Surrey.
Date of Birth: 14 June 1871, the fifth of eight children (two died in infancy): Herbert Meredyth (headmaster Seafield Engineering College, served as a temporary captain), Frank (lieutenant RN, died 1896) and three sisters: Hilda, Maud (married her first cousin, Major John Watson, youngest son of General Sir John Watson, VC, GCB) and Janet.
Father: Herbert Riversdale Mansel-Jones (formerly of Swansea) 1836–1907. He lived at Beddington Park, Beddington, Surrey (1871), Southwell Gardens, Kensington, London (1881), Fordhook, Acton (1892) and Chase Cliffe, Whatstandwell, Derbyshire.
Mother: Emilia Mansel-Jones (daughter of John Davis of Cranbrook Place, Essex). She died in 1878 and his father married Fanny Tyrell (née Baker) of Acton, London in 1888 (she died in 1929).
Father's Occupation: Barrister, County Court judge, Circuit 13 (Sheffield). Whilst at Trinity College, Cambridge he was the stroke of the winning Varsity Boat Race crew. Received the Royal Humane Society medal for lifesaving.
Education: Haileybury School (Batten House) 1885–8; RMC Sandhurst.
Pre-Service Employment: None.
Service Record: Commissioned The Prince of Wales's Own West Yorkshire Regiment, 8 October 1890; joined 2nd Bn West Yorkshire Regiment, Ambala, India 9 February 1891; served with F Company

Lieutenant Conwyn Mansel-Jones, Gibraltar, 1895. [Prince of Wales's Own Regiment of Yorkshire Museum]

2nd Lieutenant Cowyn Mansel-Jones, c.1890. [© Lieutenant-Colonel G. P. Blaker].

Mansel-Jones' decorations, orders amd medals. L–R: Victoria Cross, DSO, Ashanti Star, Queen's South Africa Medal, Africa General Service Medal, 1914 Star, British War Medal, Victory Medal (MinD), Coronation Medal 1902, Jubilee Medal 1935, Coronation Medal 1937, Legion of Honour. Below: CMG. [via Prince of Wales's Own Regiment of Yorkshire Museum]

at Port Blair, Andaman Islands (on detachment from the battalion which was in Rangoon, Burma); served Aden, November 1894-November 1895; battalion diverted from Gibraltar to serve in the Ashanti expedition of 1895–6, a bloodless campaign which deposed King Prempeh; employed by Colonial Office, August 1898, posted to Central Africa Rifles for active service in Kwamba, British Central Africa 1888–9; captain 20 March 1899; on the outbreak of South African War, he rejoined his regiment in Natal, 1 December 1899 at Frere; served with Buller's column to relieve Ladysmith and saw action at the battles of Colenso, Spion Kop, Vaal Kranz and Tugela Heights; severely wounded Pieter's Hill, February 1900 (resulting in the loss of a leg); invalided to Britain July 1900; DAAG (Recruiting) War Office, 1901–06; Recruiting Staff Officer London Area, 1903–10; retired on account of ill-health caused by his wounds, 9 March 1910; mobilised from the Reserve of Officers, August 1914, DAAG GHQ (3rd Echelon) France, August 1914. AAG and temporary lieutenant-colonel, 7 January 1916; brevet major, 3 June 1916; brevet lieutenant-colonel 1917; major and temporary lieutenant-colonel, Reserve of Officers; colonel, Reserve of Officers, 1 November 1919; Hon. Corps of Gentlemen-at-Arms, 14 December 1920–42.

Decorations, Medals and Rewards: Victoria Cross (for action at Terrace Hill, Tugela, South Africa, 27 February 1900); . CMG (1918); DSO (23 June 1915, 'For distinguished service in the field'); MinD (six times 1914–18); Officier de la Légion d'Honneur (1917).

Post-Service Employment: Called to the Bar at Lincoln's Inn, 1914.

Married: Marion Mabel Rotherham, youngest daughter of William Barton-Wright and Janet, daughter of General Forlonge, 1913. Died 1949.

Children: None.

Died: 29 May 1942 at Lymington Hospital. His home at the time was Wier's End, Brockenhurst, Hampshire.

Buried: St Nicholas's Churchyard, Brockenhurst, Hampshire.

Cowyn Mansel-Jones (front right) with his brothers Frank and Herbert, and sisters Janet, Hilda and Maud. [© Lieutenant-Colonel G. P. Blaker]

Fordhook, Acton, the home of the Mansel-Jones family and one-time home of Lady Byron (the wife of the poet) and the novelist Henry Fielding. [© Lieutenant-Colonel G. P. Blaker]

Lieutenant Cowyn Mansel-Jones (seated to the left of the central figure) with his company, c.1894. [© Lieutenant-Colonel G. P. Blaker]

Captain Conwyn Mansel-Jones, VC.
[© Lieutenant-Colonel G. P. Blaker]

Memorials: Headstone, St Nicholas Churchyard, Brockenhurst, Hampshire; the Point-to-Point Challenge Cup, 2nd Bn West Yorkshire Regiment, presented by Mansel-Jones.
Location of Victoria Cross: Privately held.
Citation for the Victoria Cross: *London Gazette,* 27 July 1900.
'On 27th Feb. 1900, during the assault on Terrace Hill, north of the Tugela, in Natal, the companies of the West Yorkshire Regt on the northern slope of the hill met with severe shell, Vickers-Maxim and rifle fire, and their advanced was for a few minutes checked. Capt. C. Mansel-Jones, however, by his strong initiative, restored confidence, and in spite of his falling very seriously wounded, the men took the whole ridge without further check; this officer's self-sacrificing devotion to duty at a critical moment having averted what might have proved a serious check to the whole assault.'
VC Investiture: By Queen Victoria at Osborne House, 20 August 1900 (in the company of Sergeant-Major William Robertson, VC).

Captain Conwyn Mansel-Jones, VC, c.1913,
possibly taken at the time of his wedding.
[© Lieutenant-Colonel G. P. Blaker]

Weir's End, Brockenhurst, the house where Mansel-Jones lived from
the late 1920s until his death in 1942.

The grave of Conwyn Mansel-Jones, in St Nicholas churchyard,
Brockenhurst. [© Lieutenant-Colonel G. P. Blaker]

Conwyn Mansel-Jones falls into the tradition of being part of a Welsh pedigree that can be traced back for many generations despite having the archetype surname of Jones. The family originated in Swansea, and several members had been notable figures in the town from the mid eighteenth century, living at Verandah on Brynmill Lane, towards Mumbles. In 1740 Calvert Richard Jones I acquired, by marriage, part of the estate of the Herberts of Swansea and his son, Calvert Richard Jones II, was a benefactor of the town, giving land for, amongst other things, the building of the market. As well as a landowner of some importance, he also owned collieries in the area. His second son, Herbert George Jones, became solicitor-general of Van Diemen's Land (Tasmania), and was one of the last barristers to be appointed to the highest rank of 'serjeant-at-law'. Herbert George gave the name 'Mansel' (after his

Herbert Riversdale Mansel Jones and his wife Emilia, the parents of Conwyn Mansel-Jones, VC. [© Lieutenant-Colonel G. P. Blaker]

maternal grandmother, Prudence, the widow of Rawleigh Mansel) to all his children, but appears never to have used it as a surname. His second child, the father of Conwyn Mansel-Jones, was born at Heathfield House, Swansea, and educated at Eton and Trinity College, Cambridge. A man with a somewhat fearsome reputation in the family, Herbert Riversdale Mansel Jones was a barrister on the South Eastern Circuit before being appointed County Court Judge for Derbyshire. He married, Emilia Davis, the sister-in-law of General Sir John Watson, VC, GCB. At some stage during his professional career, Herbert Riversdale Jones began using the surname Mansel Jones, to distinguish him amongst the legal society in which he lived and worked.

Conwyn Mansel-Jones had two brothers and three sisters with whom he had a close, happy relationship. Educated at Haileybury, he broke the family tradition and opted for a career in the army rather than the law, perhaps influenced by his mother's links with the Watson family (which had two VCs from the Indian Mutiny). He received his officer training at Sandhurst before being commissioned into the West Yorkshire Regiment which was then serving in India. He accompanied his regiment to various stations in the sub-continent, including Ambala, Lucknow, Sitapur and Port Blair (Andaman Islands), before going to Aden. Whilst en route back to Britain, the battalion was diverted from Suez, via Gibraltar, to Ashanti, in what is now central Ghana, west Africa, where it took part in operations under Major-General Sir Francis Scott against King Prempeh who was accused, amongst other things, of 'indulging in cannibalism and human sacrifices'; the 2nd West Yorkshires being the only complete British battalion to serve in the expedition. Amazingly, the Ashantis offered no resistance to the British force and accepted the presence of a permanent British Resident in their capital Kumasi to supervise the local legislative authority. For the West Yorkshires, the expedition lasted less than two months and resulted in the capture and deposition of King Prempeh who was eventually exiled to the Seychelles.

Having acquired a liking for service in Africa, Mansel-Jones was detached to the Central Africa Rifles where he remained until the outbreak of war in South Africa in 1899 when he rejoined his regiment at Frere on 1 December. It would seem that senior British commanders had little

C and D Companies, West Yorkshire Regiment at Cape Coast Castle, before start of the march to Kumasi, 1895. [Prince of Wales's Own Regiment of Yorkshire Museum]

understanding of the nature of warfare against a mobile citizen army of the type the Boers were putting into the field, and the 2nd Bn West Yorkshires, part of the 2nd Brigade, was fortunate to get through the actions at Colenso (15 December), Spion Kop (24 January) and Vaal Krantz (5 February) with relatively few losses. On 14 February, Buller launched his fourth attempt to break the siege of Ladysmith and, hill by hill, drove the Boers back across the Tugela River, capturing Cingolo, Monte Cristo and Hlangwane.

On 24 February, Major-General Hart's Brigade sustained heavy casualties trying to capture the hill that came to be known as Hart's Hill. In order to make up the losses, the 2nd Bn West Yorkshire Regiment was ordered to join the brigade. Mansel-Jones, commanding D Company, led his men along the river bank and linked up with Hart's men at Tugela Falls at 8 pm. A Boer night attack on the camp was driven off and the battalion was ordered to take up a position between the bivouac site and the 'Pom-Pom Bridge', covering a Boer foot-bridge over the Tugela. The move was successfully executed by five companies moving in line with fixed bayonets. The following day a cease-fire was called to allow the dead to be

Captain Mansel-Jones, c.1898, whilst on detachment to the Central African Rifles. [© Lieutenant-Colonel G. P. Blaker]

British troops assemble in their camp on the northern bank of Tugela River, 27 February 1900. The gully in the centre of the photograph was part of the route followed by the 2nd West Yorkshire Regiment during the assault. [Prince of Wales's Own Regiment of Yorkshire Museum]

27 February 1900. The men of the 2nd Brigade begin their advance up the steep northern slopes above the Tugela River. Shoulder-to-shoulder in a straight line, these men could easily be mistaken for the troops that scaled the heights above the River Alma in the Crimea, 1854. [Prince of Wales's Own Regiment of Yorkshire Museum]

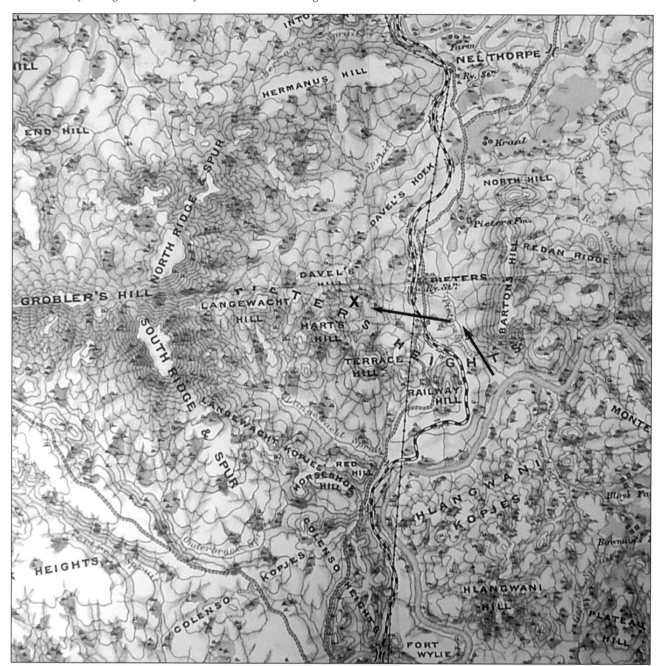

Battlefield map showing the various objectives of Buller's attempts to force open the road to Ladysmith during January and February 1900. The name of Pieter's Hill (or Height) is partially hidden by a crease in the centre of the map. The approximate route taken by Mansel-Jones is shown and the approximate location of his VC action is marked with an 'X'.
[Prince of Wales's Own Regiment of Yorkshire Museum]

buried. That evening, Mansel-Jones was detailed to lead his company,

> … on advanced outpost duty, some distance from the river towards Hart's Hill, along an open space on the Colenso side of Pieter's Hill. This being the first trial of such dangerous work round here, everyone was on the qui vive, and true to expectations, the men of D Company are never likely to forget their experience. The company had proceeded a good way on the road towards Hart's Hill, when, exactly at 9 o'clock, the Boers either wishing to let everyone know they were still in position, or perhaps were afraid that General Buller was taking advantage of the armistice to steal a 'Bronkhorst Spruit march', opened a raking fire from the different positions held by them. Then the air overhead buzzed as if some hundreds of beehives had been kicked loose, causing D Company to fairly hug mother earth. The

View across the Tugela from the artillery positions on the south bank. The railway line which was captured by the 2nd West Yorkshire Regiment can be seen running left–right across the centre of the photograph. Groups of infantry are highlighted as they make their way towards the Boer breastworks close to the summit. Mansel-Jones's VC action took place on the upper slopes seen in this photograph.
[Prince of Wales's Own Regiment of Yorkshire Museum]

company was now between the 'Devil and the Deep Sea' or rather, the Tugela. if they retired, the regiment lining the bank of the river might forget they were out in front, and only remember the naval order — 'Sink and find out afterwards'; and D Company would run a grave risk of being struck off the strength of the regiment. Fortunately the Boers did not know D Company was in their vicinity; and by lying low until morning and passing the time muttering, 'How long, Oh Lord how long?' like an oldtime congregation, enduring the rigmarole of Father Jerry's balderdash, we retired without casualties just before daybreak.

On 27 February, the anniversary of the Battle of Majuba Hill, during the first Boer War, the battalion received orders to join the 11th Brigade (commanded by their former commanding-officer Colonel Kitchener) which was ordered to attack the Boer position on Pieter's Hill in the centre of the enemy's line. No doubt because Kitchener knew the abilities of his own battalion (which he had left only four days previously), the West Yorkshires were placed in the firing line. The assault was to be led by D and F Companies (the former under the command of Mansel-Jones) under the cover of a barrage put down by artillery on the south side of the Tugela. Already fired-up at the possibility of avenging that British defeat, Buller's men were greatly heartened to hear just before the fighting began, that Field Marshal Roberts, VC, had received the surrender of the Boer General Cronje's forces in the Orange Free State.

At 10am the Fusilier Brigade began to move along the northern bank of the Tugela for about 1¹/₂ miles before forming up on the right of the British line and beginning its ascent of the steep slopes towards the enemy positions. About an hour later, the 2nd Brigade began to work its way up the slope towards the railway. They quickly gained the height of the railway line, meeting very little opposition. The two lead companies (D and F) crossed the tracks at the double and took up a position amongst rocks above from where they were able to bring a heavy fire to bear on the Boer positions. A, B, C and D companies extended the line to the right along the railway, working the right shoulder of the hill as far as the edge of a wood.

D & F Companies then wheeled to the right and advanced with fixed bayonets straight up the hill in a series of short rushes, led by Major Watts and Captain Mansel-Jones. E Company then moved to the right to secure the railway and clear the donga between Pieter's Hill and Green Hill (which was being attacked by Major-General Barton's Brigade). This subdued the Boer fire from the donga but, as D and F Companies gained the top of the hill, they came under a heavy artillery, machine-gun and rifle cross-fire from a hill to their left, causing the advance to falter and the left wing to begin to turn back. For a few minutes the situation hung in the balance until Mansel-Jones seized the initiative and impelled his men forward. Heavy volleys were poured into the positions held by the Boers who were actually standing up in their trenches trying to get clear shots at their targets. One of the Boer bullets hit Mansel-Jones in the thigh and disabled him, but inspired by his leadership his men surged up the hill and captured some 40 Boers and a Martini-Maxim gun. They also nearly managed to capture a 'Pom-Pom' gun (a small artillery piece which rapid-fired a 1lb shell,

Lieutenant Henry Singleton Pennell, VC, who was wounded alongside Mansel-Jones in the Pieter's Hill action. He was killed in an accident on the Cresta Run in 1910.

described by one of the West Yorkshires as 'those nasty little guns') but the Boers managed to get it away albeit at some considerable cost. The hill was secured a few moments later by Northcott's Brigade and the Boers were in full retreat. The battalion had five men killed and five officers (one of whom was Lieutenant Pennel, VC) and twenty-six men wounded. Mansel-Jones' action was a classic example of a junior officer seizing the initiative and, through sheer determination, carrying with him to a successful conclusion men who were uncertain whether to withdraw or advance. Whilst it is unlikely that this reverse for the West Yorkshires would have had any significant effect on the final outcome of the battle, Mansel-Jones' action served as a great morale booster to men who were in danger of doubting their ability to defeat the Boers. His VC action can be compared to that of Lieutenant-Colonel H. Jones of the Falklands where a decisive action tipped the balance in favour of the British force and brought matters to a successful conclusion more quickly than might otherwise have happened. As it was, the fight for Pieter's Hill was a victory for Buller and proved the key to unlocking the road to Ladysmith and lifting the 118 day seige on 28 February, amidst great rejoicing in both South Africa and Britain.

Mansel-Jones was a popular member of the officers mess, well-respected by the men under his command, one of whom later wrote:

Captain Mansel-Jones commanding D Company, big, bountiful and humorous, as good a company officer as ever drew a sword, distributed his company's rum with the same tact as he did everything; he divided it amongst the most deserving men after all undesirables were dispersed by him with the magic words 'Off you pop'.

Mansel-Jones had been hit in the thigh, the bullet badly smashing the bone. Lieutenant Francis of the West Yorkshires wrote 'I'm afraid he will not be able to get about for some time'. The lieutenant had under-stated the case and, far from not being able to get about, the wound nearly finished Mansel-Jones' military career. After prolonged treatment, his leg was eventually amputated, bringing to an end his active service with the battalion. By July, he was en route for Britain where he was unable to take up any appointment until the following year when he became DAAG in charge of recruiting at the War Office. He remained in various staff appointments until 1910 when, realising that his further promotion and career prospects were severely curtailed, he retired on the grounds of ill-health. Whilst one-legged soldiers had managed to have a military career, both before and after Mansel-Jones, they were usually men who had lost a leg below the knee, enabling them to adapt successfully to an artificial leg. The loss of the whole leg was another matter altogether and, although he was able to stand and move, it was not without a great deal of difficulty.

On leaving the Army, Mansel-Jones followed in his family's legal tradition and was called to the Bar just

Artist's impression of Mansel-Jones leading the assault on the Boers at Pieter's Hill. As with so many Victorian newspaper illustrations, the acuracy of the image leaves much to be desired. [© Lieutenant-Colonel G. P. Blaker]

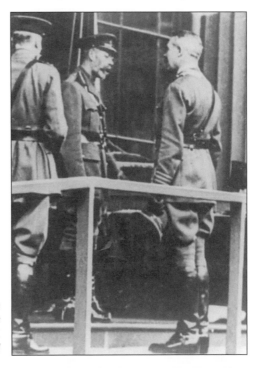

Left: Lieutenant-Colonel Conwyn Mansel-Jones, VC, back in uniform during the First World War. [© Lieutenant-Colonel G. P. Blaker]

Right: Lieutenant-Colonel Conwyn Mansel-Jones, VC, receiving the DSO from HM King George V, [© Lieutenant-Colonel G. P. Blaker]

before the outbreak of war in 1914. He was recalled to active service from the Reserve of Officers in August, with the rank of captain, and served with distinction on the staff in France throughout the war, gaining at least five Mentions in Despatches (Sir John French, 31 May 1915; Sir Douglas Haig, 9 April 1917, 7 April 1918, 30 April 1918, 16 March 1919), the DSO and a CMG; no mean achievement for an officer with his disability. By the end of hostilities he was a major (temporary lieutenant-colonel) and in November 1919 was appointed a colonel on the Reserve of Officers. Just over twelve months later, he was made a member of HM Bodyguard of the Honorable Corps of Gentlemen-at-Arms, a position which he retained until his death. Other VCs holding this office during this period were: Brigadier-General W. D. Wright, VC, CB, CMG, DSO; Major-General Ll. A. E. Price-Davies, VC, CB, CMG, DSO (see page 198); Brigadier–General J. Vaughan Campbell, VC, CMG.

Colonel Conwyn Mansel-Jones, VC, in the uniform of the Honorable Corps of Gentlemen-at-Arms, c.1920. [© Lieutenant-Colonel G. P. Blaker]

CHARLES WARD
Private
2nd King's Own Yorkshire Light Infantry

Charles Ward with his arm in a sling from one of the wounds he received during his VC action.

Full Name: Charles Burley Ward.

Place of Birth: 5 Tulip Street, Leeds, Yorkshire (demolished). The family later lived at 9 Pendulum Street, Leeds.

Date of Birth: 10 July 1876. He had a younger brother, George Burley Ward.

Father: Ward was almost certainly illegitimate and his father was probably Charles Burley of Hunslet, born Lincolnshire).

Mother: Ann Ward, born Leeds, 1854 (nail maker).

Father's Occupation: Charles Burley was a stonemason.

Education: Primrose Hill School, Leeds.

Pre-Service Employment: —

Service Record: Enlisted King's Own Yorkshire Light Infantry, 29 April 1897 (Service N° 5480); served Boer War 1899–1900; transferred to 2nd King's Own Yorkshire Light Infantry ('A' Coy) at Wynberg, Cape Colony; severely wounded at Lindley, 26 June 1900; re-enlisted, Duke of Wellington's (West Riding) Regiment, 10 September 1914 (Service N° 35893); drill instructor at Bristol training 'Kitchener's New Army'; served in France, 1918, as a company sergeant major; discharged, 21 November 1918, as no longer fulfilling the physical requirements of the army; served as sergeant major, 3rd Volunteer Battalion, West Yorkshire Regiment.

Decorations, Medals and Rewards: Victoria Cross (for action at Lindley, Orange Free State, South Africa, 26 June 1900); Queen's South Africa Medal (clasps for Cape Colony and Orange Free State); British War Medal; Victory Medal; received a Testimonial and £600 plus a commemorative gold medal from the City of Leeds.

Post-Service Employment: He owned his own newsagent and tobacconist shop at 1 Church Street, Hunslet, Leeds from 1902–08. He then became a teacher of physical education at Bridgend Grammar School, Bridgend, Glamorgan until 1914. He returned to this profession after the war, teaching at Barry County School, Barry, Glamorgan. Believed to have been working at the County Asylum, Bridgend at the time of his death. Member of the Loyal Commercial Lodge of Freemasons, Cardiff.

Married: 1) Emily Kaye, at Hunslet Parish Church, Leeds, 6 October 1904. He resided at 1 Church Street, Hunslet at this time. They separated towards the end of the Great War. She committed suicide in 1919, aged 36. 2) Annie Elizabeth McNally, at Cardiff in 1919.

Children: One son, Charles and three daughters: Lilian, Edith and Dorothy by his first wife. One son, Eric Burley (born 1920) and one daughter, Mary (born 1921) by his second wife.

Died: Glamorgan County Asylum, Bridgend, 27 December 1921. His home address at this time was 3 Soberton Avenue, Cardiff.

Buried: St Mary's Churchyard, Whitchurch, Cardiff, with full military honours. Samuel Vickery, VC attended.

Memorials: Headstone, St Mary's Churchyard, Whitchurch, Cardiff. Movie film of his return to Leeds survives in the Mitchell & Kenyon collection at the National Film Archive; portrait at the Royal British Legion Club, Whitchurch, Cardiff.

Location of Victoria Cross: With private collector.

Charles Ward, VC, wearing his Victoria Cross and, on his right breast, the commemorative gold medal which he received from the City of Leeds. [KOYLI Museum]

Charles Ward, VC's grave in St Mary's Churchyard, Whitchurch, Cardiff. The grave records that he was the last man to be presented with the Victoria Cross by Queen Victoria.

Citation for the Victoria Cross: *London Gazette,* 28 September 1900. 'On 26th June 1900 at Lindley, a picquet of the Yorkshire Light Infantry was surrounded on three sides by about 500 Boers at close quarters. The two officers were wounded and all but six of the men were killed or wounded. Private Ward then volunteered to take a message asking for reinforcements to the signalling station about 150 yards in the rear of the post. His offer was at first refused, owing to the practical certainty of his being shot; but on his insisting, he was allowed to go. He got across untouched through a storm of shots from each flank and, having delivered his message, he voluntarily returned from a place of absolute safety and recrossed the fire swept ground to assure his Commanding Officer that the message had been sent. On this occasion he was severely wounded. But for this gallant action the post would certainly have been captured.'

VC Investiture: By HM Queen Victoria at Windsor Castle, 15 December 1900. His was the last VC to be presented by the Queen before she died just over one month later.

Charles Ward enlisted in the King's Own Yorkshire Light Infantry just after his 21st birthday. After completing his basic training he joined the 1st Battalion at Mullingar, Ireland and, less than two years later, was part of a draft sent to Wynberg, Cape Colony where he transferred to the 2nd Battalion, a section of which had just arrived there from Mauritius. The detachment moved to De Aar Junction near the Orange Free State border where it was joined by the remainder of the battalion on 15 October 1899. The 2nd Bn King's Own Yorkshire Light Infantry (KOYLI) formed part of the 9th Brigade in the 1st Division under the command of Lord Methuen, part of the Kimberley Relief Force. Ward was serving in 'A' Company under Captain Withycombe and saw his first action in the assault on Belmont Station on 23 November. Two days later the KOYLI moved against the Boers at Graspan and, on 27 November, marched to Wittekop, six miles south of the Modder River where Methuen, due to poor intelligence, believed he could only cross the river by means of the bridge. Unbeknown to him, the Boer forces were in concealed and prepared positions on the opposite bank and took a heavy toll of the British troops as they struggled to cross. After nightfall, the Boers abandoned their positions and withdrew to the Magersfontein Heights where they were assaulted on 10 December. The Kimberley Relief Force remained in camp at Modder River until 16 February 1900 when they marched into and occupied Magersfontein. Six days later they raised the siege of Kimberley.

The KOYLI, still part of the 1st Division, moved to the 20th Brigade in March and were moved by rail to Warrenton near Mafeking where they were given duties to protect ox-wagon convoys and, by the end of May had advanced to Kroonstadt.

In late May, the 500 strong 13th Yeomanry Battalion was ordered to move to Lindley with orders to join up with General Colvile's force. On arriving the Yeomanry discovered that Colvile's column had left and immediately came under attack from a large Boer force under the command of Commandant De Wet. Methuen immediately moved his

Charles Ward, photographed after his return from South Africa but before being decorated with the VC. [KOYLI Museum]

division to Lindley, arriving on 3 June only to find the Yeomanry had surrendered the day before. The bulk of the division was then moved to Heilbron, leaving the 20th Brigade at Lindley under the command of General Paget.

By 4 June, De Wet's Boers were beginning to blockade the town which, as it was overlooked from several high points, was difficult to defend. Paget ordered the construction of a defensive circle of strongpoints some distance outside of the town which were manned by pickets of the 20th Brigade. These were sitting targets and regularly came under atttack. All supplies to and from Lindley had to be brought in by slow moving convoys. On 26 June one such convoy was attacked and had to be rescued. Four days later, another convoy, under the command of Colonel Brookfield of the Imperial Yeomanry, with two escort companies of the KOYLI, was attacked by a large Boer force. At noon, having successfully drawn the attention of the British forces, the Boers attacked all the positions of the eastern pickets. The heaviest assault was on No. 1 Picket, made up of Captain Withycombe, Lieutenant Hind and 25 men of 'A' Company, which included Private Charles Ward.

The picket held out with great courage but it was obvious that they would soon be overrun unless they could gain some support from other positions. The Boers, who were estimated to number about 500, closed to within 20 yards of the forward trench of No. 1 Picket and, from the cover of rocks, opened a withering fire on the defenders. As the British soldiers began to take heavy casualties, including both officers, it became obvious that nobody outside knew of their predicament and it was only a matter of a short time before they were all killed, wounded or forced to surrender. Ward then volunteered to try to run the gaunlet of enemy fire and take a message to the signalling station situated about 150 yards away. From there a message could be sent to ask for reinforcements. Realising that if Ward attempted to break cover he would become the target for every Boer marksman in the area, the officers refused to allow him to go. Ward, however, persisted and the officers, realising there was no alternative, changed their minds. There appeared to be little to gain from carefully timing his dash, and Ward hurled himself out into the open. A modern Olympic athlete can cover 100 metres in just over 10 seconds, Ward had nearly double the distance to cover and was therefore exposed to enemy fire for some 20–30 seconds. Incredibly, he reached the signalling post unharmed and sent the message. Fearing that Captain Withycombe might not realise that he had been successful, he then ran back across the open ground. This time he was not so lucky and the Boer bullets found their mark.

On receipt of Ward's message, some Yeomanry, two artillery pieces and two companies of the KOYLI were sent to the picket's rescue and managed to drive the Boers off the heights although firing continued until nightfall. The picket had lost four men killed (Corporal Lancaster and Privates Dawson, Rose and Taylor and twelve others wounded. Ward's gallant action had saved not only his own companions but almost certainly other British positions as, having failed on captured No. 1 Picket, the Boers made no further serious attempts to capture the town of Lindley before the arrival of a British relief column on 1 July.

The intensity of the fire through which Ward had run was shown by the wounds he received on his return journey. He had been wounded three times in the left arm, twice in the right arm, and once each in the head, shoulder and thigh. His war was certainly over and he was invalided back to Britain. After a lengthy period in a military hospital he was allowed a leave period (which he spent with relatives in Derby) before being discharged from the army as unfit for military service.

Following the announcement in September of the award of the Victoria Cross, Ward was presented with the decoration at Windsor Castle in December. Also present on that day to receive their VCs were Captain Sir John Milbanke, Captain M. F. M. Meiklejohn, Sergeant H. Engleheart and Driver H. H. Glasock. As Ward was the lowest ranking of the five recipients his became the last Victoria Cross presented by Queen Victoria who died just over five

weeks later. His home city of Leeds established the Ward Annuity Fund which presented him with £600 and a gold medal in February 1901, when the city centre came to a standstill for the civic reception headed by the Lord Mayor, the crowds completely filling City Square. Wearing the slouch hat which had been adopted by many British units in South Africa, Ward was filmed on this occasion by cinematic entrepreneurs, Mitchell & Kenyon, probably the first VC recipient to ever appear on celluloid.

By 1902, Ward had set himself up in business as a newsagent/tobacconist at 1 Church Street, Hunslet where he remained for six years before taking up a post as physical training instructor at Bridgend Grammar School in south Wales. That he was able to take up such a physically demanding job is a good indicator of how well he had recovered from his multiple wounds. He rejoined the army during the First World War and was appointed a drill instructor with the rank of company sergeant major, and travelled to France for 17 days in

Charles Ward, VC's last home, 3 Soberton Avenue, Cardiff.

September 1918, qualifying for the award of the British War Medal and the Allied Victory Medal.

Ward had married in 1904 and his wife had borne him four children. Sometime during the First World War, perhaps while he was away on service, the marriage broke down and in May 1918, she left the family home in Cardiff writing him a letter:

> I am leaving your house for ever, and I never wish to see you again. I know I have done wrong, and you can take what action you like. I hope you will take no action against the soldier I was speaking to on Saturday night.

Divorce proceedings were in hand when, in March 1919, she threw herself under a train on the Taff Vale Railway and was killed. The coroner's inquest returned a verdict of suicide.

In the autumn of 1919 Charles Ward married Annie McNally of Cardiff and they had two children. Ward was by this time employed at the County Asylum at Bridgend where he died on 27 December 1921. His grave in Whitchurch was originally marked with a wooden cross but, after this disappeared, the present Commonwealth War Graves headstone was erected following the efforts of local journalist John O'Sullivan. The headstone was unveiled by Mr Eddie Chapman, VC, BEM.

Two of Charles Ward's daughters at the unveiling of his headstone at Whitchurch.
[John O'Sullivan]

LLEWELYN PRICE-DAVIES
Lieutenant
1st King's Royal Rifle Corps

FULL NAME: Llewelyn Alberic Emilius Price; the additional surname Davies was added shortly after his birth. To his fellow officers he was always known as 'Mary'.

PLACE OF BIRTH: London (probably at 117 St George's Square, a house built by his father in 1868). After 1878, the main family home was Marrington Hall, Chirbury, Shropshire. He had two older brothers, Stafford Davies (later Colonel) and Hugh Arthur Lewis, and one older sister, Gwendoline Cholita Mary Sceynton.

Date of Birth: 30 June 1878.

Father: Lewis Richard Price (later Price-Davies).

Mother: Elizabeth Price, daughter of James J. Turner, JP, DL, of Pentrahylin, Llandysilio, Montgomeryshire, a former officer in the Militia.

Father's Occupation: Landowner of independent means who had spent over twenty years as a commodities broker in Vera Cruz and Mexico City, Mexico.

Education: Marlborough School (Cotton House), April 1892–December 1894; The Manor House School, Lee, 1895; RMA Sandhurst, January 1896–January 1897 (Drill Prize).

Service Record: Commissioned 2nd lieutenant King's Royal Rifle Corps, 23 February 1898; served in India 1898–9; lieutenant, 21 October 1899; served Boer War, 1899–1902; relief column for Ladysmith, present at Battle of Colenso, 15 December 1899; served operations in Natal, 17–24 January 1900; present at Spion Kop, 24 January 1900; served operations in Natal, 5–7 February 1900 (present at Val Kranz); served operations in Natal, 14–27 February 1900 (present at Tugela Heights and Pieter's Hill); served operations in Natal, March–June 1900 (present at Laing's Nek, 6–9

Lieutenant Llewelyn Price-Davies, 1901

Top L–R: Victoria Cross, CB, CMG, DSO, Queen's South Africa Medal, King's South Africa Medal. Bottom L–R: 1914 Star, British War Medal, Victory Medal, Defence Medal, Jubilee Medal 1935, Coronation Medal 1937, Coronation Medal 1953, Order of St Maurice and St Lazarus, Legion of Honour. [Royal Green Jackets Museum, Winchester]

Elizabeth Price-Davies with one of her sons.

*2nd Lieutenant Llewelyn Price-Davies, 1898.
[Shropshire Archives 631/3/3093]*

June 1900); served operations in the Transvaal, east of Pretoria, July–August 1900 (MinD with Lieutenant Massingham-Buller for the attack on De Lange's laager, 4 August); served operations in Transvaal, January–April 1901; adjutant, 24th Mounted Infantry, South Africa, 25 April 1901–3 May 1901; served Transvaal and Orange River Colony and Zululand/Natal frontier, April 1901–May 1902 (wounded slightly in right abdomen, 17 September 1901 and severely, chin and left shoulder, Ermelo, 26 January 1902); supernumary captain, 7 January 1902; adjutant and quartermaster to the School of Mounted Infantry (Irish Command), 22 March 1906–30 September 1906; captain 14 August 1906; adjutant to 5th Mounted Infantry, South Africa, 1 October 1906–26 November 1907; Staff College, Camberley, 1908–09; brigade major, 13th Brigade (Irish Command), 1 November 1910–17 June 1912; GSO 3, War Office, 18 June 1912–4 August 1914; GSO 3, 2nd Division, 4 August 1914–24 September 1914; GSO 2, GHQ (France), 2 October 1914–10th March 1915; GSO 2, 4th Division, 11 March 1915–24 November 1915; major, 1 September 1915; temporary brigadier-general, 25 November 1915; GOC 113th Brigade, 38th Welsh Division, December 1915–November 1917; brevet lieutenant-colonel, 1 January 1916; brigade commander, France, 3 April 1918–11 April 1918; special liaison officer to Italy, 19 April 1918–4 November 1918; temporary major-general, 19 April 1918–15 October 1919; brevet colonel, 3 June 1918; president, standing committee regarding prisoners of war; AAG, Aldershot, 9 January 1920–22 March 1924; GOC 145th (South Midlands) Infantry Brigade, 23 March 1924–24 February 1927; brigadier (substantive rank, back-dated to 3 June 1918); assistant-adjutant & quartermaster general (Administration) Gibraltar 1 March 1927; GOC Gibraltar (acting), local brigadier, 5 August 1929–23 September 1930; retired, 15 April 1930, honorary major-general; HM Body Guard of the Corps of Honorable Gentlemen-at-Arms, July 1933; removed from the Reserve of Officers, 1 July 1938; battalion commander, Home Guard, 1939–45.

Decorations, Medals and Rewards: Victoria Cross (for action at Blood River Poort, Transvaal, 17 September 1901); DSO (for services in South Africa, 1 April 1901); CMG (*London Gazette* January 1918); CB (*London Gazette* January 1921); ADC to HM King George V (1920–30); Queen's South Africa Medal (clasps for Tugela Heights, Orange Free State, Relief of Ladysmith, Transvaal and Laing's Nek); King's South Africa Medal (clasps for 1901 and 1902); MinD (South Africa); 1914 Star (with clasp 5th August–22nd November 1914);

Marrington Hall, Chirbury, the home of the Price-Davies family on the Welsh border in Shropshire.

British War Medal; Victory Medal (MinD); Defence Medal; Jubilee Medal (1935); Coronation Medal (1937); Coronation Medal (1953); Legion of Honour (4th Class, France); Commander of the Order of St Maurice and St Lazarus (1923, Italy); silver salver by Borough of Aldershot in recognition of his work for the town (1924).

Post-Service Employment: Secretary of the Odney Club, Cookham, Hampshire (the John Lewis Partnership sports and social club) until his retirement in 1945; vice-president Cookham British Legion; vice president YMCA War Committee; committee member of Celer et Audax Club; life member Royal British Legion; president, Hounslow Branch, Old Contemptibles Association; joint treasurer YMCA; member YMCA National Council; involved with the Boy Scouts Association.

Married: Eileen Geraldine Edith, daughter of James Wilson, DL, of Currygrane, Edgworthstone, Ireland, 8 August 1906. She was the sister of Field Marshal Sir Henry Wilson.

Children: None.

Died: Corndon, Sonning-on-Thames, Berkshire, 26 December 1965.

Buried: St Andrew's Church, Sonning-on-Thames, Berkshire.

Memorials: St Andrew's Church, Sonning-on-Thames; Distinguished Service Memorials of the King's Royal Rifle Corps, Winchester Cathedral.

Location of Victoria Cross: King's Royal Rifle Corps Museum, Peninsula Barracks, Winchester, Hampshire.

Citation for the Victoria Cross: *London Gazette*, 29 November 1901. 'At Blood River Poort, South Africa, on the 17th September 1901, when the Boers had overwhelmed the right of the British column, and some four hundred of them were galloping round the flank and rear of the guns, riding up to the drivers (who were trying to get the guns away) and calling upon them to surrender, Lieutenant Price-Davies, hearing an order to fire upon the charging Boers, at once drew his revolver and dashed upon them in a most gallant and desperate attempt to rescue the guns. He was immediately shot and knocked off his horse, but was not mortally wounded, although he had ridden to what seemed to be certain death without a moment's hesitation.'

VC Investiture: By General Lord Kitchener at Pretoria, 8 June 1902.

Major-General Llewelyn Price-Davies, VC, CB, CMG, DSO.

The grave of Llewelyn Price-Davies in the churchyard at Sonning in Berkshire.

Corndon, Sonning, the home of Llewelyn Price-Davies during his final years.

Llewelyn Price-Davies, although born in London, had strong Welsh roots, the families of both his parents originating from Montgomeryshire, with land straddling the border with Shropshire. They were connected to several notable Welsh families, including the Wynns of Wynnstay and the Prices of Rhiwlas. His father, after a precarious career as a commodities broker in Mexico and the USA, had lived in London where he built a house in St George's Square, Pimlico in 1868. Financial difficulties had resulted in the family having to live for a time in France but everything was stabilised when he inherited the Marrington estate in Shropshire on the death of his maternal uncle, John Davies, in 1877. It was in recognition of this improvement in their circumstances that

St George's Square, London, where Llewelyn Price-Davies was born.

the family adopted the name Davies as part of their surname. His son Llywelyn was named after his brother William Llewellyn, his brother-in-law (the Marquis Alberic de Balbiano of Milan) and his sister, Emelia de Balbiano. Perhaps Lewis Price-Davies was trying to guarantee a more secure financial future for his son. The family does not appear to have had any strong military connections other than an uncle, Colonel John Davies and the near commissioning of William Llewellyn Price into the Austrian army. Lewis himself served for a period in the St Georges Volunteer Rifle Corps. Despite this, his eldest son, Stafford, opted for a career in the army, being commissioned into the Royal Artillery and he was followed some years later by Llewelyn (who was thirteen years his junior) who obtained a commission in the prestigious King's Royal Rifle Corps.

Llywelyn Price-Davies' life had two interesting periods to military historians; the Anglo-Boer War, in which he first came to prominence, and the Great War where his career continued to flourish but, ironically, when in a senior command position in the 38th Welsh Division (Lloyd George's so-called 'Welsh Army Corps') he became a figure, not of ridicule, but who perhaps epitomised the weaknesses of the British staff officer corps.

Price-Davies arrived in South Africa in 1899 and served throughout the initial stages of the war with the column which eventually relieved Ladysmith, seeing action at Colenso, Spion Kop, Val Krantz, Tugela, Pieter's Hill and Laing's Nek. In late March/early April 1901, he was serving with Major Hubert Gough's mounted infantry column, 24th Bn Mounted Infantry, a composite force made up of both regulars and volunteers when he was involved in an action on 1 April, for which he was later awarded the DSO. Attempts to trace the detials of this award have drawn a blank and even Price-Davies' own diary (which is held by the National Army Museum) is a model of self-effacing modesty, providing virtually no information:

Sunday, March 31, 1901
Start at 8. 5th Brigade do scouting. We came to the place we had seen the wagons at last night, & when their scouts got well up into a kind of horseshoe a terrific fire was opened from all sides, & we came in for some of it. Luckily no scouts were hit. Bimbash Stewart came up, & we at once set about attacking the position from one end. The guns were of course some way behind but made very good shooting when they came. The J.M.R. [Johannesburg Mounted Rifles] led the way up & we followed, Stewart continually trying to persuade us not to come. All the Boers cleared & we had some shooting at the last 4 at about 600 yards.

Monday, April 1, 1901
We were all rather sick at not going

Officers of the KRRC at Wynberg, South Africa in 1899. Price-Davies is seated in the front row, second from the left.

Artist's impression of the clash between Gough's Column and the Boers at Blood River Poort.

on yesterday as we saw about 200 Boers & wagons going off. Today we saw none of the former but got plenty of the latter with a few mealies in them & the J.M.R. met the Boers at the end of the day & get a man wounded & pick up a dead Boer. We camp on a high plateau some way from the wood. Broken pom-pom found.

In mid September the column was sent to Newcastle, Natal where it was to provide a mounted escort and scouts to supply wagons which were being threatened by Louis Botha's commando. The column had already some experience of Botha's operations elsewhere in South Africa and was anxious to seize the opportunity to put an end to his activities before the year was out.

On 17 September, Major Gough was encamped at De Jaeger's Drift on the Buffalo River. At noon, a heliograph message was received from one of the forward patrols stating that 200 Boers were resting on Scheeper's Nek above the road to Vryheid. Gough immediately ordered the column to move and, when he arrived at a position overlooking the Boer camp, found the enemy still there. The distance between the two forces, over open country, meant that Gough would be unable to launch a surprise attack on the Boers and he decided to wait until dusk before making any move. Sometime in the mid afternoon, however, the Boers saddled up their horses and rode down to the Blood River and into a stony valley (poort) where they again off-saddled and made camp. Gough reckoned that he could move his force forward, unseen by the Boers, and captured a prominence overlooking the river from where they could catch the commando off-guard.

Gough gave the order to advance and three of his four companies were able to move off almost immediately. They broke into a gallop across the 1,000 yards of open grassland, followed by 69th Battery, Royal Field Artillery commanded by 2nd Lieutenant Shaw. The Boer sentries spotted the attack coming in and, instead of the expected withdrawal of the force by the river, men began to rush up to support them. As the Boers opened fire, a second force of some 500 horsemen galloped to attack Gough's right flank while several hundred more appeared on the slopes of the Drakenburg to his left. Far from launching a decisive, surprise attack on a small Boer force, Gough had stumbled across a major concentration of Boers, numbering over 1,000 horsemen. Gough later recorded the events of the next few minutes:

> I was so engaged looking at my front where a bitter fire-fight was in progress that the first intimation I had of this manoeuvre was that I saw about 20 or 30 Boers amoung my two guns shouting 'Hands up!' Price-Davies, my adjutant, was beside me. We were not 50 yards away and I shouted to the gunner 'Shoot them'. Price-Davies without a second's hesitation drew his revolver and galloped straight at the Boers, shooting one dead, but as he did so another Boer swung sharply round like a man shooting a rabbit which had suddenly bolted behind him, and fired at him point-blank. Price-Davies pitched head-over-heels over his pony's neck, and I cried: 'My God, they have killed him.' I galloped towards him, when I suddenly found that I too, was surrounded by Boers, one of whom was on his knee taking careful aim at me at a range of a few feet. To dodge his shot I threw myself off my pony, and was immediately surrounded, unarmed as I was, by half a dozen Boers.
>
> I was their prisoner. They made no attempt to seize me and I asked them at once if I might go over to Price-Davies, to which my captors readily agreed.
>
> To my great relief, I found that far from being dead he was quite conscious and not dangerously wounded, though the bullet had gone right through him … '

What should have been an easy success for Gough had turned into a major disaster. The majority of his force was captured, including the wounded Price-Davies, who wrote in his diary:

Tuesday September 17, 1901
Fine rain at night. Peyce's Farm. CAPTURED
Wires were received yesterday of the movements of Boers so Weldon & a section went out to Rooi Kopjie before dawn & we followed about 7.30 except Mott who stayed to bring on the weapons. Weldon reported seeing about 400 Boers. We off

saddled near Rooi Kopjie & Gough went on & [I] joined him later. We saw the Boers making for Blood River Poort & tried to get the Regt to saddle up or go on and occupy a ridge to surprise the Boers. Messages took too long but the Boers off saddled 200 or 300 of them in a farm. We had to make a long detour so as not to be seen but eventually we reached the ridge overlooking the farm. Dick was on the left, Cracroft [Captain H. Cracroft, 1st Royal Irish Fusiliers] in the middle & Mildmay [Captain A. R. Mildmay, 3rd Bn KRRC] on the right & the guns whose horses were rather done were in rear. On Dick's left was a big hill & he having dismounted 2 sections went under this & was met with heavy fire at 20 yards. The guns & everyone came into action as soon as possible, but we were outnumbered at least 5 to 1 & had no position worth speaking of.

Wednesday, September 18, 1901
Got up at dawn for which I had been anxiously waiting some hours & learnt later on the full extent of our loss. Mildmay, Blewitt [Lieutenant C.O.B. Blewitt, Rifle Brigade] & Lampton [Lieutenant R. R. Lampton, 1st Bn Durham Light Infantry] who I had hoped had escaped, are all hit (& died M at once, B this evening, & L of exposure in the night for he and several men were left out owing to the darkness). I find the other wounded in a barn of wool. We get very little to eat all day. Ambulance comes in at 11 & later I leave in it with some other men but get stopped. Crocker arrives with ambulances from De Jagers [sic] in the evening & others come under Blood from Vryheid. Gough and Cracroft escaped last night.

Nowhere in the diary does Price-Davies make any reference to the part he played in the action at Blood River Poort, not even hinting that he did anything that might be worthy of mention in Gough's report. The single word 'PRISONER' in block capitals at the top of the entry is the only hint that anything exceptional had occurred. The action which had promised so much had turned into a nightmare. In just over fifteen minutes Gough had lost four officers and nineteen men killed, five officers and nineteen men wounded, and 235 men, two artillery pieces, 120 ponies, 180 modern rifles and 30,000 rounds of ammunition captured. Price-Davies, despite being hit by a bullet in the abdomen, was classed as being only slightly injured as the wound was a clean one, the bullet having passed right through his body without damaging any internal organs, and he recovered remarkably quickly. The nature of the guerilla war in South Africa meant that the Boer commandos had no facility for handling prisoners of war, whether able-bodied or wounded. Their units operated fast moving, hit-and-run tactics and once prisoners had been interrogated and searched for any useful equipment or intelligence, they were often released. This was the case with the members of Gough's column who were back amongst their own within forty-eight hours.

Thursday, September 19, 1901
Start as soon as we can in the morning. Dick has to be carried on a stretcher. We out-span midday & arrive at Vryheid about 6.30. A poor welcome, nothing ready. We are put into the civil hospital & Furnell & I can get nothing to eat but luckily we get half of an orderly who looks after us.
  All the Boers were very busy yesterday & in the evening they all paraded & went off towards de Jagers [sic] … This morning we saw never a Boer & the men found a pom-pom & ammunition buried but were afraid to do anything to it.

By early 1902, Price-Davies was serving in Natal, chasing Boer commandos on the high veldt. On 26 January he was with mounted infantry in the Ermelo district operating Kitchener's policy of clearing farms and rounding up the Boer population for incarceration in the newly established, and soon to become infamous, concentration camps. It had been raining all day and the unit had been involved in some futile work chasing what they thought was a Boer commando but which turned out to be a column led by Lieutenant-Colonel Allenby.

We however see 6 or 7 Boers 1500 yards ahead of us & give chase though at the time, I must confess, I thought it a useless waste of horses, not expecting to catch them. We found ourselves gaining on them & the men were most difficult to keep back. When I saw the Boers split up I saw no reason why we should not shove on especially as I thought it very necessary to try & catch the Boers before they should get into bad country or run into more of their own men. When there were not more than 2 Boers together, Leith & I dashed on & even these two divided, we captured one & Leith halted to see that he did not escape. I went on after the next & he got off his horse & held up his hands but would not throw down his rifle until I was 10 yards past him. I was rather nervous about him but he meant no harm & was collected all right.
  The next gentleman however was a tougher customer. I called on him loudly to hands up but he took no notice. When about 20 yards from him he quietly got off his horse knelt down & took steady aim at me & missed. I then missed him with my revolver & by the time I pulled the trigger again I was almost on him. Unfortunately I had either used all my ammunition or else I had missed over a round (I lost my revolver so I dont know which). Anyway the revolver never went off & as I passed him the Boer gave me a bullet.
  In order to make myself small & in a sort of way take cover behind my pony, I had been leaning over a good deal on the side of my pony away from the Boer, which accounts for the bullet taking such a strange course.

The Boer's bullet nicked Price-Davies on the chin and cut a groove in his neck before entering his shoulder under the joint with his upper arm and travelling through the arm before exiting, fortunately missing any bones. The blow knocked him off his horse and his assailant took the opportunity to make his escape. Two brother officers, Mott and

Leith, came to his assistance, the former catching his pony whilst the latter bound up the wound. Mott went to get the help of a doctor from the 12th Hussars and it was an hour before he returned, by which time Price-Davies had recovered from the immediate effects of the wound and was able to remain with the column until it returned to Ermelo the next day and he was admitted to hospital.

Price-Davies' experience during the war in South Africa as an officer of mounted infantry stood him in good stead after his return to Britain in 1902 and he was given a number of posts where he could put it to good use culminating with his return to South Africa in 1906 as adjutant of the 5th Mounted Infantry Brigade, a similar post to that which he had held in wartime. By the time war broke out in Europe in 1914 he had held a series of important staff appointments and was ideally placed to leap-frog into a senior position in the rapidly expanding 'New Army'. Twelve years of peacetime soldiering in various staff appointments meant that he had lost touch with the day-to-day life of a regimental officer. As his career progressed up the staff ladder his reputation amongst those who served under him deteriorated, reaching an all-time low when he was given command of the 113th Brigade of the 38th (Welsh) Division in preparation for the Somme offensive of 1916.

He took over command of the brigade from Brigadier-General Owen Thomas in November 1915 and took it to France the following month. The 113th comprised the 13th (1st North Wales), 14th (Carnarvon & Anglesey), 15th (London Welsh) and 16th (2nd North Wales) Battalions, Royal Welsh Fusiliers and had a strong Welsh identity, but one that Price-Davies had difficulty relating to. Captain Wyn Griffith of the 15th Bn RWF wrote of a time when his battalion was waiting to move into the trenches in France and the men began to sing an old Welsh hymn in harmony. Price-Davies asked him:

> Why do they always sing these mournful hymns? Most depressing — bad for morale. Why can't they sing something cheerful like the other battalions? I try to explain to him that what they are singing now is what they sang as children, as I did, in chapel, in the world to which they really belong. They are being themselves, not men in uniform. They are back at home, with their families, in their villages. But he does not understand. Nor can he, with his background. I do not think I 'understand'; but the facts were there, and they still are. While they sang, they, and I, were in another country.

Price-Davies as a brigadier-general came across to those in his command as what would today be called a 'company man', a senior officer who was an efficient administrator but who had little empathy with those who served under him. His arrival on the Western Front in December 1915 was his first taste of active service since 1902 and his understanding of the demands of modern industrialised warfare was certainly weak. More accustomed to regular army soldiers, he found the volunteers of Kitchener's New Army difficult to understand and command. They were men serving for a purpose and for the duration of hostilities. More intelligent and representing a wider cross-section of society than the average regular soldier, they did not fit neatly into the traditional pattern of the British Army. Price-Davies was a hard-working and very active brigade commander, always appearing in the trenches to check that orders and directives were being carried out as intended by the GOC and in accordance with the plan of action. He was not a man to shrink from his responsibilities, with a fastidious nature which caused him to be disliked by many with whom he came into contact.

At a time when a large proportion of the army was living every day in the most appalling and dangerous conditions, his attention to detail showed a lack of understanding for the reality of the situation in which his brigade was labouring. His vision of military life and command bore little relationship to the reality of life in the trenches. One of a generation of general officers who were to be labelled as 'donkeys' by the historians of the post-war period, Price-Davies did little to enhance his

The view from the cliff, looking towards the Hammerhead, Mametz Wood, 2006. The memorial to the 38th (Welsh) Division is in the foreground.

reputation as a dynamic, astute general. He was perhaps unfortunate in those around him — including his superior officers, men such as Major-General Ivor Philipps, GOC 38th Division, who probably had even less understanding of the reality of the war — and those below him — such as Captain Llewelyn Wyn Griffith (later Dr Llewelyn Wyn Griffith, CBE), a man of intelligence and unquestioned ability and who was to later publicly record his views of the military hierarchy. Griffiths, who became brigade-major, once famously wrote that Price-Davies was 'the second biggest fool' he met in four years of soldiering. His analysis of his brigadier-general's personality and ability was summed up in his book *Up to Mametz*, first published in 1931:

> The brigadier was a daily plague. He had won the Victoria Cross and the Distinguished Service Order in the South African War. He was slight, athletic in build, and good-looking: his mind was slow in working, but tenacious to the point of obstinacy. He spoke slowly, in prim way — his fellow regular officers called him 'Jane' [sic]. It would be a misuse of words to call him brave, but he was certainly fearless. I have heard an uncharitable company commander, labouring under a grievance, say that he was too stupid to be frightened of anything but reason. He took a delight in exposing himself to fire, quite forgetting that the infantry officer who was his unwilling companion was being forced into a foolhardy challenge of the powers that troubled him day and night, when the Brigadier was far away from the line. He had little sense of humour, but I once saw him laugh at an incident that might have brought trouble upon my head.
>
> It was a cold and wet night, and I was following him along my sector, listening to an interminable catalogue of minor faults. We came to a Lewis Gun post and, as we approached it the gunner fired a drum of ammunition. He did not recognize the general who asked him:
>
> 'Was it you firing then?'
>
> 'Yes.'
>
> "What were you firing at?'
>
> 'Don't know.'
>
> 'Then why did you fire?'
>
> 'Just to bloody well amuse myself,' said the stubborn Welsh collier, in his close-clipped South Wales speech. The General turned away and laughed, to my great relief.
>
> In these days his great preoccupation was the removal of tins. All tins were to be buried behind the line, and woe to the company commander if the General found an empty tin in a trench — he was damned for the day. When the news of his coming sped before him, corporals and sergeants forsook the superintending of military tasks for a wild drive of forgotten tins into a hasty burial in the mud behind the duck boards. Great was the urgency of concealing such indecencies if peace were to reign during his visit. Fundamentally he was right in his struggle for sanitation, but to us it seemed as if this admittedly worthy enterprise were of secondary importance compared to the strengthening of our protection against shell fire. Any improvement in the parapet, or parados when it existed, was sure to gain approval, but there was a queer reluctance to encorage the building of better dug-outs for our comfort and our safety at times when more war was waged against us than we were waging.
>
> The Brigadier wore a mackintosh jacket over his uniform, a pair of mackintosh trousers over his breeches, and a steel helmet that tended to slide over his left ear. There was no visible mark of rank at first, but later he fixed on his helmet the crossed sword and baton. His real badge of office was a wooden staff exactly four feet six inches long, and with this he tested the top layer of the sandbags on the parapet over the fire-step. It was decreed that this height of four feet six inches must never be exceeded — there was little danger of any shortage, but a tall man standing on the fire-step felt acutely conscious of his upper eighteen inches. This mackintoshed figure, with boyish face and pouting expression, conscientiously measuring his staff against the trench wall, and finding a quiet satisfaction in the rare tallying of the two heights, commanded a force of three thousand men. In the stagnant condition of our war making, it might be said that though he was the titular head of this body, to which he issued orders, he commanded no one. He elaborated for our benefit orders he had received from above, but he was no prime mover. He led no one, nor did he ever taste the thrill of throwing mass against mass. We were tenants of an estate of mud, and he was the high bailiff, holding us to a careful tenancy, meticulous even in his over-seeing of our domestic economy. He was zealous in his administration, sparing not himself, nor others, struggling manfully with a burden that appeared to us to be a little too large for his capacity, and concealing this by an untiring expenditure of physical energy.

Price-Davies' ability as a commander of large forces in combat during the battle of the Somme in 1916, where he and so many other senior officers, sent men into action 'in parallel lines, with fixed bayonets, four paces between each man, 100 yards between each line', resulted in massive losses and his name was tarnished forever amongst those who walked into the teeth of the German machine-guns at Mametz Wood. Even when such tactics had been shown not to work in the first assault of 7 July, they were repeated in the second assault three days later. But, perhaps even worse as far as his reputation was concerned, when the 38th Division managed to capture the wood in accordance with the time-table laid down by the General Staff, leaving 4,000 casualties in the dense undergrowth, Price-Davies was not content. Whilst officers who took part in the actual fighting expressed their admiration for what had been achieved, he was cautious in his praise and disappointed with the overall performance. Such meanness of spirit resulted in the division being labelled as lacking in courage and determination. Later, when he discovered the true extent of the difficulties encountered in Mametz Wood and the problems faced by other adjacent divisions, he moderated his criticism but the

Major-General Llewelyn Price-Davies with his wife Eileen, c.1960 outside the Odney Club, Cookham .

damage had been done and the 38th Division had to wait a further year before redeeming itself at 3rd Ypres in 1917.

Price-Davies was a soldier whose gallantry at Blood River Poort typified his military attitude. An unthinking 'hell for leather' charge straight at the enemy was the possible solution to any problem. As an administrator he had shown considerable talent, but as a combat leader and tactician he was certainly more at home in the Victorian army than in the new citizen force of the twentieth century.

After retiring from the army in 1930, he was made an honorary major-general and embarked upon a second career as a civilian administrator. In addition to working as the secretary of the John Lewis Partnership social club at Cookham, he threw himself wholeheartedly into charity work with young people. In his private life, although he had no children, he was fortunate and happy in his marriage to Eileen, the sister of Field Marshal Sir Henry Wilson, Chief of the Imperial General Staff (1918–22) and MP for North Down in Ulster from February 1922 until he was assassinated by Irish Republicans outside his house in Belgravia in June of that year. During the Second World War he commanded a battalion of the Home Guard. In retirement, Price-Davies lived a modest life in the pleasant village of Sonning until his death aged 87.

Appendices

Associated VCs

These appendices contain outline biographical details of a number of men who were awarded the Victoria Cross and have some association with Wales or a Welsh regiment, having worked or lived there or served in a regiment which once was associated with Wales, but who were not born in Wales, who did not have a Welsh parent or who did not die in Wales. Neither were they serving with, or attached to, a Welsh regiment at the time of their VC action. Their details are included here in an effort to clarify any confusion that might arise were they to be left out of this book altogether e.g. those awards made to men who served at Rorke's Drift in 1879, but who were not serving with the 2/24th, will always be associated with that regiment.

The grave of William Coffey in Spital Cemetery, Chesterfield.

WILLIAM COFFEY
Private
34th (Cumberland) Regiment of Foot
Served for a period as sergeant instructor, Royal Cardigan Militia, Aberystwyth.

Full Name: William Coffey.
Place of Birth: Emly, near Hospital, Co. Limerick, Ireland. One of at least four sons, the other three being named Timothy, James and John. Timothy later joined him in the 82nd Regiment
Date of Birth: *c.*1829.
Father: William Coffey of Lisobyhane, Co. Tipperary, Ireland.
Mother: Johanna Coffey (née Healy).
Father's Occupation: Labourer.
Education: None recorded.
Pre Service employment: Labourer.
Service Record: Enlisted in the 82nd Regiment of Foot (Prince of Wales's Volunteers), at Fermoy, Co. Cork, Ireland, 24 November 1846, service number 3837; serving Brecon, Wales 1847, Devonport, England 1848, Wales 1851, Scotland 1851 (Glasgow and Stirling); transferred to 34th Regiment 1 April 1854 at Sheffield; posted Corfu 22 August 1854; posted Crimea 22 November (arriving at Balaclava 9 December); served in the trenches before Sebastopol; corporal 18 March 1856; returned to Britain 10 July 1856, posted to Scotland; sergeant 18 November 1856; embarked for India, 24 August 1857; served Indian Mutiny, saw action at Cawnpore and Lucknow; served Nepal 1859; granted free discharge at Calcutta, 21 December 1860 (conduct recorded as 'Very good'); re-enlisted as a private, 75th Regiment of Foot, 19 June 1861, Calcutta; transferred to 82nd Regiment, Delhi, February 1862; lance-corporal; corporal 11 July 1863; sergeant 7 September 1864; discharged at Jalandhar as 'unfit for further service', 10 October 1867 (conduct recorded as 'Very good'); admitted to Netley Hospital, Portsmouth 1868 suffering from 'chronic bronchitis', discharged 25 August 1868; appointed as sergeant instructor on the permanent staff of the Royal Cardigan Militia, Aberystwyth; musketry certificate; discharged as 'unfit for further military duty' 31 March 1875.
Decorations, Medals and Rewards: Victoria Cross (for action before Sebastopol, 29 March 1855); Distinguished Conduct Medal (for his action on 29 March 1855); Crimea Medal; Medaille Militaire (France, for 'Throwing a live shell out of a trench on 29 March

The Militia Barracks, Aberystwyth where Coffey was sergeant instructor 1868–75.

1855'); Turkish Crimea Medal; Indian Mutiny medal (clasp Lucknow); Long Service and Good Conduct Medal.

Post-Service Employment: Railway Department staff, Calcutta, 1860-1; baker, 1868;

Married: (1) Margaret Linch, in Stirling, Scotland, 27 December 1853. She was a native of Co. Fermanagh, Ireland. She died 13 May 1865 at Mian Meer, India, aged twenty-eight years. She was the adopted daughter of Corporal William Dowd and his wife, Mary (née Bernard).

(2) Margaret, daughter of Patrick Gainey, a labourer and former soldier in the 82nd Regiment, at Pembroke, 7 October 1868. They lived in the barracks at Aberystwyth until 1875 when they moved to Park View, Sheffield Road, Stonegravels, Chesterfield where her adoptive family were then living. She remarried twice.

Children: Mary Joana (1858, probably died shortly after birth), Emma Emilie (1861, died 1862), William John (1863, died aged ten months), Margaret (1865), William John (1870, died aged five months).

Died: At his home in Chesterfield, 13 July 1875, of dysentery. There are numerous erroneous references to his having taken his own life in either London or Sheffield.

Buried: Catholic Section, Spital Cemetery, Chesterfield, in an unmarked grave (No. 10657). Headstone erected by the Border Regiment 13 September 1970.

Memorials: Headstone, Spital Cemetery, Chesterfield; folk-song *Private William Coffey* by Graham Cooper.

Location of Victoria Cross: Border Regiment Museum, Carlisle Castle. Puchased at auction from Sotheby's for £320 in 1968, having previously been in a private collection.

Citation for the Victoria Cross: *London Gazette,* 24 February 1857.

'For having on the 29th March 1855, thrown a lighted shell that fell into the trench, over the parapet'.

VC Investiture: By HM Queen Victoria at the first VC investiture in Hyde Park, London, 26 June 1857.

Thomas Hale, photographed in c.1870.

Wrexham Grammar School where Hale was a pupil in the 1840s.

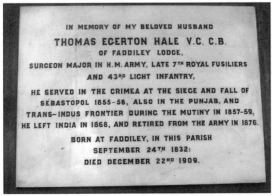

Memorial plaque to Thomas Hale in St Mary's Parish Church, Acton, near Nantwich.

L–R: The Victoria Cross, Companion of the Bath, Crimea Medal (bar Sevastopol) and Turkish Crimea Medal, awarded to Thomas Hale. His Indian Mutiny Medal is missing.
[Courtesy Army Medical Services Museum.]

THOMAS HALE
Assistant Surgeon
7th Regiment of Foot (Royal Fusiliers)
Educated at Wrexham Grammar School.

Full Name: Thomas Egerton Hale

Place of Birth: Faddiley, near Nantwich, Cheshire. In 1871 the family were living at Botterley Hill Farm, Faddiley, before moving to reside at Faddiley Lodge.

Date of Birth: 24 September 1832. He had two younger brothers: Egerton Peter Hale, a farmer who had served in Italy with General Garibaldi; and Assistant-Surgeon Albert Egerton Hale, 103rd Regiment of Foot, Royal Bombay Fusiliers, died of cholera at Gwalior, India, 1869, aged 26.

Father: George Peter Hale of Adderley, near Nantwich, Cheshire (born *c*.1803, died 25 April 1871).

Mother: Sarah Hale (third daughter of Randle Lunt of Park House, Hatherton, Cheshire, born 1813, died 1887).

Father's Occupation: Farmer and gentleman. In 1861 he was farming 66 acres at Bottley Hill Farm, Faddiley. By 1871 he was retired, living on 8 acres at Faddiley Lodge.

Education: Nantwich (1841); Wrexham Grammar School; Queen's College, Birmingham; King's College, London (BA, 1st Class Honours); St Andrew's University (MD, 1856).

Service Record: Commissioned 1854; served Crimean War with 7th Royal Fusiliers; served India, Indian Mutiny; SMO Cherat (where he established a sanitorium in 1860); civil surgeon Ferozepore, 1863; SMO 2nd Punjab Infantry, 1864–6; SMO Naini Tal Hill Sanitorium; major; retired 1876. and 43rd Light Infantry; honorary lieutenant-colonel.

Decorations, Medals and Rewards: Victoria Cross (Sebastopol, 8 September 1855); CB; Crimean Medal (clasp Sevastopol); Turkish Crimea Medal; Indian Mutiny Medal (clasps — unknown); MRCS (1854), FRGS, FRHistS.

Post-Service Employment: Justice of the Peace, Cheshire; member

Northwich Board of Guardians; author of several works on the history of Ireland; local historian; meteorologist.

Married: Emily Harriet Rowswell of Bath in 1873 (born Gibraltar *c.*1842, of English parents). She died 7 April 1922 and is buried in Bath Cemetery.

Children: None recorded.

Died: 25 December 1909, at Faddiley Lodge, Botterley Hill, Nantwich, Cheshire.

Buried: St Mary's Churchyard, Acton, near Nantwich, Cheshire.

Memorials: Headstone, St Mary's Parish Churchyard, Acton; plaque inside St Mary's Parish Church, Acton; name recorded on his wife's grave, Bath Cemetery.

Location of Victoria Cross: Army Medical Services Museum, Keogh Barracks, Aldershot.

Citation for the Victoria Cross: *London Gazette*, 5 May 1857.

'1. For remaining with an officer who was dangerously wounded (Capt. H. M. Jones, 7th Regt.) in the fifth parallel on 8 Sept. 1855, when all the men in the immediate neighbourhood retreated, excepting Lieut W. Hope and Dr Hale; and for endeavouring to rally the men, in conjunction with Lieut. W. Hope, 7th Regt The Royal Fusiliers.

'2. For having on 8 Sept. 1855, after the regiment had retired into the trenches, cleared the most advanced sap of the wounded, and carried into the sap, under a heavy fire, several wounded men from the open ground, being assisted by Sergt. Charles Fisher, 7th Regt The Royal Fusiliers.'

VC Investiture: By HM Queen Victoria, at the first VC investiture in Hyde Park, London, 26 June 1857.

Thomas Hale in old age.

Faddiley Lodge (now Faddiley House) at Faddiley, near Nantwich, the home of Thomas Hale.

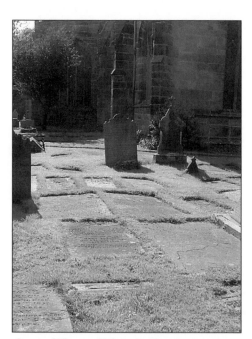

Grave of Thomas Hale in St Mary's Churchyard Acon, near Nantwich. His is the horizontal slab in the centre of the photograph. The inscription is now very indistinct.

Alfred Jones, VC c.1900.

The grave of Alfred Jones and his wife, Emily, in St James's Churchyard, Finchampstead.

ALFRED JONES
Lieutenant
9th Lancers
Lived and worked in Wrexham for part of his post-service life.

Full Name: Alfred Stowell Jones

Place of Birth: 3 Huskisson Street, Liverpool.

Date of Birth: 24 January 1832. He had an older sister, Agnes.

Father: John Jones, MA.

Mother: Hannah Jones, daughter of John Pares of Hopwell Hall, Derbyshire, founder of Pares's Bank, Leicester.

Father's Occupation: Clergyman, Church of England. He became vicar of Sefton, and later a rural dean and archdeacon.

Education: Liverpool College, RMC Sandhurst.

Service Record: Commissioned cornet, 9th Lancers (by purchase) 9 July 1852; lieutenant 21 September 1855; served India, present at siege of Delhi; saw action at Agra (Badle-ka-Serai) 8 June 1857 and 10 October 1857, when he was very badly wounded by a bullet through his left arm and suffered 22 sabre cuts; DAQMG to the cavalry forces at Delhi, 1855; captain and brevet major; graduated India Staff College, 1860; served staff officer, Cape Colony 1861–7; lieutenant-colonel; retired 1872.

Decorations, Medals and Rewards: Victoria Cross (Badle-ke-Serai, Bengal, India, 8 June 1857); Indian Mutiny Medal (clasps for Delhi, Relief of Lucknow and Lucknow); MinD three times.

Post-Service Employment: During his service as Deputy Assistant Quarter-Master General at Delhi, he became interested in the problems of sanitation which led him to pursue a career in that field on retiring from the army. He qualified as a civil engineer and became manager of the new sewage works at Hafod-y-Wern, Wrexham in the late 1870s and 1880s (living at Abenbury Cottage and Hafod-y-Wern). Whilst there he won the 1879 First Prize in the Sewage Farm Competition of the Royal Agricultural Society of England. He lived at Wallington near Croydon in 1891 when he was self-employed as a civil engineer. He was appointed manager of the Sewage Works for the 1st Army Corps, Aldershot 1895, a position which he held until 1912, living at Ridge Cottage, Riders Road, Finchampstead, Berkshire. He was the author of the books *Will a Sewage Farm Pay?* and *Natural and Artificial Sewage Treatment.* He was a founder member of the Royal Sanitary Institute and a member of the Royal Institute of Civil Engineers. Justice of the Peace, Berkshire.

Married: Emily, youngest daughter of John Back of Aldershot Place, Surrey.

Children: Five sons, one daughter. Their eldest son, Captain Harry Jones, RN, commanded HMS *Africa* (battleship), died of Bight's disease in 1914. Their second son, Captain Owen Jones, served in the Royal Naval Reserve. Their third son, Lieutenant Tertius Jones, RHA, died at Meerut, India, 1896. Their fourth son, Percy Jones, an indigo planter in India, was commissioned into the 13th Lancers and served with the Mesopotamia Field Force. He was killed in action at Samara on 2 November 1917 (rank captain). Their youngest son, Martin (born Wrexham), a lieutenant in the 11th Hussars, was killed in a polo accident in India in 1895. Their daughter, Mary Audrey, married Major-General W. Arthur Watson,

CB, son of General Sir John Watson, VC, GCB.

Died: 29 May 1920, Finchampstead.

Buried: St James's Churchyard, Finchampstead.

Memorials: Headstone in St James's Churchyard, Finchampstead. Colonel Jones VC Award.

Location of Victoria Cross: Privately held.

Citation for the Victoria Cross: *London Gazette*, 18 June 1858.

'The Cavalry charged the rebels and rode through them. Lieut Jones with his squadron captured one of their guns, killing the drivers and, with Lieut-Colonel Yule's assistance, turned it upon a village occupied by the rebels, who were quickly dislodged. This was a well-conceived act, gallantly executed. (Despatch from Major-General Hope Grant, KCB, dated 10 Jan. 1858.)'

VC Investiture: By HM Queen Victoria at Southsea Common, Hampshire,

Hafod-y-Wern, Wrexham, home of Alfred Jones, VC when manager of the Wrexham Sewerage Works.

• When the VC was established, Lieutenant Jones and Lieutenant Robert Blair (see p.77) are on record as having decided to do everything possible to win the award. Both achieved their ambition.

Henry Addison, wearing his VC, Indian Mutiny Medal and LSGC Medal. He lost his left leg in the VC action.

HENRY ADDISON
Private
43rd (Monmouthshire) Light Infantry
Regiment was, at time of VC action, associated with Monmouthshire; now part of the 1st Bn. Royal Green Jackets.

Full Name: Henry Addison
Place of Birth: Bardwell, Suffolk.
Date of Birth: 1 February 1821. He had a brother, William, who served in the Royal Marines.
Father: George Addison.
Mother: Susan Addison.
Father's Occupation: Farmer.
Education: —
Service Record: Enlisted in 94th Regiment (Connaught Rangers), 9 February 1841; transferred to 43rd (Monmouthshire) Light Infantry, 1854; served India; Indian Mutiny (wounded twice, leg amputated); invalided out of the service, 1860, after 19 years 6 months.
Decorations, Medals and Rewards: Victoria Cross (Punnah Jungle, near Kurrereah, India, 22 January 1859); Indian Mutiny Medal (no clasps); Long Service and Good Conduct Medal.
Post-Service Employment: —
Married: Charlotte, born Madras, East Indies, *c.*1835. British subject.
Children: One son, William, born East Indies, 1860. Appears on the 1861 census, aged seven months, but not thereafter.
Died: 18 June 1887, Bardwell, Suffolk.
Buried: Parish Churchyard, Bardwell.
Memorials: Headstone, Parish Churchyard, Bardwell, Suffolk.
Location of Victoria Cross: Royal Green Jackets Museum, Winchester.
Citation for the Victoria Cross: *London Gazette*, 2 September 1859. 'Near Kurrereah, in defending against a large force and saving the life of Lieut Osborne, Political Agent, who had fallen on the ground wounded. Private Addison received two dangerous wounds and lost his leg in this gallant service.'
VC Investiture: By HM Queen Victoria at Windsor Home Park, 9 November 1860.

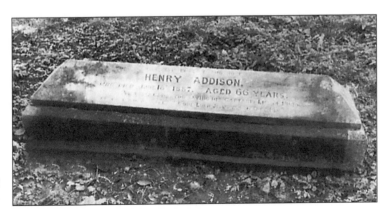

The grave of Henry Addison at Bardwell Parish Churchyard, Suffolk.

JOHN CHARD
Lieutenant
Royal Engineers

VC award for action whilst in command of the British troops at Rorke's Drift, 1879.

Full Name: John Rouse Marriott Chard.

Place of Birth: Boxhill, Pennycross, near Plymouth, Devon.

Date of Birth: 21 December 1847. He had two brothers, Colonel William Wheaton Chard and the Reverend Charles Edward Chard and four sisters, Charlotte, Florence, Mary and Jane.

Father: Dr William Wheaton Chard of Pathe House, Othery, Somerset and Mount Tamar, Devon.

Mother: Jane Chard, the only daughter of Dr John Hart Brimacombe of Stoke Climsland, Cornwall.

Father's Occupation: Landed proprietor.

Education: Plymouth New Grammar School; Cheltenham; RMA Woolwich.

Service Record: Commissioned Royal Engineers, 15 July 1868; served Chatham; served Bermuda October 1870–3 constructing naval defences at Hamilton; served Malta, February 1874–April 1875, constructing fortifications; served Devonport, September 1875–April 1878; embarked as senior subaltern with No. 5 Company, Royal Engineers, 2 December 1878, arrived South Africa, 5 January 1879; arrived Rorke's Drift to construct a pont bridge system across the Buffalo River, 19 January 1879; present as senior officer at the defence of Rorke's Drift, Natal, 22/23 January 1879 and Ulundi, 4 July 1879; captain and brevet major w.e.f. 23 January 1879; served Devonport January 1880; Cyprus December 1881–March 1887; major, 17 July 1886; Preston 1887–92; served Singapore 1892-6; lieutenant-colonel 8 January 1893; Chief Royal Engineer, Perth, September 1896; colonel, 8 January 1897; retired August 1897.

Decorations, Medals and Rewards: Victoria Cross (for action at Rorke's Drift, Natal, 22/23 January 1879); South Africa medal (clasp for 1879); Diamond Jubilee Medal (1897); Sword of Honour, given by the people of Plymouth, 1879; Illuminated Addresses from Langport, Chatham, Brompton and the St George's Freemasons' Lodge, Exeter.

Post-Service Employment: None.

Married: Unmarried.

Children: None.

Died: He was diagnosed as having cancer of the tongue which resulted in his retiring from the Army. He underwent surgery to remove his tongue but died on 1 November 1897, at his brother's home, Hatch Beauchamp Rectory, near Taunton, Somerset.

Buried: St John the Baptist Churchyard, Hatch Beauchamp, Somerset. Queen Victoria sent a wreath inscribed 'A mark of admiration and regard for a brave soldier from his sovereign'.

Memorials: Headstone, St John the Baptist Church, Hatch Beauchamp, Somerset; memorial window in St John the Baptist Church, Hatch Beauchamp, Somerset; plaque in Jesus Chapel, Rochester Cathedral; plaque in Ottery Church, Somerset; bust in Shire Hall, Taunton, Somerset, now in private hands; 'John Chard VC House' TA Centre, Swansea; the 'John Chard Decoration' and

Brevet Major John Chard, VC, photographed c.1880.

The grave of John Chard, VC outside the door of St John the Baptist Church, Hatch Beauchamp, Somerset.

John Chard, VC.

'John Chard Medal' are given as long service awards by South Africa to their Citizen Force; Sword of Honour and various other items displayed at the Royal Engineers Museum, Chatham; a memorial window at the Guildhall, Plymouth was destroyed by bombing in 1941.

Location of Victoria Cross: Whereabouts unknown, probably in a private collection. A duplicate Victoria Cross was sold at Glendinings, London, 17 May 1972, for £2,700 to the actor Sir Stanley Baker who had played Chard in the film *Zulu*. Following Baker's death in 1976, this again came on the market and the replica underwent analysis, the results of which showed it to be almost certainly the original VC.

Citation for the Victoria Cross: *London Gazette,* 2 May 1879 (joint citation with Lieutenant Gonville Bromhead).

'For their gallant conduct at the defence of Rorke's Drift, on the occasion of the attack by the Zulus, on the 22nd and 23rd Jan. 1879. The Lieut-General commanding the troops reports that had it not been for the fine example of these two officers under the most trying circumstances, the defence of Rorke's Drift post would not have been conducted with that intelligence and tenacity which so essentially characterized it. The Lieut-General adds that its success must, in a great degree, be attributed to the two young officers who exercised the chief command on the occasion in question.'

VC Investiture: By Sir Garnet Wolseley at Inkwenken Camp, St Paul's, Natal, 16 July 1879.

The John Chard Memorial Window at St John the Baptist Church, Hatch Beauchamp, Somerset. Note the Victoria Cross depicted in the second small light from the left at the top of the window.

JAMES REYNOLDS
Surgeon-Major
Army Medical Corps
VC award for action whilst acting as medical officer to a small detachment of the 24th Regiment of Foot at Rorke's Drift, 1879.

Full Name: James Henry Reynolds

Place of Birth: Kingstown (now Dun Laoghaire), Co. Dublin, Ireland. At the time the family were living at 7 Queen Street, Dublin. The family moved to Lower Gardiner Street, Dublin in 1860 and, three years later, to Rockfield House, near Granard, Co. Longford (900 acres, later re-named Dalystown House).

Date of Birth: 3 February 1844. He was the middle of five children: Rose, Laurence Patrick, Ellenor and Margaret.

Father: Laurence Patrick Reynolds, JP (son of Rev. James Reynolds).

Mother: Margaret Savage (née Kearney). She was the widow of Patrick Savage (died 1833) a hotelier in Dublin.

Father's Occupation: Hotel proprietor (The Sun Inn, corner of Queen Street and Bridewell Lane, Dublin) and racehorse breeder.

Education: Castle Knock College and Trinity College, Dublin (BA 1864, MB and Master of Surgery (1867). Passed examination (16th out of 60 entrants) for entry into the Army Medical Department, 1868.

Service Record: Commissioned Medical Staff Corps as assistant-surgeon, 31 March 1868, Gosport Military Hospital (Netley); posted to India as medical officer to the 36th Regiment, 1869; invalided home after three months; returned to India 1 May 1869; received thanks of C-in-C India, Lord Sandhurst for services during a cholera outbreak; surgeon 1 March 1873; served South Africa, Griqualand Campaign, 1875; served Kaffir War 1877–8 (present at engagement at Impetu); served Zulu War 1879 (present at defence of Rorke's Drift, 23/24 January 1879, and Ulundi); special promotion to surgeon-major; lieutenant-colonel 1 April 1887; brigade-surgeon lieutenant-colonel 25 December 1892, attached 2nd Bn Warwickshire Regiment; retired 1896.

Surgeon-Major James Reynolds with his dog, c.1880.

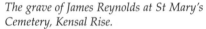

The grave of James Reynolds at St Mary's Cemetery, Kensal Rise.

L–R: The Victoria Cross, South African War Medal. [Courtesy of Army Medical Services Museum]

The medical kit used by James Reynods during the defence of Rorke's Drift. This was sold at auction by Spink in 2001 for £41,400.

James Reynolds, VC c.1895.
[Army Medical Services Museum]

Decorations, Medals and Rewards: Victoria Cross (for action at Rorke's Drift, 22/23 January 1879); South African War Medal (clasp for 1887-8-9); Gold Medal presented by the British Medical Association for his services at Rorke's Drift; LLB, University of Dublin, 1879 (in recognition of his action at Rorke's Drift).

Post-Service Employment: Medical officer in charge of the Royal Army Clothing Factory, London. Also worked as a general practitioner in London.

Married: Elizabeth Mary, daughter of Dr McCormick, 1880. Her father had been the Reynolds family doctor in Dublin.

Children: Percival, George Cormac, Henry Laurence.

Died: 4 March 1932, Empire Nursing Home, Victoria, London.

Buried: St Mary's RC Cemetery, Kensal Rise, London, grave RC 504.

Memorials: Headstone, St Mary's RC Cemetery, Kensal Rise, London. Biography *The Rorke's Drift Doctor, James Reynolds VC and the defence of Rorke's Drift* by Lee Stevenson, 2001.

Location of Victoria Cross: On loan to the Army Medical Services Museum, Keogh Barracks, Aldershot.

Citation for the Victoria Cross: *London Gazette,* 17 June 1879.

'For the conspicuous bravery during the attack at Rorke's Drift, on the 22nd and 23rd Jan. 1879, which he exhibited in his constant attention to the wounded under fire, and in his voluntarily conveying ammunition from the store to the defenders of the hospital, whereby he exposed himself to a cross-fire from the enemy both in going and returning.'

VC Investiture: By Colonel R. T. Glynn, CB, at a brigade parade, at Pine Tree Camp, Durban, Natal, 22 August 1879. Edward Stephenson Browne (see p.162) was also decorated with his VC at the same parade.

The BMA Gold Medal awarded to James Reynolds, VC c.1895. [Army Medical Services Museum]

JAMES DALTON
Acting Assistant Commissary
Commissariat and Transport Corps

VC award for action whilst serving with a small detachment of the 24th Regiment of Foot, now part of the Royal Welch (Royal Regiment of Wales).

James Dalton, VC, photographed in Portsmouth, 1880.

Full Name: James Langley Dalton
Place of Birth: St Andrew's, London
Date of Birth: December 1832
Father: —
Mother: —
Father's Occupation: —
Education: —
Service Record: Enlisted 85th Foot November 1849; transferred Commissariat Corps 1862 as corporal; sergeant 1863; clerk and master-sergeant 1867; served Red River expedition, Canada, in 1870; retired 1871; sergeant-major; volunteered Commissary and Transport Department, 1877, South Africa; present at defence of Rorke's Drift, Natal, 22/23 January 1879; permanent commission Commissary and Transport Department, 1879;
Decorations, Medals and Rewards: Victoria Cross (for action at the defence of Rorke's Drift 23/24 January 1879); South Africa War Medal (clasps for 1877–78 and 1879); Long Service and Good Conduct Medal. He was almost certainly entitled to the Canada General Service but there is no record of his being awarded it. His South Africa War Medal is a replacement and should have the clasp 1877–8–9. The original of this medal, and his LSGC Medal were badly damaged in a fire.
Post-Service Employment: Part shareholder in a South African gold mine, 1880.
Married: —
Children: —
Died: 8 January 1887, at Grosvenor Port Hotel, Port Elizabeth, Cape Province, South Africa.
Buried: Russell Road RC Cemetery, Port Elizabeth, Cape Province, South Africa. Plot E.
Memorials: Headstone, Russell Road Cemetery, Port Elizabeth, South Africa.
Location of Victoria Cross: Royal Logistic Corps Museum, Blackdown, Camberley, Surrey.
Citation for the Victoria Cross: *London Gazette*, 17 November 1879. 'For his conspicuous gallantry during the attack on Rorke's Drift post by the Zulus on the night of 22nd Jan. 1879, when he actively superintended the work of defence, and was amongst the foremost of those who received the first attack at the corner of the hospital, where the deadliness of his fire did great execution, and the mad rush of the Zulus met with its first check, and where, by his cool courage, he saved the life of a man of the Army Hospital Corps, by shooting the Zulu who, having seized the muzzle of the man's rifle, was in the act of assegaiing him. This officer, to whose energies much of the defence of the place was due, was severely wounded during the contest, but still continued to give the same example of cool courage.'
VC Investiture: By General Hugh Clifford, VC, at a special parade at Fort Napier, 16 January 1880.

The grave of James Dalton, VC, in Russell Road RC Cemetery, Port Elizabeth, South Africa.

FRIEDERICH SCHIESS
Corporal
Natal Native Contingent
VC award for action whilst serving at Rorke's drift, 1879.

The VC awarded to Friederich Schiess is now held by the National Army Museum, London. The whereabouts of his South Africa Medal is unknown.

Full Name: Christian Ferdinand Schiess (known as Friederich). His name is also recorded as being Ferdinand Christian Schiess.
Place of Birth: Burgdorf, Bern Canton, Switzerland.
Date of Birth: 7 April 1856.
Father: —
Mother: —
Father's Occupation: —
Education: —
Service Record: Volunteered for service with the French Army; discharged; volunteered for service with the 2nd Battalion, Natal Native Contingent, South Africa; served in the 9th Frontier War; corporal; served Zulu War; present at defence of Rorke's Drift, Natal, 22/23 January 1879; discharged.
Decorations, Medals and Rewards: Victoria Cross (for action at the defence of Rorke's Drift, 23/24 January 1879); he would almost certainly have also been awarded the South Africa Medal (bar 1878–9).
Post-Service Employment: Emigrated to East London, South Africa from Hamburg, 1877. After the end of the Anglo-Zulu War hostilities he was unable to obtain employment. In 1884 he managed to obtain a passage aboard a ship bound for Britain, the ticket being paid for by public subscription, organised by the Royal Navy.
Married: No details recorded.
Children: No details recorded.
Died: 14 December 1884, aboard the *Seraphis*, off the coast of Angola, *en route* to Britain.
Buried: Buried at sea off the coast of Angola having died on 14 December 1884
Memorials: Plaque at the Rorke's Drift Museum, Kwazulu-Natal, South Africa.
Location of Victoria Cross: National Army Museum, Chelsea, London.
Citation for the Victoria Cross: *London Gazette*, 29 November 1879. 'For conspicuous gallantry in the defence of Rorke's Drift Post on the night of 22nd Jan. 1879, when, in spite of his having been wounded in the foot a few days previously, he greatly distinguished himself when the garrison were repulsing with the bayonet a series of desperate assaults made by the Zulus, and displayed great activity and devoted gallantry throughout the defence. On one occasion, when the garrison had retired to the inner line of defence, and the Zulus occupied the wall of mealie bags which had been abandoned, he crept along the wall, without any order, to dislodge a Zulu who was shooting better than usual, and succeeded in killing him and two others before he, the Corporal, returned to the inner defences.'
VC Investiture: By Sir Garnet Wolseley at a special parade in Pietermaritzburg, 3 February 1880.

ALEXANDER COBBE
Captain (local Lt-Colonel)
1st Central Africa Bn, King's African Rifles, Indian Army
A former officer in the South Wales Borderers, and later Colonel of the Regiment.

Major-General Alexander Cobbe, VC, c.1916.

Full Name: Alexander Stanhope Cobbe.
Place of Birth: Naini Tal, India.
Date of Birth: 5 June 1870. His elder brother was Colonel Henry Hercules Cobbe, CMG, DSO, Indian Army.
Father: Sir Alexander Hugh Cobbe, KCB (1825–99).
Mother: Emily Barbara (née Jones).
Father's Occupation: Lieutenant-General, Colonel Princess Victoria's (Royal Irish Fusiliers) 1897–99.
Education: Eagle House School, Wimbledon; Wellington College; RMC, Sandhurst.
Pre-service Employment: None.
Service Record: Commissioned 2nd lieutenant South Wales Borderers, 21 September 1889; lieutenant, 4 March 1892; tfd Indian Staff Corps 1892; posted 32nd Bengal Native Infantry, 12 August 1892; served Chitral Relief Force, 1895 (MinD); seconded to 1st Bn King's African Rifles, 13 May 1898; served Angoniland Expedition 1898; served expedition against Nkwamba, 1899 (MinD); served Ashanti, 1900 (local major), severely wounded (MinD 4 December 1900 and 8 March 1900); captain, 21 September 1900; seconded 2nd Bn King's African Rifles, 1902; served Somaliland, 1903 (local lieutenant-colonel, MinD 3 September 1904); GSO3 Army HQ India; major, 21 September 1907; brevet lieutenant-colonel, 22 September 1907; GSO1 CGS Division, India, 1 April 1910–3 March 1914; colonel 1 December 1911; GSO1 Lahore Division, 18 October 1914–4 January 1915; served France and Flanders 1914 (MinD three times); DAQMG and temporary major-general, 5 January 1915– 16 July 1915 (MinD 17 February 1915 and 22 June 1915); brigadier-general, Staff 1st Army Corps, 17 July 1915–28 January 1916 (MinD 1 January 1916); director of staff duties and military training, Army HQ India, March 1916; major-general, 3 June 1916; GOC 7th (Meerut) Division, India and Mesopotamia; served Mesopotamia, including fall of Baghdad (MinD 10 July 1917, 10 January 1918, 12 March 1918, 27 March 1918 and 5 June 1919); GOC 3rd Indian Army Corps then 1st Indian Army Corps; temporary lieutenant-general, 3 June 1919; Military Secretary India Office, London 20 October 1919–13 June 1920; general, 14 February 1924; GOC Northern Command, Rawalpindi, India, 9 May 1926; Military Secretary, India Office, London, May 1928; ADC to HM King George V, 1 December 1911–2 June 1916; ADC (General) to HM King George V, June 1928; Colonel South Wales Borderers, 22 February 1922–his death.
Decorations, Medals and Rewards: Victoria Cross (for action at Erego, Somaliland, 6 October 1902); GCB (*London Gazette*, 2 January 1928); KCB (*London Gazette*, 10 March 1917); KCSI (*London Gazette*, 5 March 1919; Distinguished Service Order (for actions in Ashanti, *London Gazette*, 26 April 1901); CB (*London Gazette*, 3 June 1915); CSI (*London Gazette* 1 January 1918) India Medal (clasp Relief of Chitral, 1895); Central Africa Medal (clasp CentralA frica 1894–98); East and West Africa Medal; Africa GSM (clasps for Jidballi, Somaliland

General Sir Alexander Cobbe, VC, c.1928.

The overgrown grave of Sir Alexander Cobbe, VC alongside the boundary wall of St Peter's Churchyard, Sharnbrook.

1902–04 and BCA 1899–1900); Ashanti 1900 medal (clasp Kumassi); 1914 Star (clasp 5th Aug–22nd Nov 1914); British War Medal; Victory Medal; Coronation Medal (1910); Commander Legion of Honour (France); Commander Order of St Maurice and St Lazarus (Italy).

Post-Service Employment:

Married: Winifred Ada Bowen, eldest child of Sir Albert Edward Bowen, 1st Baronet Bowen of Coleworth), JP, HS of Bedfordshire (1910) and Alice Anita (née Crowther), of Coleworth, Bedfordshire, on 1 October 1910. She died in 1956.

Children: One son, two daughters.

Died: 29 June 1931 at Sharnbrook, Bedfordshire.

Buried: Full military honours on 3 July 1931, from the Guards Chapel to St Margaret's Westminster before interment in St Peter's Churchyard, Sharnbrook, Bedfordshire.

Memorials: St Peter's Churchyard, Shambrook; Havard Chapel, Brecon Cathedral.

Location of Victoria Cross: RRW Museum, Brecon.

Citation for the Victoria Cross: *London Gazette* (20 January 1903)
'During the action at Erego on 6th October 1902, when some of the companies had retired, Lieutenant-Colonel Cobbe was left by himself in front of the line with a Maxim gun. Without assistance he brought in the Maxim and worked it at a most critical time. He then went out under an extremely hot fire from the enemy about twenty yards in front of him and from his own men who had retired about the same distance behind and succeeded in carrying in a wounded orderly. Colonel Swayne, who was in command of the force, personally witnessed this officer's conduct, which he described as most gallant.'

VC Investiture: By Brigadier-General W. H. Manning, 22 February 1903, at Obbia, Somaliland. 'All the available men were drawn up on three sides of a square formation, a flagstaff had been erected on a little mound, and General Manning, standing close by it, made a pretty little speech to the troops. Then Colonel Cobbe was asked to step forward, and the General pinned the much-coveted prize on his breast. Congratulations all round, 'God Save the King!' and the show was over.' (Melton Prior, *Campaigns of a War Correspondent*, London, 1912.)

BIBLIOGRAPHY

ABBOTT, P. E. and TAMPLIN, J. M. A., *British Gallantry Awards*, London, Guiness Superlatives Ltd., 1971.

ARTHUER, MAX, *Symbol of Courage, a complete history of the Victoria Cross*, Sidgwick & Jackson, London, 2005.

TKINSON, C. T., *The South Wales Borderers, 24th Foot, 1689-1937*, Cambridge, Regimental History Committee, 1937.

BARTHOP, MICHAEL, *The Zulu War*, Blanford, 1980.

BEETON, 5. 0. (Ed.), *Our Soldiers and the Victoria Cross*, London, Ward, Lock & Tyler, n.d.

BENSON, W. H. D., *Gallant Deeds*, London, Gieves, 1919.

BILCLIFFE, JOHN, *Well Done the 68th , the Durhams in the Crimea and New Zealand 1854–1866*, Picton Publishing, Chippenham, 1995.

BRANCH, N., *Boys' Book of VC Heroes*, London, Publicity Products, 1953.

BULLETIN, THE, Military Historical Society, Various issues.

BURLEIGH, B. *Khartoum Campaign 1898 or the Re-Conquest of the Sudan*, London, Chapman & Hall, 1899.

CREAGH, General Sir O'Moore, and HUMPHRIS, H. M., *The VCandDSO*, (Vol. 1), London, Standard Art Book Co., 1924.

CROOK, M. J., *The Evolution of the Victoria Cross*, Tunbridge Wells, Midas Books, 1975.

DE LA BILLIERE, GENERAL SIR PETER, *Supreme Courage, heroic stories from 150 years of the Victoria Cross*, Little Brown, London, 2004.

FFRENCH BLAKE, R. L. V., *The Crimean War*, Leo Cooper, London, 1971.

GAINE, S., *The Story of Sergeant William Coffey, V.C., D.C.M.*, internet site.

GLANFIELD, JOHN, *The Bravest of the Brave, the Story of the Victoria Cross*, Sutton Publishing, Stroud, 2005.

GLOVER, MICHAEL, *That Astonishing Infantry, the history of the Royal Welch Fusiliers, 1689–1989*, Leo Cooper, London, 1989.

GORDON, Major L. L., *British Battles and Medals*, (5th Edition), London, Spink & Son, 1979.

GON, P., *The Road to Isandlwana*, Johannesburg, Ad Doiiker, 1979.

HALL, D., *British Orders, Decorations and Medals*, Huntingdon, Balfour, 1973.

HARE-SCOTT, KENNETH, *For Valour*, Peter Garnett, London, 1949.

HARRINGTON, Peter & Frederick A. SHARF, *Omdurman 1898: the Eye-Witnesses Speak*, London, Greenhill Books, 1998.

HARVEY, David, *Monuments to Courage, Victoria Cross Headstones and Memorials* (2 Vols), 1999.

HASTINGS, MAX, *Battle for the Falklands*, Michael Josephj, 1983.

HAYDON, A. L., *THE BOOK OF THE VICTORIA CROSS*, Melrose, London, 1906.

HOLME, NORMAN, *The Silver Wreath, being the 24th Regiment at Isnadhlwana and Rorke's Drift, 1879*, Samson Books, London, 1979.

ILLUSTRATED LONDON NEWS, Various issues.

JOURNAL OF THE ORDERS AND MEDALS RESEARCH SOCIETY, Various issues.

KNIGHT, IAN, *The National Army Museum Book of the Zulu War*, Pan Books, London, 2003.

KNOLLYS, W. W., *The Victoria Cross in the Crimea*, London, Dean, 1887.

LUMMIS, Rev. Canon W. M., *Padre George Smith of Rorke's Drift*, Norwich, Lummis, 1978.

LUMMIS FILES, Compiled by the Rev. Canon W. M. Lummis, MC. Held by the Imperial War Museum.

MACKINNON, J. P., and SHADBOLT, S., *The South African Campaign, 1879*, London, Hayward, 1973.

MASSIE, ALASTAIR, *The National Army Museum Book of the Crimean War, the Untold Stroies*, Sidgwick & Jackson, London, 2004.

MAXWELL, LEIGH, *THe Ashanti Ring, Sir Garnet Wolseley's Campaigns 1870–82*, Leo Cooper, London, 1985.

MORRIS, D. R., *The Washing of the Spears*, London, Jonathan Cape, 1971.

PARRY, D. H., *Britain's Roll of Glory*, London, Cassell, 1906.

PRATT FILES, Compiled by Mrs. Margaret Pratt. Held by Mr. John Winton.

RANKEN FILES, Held by the Imperial War Museum.

RATTRAY, DAVID, Guidebook to the Anglo-Zulu War Battlefields, Leo Cooper, Barnsley, 2003.

REGISTER OF THE VICTORIA CROSS, Cheltenham, This England Books, 1981.

SHANNON, STEPHEN D., *Beyond Praise, the Durham Light Infantrymen who were awarded the Victoria Cross,* Durham, County Durham Books, 1998.

SMYTH, Brigadier The Hon. Sir J., *The Story of the Victoria Cross, 1856–1963,* London, Muller, 1963.

SNOOK, LIEUTENANT-COLONEL MIKE, How Can Man Die Better, the Secrets of Isnadlwana Revealed, Greenhill Books, London, 2005.

SNOOK, LIEUTENANT-COLONEL MIKE, Like Wolves on the Fold, the Defence of Rorke's Drift, Greenhill Books, London, 2006.

SOLDIERS OF THE QUEEN, journal of the Victorian Military Society, Various issues.

STEVENSON, L, *The Rorke's Drift Doctor, James Reynolds VC and the defence of Rorke's Drift,* Stevenson, 2001.

STEWART, R., *The Victoria Cross: The Empire's Roll of Valour,* London, Hutchinson, 19

SWETTENHAM, J., *Valiant Men: Canada's VC and GC Winners,* London, Seeley Service & Cooper, 1975.

TOOMEY, T. F., *The Victoria Cross and How Won,* London, Boot, 1890.

UYS, I. S., *For Valour — The History of Southern Africa's Victoria Cross Heroes,* Johannesburg, Uys, 1973.

WARD, Major C. H. D., *Regimental Records of the Royal Welch Fusiliers (23rd Foot),* London, Forster Groom & Co., various dates during the 1920s.

WARD, S. G. P., *Faithful — the story of the D.L.I.,* Naval & Military Press, Ukfield, n.d.

FFRENCH BLAKE, R. L. V., *The Crimean War, Sphere, London, 1973.*

WHITEHORN, Major A. C. and MARDEN, Major-General Sir T. O., *The History of the Welch Regiment,* Cardiff, Western Mail & Echo Ltd., 1932.

WHITTON, F. E., *Rorke's Drift,* booklet reprinted from *Blackwood's Magazine,* January 1979.

WILKINS, P. A., *The History of the Victoria Cross,* London, Constable, 1904.

WILLIAMS, W. ALISTER, *The VCs of Wales and the Welsh Regiments,* Bridge Books, Wrexham, 1984.

WILLIAMS, W. ALISTER, *Commandant of the Transvaal, the life of General Sir Hugh Rowlands, VC, KCB,* Bridge Books, 2001.

WINTON, J., *The Victoria Cross at Sea,* Michael Joseph, London, 1979.

ZIEGLER, PHILLIP, *Omdurman,* Collins, London, 1973.